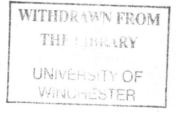

METHUEN'S
MANUALS OF MODERN PSYCHOLOGY

General Editor 1946–68 C. A. Mace
1968–   H. J. Butcher

Human Intelligence
Its Nature and Assessment

Human Intelligence

Its Nature and Assessment

H. J. BUTCHER
Professor of Higher Education
University of Manchester

METHUEN & CO LTD
11 New Fetter Lane London E C 4

Distributed in the USA
by Barnes & Noble Inc.

To M.B.

Acknowledgments

My first and foremost debt is to Professor R. B. Cattell, who provided an outstanding example of dedication to psychological research.

Professor Sir Cyril Burt very generously commented on the manuscript almost word by word, and it has been greatly improved by his criticisms. He has allowed me to include his lucid account of the principles of factor analysis as an appendix to chapter 2.

Mr Michael Hutchings also criticised the whole book in detail, and I have incorporated many of his useful suggestions.

Other friends and colleagues who have advised on particular aspects include Mr T. Bates, Miss J. Cookson, Dr R. Corteen, Dr Margaret Donaldson, Prof. H. J. Eysenck, Dr W. Mays, Prof. F. W. Warburton and Mr P. O. White. None of these bears any responsibility for the defects that remain.

I am greatly indebted to Miss N. Boothby, Mr Harry Pont, Mrs Barbara Muir, and the staff of the Godfrey Thomson Unit for Educational Research for various kinds of help in preparing the book; also to Miss C. Stewart and Mrs A. Turnbull for their indefatigable work in typing successive drafts.

Mr C. W. Butcher, Mr M. Giles and Mrs M. King have been of great assistance in compiling and checking the bibliography.

The author would like to thank all authors, publishers and journals for permission to quote tables, diagrams and passages, in particular:

Baillière, Tindall and Cox, *The British Journal of Psychology*, *The British Journal of Statistical Psychology*, Harper and Row, Holt, Rinehart and Winston Inc, The McGraw Hill Book Company, Penguin Books, Prentice-Hall Inc, Rand McNally and Company, *Science*, *Scientific American*, *The Scottish Educational Journal*, The University of Chicago Press, The University of London Press, John Wiley and Sons Inc., William and Wilkins.

Contents

Introduction

This book has three main aims: (1) to treat the subject of human intelligence not as a narrow speciality, but as a fundamental topic in psychology, to which many different kinds of survey, experiment and speculation are relevant; (2) to provide an up-to-date guide to much of what is known and where it can be found with particular reference to work done in the last decade; (3) to swing the pendulum a little against the current state of opinion, in so far as this holds that 'intelligence' is an out-dated concept.

It is intended primarily as a textbook for students in University Departments of Psychology and Education and in Colleges of Education, but I have tried also to bear in mind the needs and interests of both more and less specialised groups. In one or two chapters, where the amount of relevant research is not overwhelmingly large, it has been possible to provide a review of the literature which may be useful to the intending specialist. Thus in Chapter 4, which deals with the fashionable but undeniably important topic of 'creativity', the coverage may be more adequate than elsewhere, since much of the relevant research has been carried out during the last ten years, and, although voluminous, is still perhaps capable of being condensed into twenty or thirty pages without drastic over-simplification. On the other hand, Chapters 1 and 5, which purport to summarise the state of knowledge and opinion about 'the concept of intelligence' and 'brains and machines', could hardly be both comprehensive and detailed. Either topic, to be dealt with at all fully, would require a complete book. In chapters such as these I have therefore aimed at a broad treatment rather than an accumulation of detail, and they may be of most value to readers who are interested in the subject without being required to be examined in it. Another necessary limitation is that for the most part only intelligence within the 'normal' range will be dealt with. Retardation, mental deficiency and disorders of mental functioning lie outside this book's scope.

These differences in amount of detail are relative, and intended to be subject to a common and over-riding intelligibility. In some sections individual researches are described, with comments about their experimental design and sampling plan when it seems vital to explain the

degree of generalisation of results that is possible; in other places it has
been necessary to summarise a dozen experiments in a single sentence.
In either case the aim has been to avoid excessively technical language,
and to enable the student to see something of the whole wood without
neglecting important trees. Short reading lists have been included at the
end of each chapter, together with fairly frequent references in the
text to original sources, and a large, though certainly not comprehensive, bibliography.

A few words are required about why one needs to stress that intelligence is a fundamental topic in psychology. For a century or so there
has been a school or succession in Britain of very competent writers
on individual differences in ability, including, for instance, Galton,
Spearman, Burt, Thomson, Vernon and Wiseman. In the USA similar
work has been done, and, on the whole, similar conclusions reached by
Terman, Thorndike, Hull, Kelley, Thurstone, R. B. Cattell, McNemar
and Humphreys. Detailed and solid as this work has been, it has remained rather isolated from other branches of psychology, and has
overlapped comparatively little, extraordinary as this must seem, with
the experimental study of learning and problem-solving, to mention
only one field of general psychology with which one would expect
contact and cross-fertilisation. Although the authors just mentioned
have been conspicuous for breadth of outlook and for developing and
using statistical methods as means to an end, the same cannot be said
of all their followers. 'Psychometrics', or the technology of mental
testing and its associated armoury of statistical methods, has, as often
practised, taken on the appearance of a barren subscience, and arguments about rival techniques of factor extraction and rotation have
sometimes seemed like mediaeval disputations about how many angels
could dance on the head of a pin. There has also been a relative lack of
research into individual differences in high-level cognitive performances,
except as represented by a few limited kinds of test. These established
tests have proved effective in practice, but their very success has tended
to impoverish psychological theories of intelligent behaviour and sometimes also to persuade both psychologists and the general public to
accept the IQs based on them as definitive and as requiring little sup-
plementation. It would usually be wise, on the other hand, to think of
an IQ as like documentation of a patient's height, weight and external
symptoms, which is only a preliminary to detailed diagnosis.

The study of intelligence has tended to suffer at the hands of over-
specialised psychometrists and of those who maintain that intelligence
is simply what is tested by existing intelligence tests. For many practical

purposes we have to act as though this were so, but to accept this as finally agreed and settled would misrepresent the actual state of affairs and would seriously restrict discussion of related issues. The chapter headings of the present book will confirm at a glance that in the writer's view the study of human intelligence should cover far more than performance on intelligence tests. The subject is a huge one – perhaps, as Piaget suggests, amounting to half of psychology.

'Psychometrics' and 'experimental psychology' correspond approximately to what Cronbach (1957) has described as the two disciplines of scientific psychology, that is to say the study of individual differences and the study of the basic laws of human functioning that apply to everyone. From the latter point of view, individual variations produce an inconvenient perturbation, but from the former they are the main subject of interest. The study of human intelligence has yielded a large accumulation of knowledge about individual differences, and relatively little about basic laws of cognitive functioning. Least work of all has been done on combining and integrating the two approaches.

Not only these two approaches require to be considered, but also findings from half a dozen other fields, including for instance genetics, sociology and the new science of computer simulation. Throughout this book, therefore, unity of theme is precarious and many of the topics discussed *ought* to be inter-connected and inter-dependent, but the links and dependences have often been inadequately demonstrated. In part, the lack of connections reflects a genuine absence of research bridging the different areas. Many previous accounts have been *either* psychometric *or* philosophical *or* sociological; this book, if only a sketch, is a sketch of the comprehensive kind of treatment that seems to be needed.

The second aim, that of providing a more up-to-date general account than most of the texts in current use, needs little further explanation. At the time of writing (March 1967), there are few, if any accounts, either British or American, that provide a general survey of work in the area of intelligence and abilities and that include any reference to books or journal articles later than about 1960.[1] Psychology is a rapidly developing subject, and a new text is needed every few years to cover each major area. Examples of work published since 1960 that requires mention in any survey of the literature are, selected almost at random, Cattell's attempt to separate fluid from crystallised intelligence (Ch. 2),

[1] Since this introduction was written, Guilford (1967) has published a comprehensive text which, although to a great extent concerned to expound his own 'structure-of-intellect' system, also contains sections, for instance, on the physical basis of intelligence, on computer simulation, and on the work of Piaget.

the books on concept identification and concept formation by Hunt, by
Klausmeier and Harris, and by Gagné (Ch. 3), a great deal of the
research on creativity, and in particular the work of Wallach and Kogan
(Ch. 4), the collections of papers on machine intelligence by Feigenbaum and Feldman and by Collins and Michie (Ch. 5), some of the
recent studies of identical twins such as Shields', and also Vandenberg's
symposium on the genetics of human behaviour (Ch. 6), the repetition
and extension in Montreal of some of Piaget's work by Laurendeau and
Pinard and by Décarie (Ch. 7), Anstey's book on test construction
(Ch. 8), Elithorn's interesting new perceptual maze test (Ch. 9),
J. McV. Hunt's book on 'Intelligence and Experience', Vernon's
comparative study of West Indian and English children (Ch. 10) and
Lavin's survey of factors determining academic performance (Ch. 11).
Since the subject-matter relevant to the study of human ability has
been widely construed, and since the output of papers in many of these
areas is enormous, there has been some danger of certain sections
degenerating into mere strings of references interspersed with brief
comments, rather as in the Annual Reviews of Psychology. A series of
review chapters of this kind would be quite useful, but would serve a
more limited purpose than is intended here. Even where the references
come thick and fast, I have tried to provide more than a bibliographical
catalogue, and to outline at least the main trends in recent research.

The third aim, that of restoring to the concept of general intelligence
some of its waning respectability, can be justified only by a reading of
the book as a whole. The reasons for many people's increased scepticism about the value of the concept are complex, and are discussed at
some length in Chapter 1, but even at this point a brief indication of
why such an aim is necessary may be useful. There can be little doubt
that the status of intelligence as a useful concept *has* been showing signs
of decline or at least that there are people who feel that it should be
doing so. Floud (1963), for example, reviewing Jenkins and Paterson's
collection of readings on individual differences in ability, finds that this
extensive selection from the literature fails to provide her with any clear
picture of the nature of intelligence, and implies that the concept itself
is not very valuable. Armer (1963), in a discussion of the simulation by
electronic computers of intelligent behaviour, writes – 'Intelligence is a
slippery concept – in explaining it you explain it away.'

Another trend is that, whereas in the past the effects of social class
have often been underestimated, today it is sometimes implied that
differences in measured intelligence reflect *only* differences in social
class or in early environment. Swift (1967) for instance, in an excellent

attempt to study the social and environmental factors affecting success in the '11+' selection procedure, and to refine the rather crude indices of 'social class' that have generally been used in experimental studies writes of 'ability' in inverted commas, as if to imply that individual differences ascribable to factors other than social class do not exist. Similarly, Stott (1967) criticising a recent article by Burt, writes

> It is a fact of observation that individual children show varying success in solving certain standardised problems. But it is not neces sary to attribute this variation to differences in some cognitive factor. No problem can be solved by pure 'intelligence'. A person has to know about the nature and qualities of all the things that he is dealing with, and such knowledge comes in large part from experience. Even apart from the advantages enjoyed by children in different cultural groups, the extent to which an individual learns about his environment depends upon his curiosity, his eagerness to understand, and his habits of cogitating upon his observations. In other words, his contemporary problem-solving ability is a function of the strength of his intrinsic motivations during the earlier stages of his development. Developing the argument further, the ability to solve problems of a given type depends upon the acquisition of a stock of trial solutions or 'mental templates' which are applied as analogies from similar, previously solved problems. Their possession by any individual depends upon the extent to which he has, up to that point, engaged himself in problem-solving. This in turn depends upon the strength of his 'effectiveness-motivation' (Stott, 1961), and his choice of problem-solving as a sphere of effectiveness. A child without the confidence or desire to widen the scope of his effectiveness will remain at a low level of cognitive development.
>
> In short, the conceptual equipment of any individual, upon which his problem-solving ability and success at intelligence tests depend, is in large part determined by his motivational history.

There is a plausible case to be made along these lines, that motivational factors have been underestimated in assessing intelligence and abilities, but their influence has not been so fully demonstrated as Stott's statement suggests. Moreover, many of the criticisms which have been directed against intelligence as a useful concept would apply more strongly to one such as 'effectiveness-motivation', which might well prove even more elusive to assess. American psychologists have devoted much research to appraisal of 'need for achievement', and useful results have been obtained, but few would maintain that concepts of ability have thereby been superseded. So far they have at best been *supplemented*.

These examples of current dissatisfaction with accepted views of human intelligence, or at least with views that have until recently been widely accepted, have been quoted to illustrate the changing climate of opinion. There are signs indeed that, in a rush of enthusiasm to investigate motivational or social-class influences on cognition, the baby may be thrown out with the bathwater and that firmly established knowledge about individual differences in ability may be neglected or forgotten. A main purpose of this book is to discourage any 'nothing-but' type of explanation and to provide some kind of picture of the wealth and variety of evidence that needs to be taken into account.

I

The Concept of Intelligence

RECENT DEVELOPMENTS IN THE STUDY OF HUMAN INTELLIGENCE

During the first forty years of this century the idea of intelligence or general mental ability was found useful and important by psychologists. Many of the most talented devoted their lives to its study, and the early volumes of the British Journal of Psychology and of many American journals contained a high proportion of articles on the subject. Recently, however, the concept has become less generally acceptable and more exposed to various kinds of criticism. It seems time to take stock of the situation, to review the current state of knowledge and opinion, and to estimate how far this apparent decline is justified.

How 'intelligence' came to be an important scientific concept and how the word became common in popular usage has been described in detail in numerous scholarly articles by Sir Cyril Burt (e.g. 1955a; 1955b). He has pointed out that even in his own boyhood the word was rarely used and that he never heard either teachers or parents talk of a child's 'intelligence' or describe him as 'intelligent'. The introduction of the concept was mainly due to the writings of Herbert Spencer and of Francis Galton in the nineteenth century and the word came into general use considerably later.

Both Spencer and Galton believed in the importance of a general ability super-ordinate to and distinct from special abilities, and their views were adopted and amplified by leading neurologists around the turn of the century. Hughlings Jackson and Sherrington were particularly influential in this respect and most psychologists with a physiological training, such as Burt himself (who worked as Sherrington's assistant) accepted the theory of a general cognitive capacity probably dependent upon the number, complexity of connections, and organisation of the nerve-cells in the cerebral cortex. This general hypothesis is still perfectly tenable and accepted by many modern neurologists (e.g. Sholl, 1956).

Early in this century powerful support for these ideas came from two sources. Spearman, developing the technique of factor analysis first suggested by Karl Pearson, produced extensive statistical evidence for the predominance of general ability or intelligence, and was a formidable advocate of this predominance, even to the extent of denying any importance to more specific abilities. At about the same time Binet in France produced the first satisfactory scale for assessing differences in intelligence, and in this country Burt, who had just been appointed psychologist to the London County Council, was by 1909 using standardised tests to demonstrate that many children certified as 'mentally deficient' were in fact within the normal range of intelligence and were backward rather than defective.

In the succeeding thirty or forty years the work of these pioneers was extended and refined, but few fundamental developments occurred. Since the Second World War, the importance of general mental ability has been more widely questioned, particularly in the USA. The rest of this section will attempt to summarise recent trends.

Four or five main causes can be distinguished, all contributing in different degrees to the changing picture of human intelligence; some of these have been briefly mentioned in the introduction. Within psychology there have been developments in the last two or three decades that have made necessary considerable modifications in attitude, and an additional factor has been the rapid development of sociology and the spread of knowledge about sociological findings.

As already mentioned, Spencer and Galton, while stressing the predominant and integrating function of *general* ability, had by no means denied the existence of more *specific* abilities. Since the earliest days of testing and statistical analysis, the relative importance of the two kinds of ability has been hotly disputed. There was prolonged technical dispute about the extent of correlation or overlap between various abilities and about whether the statistical evidence pointed in the direction of one important factor of general ability or whether other major factors were indicated, supplementing or supplanting it. This particular controversy, briefly summarised in Chapter 2, has now died down, and it is widely accepted that the question cannot be answered by statistical means alone. Many alternative classifications are possible, but in most of these general intelligence emerges implicitly or explicitly as an important and pervasive factor.

Recently there has been considerable interest shown and a great deal of research carried out into 'original', 'creative' or 'divergent' thinking, which has been contrasted with the analytic or 'convergent' kind of thinking studied in the past and assessed by conventional kinds of intelligence test. This distinction had been drawn by many psychologists, including for instance, Stout, Sully, Woodworth and Thurstone, but became much more prominent when discussed by Guilford (1950). Often, particularly in America, convergent thinking only is described as intelligence, and divergent thinking is called 'creativity'. Hudson (1966) accepts the importance of this distinction between convergent and divergent thinking and found that the British public schoolboys he studied fell into one or other of two contrasted types, 'convergers' and 'divergers', but he denies that this distinction has any close connection with creativity. He also quite rightly points out that the study of creativity (often rather inadequately specified and defined) has become something of a bandwagon, particularly in the USA. It has in fact become the fashionable quality to possess, with a consequent denigration of mere analytic intelligence. This is only one side of the picture, however, and many serious and important investigations of creativity have been carried out. It is a sign of the climate of opinion that the recent extensive survey by the National Child Development Study of 11,000 children born in 1958 included among its measures a rating on creativity but omitted any measure of general ability (Kellmer Pringle et al., 1967). The consensus of opinion among psychologists however is that, while several of the new, open-ended tests of 'creativity', or of 'divergent thinking' are distinctly promising their practical value has not as yet been adequately demonstrated. This topic will be discussed in Chapter 4.

Another important field of research concerns the development of children's thinking as studied by the Swiss child psychologist Jean Piaget. Like many brilliant psychologists of the older generation, Piaget was attracted to the subject after being trained in another discipline. Having established while still a student a high reputation as a biologist and zoologist, Piaget, early in his career, worked under Simon on the development of intelligence tests. His interest, however, was never in individual differences in intelligence as such, but in modes of functioning (and, in this early work, in mistakes made by children in attempting test problems). His main contributions can be very roughly summed up as follows. Firstly, by observing children's processes of thinking from the detached viewpoint of a biologist, Piaget discovered many previously unsuspected basic differences between the concepts of children at various stages of development, and between those of children and of adults. Most of this observation was in the first place devoted to his own three children. Secondly, he devised ingenious

A*

semi-experimental methods to test whether his interpretation of his observations was the correct one. Thirdly, he formalised these observations by showing that all children passed successively through certain stages in a fixed order, and that many basic concepts essential to formal adult thinking only became available at a late stage. Finally (and this part of his work is the most difficult, theoretical and debatable) he maintained that the structure of the logical operations available at a particular stage was paralleled by certain mathematical groups, near-groups, and lattices.

This work of Piaget and his followers, which will be discussed in Chapter 7, has obvious importance for the study of intelligence, and also important educational implications. If Piaget is right, the nature and functioning of intelligence change quite radically from one age to another. Formal intelligence, as displayed and exercised by the adult, works in a different manner and makes use of different kinds of concept from concrete intelligence (typical of mid-childhood), and is still more different from sensori-motor intelligence, which is all that is available to the young infant. How meaningful therefore is it to use one word for such a variety of processes?

It is more legitimate than might appear from the preceding, harshly simplified, sketch of Piaget's findings. Firstly, the successive stages and kinds of thinking are not absolutely different in kind. Piaget, confirming by experiment a hypothesis suggested by Herbert Spencer, has made it clear that each stage incorporates the preceding one rather than supersedes it, and that cognitive development is in this sense hierarchical; he has himself used 'intelligence' as a description of what is essential to all these stages. Also, significant and revolutionary as the findings of Piaget and his school certainly are, they cannot be the whole story. Considerable cognitive differences can be observed between children who, in Piaget's terms, have reached the same stage of intelligence. Moreover, when the final stage of development has been attained, that is the achievement of formal reasoning, differences still remain to be accounted for. Keynes, Einstein, Mozart, Piaget himself, and the man-in-the-street all attained this stage, but it would be nonsense to claim that their cognitive behaviour shows only minor differences.

These two kinds of psychological research, the work on divergent thinking and that on stages of concept formation in children, have made necessary some revision of the traditional picture of intelligence, but they do not seriously affect the need for such a concept. There are other trends that may eventually alter the idea of intelligence out of all recognition. What may be called the computer revolution has already influenced psychology and education in several ways. The first and most obvious effect has been the provision of enormous computational facilities, making possible kinds of research and techniques which would previously have been prohibitively long and laborious. It has been said, in fact, that an unmistakable sign of progress in psychological research is that from year to year misuse is made of ever more sophisticated techniques! Even this advance has not been fully appreciated by most psychologists (Green, 1966). A more exciting and fundamental development arising from the existence of flexible, general-purpose electronic computers of large capacity is that they can in principle mimic, represent or perform intelligent processes of any kind. Computers are still a relatively new invention, and only a small proportion of the time and effort given to their development and programming has been spent on research into the simulation of human thought processes. The impact of computers on cognitive psychology is described in more detail in Chapter 5.

Another development which is less easy to pin down may be described as a liberalised neo-behaviourism. In its original form, behaviouristic psychology was a necessary but naive reaction against the subjectivity involved in introspective accounts of activities such as thinking. To a large extent, this reform has proved a permanent one. Psychologists still look, where possible, for behavioural responses in preference to subjective impressions, and still distrust unaided introspection. Behaviouristic psychology, however, in its early forms contained many elements that were irrelevant to its main purpose and that tended to weaken its strong central tenets (Broadbent, 1961). Watson, for instance, the earliest articulate and systematic exponent of behaviourism, was dogmatic about the overwhelming importance of environmental factors. Often, also, behaviouristic or objective psychology has been interpreted as more or less synonymous with or dependent upon stimulus-response theories of behaviour. In the cruder and more reductionist versions of these theories it was supposed that thinking could be described in terms of stimulus-response connections established according to the principles of classical or operant conditioning, and the very use of terms such as 'thinking', still less of such abstractions as 'intelligence', was tabooed as implying an unwelcome introspective or subjective kind of theorising. The newer, liberalised behaviourism of contemporary experimental psychologists has quietly abandoned many of these earlier restrictions. Their aim, however, is still to describe and explain even the most complex and abstract human thinking in terms of simpler mechanisms, whether these operate by chains of stimulus-response connections, by feedback loops, or by other kinds of element. Although in the past this goal has receded almost as fast as experimental results have accumulated, the hope has not been abandoned, but has been strengthened by the recent developments in cybernetics and computer applications already mentioned. Many experimental psychologists and cyberneticists would argue that 'intelligence' is a cloak for our ignorance of the mechanics of thinking and little else. There is still a long way to go before the cloak is no longer needed.

Probably the most influential factor in changing attitudes to the study of human intelligence has been the growth of educational sociology. The result has been a reaction against the too static and narrow idea of differences in intelligence that seemed to be the orthodox view of educational psychologists a few years ago. In its extreme form this view implied that a child is born with a fixed or pre-determined level of intelligence, that this innate intelligence level can, at least in principle, be assessed by standardised tests, that the resulting intelligence quotient will vary hardly at all from infancy to old age, and that the kind of test used (relatively unchanged since the pioneer days of testing some forty or more years ago) is so superior in predictive power for almost all purposes that it is hardly worth experimenting with new kinds of cognitive test, let alone with measures of temperament or motivation.

The reaction to this kind of view has sometimes involved an excessive swing in the opposite direction, particularly in so far as intelligence testing has become a matter of political dispute. Many of the pioneers of psychological testing, such as Godfrey Thomson and Cyril Burt, saw it as a potent means of furthering social equality and of ensuring that able children, whose ability would otherwise have been submerged by poverty and environmental handicaps, should have the opportunity of an education commensurate with their talent. Inglis (1967) rightly comments: 'It is hard to believe that Thomson would have kept silent when his desire to give an equal educational chance to children of different classes in society and in different districts is misconstrued, as it now is, as a device to perpetuate social privilege and to protect an established elite.' As early as 1929, in *A Modern Philosophy of Education*, Thomson produced powerful arguments in favour of comprehensive secondary schooling. Ironically, intelligence testing is now often regarded as a reactionary practice, particularly by left-wing critics, mainly because it is associated with the obsolescent allocation of children to different types of school at the age of eleven. The merits of psychological testing and of the tripartite system of secondary education are entirely different issues, although not always recognised as such. In the USA psychological testing flourishes, although the system of secondary education is predominantly comprehensive. In the USSR by contrast, psychological testing is not encouraged, but, if newspaper reports are to be believed, special schools and classes for exceptionally able children are not uncommon, and there is even a special school in the new 'science city' of Akademgorodok in Siberia for children of outstandingly high mathematical ability.

For all the reasons mentioned, the practice of intelligence testing and the conception of intelligence fostered by the use of conventional tests have tended to be held in lower repute during the last few years, on the grounds that they have been associated with a too narrow and static view of intelligence, and because of a healthy change in public and official attitudes to the whole question of educational opportunity. The rapid growth and acceptance of sociology as an academic discipline has been both cause and effect of the changing climate of opinion.

By its very nature, sociological enquiry is likely to emphasise environmental and to neglect hereditary factors, and thus to help correct the previously current picture of intelligence which now appears to have been in some respects one-sided and to have laid too much stress on, for instance, the constancy of the IQ. In addition, sociological studies are bound to place strong emphasis upon the common features and mutual influence within social groups, and relatively to discount psychological differences between individuals. An example is to be found in the Plowden report (Department of Education and Science, 1967), in which, it seems fair to say, much more attention has been given to sociological than to psychological factors. In Chapter 3 of the report, a rather elaborate statistical analysis by multiple regression has been applied to survey data. The conclusion drawn, which forms one of the major empirical findings of the report, is that educational achievement in primary school children is strongly affected by parental attitudes. It is noticeable, however, that whereas 20% of variation in achievement within schools (assessed by a test of reading comprehension) is ascribed to parental attitudes, 54% is described as 'unexplained'. Most of this major category of variation must be ascribed to readily assessable differences in ability after social factors have been taken into account. It is odd to see it labelled 'unexplained', as though it were inexplicable. Undoubtedly, however, psychologists have been justifiably influenced by the growth of sociology, in the direction of paying more attention to environmental factors in general and to group influences in particular. Some indeed are convinced of the primacy of group influences, though few would go as far as Meredith, who writes (1966, p. 577):

.. in an ordinary situation the behaviour of an individual is so dependent on the behaviour of others that its effectiveness must be dependent on the integrated intelligence of the whole group. Thus in so far as we can improve the working conditions of the group we can raise their effective intelligence. It is as serious a categoreal error to speak of the 'intelligence' of a single individual as to speak of the 'temperature' of a single molecule.

The great increase in the prestige of sociological studies and the rapid expansion of sociology in recent years (and particularly the application of sociological methods to research in education) have all combined not only to produce a needed re-assessment of the relative effects of heredity and environment on intelligence, but also to play down individual psychological differences as compared with group influences.

It would be interesting and useful to see how far these changes have affected educated public opinion. Flugel (1947) carried out a survey to investigate popular views on intelligence and related topics; it is probable that the developments summarised in the last few paragraphs have begun to affect public opinion and that detectable differences from Flugel's results would now be found. In some respects it seems possible, however, that public opinion and 'common sense' fluctuate less sharply than expert views. Some of the answers to his questions, such as those about the distinction between intelligence and achievement and about the constancy of the IQ, appear closer to 'accepted' views today than to those of twenty years ago.

THE NATURE OF INTELLIGENCE

Before we consider the numerous definitions and descriptions that have been offered, it will be advisable to clear away one or two common preconceptions that can hinder understanding of 'intelligence' and of the kind of concept it exemplifies.

The grammatical form itself can be misleading. 'Intelligence' is a noun, and nouns often refer to things or objects. Even when we know perfectly well that intelligence is not a 'thing', but a sophisticated abstraction from behaviour, we may sometimes half-consciously endow it with a kind of shadowy existence distinct and separate from the intelligent organisms which alone give it meaning, or, more insidiously, think it is a 'thing' that these organisms 'have', rather than a description of the way they behave. This kind of misconception is often described as 'reification' of the concept. It is better, therefore, to think of the adjective 'intelligent' as more basic (and less dangerous) than the noun, and perhaps of the adverb 'intelligently' as still more basic.

This warning need not be pushed too far. Provided the main point is taken, we shall find it infinitely more convenient to talk about intelligence than to use circumlocutions about the common characteristic of organisms behaving intelligently. Reification is dangerous in so far as it sometimes makes us misinterpret behaviour, but it would be absurd on that account to discard all theoretical concepts describing human differences, which are essential in any scientific description.

Among these concepts, the class of traits (including traits of ability) forms a large and useful subset. Psychological traits can differ both in mode of functioning and in degree of generality. The most widely accepted distinction between modes of functioning, and one that seems to represent an important difference, is between traits of personality and traits of ability. The former describe how a person generally behaves, the latter what problems he can solve, if sufficiently motivated. This distinction between ability and personality traits is a useful one, but it is obviously not clearcut. One aspect of the difference is that direction of assessment of personality traits usually seems more arbitrary. If one considers a typical personality trait such as introversion–extraversion, which has been shown to account for a high proportion of variation in personality among normal people, and attempts to assess it as a scale or dimension, there is no particular reason why it should be scored in one direction rather than the other. Neither quality seems more creditable than the other; if there are things introverts can typically do that extraverts cannot, the reverse applies equally, and the dimension is not readily described in such a way that people at one end seem better favoured or more talented than at the other. The natural way to assess introversion–extraversion is from the middle outward, and to think of people as deviating towards either pole from the average of the whole population.

With abilities, on the other hand, there is an inevitable tendency to see one end of the scale as high, and the other as low, to describe in favourable terms anyone believed to deviate towards one pole, and to denigrate someone nearer the other. Admittedly, some writers try hard to avoid these tendencies, speaking of gifted children as 'super-normal deviates', but even in this jargon, 'super' and 'sub' still imply directionality in the scale. This question of the uni-directionality or bi-polarity of psychological scales of assessment is discussed in detail by Thompson (1963), but is only of concern in the present context as one of the features that approximately distinguish ability from personality traits. Only approximately, since some personality traits, such as ego-strength (or 'will-power') seem analogous in this respect to abilities, and abilities themselves for many purposes are best expressed on a scale anchored at the mid-point rather than at one end. As a rough guide, however, assessment of abilities recognises a 'high' and a 'low' end, assessment of personality traits does so less often.

Traits, whether of ability or personality, vary in generality. The most specific traits, such as perhaps being expert at lacrosse or liking the music of Sibelius, although they may give interesting information about an individual, are usually of less concern to the psychologist, both because they vary relatively little in the population as a whole (90% of people will score zero) and because, even in the individual, they do not typically represent his pattern of abilities and personality or more than a small fraction of his life-style. As a first step, the psychologist seeking valid generalisations must seek to study traits that are as broad and unspecific as possible, or in more technical language, those that account for the maximum assessable variance in the population. This is the prime importance of intelligence or general ability, that by definition it is the broadest and most pervasive cognitive trait, and is conceived of as being involved in virtually every kind of intellectual skill.

To say that intelligence is of great importance because it is *defined* as being the most general kind of ability gets us very little further unless other conditions are fulfilled, two in particular. If a general trait is thought of as entering into a wide range of performances, and is in fact an abstraction from common features in them, these performances must be shown to have common features in the first place, to overlap in some degree, to be correlated and not independent. This overlap has generally been found in the case of intellectual performance, although the evidence is complex and will be discussed in detail in the next chapter. In addition, for the concept to be really valuable, it should have more than purely statistical support, and be more than a blind abstraction from a set of correlated performances. Its unity should be demonstrably functional and psychological, not merely mathematical and logical. To show that intelligence is a satisfactory unitary trait in this sense, one should be able to point to its integrating function in the individual as well as to its emergence as a statistical factor averaged over a large number of people.

A concrete illustration may make this point clearer, although the analogy is by no means exact. Events such as the decathlon in the Olympic games were presumably instituted to be a measure of some sort of 'all-round athletic ability'. But it is by no means clear or even probable that this is a useful or unitary concept. Success is based on a hotchpotch of unrelated, possibly conflicting skills, and it seems unlikely that the supposed general ability has any integrating function. Consider by contrast the idea of skill at bridge (or at some other game requiring complex intellectual co-ordination). At first glance this may appear similar, since a good player will need to possess various subsidiary skills, which may not be highly correlated, such as knowledge of bidding conventions, capacity to memorise without undue cognitive strain which cards have already been played, ability to draw inferences from his opponents' play, and so on. But 'being a good bridge player' also involves co-ordinating these separate skills and subordinating them to a plan, pushing them down the hierarchy, so to speak, so that both logically and psychologically they become means to an end or parts of a whole. Similarly, when people learn morse code, they first have to learn the elementary skills involved in knowing the letters. As they progress, they work in larger units, words, phrases and so on, again pushing the simpler skills down the hierarchy (Bryan and Harter, 1897, 1899). Many, if not all, complex skills are developed in this way.

It is remarkable that co-ordinating skills such as those of the expert bridge player have received so little attention from psychologists. The only such study known to me is an unpublished attempt by F. H. George in 1960 to program a computer to play bridge. Even the thinking of expert chess players, which would seem much simpler to investigate, as being a game played by one individual, not in partnership, has been a neglected field of study, with only two main exceptions, the pioneering work of Binet and the research described by De Groot (1965, 1966). (For a summary of this sparse literature on the psychology of chess by a chess master who is also a psychologist, see Penrose, 1966). De Groot conducted a variety of experiments with chess players of differing standards, from good amateur to grandmaster, including, for instance, setting up game positions and asking the subjects to assess them in detail, and to comment on the best moves available and the chances of a win for each side. Most of his findings appear to have confirmed the argument just outlined about the expert bridge player. De Groot's experts at chess were not particularly superior in memorising ability, or even in power of looking ahead at all the possible combinations. Their superiority appeared rather to reside in superior powers of selection, integration and co-ordination.

Intelligence, on the view suggested here, is more than a common factor emerging from the statistical analysis of a wide variety of intellectual performances. It is a quintessentially high-level skill at the summit of a hierarchy of intellectual skills. It will always function in the integrating manner described, but on different materials, with different hierarchies, and with varying ceilings of complexity according to the experience of the individual. This is very much what Piaget has demonstrated in his studies of children's cognitive development, and one must suspect that the principle can be carried further, that even among adults who have all reached the last stage of development in his system, i.e. the attainment of formal reasoning, there still remain important qualitative differences. The power of quite short standardised tests of intelligence to discriminate with considerable validity among young adults with very similar experience and educational background is demonstrable, even though inadequately supported by any body of theory. Such tests are of value, for instance, in discriminating among British Civil Service Administrative Class candidates, in spite of the highly selected nature of the group, which normally consists only of first and second-class honours graduates.

If human intelligence is best described as statistically a unitary trait but also as diverse in its manifestations, owing to the different experiences and degrees of development among individuals, it is natural that attempts to define it have proved very various. In fact it will probably always be a misguided labour to try to pin down *one and only one* logically essential feature of such a flexible and superordinate concept.

Miles (1957) has written an interesting paper on defining intelligence, though, as McNemar (1964) rather scathingly points out, it is at least as much concerned with defining 'definition'. While Miles' essay may seem to the student of education or psychology a little rarefied and reliant on the technicalities of philosophy, it probably throws as much light on what can and cannot be expected from a definition of intelligence as any other account. It should also be supplemented by Donaldson's (1963) lucid and thoughtful discussion. Both these writers have been influenced by the analysis of psychological language by Ryle (1949), who points out that 'intelligent' is a dispositional concept, and not an attribute in the same sense as 'tall' or 'British' or 'born in 1925'. According to Ryle (though it is an arguable point) there is no kind of performance or behaviour which can be described without qualification as 'intelligent', and still less any 'essence' of intelligence. Playing chess or theorising about relativity, or any other activity to which intelligence is relevant, can be performed intelligently or unintelligently. Ryle spells out in detail what I have attempted very briefly to show, namely that 'intelligent' and 'intelligence' are, by their grammatical form, capable of misleading if taken as sharing the characteristics of many other nouns and adjectives. When we speak of 'intelligence', we might do better to talk of 'a general tendency in an individual to perform a wide variety of tasks intelligently', bearing in mind that some tasks may serve much better than others as indicators of this disposition.

In Miles' language, 'intelligent' is not only a 'disposition-word', but is also 'polymorphous' and 'open'. The two last adjectives require elucidation. 'Grocer', for instance, is a polymorphous concept, and 'baker' is not, because a grocer, by the nature of his trade performs a wider range of activities than a baker, who by the nature of *his* trade only bakes. 'Intelligence' is also an 'open' concept, because the number of activities legitimately characterised as indicators has never been listed – would indeed hardly be capable of being listed if the argument in the last paragraph is accepted.

It is not surprising therefore that very diverse definitions and descriptions of intelligence have been put forward, nor that many of them can be readily criticised as naive, question-begging, circular, over-inclusive or unsatisfactory in other respects. Often the main value of a particular writer's description is to show that *he* proposes to interpret the concept in such-and-such a way and that his experimental work and the conclusions drawn from it should be interpreted accordingly. This diversity of emphasis was made very evident in the well-known symposium published in the Journal of Educational Psychology in 1921, when the editor invited 17 leading American authorities to write on the two following topics

(1) What I conceive 'intelligence' to be, and by what means it can best be measured by group tests. For example, should the material call into play analytical and higher thought processes? Or should it deal equally or more considerably with simple, associative, and perceptual processes, etc.?

(2) What are the most crucial 'next steps' in research?

13 of the 17 invited actually contributed to the symposium, and the strikingly different interpretations offered have often been commented on. Of the particular definitions and descriptions offered, some have become well-known, such as Terman's 'the ability to carry on abstract thinking', Woodrow's 'the capacity to acquire capacity' and Thorndike's 'the power of good responses from the point of view of truth or fact'. Thurstone's view is interesting and important, as briefly sketched in his symposium contribution and more fully developed in his (1924) book. In his view, the most important aspect of all cognition is that it is action in the process of formulation; various kinds of thinking can be distinguished mainly by the extent to which the action has to be carried out, or can be inhibited. Thurstone therefore concluded that intelligence

could be described as the capacity to live a trial-and-error existence with alternatives that are as yet only incomplete conduct. Anderson (1962) carried out a study of 13-year-old Canadian children which was a test of the hypothesis that IQ would, following Thurstone's ideas, correlate with capacity to inhibit motor responses, and found some degree of positive confirmation.

It is obviously not possible to describe these thirteen different views in detail, but later commentators have attempted to group them into a few main categories, which also include most other accounts of the nature of intelligence. Vernon (1960) for instance classifies descriptions of intelligence as biological, psychological or operational. Freeman (1962) divides them into those emphasising (a) power of adaptation to the environment, (b) capacity for learning, (c) ability for abstract thinking.

Standing a long way back, seeing man as one kind of organism among a million and interpreting psychology as a biological science, there is little doubt that one must also interpret intelligence as adaptation and see any other description as relatively specific and superficial. This is the most far-reaching and general view. But for many practical purposes, as Vernon points out, this idea of intelligence is too fundamental and general. Many human beings, to whom one could hardly deny an assessment of exceptional intelligence (Pascal, Kafka, numerous academic experts) have been spectacularly ill-adapted to their physical and social environment. The biological picture of intelligence is therefore, although important as a bird's-eye view, not necessarily of practical use in the study of individual differences within a given culture. Modern civilisation has, by and large, provided a stable environment within which trends of biological adaptation are hard to discern, and specialised psychological differences have therefore assumed a greater importance. If we reject the biological picture of intelligence as too general and fundamental to be very relevant to the study of individual differences in human beings, we are left with the two remaining kinds of definition, the psychological and the operational in Vernon's terms. The rest of this chapter will discuss the implications of these two approaches.

Few of the definitions and descriptions offered by experts have contained a clear commitment about the relative effects of hereditary and environmental factors, although some have implied a leaning in one or the other direction. Burt (1955) is almost alone in grasping this nettle firmly and *defining* intelligence as 'innate general cognitive ability'. Since scores on existing tests have often been shown to be susceptible to environmental influences, a consequence of this definition is that intelligence as defined differs from intelligence as measured by tests. To many, this is scientifically uncomfortable, since it appears more satisfactory to be able to relate one's concepts directly to actual observations or measurements.

Psychologists have attempted to escape from this dilemma in one of two ways. Either, like Hebb and R. B. Cattell, they have distinguished two kinds of intelligence, calling them 'Intelligence A and Intelligence B' (Hebb) or 'Fluid and Crystallised Intelligence' (Cattell), or they have plumped for an operational definition in an attempt to parallel procedure in other sciences, and have maintained that intelligence should be defined as 'what the tests test'.

The distinctions made by Cattell and Hebb are quite similar. In each case one kind of intelligence is thought of as genetic potentiality, or the basic, given qualities of the individual's central nervous system, and the other kind as mainly the result of experience, learning and environmental factors. The need for such a distinction is suggested, for example, by observations that an astonishingly large proportion of the cerebral cortex has been surgically removed from some adult patients with very little effect on their scores on standardised intelligence tests, whereas cognitive development in children is severely impaired by similar damage. It thus appears that brain cells needed for the development of intelligence are no longer essential to maintain a high level once it has been developed. Similarly, it has been widely confirmed (see Chapter 7) that many aspects of intelligence continue to develop well into middle age in many people, but that speed and capacity to cope with entirely new problems universally decline. It is therefore tempting to specify two kinds of intelligence which will in normal circumstances overlap so much as to be in practice indistinguishable, but which can be distinguished conceptually and perhaps statistically, and which will be clearly revealed as distinct in the drastic circumstances of some brain operations. Cattell goes further, attempting to distinguish the two kinds of intelligence in normal populations by the use of different kinds of test. This is certainly not impossible in principle, because different tests do produce rather different age trends in adults over the life span, but most experts would hold that all tests measure an indissoluble mixture of Intelligence A and Intelligence B (or of fluid and crystallised intelligence), that any differences are ones of degree rather than of kind, and that it is impossible to assess genetic potential uncontaminated by the effects of experience.

The other line of escape from the dilemma is to adopt an operational definition of intelligence. As sometimes stated, this kind of definition, i.e. 'what the tests test', appears impossibly crude and unhelpful and, even if modified and refined, essentially circular. Nevertheless, a definition on these lines appeals strongly to a large number of psychologists, and particularly to those most eager to establish psychology as a satisfactory scientific discipline. The arguments for and against an operational definition of traits such as intelligence take us immediately to fundamental questions about scientific method, about the scientific status of the social and behavioural sciences, and about the strategy of psychological research.

The importance of being able to define scientific concepts in terms of physical operations was first made fully clear by Bridgman (1931). An illuminating discussion of the advantages and limitations of 'operationism' and of operational definitions is provided by Hempel (1966). Typically the advantages are most evident at a relatively early stage in the development of a science. 'Acid' might be operationally defined as any substance that turns blue litmus paper red, or a 'magnet' as a bar of iron or steel to which iron filings are attracted in certain standard conditions. Operational definitions have the advantage that they prescribe standard procedures, ensure agreement about concepts between different observers, and eliminate those that are too ambiguous or hazy to be translated directly or through a chain of operations into an observable and measurable physical occurrence. Their disadvantage is that they may be arbitrary and restrictive unless they are continually changed as knowledge expands. At one stage of knowledge, to base measures of time on the rotation of the earth provided the best definition that could be achieved. Once it was realised that this rotation was gradually slowing, new criteria of greater generality became necessary. For an operational definition to be useful in the first place, certain lawful regularities in nature must have been detected; for it to be superseded, new and more far-reaching regularities, making possible the prediction of a wider range of phenomena, must be found.

There is a strong case for stating that in the physical sciences, operational definitions can and should be adopted at an early stage. How far this is also true of the social and behavioural sciences is a debatable issue. Hempel suggests that the concept of intelligence is readier for such treatment than are, say, measures of differences in personality, if only because the latter, as commonly assessed, have low inter-observer reliability. But it is still arguable whether the relatively more stable and objective measures of ability and intelligence rest on a firm enough basis to justify definition of human intelligence in terms of them. Hunt (1961), for instance, in his influential book 'Intelligence and Experience' argues that the whole idea of representing intelligence on a numerical scale is misguided, and that it would be preferable to substitute 'a sampling of schemata'. On this view, it would be a retrograde step to give IQ a kind of official recognition by making it the basis of agreed operational definition. Presumably he would also argue that when, and only when, much more detailed information is available about the acquisition of these schemata in entire populations, enabling norms to be established, these norms might provide a basis for objective definition and for a kind of quantification, though not on a single dimension.

The case for an 'open' view of the nature of intelligence has already been stated, and the arbitrary and restrictive effect of defining someone's degree of intelligence by a single numerical score is obvious enough, particularly to the eye of 'common sense'. It has been pointed out that the status of research into intelligence and the breadth of enquiry can be impoverished by a narrow operationism or a pedantic reliance on psychometric techniques. In the long term, however, the opposing arguments are also very strong. The arguments *against* operational definition are undoubtedly a reflection on the present state of psychology as a science. Future trends are likely, almost certain, to be in favour of the hard-headed fraternity of psychologists that insists on operational definitions and distrusts 'open' concepts with their seductive penumbra of vagueness.

Brodbeck (1963) has put this latter case clearly and powerfully.

The characteristic abstractness of scientific concepts, like mass or IQ lies in the fact that these terms cannot be defined by simply listing a cluster of directly observable attributes. Merely by looking at a surface we can tell whether it is red or by looking at an object whether it is a gnu. We cannot so simply tell what the mass of an object or the IQ of a child is. Yet a body has mass as well as color; a child has an IQ as well as blond hair. However, more complicated observations are required to know that a body has a certain mass than to know that it has a certain color. This greater complication is reflected by the way the concepts of science are defined, for scientific definitions are rarely of the simple dictionary type, illustrated by 'gnu'. They are not, precisely because they name features of the world that can be discerned only under certain conditions. And these conditions are part of the meaning of the concept. They must therefore be included in the defining properties of it. To do this requires an operational definition. . . .

Scientific terms are defined, not in isolation, as in a dictionary, but by stating the observable conditions under which a sentence containing the term is true or false. Instead of defining the word by itself,

as 'gnu' was defined, it is defined by giving the conditions for the truth
of a sentence in which the term occurs. Such definitions are called
'operational', for they frequently state what must be done in order to
make certain observations. For instance, in order to determine a child's
IQ, we must first administer a test of a specified kind, then observe
his performance on the test, and finally make certain calculations. All
of these conditions define the meaning of IQ as it appears in the
sentence 'John has an IQ of 115.' . . .

There has always been criticism from the right, that is, from sources
essentially hostile to a science of behavior. Life and space are too short
for more than a few brief comments on these last-ditch defenders of
lost causes. Their essentially antiscientific plaint is to the effect that
definition, operational or otherwise, deprives science of the rich halo
of meanings surrounding terms in ordinary use. Far from being a
weakness, this is as it should be. A concept means what its definition
says it means. If it does not say this clearly so that we know when we
do or when we do not have an instance and, if it is quantified, how
much of it, then the concept may be criticized legitimately as inadequately defined.

On the other hand, it makes no sense to criticize a concept on the
ground that its definition is not 'really' what the concept means. It
is, for instance, improper to criticize a definition of political 'conservatism' on the grounds that the defining terms do not really cap-
ture the 'essence' of conservatism, or something of that sort. The
scientist's concept is not that of common sense. His concept means
only what he says it means. This meaning need not include all or even
any of the meanings various people associate with the concept.
Generally, in fact, it will include some of these associated meanings,
since the scientist has picked this particular term and not some other
from common sense. But it is unlikely to include all of them and need
not include any. The scientist may draw upon the halo surrounding
terms which also have a commonsensical use for hunches about laws,
but if he wants objective knowledge of behavior, he cannot carry over
the vagueness of ordinary use into his technical vocabulary. The concept of IQ, for instance, is by now a classic target for this kind of mis-
placed criticism. It does not, so the complaint goes, measure intelligence in the common-sense use of that term. Of course not, but the
criticism is irrelevant. If IQ is a good concept, it is so not because it is
consonant with common sense, but because we can measure it with
fair reliability and because we know, with moderately high probability,
its connection with other attributes and kinds of behavior. Some of

these other things, like general information, success in school, professional achievement, and social adjustment, are part of the meanings commonly associated with 'intelligence'. But this merely shows that when choosing the ordinary word for their particular concept, the scientists made some rather successful hypotheses about laws connecting performance on certain kinds of tests with some components of the common-sense notion of intelligence. Because certain of its concepts, like 'force' and 'energy', are also in common sense, physics once had to endure similarly irrelevant criticism. By now, social science remains the only target.

It would certainly be of great advantage to have an operational definition of intelligence that everyone would accept for scientific work and would distinguish from vague popular conceptions. Up to a point this has already been achieved, but there are still too many different tests and too many different ideas about their merits and demerits for IQ to be considered a satisfactory operational dimension at all comparable with corresponding yardsticks in more developed sciences. If we want to define intelligence as what is measured by an intelligence test or battery of tests, we must first agree on what test or combination of tests to accept.

Most fundamentally, what is urgently needed before major scientific advance can be achieved in the study of intelligence is *a law*, or better still, a number of laws. Such laws are scarce enough in any branch of psychology and virtually non-existent in the study of cognition. Until something of the kind is found, any operational definition of intelligence is bound to remain very largely arbitrary, and dependent, say, on the decision of a committee, rather as usage of the French language is defined and settled by Academicians.

Eysenck (1952) quotes a passage from Bertrand Russell that is relevant and informative, but too long to reproduce here in full. Russell is discussing the problem of establishing an agreed criterion of physical length. Even this problem, though lacking in most of the characteristic difficulties of psychological measurement, is nowhere near so straightforward as most people would imagine.

If you assume that a certain steel rod, which looks and feels rigid, preserves its length unchanged, you will find that the distance from London to Edinburgh, the diameter of the earth, and the distance from Sirius, are all nearly constant, but are slightly less in warm weather than in cold. It will then occur to you that it will be simpler to say that your steel rod expands with heat, particularly when you find that this enables you to regard the above distances as almost

B

exactly constant, and, further, that you can see the mercury in the thermometer taking up more space in warm weather. You therefore assume that apparently rigid bodies expand with heat, and you do this in order to simplify the statement of physical laws. . . .

This process is the same in all physical measurements. Rough measurements lead to an approximate law; changes in the measuring instruments (subject to the rule that all instruments for measuring the same quantity must give as nearly as possible the same results) are found capable of making the law more nearly exact. The best instrument is held to be the one that makes the law most nearly exact, and it is assumed that an ideal instrument would make the law quite exact.

Russell's analysis is more subtle and detailed than this excerpt conveys, but, for our purpose, the main point emerges clearly, that any kind of measurement is arbitrary unless tied in detail to a scientific law or combination of laws. From this viewpoint the assessment or measurement of intelligence seems a long way from being anything more than extremely crude and arbitrary.

Granted that scientific laws form a logical pre-requisite for adequate definition of such concepts as intelligence, what form might such laws take? It is not impossible, it is even fairly likely, that sooner or later physiologists will discover a method for assessing quantitatively the growth and decline in function of brain cells with increasing age (possibly related, for instance, to the amount of RNA, which also increases and then declines) and for plotting these trends. Such an advance, if ever achieved, would provide an objective measure against which to calibrate growth and decline of performance on cognitive tests. This possibility underlines the usefulness of the formulations by Hebb and Cattell of two kinds of intelligence, one directly dependent on neural structure, the other mainly on acquired knowledge. It also underlines the great difficulties that would arise from many alternative formulations, particularly those that ascribe cognitive differences very largely to motivational factors, such as the theory of Hayes (1962) and the views expressed by Stott, as quoted on p. 13. It will be difficult enough to give 'intelligence A' or 'crystallised intelligence' an agreed, non-arbitrary and operational definition. If we define individual differences in ability in terms of 'curiosity', 'eagerness to understand', 'habit of cogitating upon observations', 'effectiveness-motivation', and so forth (as suggested by Stott) it is difficult even to imagine a satisfactory means of objective definition.

The idea of tying measures of ability to physiological measures is, one need hardly say, still hypothetical, and mentioned more as an example of the sort of development that might provide an operational definition than as a likely programme for the near future. Is there then any sign of psychological as distinct from physiological laws that might serve this crucial purpose of tying down a definition? The short answer is that none have been found that have been generally recognised as such. Eysenck (1967), however, has just published an important article in which he draws attention to a finding by Furneaux.

This is to the effect that *speed* in attaining the correct answer is the main individual difference in measured intelligence. In addition a law is claimed to have been found as follows. (See figure 1.1). If, for each

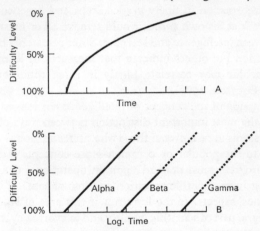

Figure 1.1. Relation between difficulty level of test items and time (A) and log time (B) needed for solution. Alpha, beta and gamma are three imaginary subjects of high, medium and low mental ability, respectively. From Eysenck (1967)

individual, speed of attaining a correct answer is plotted against item difficulty a series of individual curves is obtained. When each individual curve is then transformed (so that speed is represented not by length of time taken but by its logarithm), a set of parallel straight lines results, one for each person. This is taken to mean that people differ basically only in the points of origin of these lines, which represent different individual rates of working. A fuller account of the experiment in which this result was found is provided by Furneaux (1960), but is decidedly obscure.

It is not immediately obvious whether or not this finding is of far-reaching importance for the purposes we have been considering, nor even (without replication in other experiments) whether it attains the status of a psychological law at all, but it certainly cries out for fuller investigation. It is surprising that more work has not been done in this direction, particularly as these results were also briefly reported in a widely read Pelican book fifteen years ago (Eysenck, 1953).

Another suggestion (Sorenson, 1963) which deserves to give rise to research that might be combined with the testing of the Eysenck–Furneaux hypothesis, is that speed of learning on teaching machines in certain standardised conditions could be developed into an objective measure of individual differences supplementary to the conventional IQ. Research evidence about this topic is conflicting (Cronbach 1967, p. 31). At one time it was believed that programmed instruction, by presenting information in finely graded steps and by encouraging the learner to work at his own speed, would remove all or most of the correlation between intelligence and learning. Some researches have pointed in that direction but others indicate that measures of learning from a teaching machine may correlate highly in some conditions with IQ (Lewis and Gregson, 1965).

This discussion of the concept of intelligence has ranged widely. To summarise, the most important distinction between ways of conceiving intelligence seems to be between those who prefer an 'open' view, somewhat allied to the popular or common-sense concept, and those who insist that progress must depend upon an operational definition, with consequent gain in scientific precision and loss of some of the rich and 'polymorphous' aspects. In the long run, if this area of study is ever to form an integral part of scientific enquiry and to evolve beyond the status of quasi-science, the latter view must prevail and the loose, 'open' concept be replaced, for experimental and statistical enquiries, by an agreed and measurable dimension or set of dimensions. Nothing that has been said so far about the failings of narrow psychometrists and operationists should be taken to invalidate this basic point.

What is desirable in principle in the long run, however, is not necessarily good policy immediately. Operational definitions not tied to demonstrable laws and regularities will tend to have the worst of both worlds, being narrow and arbitrary, and offering small prospect of forming part of the network of invariant relations that we call scientific knowledge. Even in the most highly developed area of experimental psychology, i.e. the study of simple forms of learning, attempts, such as that of Hull, to apply rigorous hypothetico-deductive methods and to develop a general set of axioms and predictable relations have proved premature. The study of high-level human abilities is fundamentally much less advanced, in spite of the mass of published research, and the degree of divergence among authoritative experts will rapidly become apparent. If Guilford believes that some 120 independent measurable abilities are required to describe human capacity, whereas Vernon finds that general intelligence accounts for far more variation than all other factors put together in representative samples whether of children or adults; and if Cattell asserts that with a 'culture-fair' test he can derive scores that are genuinely comparable, obtained from Americans, Italians and Formosans, whereas educational sociologists question the significance of differences in measured ability within a single school in one country, we are still a long way from establishing the agreement on valid procedure that is one important sign of a developed science. In this state of affairs it would be highly misleading to publish a textbook that was anything but broad and eclectic. One must conclude that satisfactory operational definition of intelligence, though by no means impossible in principle, has not yet been achieved. There are many ways in which approximations to it could be improved, even before basic laws of cognitive functioning are established, but until then they are likely to be no more than blind, empirical approximations.

Both in the introduction and in parts of this chapter too much has probably been made of the deficiencies, ambiguities and disagreements associated with the concept of intelligence and with difficulties encountered in providing a satisfactory agreed definition. Many of these deficiencies and difficulties are far from being confined to the study of intelligence, but are almost universal in the whole field of psychology and of the social sciences in general. Wallace (1965) in his book 'Concept Growth and the Education of the Child' discusses an article by Skemp on 'mathematics and reflective intelligence' and takes him to task for using the term 'intelligence' on the ground that it involves 'a reification'. This seems little more than a criticism of the use of abstractions. It certainly applies with no more force to the concept of intelligence than to any other psychological trait, such as introversion, adaptability or ego-strength. Short of abandoning the use of *any* description in terms of traits, the use of such abstractions is an inevitable practical necessity. Nor is criticism of this kind especially appropriate only to trait psychology. 'Concept Growth' itself is a decidedly abstract concept – in fact a second-order concept incorporating a metaphor.

The concepts of general intelligence and of more specialised abilities are no less satisfactory than other psychological abstractions and a great deal more useful than many of them. Intelligence has proved a valuable independent variable in a remarkably wide range of psychological experimentation. One would have to comb the whole literature of experimental and clinical psychology to demonstrate this adequately, but one or two recent examples may be quoted. Clarke and Olson (1965), studying 15-year-old boys who had displayed outstanding achievement in athletics, science, leadership, and in the arts, found high intelligence the only quality out of 32 studied that characterised all these different groups. Davitz (1964) found intelligence a crucial variable in studying 'the communication of emotional meaning'. Haan (1963) related both level of intelligence and fluctuations in IQ to various measures of 'coping' and to psychological defence mechanisms. Carment, Miles and Cervin (1965) found intelligence a relevant variable in the study of persuasiveness and persuasibility. Kohlberg and Zigler (1967) found significant interactions between intelligence and other variables in studying the development of sex roles and sex-typing in young children. Kipnis (1965) studied intelligence as an important modifying variable in certain character disorders. Entwisle (1966) found it necessary to take intelligence into account in providing a new and thorough set of norms for children's word-associations. Kogan and Wallach (1964, Ch. 5) found verbal ability relevant to risk-taking, with interesting findings about a sex difference in the extent of this relationship. Hamilton (1967) reviewed the literature on the relation between size constancy and intelligence. Although the findings are not entirely clear-cut, it appears that there is ample evidence for the importance of intelligence even in the fundamental processes of visual perception (cf. Houssiadas 1964, Hodges and Fox, 1965). The degree of intelligence of the investigator, although varying only within quite a narrow range, may have a direct effect on the results of experiments in social psychology (Rosenthal, 1966). Even in the study of extra-sensory perception (Nash and Nash, 1964) it has been suggested that intelligence is relevant – not, as one might suppose, that more effective extra-sensory perception is dependent on superior intelligence, but that high measured intelligence may depend upon ESP! These few recent illustrations of the continuing usefulness of intelligence as an independent or classifying variable in the study of very diverse kinds of behaviour have been chosen from areas to which it might be expected to have *least* relevance. Obviously it is an even more crucial variable in work on problem-solving, learning, creativity, scholastic attainment and vocational success. These relations will be reported in subsequent chapters.

Suggested additional reading

BURT, SIR CYRIL, 'The evidence for the concept of intelligence'. *Brit. J. educ. Psychol.* 25, 158–177 (1955).

MCNEMAR, Q., 'Lost: Our Intelligence? Why?' *Amer. Psychologist.* 19, 871–882 (1964).

DONALDSON, MARGARET, *A Study of Children's Thinking.* London: Tavistock (1963) Chs. 1 and 2.

MILES, T. R., 'On defining intelligence'. *Brit. J. educ. Psychol.* 27, 153–165 (1957).

EYSENCK, H. J., 'Intelligence assessment: a theoretical and experimental approach'. *Brit. J. educ. Psychol.* 37, 81–98 (1967).

SPIKER, C. C. and MCCANDLESS, B. R., 'The concept of intelligence and the philosophy of science'. *Psychol. Rev.* 61, 255–266 (1954).

Note. This short series of recommendations and the similar ones at the end of other chapters are arranged in a rough order of priority for the student. Those that seem important and are not too long, obscure and specialised will appear early in the list. This arrangement should not be taken as disparaging books and articles placed lower or omitted altogether. They will often be more original and profound (but also perhaps less general or less easily assimilated) than those included.

II

The Structure of Abilities

When we talk about intelligence, we imply that there is one principal kind of cognitive ability. It sounds wrong to speak of 'intelligences' in the plural. Admittedly we can talk of different 'kinds of intelligence', but we still tend to imply one over-riding capacity which can manifest itself in different forms, rather than separate, non-overlapping skills. The idea of one dominating intellectual trait is very widely accepted.

The more extreme version of this view, which holds that fundamentally there is only one kind of ability, is far from being self-evidently correct, and many alternatives are possible. There may be *no* single common ability involved in all kinds of intellectual task, and different kinds of problems or situation may all require separate, distinct skills. Alternatively, *both* general intelligence *and* particular, less general, abilities may need to be employed in varying degrees for various tasks. All these possibilities and many other variations are conceivable and in fact the debate about one intelligence or many abilities is centuries old, which suggests that there may be good arguments on either side. The purpose of this chapter is to examine some of these arguments, and particularly the evidence for them from experimental and statistical research. It will be necessary to introduce a few statistical concepts, but this will be done as untechnically, non-mathematically and painlessly as possible, with all the emphasis on their logic and use, not on computation.

THE TECHNIQUES OF CORRELATION AND FACTOR ANALYSIS

Correlation is a technique for finding the extent to which two psychological traits or other qualities vary together. It may appear to a teacher studying his class that, say, performance in geometry and performance in algebra go together so that, on the average, pupils good at one are good at the other, and vice versa. This would suggest a *positive corre-*

lation. If this impression proved wrong, and it was found that there was no systematic relation between algebra and geometry marks, it could be said that these two showed no correlation. But it might happen that those who were good at algebra were poor at geometry. This would be an example of *negative correlation.*

The closeness of the relation is measured by a *correlation coefficient*, which is an index ranging from -1.0 to $+1.0$. A correlation coefficient of $+1.0$ would mean perfect positive correlation. If there were a correlation of $+1.0$ between algebra and geometry, the same boy or girl would be top at both, the same would be bottom, and so on. A correlation of -1.0 indicates that the pupil who was top at algebra would be bottom at geometry. A correlation of 0 indicates no positive or negative relation. In practice, of course, such results are rare, and one more often finds values like $+0.7$, meaning quite a high degree of positive relation or -0.2, meaning a slight degree of negative relation. There are different kinds of correlation coefficient to suit different kinds of data. The one most commonly used, and most suitable where both performances to be correlated can be expressed as continuous measurements, is the product-moment coefficient.

In studies of the inter-relation and structure of human abilities, one usually collects the scores of a group of people on a number of mental tests or other cognitive tasks. This requires careful planning and the formulation of hypotheses or it may become a meaningless exercise; the way in which both people and tests are sampled will have a crucial bearing on the results. When all the tests or other performances have been correlated with each other, the resulting coefficients are tabulated in what is called a matrix of inter-correlations, or simply a *correlation matrix*. An example of a small correlation matrix is shown in table 2.1.

It can be seen from this table that, although correlation matrices are often presented in rectangular form, as here, one half of the table is

TABLE 2.1 *Inter-correlations among creativity and intelligence tests (from Getzels and Jackson, 1962). Based on 292 boys.*

Variable number	Test	1	2	3	4	5	6
1	Word association		·369	·344	·303	·420	·378
2	Uses	·369		·206	·222	·175	·186
3	Hidden shapes	·344	·206		·159	·414	·366
4	Fables	·303	·222	·159		·220	·131
5	Make-up problems	·420	·175	·414	·220		·246
6	I.Q.	·378	·186	·366	·131	·246	

redundant, since each triangular section, on either side of the diagonal from top-left to bottom-right, repeats the other; one can read from the table the correlation of variable 1 (word association) with variable 2 (uses) either in row 1, column 2, or in column 1, row 2. In this particular table all the correlations are positive, though they need not have been. This prevalence of positive correlations is usual when tests of ability and other cognitive measures are compared, although in some areas of psychology, such as personality study, negative correlations may be as numerous as positive. Secondly, there is an empty line of spaces down the diagonal of the table. This arises from a lack of entries where any correlation appearing would be the correlation of a test with itself.

A common-sense or intuitive interpretation of the fact that two measures vary together, as indicated by a sizeable correlation coefficient, is that they share something in common. If marks in algebra and geometry show a substantial positive correlation, but in algebra and woodwork virtually no correlation, this suggests that the performances on the tests of algebra and geometry were similar in some way, or shared some common factor, which was not shared by algebra and wood-work. This is a reasonable interpretation, and the correlation coefficient (or strictly the square of the coefficient) may be statistically interpreted as the proportion of variability that is *common* to the two measures.

Factor analysis is a technique which extends and generalises this kind of interpretation. Even a matrix of the size illustrated in table 2.1 may contain complex inter-relations between the variables that are hard to discern by inspection. By using factor analysis one may analyse the whole matrix to find out how much of the variation in performance on all six tests may be accounted for by one common factor and how far supplementary factors are required. If one has tested a large sample of people, it may be possible to 'take out' statistically the effect of the factor common to all the variables (the general factor) and still find patterns of correlation which indicate further common influences – common not to every variable or test, but to several (group factors). The process is repeated until all the general and group factors have been 'extracted' and the residual correlations are statistically non-significant. The whole procedure is explained in detail in the appendix to this chapter provided by Sir Cyril Burt.

As may be imagined, this is a powerful mathematical technique for unravelling a complex pattern of overlapping influences, and is in many ways ideally suited to provide an answer to the questions that have been asked about the structure of human abilities. Indeed, the views of psychologists at the present time about this structure have been more strongly influenced by the results of factor-analysing test scores than by any other approach. But the technique is by no means a panacea. Various qualifications that have to be made in interpreting the results of factor analyses will gradually become clearer in the course of this chapter, but the three most important ones can be stated at once.

First, although it is often reasonable to interpret these statistical factors as fundamental psychological qualities, they do not emerge conveniently labelled 'intelligence', 'spatial ability' and so on. They are simply evidence of co-variation between several variables, and this may be due to other properties in common; if in a battery of tests, three shared a common layout or format, perhaps being the only multiple-choice tests, this might give rise to a common factor linking these three. Even when the possibility of such unwanted or artificial factors is excluded, it is a big jump from observing a pattern of co-variation to claiming that this pattern indicates a significant psychological function. Burt (1940, p. 249), though a strong proponent of factor-analytic methods and a pioneer in developing them, goes so far as to say that 'factors as such are only statistical abstractions, not concrete entities. To resolve a test-performance into g and s no more demonstrates the existence of a general and specific "ability" than describing a breeze as north-west implies the combination of two currents from separate quarters of the sky.' Thus the interpretation of a statistical factor as a consistent psychological quality always requires careful justification.

Secondly, no method of analysis, however objective or sophisticated, can analyse what is not there. The method of factor analysis gives no information about what material to analyse in the first place. Although it may throw a great deal of light on the structure of various measures of ability which have been administered and scored, it can tell us nothing at all about abilities for which there are no adequate tests, or which are not quantifiable, or which no one has imagined to be important. When one writes, as psychologists are liable to, about 'the structure of abilities as revealed by factor analysis', it would be more accurate to say 'the structure of those abilities which psychologists have thought to be worth testing and have gone on to test by methods which yield adequate numerical scores'. The question of whether important kinds of ability have been left out of the traditional framework will be discussed in Chapters 3 and 4, and what is meant by 'adequate numerical scores' in Chapter 8.

A third qualification about the technique of factor analysis is that in itself it does not provide a unique and objective description of the structure of abilities or about any other data to which it is applied. It can provide a number, in fact an infinite number, of mathematically equivalent answers. To select one of these and say that 'such and such is the structure', that general intelligence, for instance, accounts on the average for 50% of success at a particular task, and spatial ability for a further 20%, depends on extra assumptions, either mathematical or psychological. Mathematical considerations may indicate one kind of answer as the most elegant and economical but psychological considerations may suggest an alternative solution as more easily interpretable in terms of accepted concepts.

This last qualification, although it accounts for much of the apparent disagreement about the structure of abilities, sounds more damaging than it really is. It certainly does *not* mean that any or every kind of answer can be produced, nor is it at all impossible that an agreed solution should be reached. Burt has suggested an analogy between psychological factors and lines of latitude and longitude on a map. These are in a sense arbitrary, and without an agreed scale and origin an infinite number of different systems is possible. Once a system is agreed, the convention may be extremely useful. The alternative answers that can be provided by factor analysis should be thought of as alternatives in a similar sense and this should become clearer when we discuss some of the main findings.

THE ISOLATION OF A FACTOR OF GENERAL INTELLIGENCE

Charles Spearman (1863–1945) is generally recognised as both the inventor and first user of factor-analytic methods, although his ideas were partly foreshadowed by Karl Pearson. His work has been extensively discussed in psychological journals and textbooks for fifty years, and the following account will therefore be condensed and selective. Useful summaries of his contributions to psychology may be found in Vernon (1950), Peel (1956), Flugel and West (1964) and Hearnshaw (1964).

Unlike many of his successors, Spearman was not content merely to carry out statistical analyses, to isolate factors and to describe structure. He also theorised ambitiously about the nature of intelligence and its mode of operation, and it is due more to Spearman than to any other one man that the idea of 'general intelligence' as an important psychological factor (in both the technical and the more general sense of the word) has become part of the body of psychological knowledge, and indeed of most people's way of thinking. But the details of his theories, and some of his suggested 'psychological laws' have not worn so well, and this decline of interest was probably speeded by the over-ambitiousness of many of his claims.

Spearman's first paper on the empirical study of general cognitive ability, entitled 'General intelligence objectively determined and measured', was published in the American Journal of Psychology in 1904, and has been described by Hearnshaw as 'epoch-making'. Already in this early publication, several of the most characteristic features of his later theory of intelligence are made explicit. After criticising the earlier experimental and statistical work in this area as being methodologically unsound, Spearman describes his own findings on several small groups of schoolchildren. Two of his conclusions from these data are, in his own words, and with his own use of italics,

> The above and other analogous observed factors indicate *that all branches of intellectual activity have in common one fundamental function (or group of functions), whereas the remaining or specific elements of the activity seem in every case to be wholly different from that in all the others*. The relative influence of the general to the specific function varies in the ten departments here investigated from 15:1 to 1:4.

> As an important practical consequence of this universal Unity of the Intellectual Function, the various actual forms of mental activity constitute a stably interconnected Hierarchy according to their different degrees of intellective saturation.

The first of these paragraphs is the earliest statement of Spearman's celebrated two-factor theory. The second implies that every kind of mental task will have its own factor loading (or 'saturation') on the factor of general intelligence, which will be an indication of the part general intelligence plays in that task. Much of the rest of Spearman's life was spent elaborating this view and in developing techniques to provide evidence for it.

According to this celebrated 'two-factor theory', which might have been called a 'one-factor theory' (since it depends on the existence of only one *common* factor), the performance of every cognitive task depends only on general intelligence and on another factor entirely specific to the particular task. Spearman stresses that this is a new idea, and distinguishes it from three kinds of earlier theory about abilities, which he calls the monarchic, the oligarchic and the anarchic. The monarchic view would imply a truly 'one-factor' theory, with general intelligence supreme, and equally important in every cognitive task; the oligarchic would imply several large ability factors of roughly equal influence; the anarchic view would make every task depend upon its own specific ability. Spearman's two-factor theory is thus a refined version of the

46 Human Intelligence

monarchic type, with the important qualification that general intelligence enters into different tasks in different degrees.

The picture is beautifully simple, too simple to be true, one might say. If true, it has important consequences, particularly for educational and vocational guidance. As Vernon (1950) has pointed out, this view, if interpreted strictly, excludes the possibility of linguistic or mechanical aptitudes and of tests to assess them, since such tests would measure only general intelligence plus something extremely specific – a consequence that would make guidance very difficult. Spearman has, however, proved more nearly right than vocational and educational psychologists would wish him to be.

Towards the end of his life, Spearman acknowledged that his theory did not meet all the observed facts, though he continued to maintain that it met the most common and most important ones. Thus Spearman and Wynn Jones (1950, p. 10) say that the two-factor theory 'only indicates the initial degree of analysis; certainly not the ultimate'. They consider the accumulated evidence for group factors, i.e. for abilities that cover many activities but not all and their conclusion is that such factors have been found but that they are either small or rare.

Most psychologists today would disagree, and would maintain that certain abilities, distinct from general intelligence but covering a large range of cognitive activities, are neither small nor rare but of considerable importance, and that Spearman's theory, even in the slightly modified form it finally reached, was still too simple. Nonetheless Spearman was probably more nearly right than many people in the current state of psychological opinion might admit, and his work was important for two main reasons. Firstly, he was a doughty pioneer in introducing empirical and statistical methods of studying material and phenomena which had earlier appeared too complex to analyse. Secondly, his basic concept of general intelligence, which following Galton, he made the main plank in his programme, has weathered the storms of adverse criticism more satisfactorily than many other plausible-seeming concepts in the short history of psychology as a science.

SUBSEQUENT BRITISH MODIFICATIONS OF SPEARMAN'S THEORY
OF GENERAL INTELLIGENCE

After Spearman, the strongest influence on British psychologists' ideas about intelligence has been that of Sir Cyril Burt. Since his first published paper on the subject (Burt, 1909), which describes a thorough and extensive experimental study, he has produced a flood of authoritative articles on all aspects of intelligence and abilities. His early article concludes with the words, 'Parental intelligence, therefore, may be inherited, individual intelligence measured, and general intelligence analysed; and they can be analysed, measured and inherited to a degree which few psychologists have hitherto legitimately ventured to maintain.'

Of these three statements, two have been abundantly justified; that concerning the effects of heredity is still arguable and has stimulated debate in a very recent issue of the British Journal of Psychology (March, 1967). This will be discussed in Chapter 6, and there will be continual need to refer to various aspects of Burt's work and views throughout this book. In the writer's opinion, his contributions to psychology have been grossly under-estimated, particularly in the USA.

Burt's major innovation was the rejection of the view, to which Spearman clung so stubbornly, that only two kinds of factor are needed to account for the correlations among cognitive performances, (1) a general factor (2) a factor specific to each different task. In the early paper just quoted, Burt foresaw to some extent that intermediate factors would be needed to provide a full account of the structure of abilities. In the twenties and thirties of this century, enough evidence was amassed, by Kelley (1928), Stephenson (1931) and El Koussy (1935) among others, to show conclusively that group factors did occur, common, for instance, to verbal problems or spatial problems, but not represented in other kinds of task. These findings are excellently summarised by Vernon (1950, Chapter 2).

Burt was able to combine the central idea of Spearman about the importance of general intelligence and these newer modifications into one integrated scheme, which is still in many ways the most satisfactory and convincing. Its central feature is the idea of a hierarchy of abilities. In any study of cognitive behaviour where the data are subjected to a thorough analysis, four main kinds of factor are likely to be found; these are general, group, specific and error factors.

> The measurement of any individual for any one of a given set of traits may be regarded as a function of four kinds of components: namely, those characteristic of (i) all the traits, (ii) some of the traits, (iii) the particular trait in question whenever it is measured, (iv) the particular trait in question as measured on this particular occasion. (Burt 1940, p. 103).

In his book *The Factors of the Mind*, Burt provides an exhaustive and persuasive account of the logic of factor analysis and, in particular, of his reasons for defining these four kinds of factor, which he relates to traditional categories of classification.

General factor, group-factors (or bipolar factors), specific factors and chance factors – this fourfold scheme is thus in effect an independent rediscovery, in a special application, of the fourfold scheme of predicables handed down by traditional logic. Indeed, nearly every one of the fundamental controversies that have perplexed the psychological factorist could be paralleled by the ancient disputes that have arisen out of the famous schemes originally set forth by Aristotle and his commentator Porphyry.

Why then the mathematical disguise? Simply because, as we have already seen, the popular notion of personal characteristics as being merely present or absent, and of individual persons as being assignable to a few non-overlapping classes, each comprising relatively homogeneous members, is far too crude and inexact for a scientific description. Hence, what were originally plain principles of qualitative classification have taken on a quantitative form, and have become 'factors' instead of mere fundamental divisions.

This way of looking at abilities as forming a hierarchical tree in descending degrees of generality is widely accepted among British psychologists. The most general source of variation, Spearman's *g* factor, or general intelligence will retain most of its explanatory status. When its effects on a variety of performances have already been taken into account, there will still remain factors, such as for instance verbal ability or spatial ability, common to large groups of performances. Within these groups it may be possible to find smaller groups, each of which still has something in common, even after the effect of the major group factor has been taken into account, and so on, until all the common variation has been accounted for, and one is left with the variation specific to a particular performance. This specific variation can itself be divided into 'true' and 'error' variation.

After the effect of the general factor has been removed, the next most important factor has very commonly been found to be one that distinguishes verbal from non-verbal abilities. This is a very pervasive factor and has been identified in researches using a wide variety of tests (and examinations) on subjects of all ages (Burt, 1949). The total picture current among British psychologists is probably similar to the illustration provided by Vernon (1950), which is reproduced as figure 2.1.

But, as Vernon warns us, this picture should only be treated as a general approximation, and the details are left vague in the diagram not only because they are not fully known, but also because they will vary according to circumstances. There is some danger in the whole factorial approach, at least to those who read summaries of its findings; they may be tempted to think that the pattern of human abilities is such and such, and that any variations from it are exceptional. On the contrary, one must *expect* the pattern to vary according to the sampling of variables, the sampling of people, and many other circumstances. We have already seen that Spearman's original theory was based on too limited a set of performances, and that modifications were required when later workers analysed larger sets. Similarly we shall see that Thurstone's original theory depended on too limited a selection of people. The hierarchical theory first suggested by Burt and illustrated in figure 2.1 is

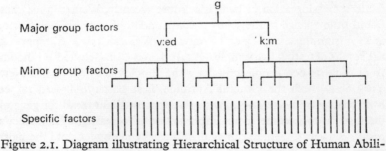

Figure 2.1. Diagram illustrating Hierarchical Structure of Human Abilities. From Vernon (1950)

an improvement, not least because it recognises this dependence of the factor pattern on the selection of tasks and of people, and explicitly allows that a factor at a given level may at one time appear general and important (if the analysis is confined to a rather similar set of tests), and at another time relatively narrow and specific when a much larger range and variety of performances is analysed. One of the most salient virtues in Burt's account has been his keen awareness of the relativity of factor structures and their dependence on the sampling of variables to be included in the battery.

Thus the major group factors *v:ed* and *k:m* (verbal-educational and spatial-mechanical) may sometimes appear as such. But if, for instance, a comprehensive set of tests demanding verbal skills and educationally-acquired skills is analysed, one will expect the *v:ed* factor to break down into its two distinguishable components, verbal and educational respectively. And if one carried this process further, limiting the analysis, say, to an extensive selection of tests involving verbal skills, one would find that the verbal factor would split into factors lower in the hierarchy and relatively more specific. Other circumstances, too, will affect the relative prominence and importance of general and group factors. It is generally accepted, for instance, that with increasing age the relative importance of *g* becomes less, owing to the progressive differentiation of more specialised kinds of ability. This was presented as a general theory of human development by Garrett (1946), but as Maier has pointed out in his (1965) book on developmental psychology, it is by no means clear whether it is age as such which produces this increasing differentiation, or perhaps education or some other combination of influences. There is some evidence available about such specific points as the age at which a spatial factor can be separately assessed in children (Emmett, 1949), but very few relevant longitudinal studies extending throughout life. Balinsky (1941), however, showed the relative importance of the general factor increasing again in later life. More recently, Weiner (1964) has found little change in the relative contribution of general intelligence, at least from the age of 13 or 14 onwards. Weiner's research, reporting the results of testing two samples of 1,400 cases each (selected at random from some 10,000 people tested by the Employment Service in New York State) with the General Aptitude Test Battery, showed rather little change from age 14–54, with an apparent slight trend for general intelligence to become more important with increasing age. Weiner's results, however, seem to run against the general opinion, and the most recent study of this question supports Garrett's theory of progressive differentiation. This is by Quereshi (1967), who found a continuous decrease in the percentage of total variation attributable to the general factor with increasing age, and a gradual decline in the interdependence of factors in the older age groups.

The hierarchical theory has major advantages over almost all other models of human abilities. It accounts for the proliferation of apparently conflicting findings and the multiplicity of ability factors that have been described and labelled. Much of this apparent confusion has been caused by the comparison of factors operating at different levels in the hierarchy, and this in turn is largely due to the initial selection of tests and people. To this extent, the criticism of factorial methods, 'that you only get out of a factor analysis what you put in' is correct. The second major advantage is that one is thus enabled to recognise that different kinds of factor, and the tests based on them, serve very different purposes in assessment and prediction. Other things being equal, measurement of a general factor will account for more variation in performance and provide prediction over a wider range of tasks than measurement of a major or minor group factor. This is of course the fundamental reason for the continued use of measures of general intelligence both in this country and the USA. But for particular families of skills and for greater accuracy in a more limited area (where 'fidelity', in the language of communications specialists, is more important than 'bandwidth') it may well be necessary to use tests that measure a major or minor group factor.

AMERICAN RESEARCH AND THEORY UP TO 1945

American psychologists, since the earliest extensive empirical work on abilities at the very beginning of the twentieth century, have, in contrast to their British counterparts, tended to favour an 'oligarchic' or 'anarchic' view (in Spearman's language) rather than a 'monarchic' one. It is tempting to ascribe the difference in approach to pre-suppositions arising from national temperament and national culture-pattern. One is reminded of Bertrand Russell's observation that animals studied by American learning theorists learned by an energetic process of trial and error, whereas those studied by German theorists sat down and waited for a flash of insight. Be this as it may, there is no doubt that on the whole, with a few conspicuous exceptions, theories of general intelligence as the prime mover, perhaps modified or 'perturbed' by subsidiary influences, have flourished in Britain, whereas the generally preferred picture in the United States has been of multiple abilities of more or less equal status and influence.

Early research in America has been summarised by Tuddenham (1961), who points out that, after a period of great enthusiasm for mental testing in the eighteen-nineties, which was stimulated and led by J. McK. Cattell, theoretical studies of the structure of abilities were discouraged by the findings of Sharp (1899) and Wissler (1901), from which it appeared that there was very little overlap between performance on various mental tasks. Two reasons mainly account for this premature conclusion, firstly the fact that most of the tests which showed such a low degree of inter-correlation were of simple sensory functions, such as reaction times, time estimation and judgments of weight, and few tests of reasoning or abstraction were included. Secondly, where tests of more complex mental processes were employed, these were in general unreliable. As Tuddenham says, 'in retrospect it is surprising that the Wissler and Sharp studies should have counted so heavily against the "method of tests". Nevertheless the conclusions were taken as a condemnation of mental measurement. When modern intelligence tests were introduced a few years later, it was under non-academic auspices.

University departments were often uninterested when they were not hostile.'

Even when this hostility or lack of interest had been largely overcome, the belief in a large number of separate abilities, each specific to a particular task or narrow range of tasks, remained strong. In particular, this was due to the influence and high reputation of E. L. Thorndike (1874–1949), whose views on this issue were absolutely opposite to those of Spearman. It was not until about 1930 that Kelley and later Thurstone, by extensive testing programmes and by the introduction of new methods of analysis, confirmed and re-interpreted the complex overlapping of abilities that is now generally accepted.

(a) *Thurstone's innovations in technique.* L. L. Thurstone (1887–1955) has been by far the most influential American analyst of abilities, both in methodology and in findings. Indeed, as so often in this field, the two are closely related, and one must therefore provide an outline of his technical innovations.

As we have seen, the technique of factor analysis usually starts from a matrix (or table) of the inter-correlations between a number of tests or other psychological measures. From this table it produces a further matrix or table, known as a factor matrix, which shows the relation between the original tests and the common factors which have been 'extracted' from them. In the special case where the data fit the Spearman theory of general intelligence, there will be only one such common factor, but more generally there may be several. In this factor matrix, each row represents a test, and each column a common factor. The figures in the body of the table are the 'loadings' of each test on each factor, indicating the extent to which the test involves the ability represented by the factor. These loadings are like correlation coefficients in that they can take any value from $+1\cdot0$ through zero to $-1\cdot0$, and may be thought of as correlations between the tests and the abilities. A simple example of a factor matrix, taken from Vernon (1950), is shown in table 2.2 opposite. Here three factors have been extracted from the correlations between six tests (by a computational method described in Vernon's text) and have been identified as g, v and k, i.e. as a general intelligence factor, a verbal factor and a spatial factor. From the relative size of the factor loadings it appears, for example, that of the tests used, 'vocabulary' and 'classifications' are the best measures of general intelligence, and that 'vocabulary' is also the best measure of verbal ability (though not such a good measure as it is of intelligence).

We have already seen in an earlier section that any such table of factor loadings is in an important sense arbitrary, but that it is not *completely* arbitrary, since it must be derived mathematically from the observed correlations. However, an infinite number of different solutions is possible, all of which are mathematically permissible. Factor analysis as such enables us to simplify and interpret complex overlapping performances in terms of relatively few abilities, but it does not in itself tell us *how* to do this. It offers a set of economical interpretations, but to choose between them we need some further mathematical or psychological principle.

Thurstone introduced a new principle which he called 'simple structure'. He developed this principle from an intuitive belief that, in a large and representative set of mental tasks, abilities will be involved that greatly facilitate some of the tasks but have no effect on others. For example, one would not expect numerical ability to influence performance on a task of verbal fluency. Thurstone therefore imposed a condition about the number of zero factor loadings that must occur in each row and column of the factor matrix for the analysis to be acceptable. To quote part of this principle in his own words (Thurstone 1938, p. 8)

> If there are six fundamental abilities involved in an experiment with fifty tests, then it is not likely that every test requires all six fundamental abilities. The factorial matrix would have fifty rows and six columns. If the abilities were known, it would probably be very difficult to construct a set of fifty tests each one of which required all the abilities. It is much more likely that each test will require one or more abilities but that these will differ from one test to another. For example, if one of the tests calls for the ability to visualize, it is not likely that all the verbal tests will contain this ability. If one of

TABLE 2.2 *Completed factor analysis of six psychological tests*[1]

	Loadings			Squares of Loadings			Commun-ality h^2	Speci-ficity $1—h^2$
	g	v	k	g	v	k		
1. Vocabulary	·8	·5		·64	·25		·89	·11
2. Analogies	·7	·4		·49	·16		·65	·35
3. Classifications	·8	·3		·64	·09		·73	·27
4. Block Design	·6		·4	·36		·16	·52	·48
5. Spatial	·5		·7	·25		·49	·74	·26
6. Formboard	·4		·5	·16		·25	·41	·59
Variance				42·3	8·3	15·0	65·7	34·3

[1] From Vernon 1950, p. 7

the tests involves a number factor, it is not likely that all the tests require this factor. It is to be expected, therefore, that even for a random battery of tests there will be a large number of zero entries in the factorial matrix which describes the tests in terms of the fundamental abilities. There will be one or more zeros in every row. This circumstance can be capitalized in finding a unique solution for the factor problem in which the fundamental abilities shall be simple and meaningful.

At this point two questions may occur to the reader who has been following the argument closely. Does not this principle of 'simple structure' automatically preclude the possibility of finding a general factor? A general factor, such as Spearman's *g*, will, in contrast to Thurstone's intuitive picture of abilities, affect *all* cognitive performances. Secondly, if this is so, is it not begging the question to devise, as Thurstone does, a method which makes it impossible to find a factor of general intelligence? The answer to the first question is that Thurstone's criterion of simple structure does indeed rule out the possibility of finding a general factor. But the answer to the second is, on the whole, negative. If the pattern of performances and the observed correlations are to a large extent accounted for by one general ability, the technique may minimise the apparent effect of this general ability, but cannot abolish it entirely. If the observed results do not fit, no satisfactory simple structure can be found.

Satisfactory simple structure was *not* always found when a representative selection of tests and subjects was sampled and this result led to Thurstone's second major technical innovation, the introduction of *correlated* factors. All the factors we have discussed so far have been statistically independent, with the result that there would be no systematic relation between someone's degree of general intelligence, and, for example, his degree of verbal ability. These uncorrelated factors are also known as orthogonal, and correlated factors as oblique, since the former can be represented as two axes at right-angles, and the latter as two axes crossing at an oblique angle.

Thomson (1951) describes this innovation lucidly.

(So far) we have kept our factors orthogonal; that is independent, uncorrelated with one another. It is natural to desire them to be *different* qualities, and convenient statistically. In describing a man, or an occupation, it would seem to be both confusing and uneconomical to use factors which, as it were, overlapped. Yet in situations where more familiar entities are dealt with, we do not hesitate to use correlated measures in describing a man. For instance, we give a son's height and weight, although these are correlated qualities.

Often, moreover, a battery of tests which will not permit simple structure to be reached if orthogonal factors are insisted on will nevertheless do so if the factors are allowed to sag away a little from strict orthogonality. Even as early as in *Vectors of Mind* (1935), Thurstone expressly permitted this. It can clearly be defended on the ground that even if the factors were uncorrelated in the whole population, they might well be correlated to some extent in the sample of people actually tested. I was at one time under the impression that this comparatively slight departure from orthogonality was all that was contemplated by Thurstone. But he and his fellow-workers now have the courage of their convictions, and permit factors to depart from orthogonality as much as is necessary to attain simple structure, even if they are then found to be quite highly correlated.

(b) *Thurstone's 'Primary Mental Abilities'*. We have discussed Thurstone's new technique at some length, since an understanding of it is necessary to compare his findings about the structure of abilities with those of other psychologists. Thorough and large-scale studies were made both of college students and of fourteen-year-old school children (Thurstone, 1938; Thurstone, T. G., 1941; Thurstone and Thurstone, 1941), and the results analysed by the new methods just described.

In the first research, in which 56 very varied tests (ranging from 2 to 20 minutes in length) were administered to 240 students, seven main factors were identified, with two more provisionally interpretable. The seven factors recurred in other studies (with minor modifications and exceptions), and became the basis for the sub-tests in Thurstone's well-known tests of 'primary mental abilities'. These seven factors (Thurstone, 1938) were

> S – spatial ability
> P – perceptual speed
> N – numerical ability
> V – verbal meaning
> M – memory
> W – verbal fluency
> I or R – inductive reasoning.

With young children, not all of these were found, but a 'motor' factor appeared. In later versions of the tests, the memory factor was dropped, so that the final versions, designed for three age-groups, were designed to measure factors as follows:

Age 5-7. V, P, S, quantitative, motor.
Age 7-11. V, P, S, R, N.
Age 11-17. V, S, R, N, W.

An important point is that, since scores on these factors are correlated, it is possible to perform a second-order analysis of the factors themselves, and the resulting super-factor that is found can only be interpreted as a factor of general intelligence! In his earlier studies Thurstone believed he had analysed abilities without any need to admit 'general intelligence', but later realised that the system of correlated factors implied a second-order general factor, with the result that the published tests include instructions for estimating general intelligence from a combination of scores on the primary factors.

It is probably unfortunate that Thurstone in the first flush of enthusiasm should have called his factors 'primary' mental abilities. There is no evidence that they are primary in any neurological or psychological sense, although innocent users (and some writers of textbooks) have supposed them to be. The claims of Thurstone's scheme to be the most satisfactory must rest either on the methodological superiority of the technique of rotation to simple structure, or on the convenience for practical purposes (e.g. in vocational guidance) of prediction from his correlated factors. These are both arguable questions. The first will be considered in the final evaluatory section of this chapter. On the second question, whether the use of Thurstone's primary mental abilities is more useful than other approaches for practical predictive purposes, one can at least say that no overwhelming advantages have been demonstrated. In practice, the tests of V and R have proved most useful in predicting academic success, and those of S and N have been moderately useful for particular purposes, while W (word-fluency) has shown very little predictive value.

AMERICAN WORK SINCE 1945

A great deal of interesting research has been done by J. P. Guilford and his associates at the University of Southern California. This is presented in some 40 reports over the last 16 years. A useful and up-to-date account of the present state of these findings is contained in report No. 36 which also lists all the earlier publications up to August, 1966 (Guilford and Hoepfner, 1966).

Guilford starts by classifying possible kinds of ability under three heads. Abilities may vary according to (a) the basic psychological processes involved, which are cognition, memory, evaluation, divergent production and convergent production, (b) the kind of material or content, such as symbolic (e.g. letters, numbers and words, when meaning as such is not considered), or semantic (meaningful material, particularly verbal), (c) the forms that information takes in the course of being processed, such as classes, systems, relations or transformations.

The possible processes or operations according to Guilford are 5 in number, the kinds of content 4, and the kinds of product 6. Since these

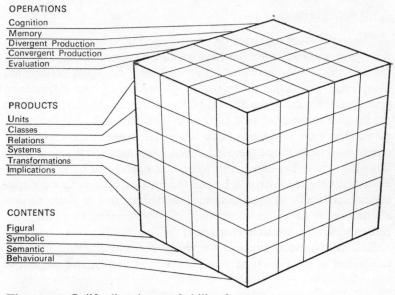

OPERATIONS
Cognition
Memory
Divergent Production
Convergent Production
Evaluation

PRODUCTS
Units
Classes
Relations
Systems
Transformations
Implications

CONTENTS
Figural
Symbolic
Semantic
Behavioural

Figure 2.2. Guilford's scheme of ability factors

are independent cross-classifications, this system yields a large number of possible different abilities, i.e. $5 \times 4 \times 6 = 120$. This 3-dimensional classification is shown in figure 2.2 above.

This way of classifying abilities according to logical principles is similar to ideas suggested independently by Guttman (1965) and by Humphreys (1962), although these two writers would not necessarily agree with Guilford's actual bases of classification.

Merrifield (1966, p. 22) one of Guilford's associates, attempts to throw a little light on what may appear the rather arbitrary aspects of this system.

One may question the choice of the three-category scheme – why not a two-category description, or one with four categories? Two categories seemed too few to account for the observed differences among factors, and four categories seemed more than necessary. Without straining too hard to find historical referents, one may recall the distinction between sensation, percept and concept as compared to content in the model; the variety of tasks in the complication experiments at Leipzig and, later, the emphasis on totality of phenomena at Berlin as possible precursors of the different products; and Brentano's division of psychic acts into sensing, imagining, acknowledging, perceiving, and recalling, among others, as foreshadowing the five operations.

The five kinds of operation or psychological process contained in the first basis of classification are largely self-explanatory, except perhaps for the distinction between convergent and divergent production. Convergent production refers to 'the generation of information from given information, where the emphasis is upon achieving unique or conventionally accepted best outcomes' (Guilford and Hoepfner 1966, p. 3). Divergent production is conceived of as more concerned with open-ended tasks, where there is no such single agreed correct outcome. This distinction has been an influential one, and will be further discussed in Chapter 4. It will be seen there that both Guilford's conceptualisation and his construction of numerous tests to assess various abilities under the general heading of 'divergent production' have been reflected in recent work on 'creativity'.

Each of these five kinds of operation or psychological process is thought of as comprising 24 possible forms of ability, and the aim of

TABLE 2.3 *Cognition factors*[1]

	Figural	Symbolic	Semantic	Behavioral
Units	CFU-V CFU-A	CSU-V CSU-A	CMU	CBU
Classes	CFC	CSC	CMC	CBC
Relations	CFR	CSR	CMR	CBR
Systems	CFS	CSS	CMS	CBS
Transformations	CFT	(I)	CMT	CBT
Implications	CFI	CSI	CMI	CBI

[1] From Guilford and Hoepfner 1966, p. 5.

Guilford and his associates has been to make up several tests for each of the 120 resulting abilities, and to define each ability as a factor, independent of or orthogonal to all the other factors. Each is given a code-name in terms of the three bases of classification, and sometimes also a psychological name. Thus the ability resulting from divergent production applied to symbolic material to produce units is referred to as DSU, and has also been called 'word fluency'. As an illustration, one of the blocks of 24 abilities, those falling under the heading of cognition, is shown in table 2.3 above. It can be seen that every cell has an entry, but that one, where one would expect to find CST is marked (I.). This means that Guilford claims to have defined a factor empirically for each of these combinations, with one exception, which is still under investigation. The report by Guilford and Hoepfner (1966), from which figure 2.2 and table 2.3 are reproduced, also provides a useful short summary of the kinds of tests used to define each of these numerous factors. Thus, one of the tests used to assess CMU is a multiple-choice vocabulary test (the Guilford-Zimmermann Verbal Comprehension Test) and CFC is assessed by a picture classification test.

Guilford and his associates have been working for almost twenty years on the ambitious task of constructing tests to measure this large number of rather specific abilities, but not all the areas are so well charted as appears from table 2.3.

In some of the other blocks, the column representing 'behavioral' content for instance is still blank, but recent developments in that area have been described by O'Sullivan et al (1965). The idea is a useful one, that a set of abilities might be identified which deal with the handling of information about human behaviour; as Guilford and Hoepfner (1963) put it, 'information, essentially non-verbal, involved in human interactions, where awareness of the attitudes, needs, desires, moods, intentions, perceptions, thoughts, etc., of other people and ourselves is important'. A similar idea was described in some detail by Alfred Adler (see the Ansbachers' 1965 selection of his writings), who described reason or common sense as intelligence combined with social interest (*gemeinschaftsgefühl*) and therefore directed to socially useful ends. E. L. Thorndike also thought that 'social ability' was an important facet of intelligence. One might expect a sex difference in favour of girls in this kind of ability, and it is interesting that 'social competence' has been found to be more closely associated with intelligence (Terman-Merrill test) in girls than in boys (Wall and Kellmer Pringle, 1966).

What are the advantages and defects of this complex classificatory scheme, which it has not been possible to describe except in brief outline? How important is it to the psychologist who wants to form a rational picture of the nature of abilities and what practical value does it possess?

Firstly, Guilford's account of the nature and structure of abilities has the advantage of being systematic and giving the appearance of a scientific classification, unlike much research in the field of abilities which has rightly been criticised as blindly operational and undirected by theory. The three-fold classification of intelligent behaviour according to how it operates, what it operates on, and what is produced by the operation, although not the only possible or necessarily the best system, undoubtedly forms a logical and useful frame of reference. It has even been hailed by some as comparable to Mendeleev's discovery of a periodic table of chemical elements (Gowan and Demos, 1964, p. 19). In some ways this account of abilities is also more easily related to the general body of psychological knowledge than are most factorial analyses. An attempt of this kind to demonstrate connections between (a) the theory of abilities and (b) problem-solving and learning theory is made by Guilford (1961). Similarly Merrifield (1966) has produced a systematic set of hypotheses (p. 30) about the particular Guilfordian or 'structure-of-intellect' factors that contribute to a wide range of learning, concept formation and problem-solving. Finally, Guilford's theory, his analysis of many of the cognitive components in creative production, and the prolific flow of tests from his laboratory have all provided a good deal of stimulus to a new and more varied approach to the study of intellectual functioning.

As for disadvantages, these mainly amount to a lack of demonstrated predictive value. Vernon (1964b) has pointed out that Guilford's factors are too narrow and specific to be much use except in predicting narrow and specific criteria. Sultan (1962) found rather discouraging results when using a large battery of Guilford's tests with English grammar school pupils aged 13–14, being unable with this sample to find the expected factor structure in terms of such factors as Spontaneous Flexibility and Adaptive Flexibility. Hunt (1961) states flatly (p. 301) that these highly specific factors have no predictive value in any situation. Undoubtedly Guilford goes to extreme lengths in extracting a very large number of factors that are at the opposite end of the scale from 'general intelligence' in terms of generality, and apparently also at the opposite end in predictive power. Humphreys (1962) has commented that Thurstone (although himself a proponent of multiple abilities) supposed he had adequately sampled the whole area of abilities with less tests than Guilford has factors!

Finally, mention must be made of recent work by R. B. Cattell. Cattell's view of human abilities is in a sense a synthesis of the typical British and American views, since he retains a belief in the importance of general intelligence, but believes that this is best reached and assessed as a second-order factor via Thurstone's primary mental abilities. His reason for this preference is the further belief that Thurstone's technique of correlated factors and simple structure produces a more objectively defined factor of general intelligence in the long run, particularly in the sense that its nature will remain more constant even with considerable variation in the initial measures from which it is derived. Cattell also makes a distinction between two kinds of general intelligence, which he describes as 'fluid' and 'crystallised'. These bear some resemblance to Hebb's (1949, 1966) intelligence A and intelligence B, and the two formulations were proposed independently at about the same time. A third formulation, which Cattell sees as rather similar to his own distinction is that of Newland (1962), who distinguishes between 'process' and 'product'.

Crystallised general ability is defined as represented by those cognitive performances in which habits of skilled judgment have become crystallised from the application of some prior, more fundamental general ability to these fields. Thurstone's Verbal and Numerical primaries, or achievement in geography or history, would be examples of such products. Fluid general ability, on the other hand, shows more in tests requiring adaptation to new situations, where crystallised skills are of no particular advantage. Before biological maturity (15–20 years of age) individual differences between gf and gc will reflect mainly differences in cultural opportunity and interest. Among adults these discrepancies will reflect also differences in age, since the gap between gc and gf will tend to increase with experience and the time-decay of gf.

Cattell (1963b) goes on to develop in considerable detail other expected consequences of this distinction and to suggest experimental tests for some of these hypotheses. What is of particular interest is that, alone of the many authors who have seen the conceptual advantages of distinguishing two kinds of intelligence, one largely innate and unmodifiable and one highly dependent on cultural influences and experience, Cattell attempts to separate these experimentally. It is interesting to note, however, in this connection the work of Renshaw (1952) who found two second-order factors which he interpreted as general intelligence and 'schooling' respectively. Further details of recent work along these lines may be found in Horn and Cattell (1966, 1967) and

Cattell (1967). The fullest recent account of this theory of Cattell's is provided by Cattell and Butcher (1968).

AN EVALUATION OF THE FACTORIAL APPROACH

It is often extremely difficult for the student to arrive at a just appreciation of what has been achieved by the extensive attempts during the last sixty years to analyse human abilities into distinct components. Many psychologists would dismiss this work as devoted and industrious, but quite misguided. Chambers (1943), Zangwill (1950), Heim (1954) and others of the Cambridge school have expressed the conviction in various forms that mental measurement in general, and the technique of factor analysis in particular, lack a proper psychological basis and misguidedly exalt minutiae of statistical method above controlled experiment and psychological understanding. Cohen (1964), from a similar viewpoint, has poked fun at the whole approach, remarking that 'in some dim and esoteric way the fabulous visions of a Swedenborg, a Factor Analyst, or even a Learning Theorist undeniably constitute an attempt to understand his world!'

Statements of this kind are, one hopes, not intended to be taken entirely seriously, but there is *some* foundation to these criticisms. Much factorial work has been psychologically naive, and the mystique of the method has often induced people to make sweeping claims for the importance of their factors. Often there has seemed to be an implication that the factors, like Platonic 'Forms' or 'Ideas', are more real than the scores from which they are derived, and that their structure is constant over changes in the sample of people, in the environmental conditions and in the period of time. Sometimes indeed it may be, but this can never be simply assumed. Hofstaetter (1954) has demonstrated the changing factorial structure of abilities in a longitudinal study of children, and Fleishman and Hempel (1954) have shown that the factorial structure of a complex task can change in a short period of time according to the stage of practice reached. A number of studies, such as that of Maxwell (1961), have shown that the pattern of abilities involved in performance on the Wechsler adult scale changes in late middle age and old age, and that a verbal comprehension factor then accounts for much more of the variance. Berger et al. (1964) even found a greater change in structure occurring with ageing than in some pathological states. Findings of this kind can of course be interpreted as indications of the sensitivity of the method to variations in structure, but genuine difficulties have arisen from two aspects of factor analysis already discussed, from the multiplicity of alternative solutions, and from the enormous differences in importance and generality of the factors discovered which arise from different ideas about the sampling of variables.

In answer to these various objections, it may be said in the first place that some criticisms of the factor-analytic method appear to be founded on a disinclination for statistics as such, which is certainly a severe handicap to a biological scientist. Geneticists, for instance, have had occasion to employ formidably complex methods of statistical analysis and require a competence of this kind far beyond the reach of many eminent psychologists. Counter-polemics apart, in discussing individual differences in ability, we all, whether we like it or not, experience the need to quantify and categorise them in dimensions of one kind or another. Until about 1900, there were no methods available, other than armchair speculation, to determine which of the innumerable kinds of classification best fitted actual human performance. Factor analysis, with all its inherent drawbacks, and with all the additional hazards of misguided application and faulty drawing of conclusions (which it shares with most other techniques of any value), has been and is the only available method to show clearly what is common and what is specific in a complex set of performances. The work summarised in this chapter has provided no simple answer about the structure of abilities, much as some of its most able practitioners wished for one. We have seen that Spearman's attempt to make general intelligence the only common element in cognitive performance and Thurstone's attempt to exclude it altogether were both unsuccessful. The joint result of these two men's work is important, not least in this negative aspect. Both were at fault also in being over-optimistic about the status or 'reality' of their factors. Burt's view of factors as convenient principles of classification rather than as 'real', causal entities is the only scientific one *except when other lines of evidence besides the correlational and factor-analytical one* converge to support something beyond a merely statistical unity.

Probably, the main value of factor analysis unsupported by other evidence is a negative one, which is none the less important. It cannot conclusively demonstrate that a particular method or system of classifying abilities is the *correct* one, or even the most neat and economical one, since over sixty years agreement has not been reached about what kind of classification is nearest and most economical. Whatever scheme is put forward, it is perfectly permissible for another factorist to substitute an alternative, mathematically equivalent, but quite different in apparent structure and nomenclature. Thus a representative selection of test scores may be analysed to produce Thurstone's 'primary mental abilities' with their implicit general factor, or to produce the Burt-Vernon hierarchical set of uncorrelated abilities headed by general intelligence. While the factor-analytic method is not capable of specifying one best scheme of classification, it is perfectly capable of *rejecting* schemes that do not fit the observed figures, as we have already illustrated in the attempts of Spearman and Thurstone respectively to enthrone and to abolish general intelligence.

Factor-analysis may therefore be considered as a method of testing hypotheses, but more thought and work is needed before its uses and limitations in this respect are fully understood. Techniques such as Hurley and Cattell's (1962), aptly-named 'Procrustes' (cf. also Hendrickson and White, 1964, 1966; Schönemann, 1966), are interesting and promising. The idea behind this is to specify in advance what one believes on psychological grounds to be a likely factor structure, and then to employ the program to manipulate the data to the best possible fit. An account of its use to test hypotheses about the ability structure of young children is given by Meyers et al. (1964). There are two obvious dangers here. Firstly, the choice of test scores or other measures that one feeds into the analysis may be biased or unrepresentative of the whole domain one is trying to study. Secondly, an electronic computer searching for combinations of oblique factors may be able to produce a plausible-looking fit to a wide variety of hypothetical structures. But if the troublesome problem can be solved of obtaining a set of measures which is agreed to be representative of a given domain, and if objective measures of goodness of fit between a hypothesised and obtained structure can be improved, this approach may transform factor analysis from relatively undirected search to a rigorous method of testing hypotheses.

The increasing use of electronic computers for factor analysis holds promise in another way. It is possible that this account has laid too much stress on disagreements between factorists and on drawbacks in the method. This has been deliberate, since the commonest misunderstanding in the past has been a too naive acceptance of any and every factorial result at its face value. But it seems likely that the increasing use of computers to analyse large batteries of tests (as is already common practice in the USA) can lessen some of the most serious difficulties.

Two of these problems as already stated have been the adequate sampling of variables and the finding of an agreed method of analysis. The capacity of electronic computers enables much larger collections of variables to be analysed in one operation, and consequently eases the sampling problem. The use of 'analytic' programmes of rotation, in which the factor structure is objectively determined without the intervention of human judgment, goes some way towards solving the second problem; only some way, because human judgment is pushed back one stage, to the point of deciding on what principles these programs should be compiled. Most have consisted of attempts to objectify Thurstone's intuitive concept of simple structure (e.g. Carroll, 1953; Neuhaus and Wrigley, 1954; Kaiser, 1958), but there is no reason why alternative criteria should not be programmed. These attempts have been summarised by Warburton (1963), and other recent technical advances and changes in viewpoint are very lucidly reported in non-technical language by Harris (1964) and by Tatsuoka (1966). One important new development outlined by Tatsuoka (and originated by Ledyard Tucker) is the extension of factor analytical methods to more than two modes. Normally the data subjected to analysis is in a two-way table, and consists of the scores of people on tests. Multi-mode factor analysis can deal with more complex data, such as scores of people on tests on several occasions.

The contribution of these statistical studies to our knowledge of the structure of human abilities may be summed up as follows.

(1) If any broad selection of mental tasks is given to a representative sample of people in a particular culture, the pattern of performance generally reveals a component common to all tasks, which may be interpreted as general intelligence.

(2) This general factor is not sufficient to account for all the overlap in performance. Supplementary common factors, independent of general intelligence, are found, and may be interpreted as abilities such as verbal ability and spatial ability.

(3) The effect of general intelligence, as assessed from the amount of overlap between performances for which it accounts, is important. Quite often, the amount of variation in performance ascribable to general intelligence has been greater than that ascribable to all other factors together.

(4) It is possible to analyse a representative set of mental performances in such a way that no factor of general intelligence is found, but this generally involves the use of factors which are themselves to some degree correlated, with the result that further analysis reveals a hidden general factor.

(5) Many alternative accounts of the structure of human abilities have claimed support from the technique of factor analysis. These analyses, although apparently very different, have often been mathematically

c

equivalent. If they have actually been different, this has usually been due to different choices of the kind of data to analyse.

(6) Factor analysis by itself is unable to indicate one best picture of the structure of abilities. A choice among alternative pictures must be made on psychological rather than statistical grounds. This is a matter of emphasis rather than of factual disagreement. In Britain, the emphasis has generally been on paragraphs (1) and (2) of this summary, in the USA on the first part of paragraph (4).

(7) Although the statistical techniques described in this chapter have produced no universally agreed scheme of classification, they are capable of rejecting schemes that do not fit the facts. They are still being rapidly developed, partly due to the availability of electronic computers; likely future developments are (a) that factor analysis may become less a method of blind exploration and more a method of hypothesis testing, (b) that increased use will be made of relatively objective methods of analysis by computer.

Suggested additional reading

VERNON, P. E., 'The psychology of intelligence and g'. In *Readings in Psychology* (Ed. J. Cohen). London: Allen and Unwin (1964).

TUDDENHAM, R. D., 'The nature and measurement of intelligence'. In *Psychology in the Making.* (Ed. L. Postman). Knopf (1961).

VERNON, P. E., *The Structure of Human Abilities.* London: University of London Press (1950).

BURT, SIR CYRIL, *The Factors of the Mind.* London: University of London Press (1940). Chs. 1–4.

GUILFORD, J. P., *The Nature of Human Intelligence.* New York: McGraw Hill (1967).

HEBB, D. O., *A Textbook of Psychology.* 2nd edn. London: Saunders.

WISEMAN, S. (Ed.), *Intelligence and Ability.* Penguin Books (1967).

Appendix to Chapter II. An Illustration of Factor Analysis.
Extract from note by Sir Cyril Burt

As used in psychology factor analysis (as its earliest introducers explained) is essentially a statistical technique for confirming or refuting certain hypotheses regarding the possible factors or components of certain mental measurements. It is really an extension of the well-known formulae, based on the so-called 'parallelogram of forces', which, (as students of elementary physics are aware) are used to resolve composite forces into orthogonal (i.e. uncorrelated) components, and to combine hypothetical components into observable tendencies.

In psychology it was in fact first used by Burt to decide between the three alternative hypotheses set out in section 1.

1. Consider the first of the views there formulated – that there is only a 'single common ability' involved in all the various kinds of intellectual tasks, measured by cognitive tests or otherwise assessed. Let us for simplicity imagine we have applied six tests to a large group of children. Suppose that their performances are fundamentally determined by a single common factor only and that the hypothetical correlations of each test with this factor are as shown in the margins at the top and left-hand side of Table 2.4.

These are the so-called factor loadings. A well known algebraic formula states that, if the correlations of (say) tests 1 and 2 with the common or general factor are ·80 and ·70, then the resulting correlation between the two loadings, viz., ·80 × ·70 = ·56. And similarly for all other pairs of tests.

TABLE 2.4 *A general factor only*

Test	Factor Loading	1 ·80	2 ·70	3 ·60	4 ·50	5 ·40	6 ·30	Total
1	·80	[·64]	·56	·48	·40	·32	·24	2·64
2	·70	·56	[·49]	·42	·35	·28	·21	2·31
3	·60	·48	·42	[·36]	·30	·24	·18	1·98
4	·50	·40	·35	·30	[·25]	·20	·15	1·65
5	·40	·32	·28	·24	·20	[·16]	·12	1·32
6	·30	·24	·21	·18	·15	·12	[·09]	·99
Total	3·30	) 2·64	2·31	1·98	1·65	1·32	·99	10·89
		·80	·70	·60	·50	·40	·30	3·30

Thus, according to the first hypothesis, the correlations observed should form a pattern similar to that shown in Table 2.4. The correlations in the several rows are proportional to each other. Owing to the errors resulting from sampling and other irrelevant influences we can hardly expect the correlations actually obtained to fit this pattern with absolute accuracy. However, if the errors are merely minor fluctuations due to accidental causes, we may expect them to cancel out on addition. Hence we may still attempt to estimate the factor loadings by the method shown in the table, a method analogous to the process of averaging. We calculate the sum of the coefficients in each column, and then divide, not by their number, but by the sum of the six factor loadings. It is easy to see that the grand total of all the correlations (10·89 in the present case) must necessarily be the square of the sum of factor-loadings. Hence we take the square root of the grand total ($\sqrt{10·89}$ = 3·30), and use this figure to divide the sums of the several columns. The quotients, shown in the last line of all, are the factor loadings.

Here I have kept to simple round figures so that the student can carry out the calculations in his head. In an actual experiment, having obtained the factor loadings in this way from the correlations observed, we should proceed to reconstruct the correlation table by multiplying pairs of loadings; and then compare the reconstructed theoretical table with the correlations actually observed. There will of course be discrepancies. To determine their size the theoretical figures are subtracted from the figures observed, and their statistical significance tested by the appropriate formula. If any of the discrepancies are large enough to be statistically significant, then clearly the hypothesis that a single factor only is sufficient to account for the correlations can no longer be entertained.

Footnote

(1) This method was first used by Burt and his research students in early studies from 1907 onwards. It is essentially a simplification of the method proposed by Karl Pearson (1901), commonly known as 'principal components'. With that method it is necessary to weight each row of correlations by the corresponding factor loading before calculating the sum. Since the factor loadings can only be roughly estimated at the start, this involves a long and tedious process of successive approximation (which, however, can readily be undertaken by an electronic computer). The resulting modifications are so slight that as a rule the extra labour is hardly justified: as is well known a 'weighted average' differs very little from a 'simple average'. The simplified procedure was originally termed 'factor analysis by simple summation', in contrast to Pearson's 'weighted summation'. Thurstone, however, who later used exactly the same formula, termed it the 'centroid method'. Under one name or the other it is the procedure which has been most frequently used by psychologists.

(2) The hypothesis of a single common factor only was put forward and defended by Spearman. His opponents inclined rather to the traditional faculty theory, viz., that intellectual performances and tests could be divided into groups of similar activities, each group being due to a special ability or faculty – a 'primary ability', as Thurstone preferred to say – which thus formed not a general factor but a 'group factor'. For simplicity, let us suppose that we are concerned with two contrasted types of thinking – 'convergent thinking' of the type required for many of the more popular intelligence tests and 'divergent thinking' such as is said to be distinctive of 'creative' processes. We devise two sets of tests – tests 4, 5 and 6 for 'creativity' and tests 1, 2 and 3 for 'convergent thinking'. The question is – are these two abilities distinct and separate (as assumed by the second hypothesis described in section 1)? If these were perfectly distinct and separate, then the cross correlations would be zero; and we should have a factor pattern similar to that in Table 2.5.

As before, the actual figures obtained in any empirical research will inevitably be affected by minor errors, since in psychological research it is seldom possible to eliminate all irrelevant influences. Hence instead of

TABLE 2.5 *Distinct group factors*

Test			1	2	3	4	5	6
	Factor		·50	·60	·40	·00	·00	·00
	Loadings		·00	·00	·00	·60	·30	·20
1	·50	·00	[·25]	·30	·20	·00	·00	·00
2	·60	·00	·30	[·36]	·24	·00	·00	·00
3	·40	·00	·20	·24	[·16]	·00	·00	·00
4	·00	·60	·00	·00	·00	[·36]	·18	·12
5	·00	·30	·00	·00	·00	·18	[·09]	·06
6	·00	·20	·00	·00	·00	·12	·06	[·04]

zero we shall probably get small coefficients, sometimes positive, some-times negative. But, if the second hypothesis is true, the vast majority of the cross-correlations should be statistically non-significant.

(3) In actual practice, unless the persons tested have been carefully selected so as virtually to exclude differences in the general factor, and unless the tests used have been carefully constructed so as to eliminate any common factor (which as a rule is only possible with tests of relatively simple capacities such as visual, auditory, or tactual discrimination), this second pattern is hardly ever found. The commonest type of pattern is a table in which there appear to be clusters of augmented correlations superposed upon proportionate correlations suggestive of a general factor, resembling (when there are only comparatively few tests) the pattern shown in Table 2.6. This, it will be seen, has been constructed by adding Table 2.4 to Table 2.5. It is the pattern implied by the third of the above hypotheses.

TABLE 2.6 *General and group factors*

Test				1	2	3	4	5	6
	Factor			·80	·70	·60	·50	·40	·30
	Loadings			·50	·60	·40	·00	·00	·00
				·00	·00	·00	·60	·30	·20
1	·80	·50	·00	·89	·86	·68	·40	·32	·24
2	·70	·60	·00	·86	·85	·66	·35	·28	·21
3	·60	·40	·00	·68	·66	·52	·30	·24	·18
4	·50	·00	·60	·40	·35	·30	·61	·38	·27
5	·40	·00	·30	·32	·28	·24	·38	·25	·18
6	·30	·00	·20	·24	·21	·18	·27	·18	·13

If we are dealing with abilities (rather than with temperamental qualities or other dichotomous variables), it is natural to seek factors which have positive factor loadings only. Confronted with a complex table like the above, it is usually possible to estimate first the factor loadings for the general factor; and then, after subtracting the hypothetical correlations which these produce (viz. Table 2.4) and testing the residuals for statistical significance, these can also be factorised in the same way.

When dealing with temperamental qualities (introversion *versus* extraversion, etc.), the supplementary factors are better expressed as 'bipolar' components with both positive and negative loadings. Often with highly complex tables it is best to begin in this way even when dealing with mental abilities, since this provides the clearer lines of division between the successive 'groups'. The latter can then be obtained by mechanically 'rotating' the factors, a technique which need not be discussed in detail here (see 'Group Factor Analysis', *Brit. J. Psychol. Statist. Sect.*, III, 1950, pp. 40–75).

Sir Karl Popper, it may be remembered, has insisted that a scientific experiment can at best only disprove a hypothesis, never prove it. The nearest approach to proof consists in disproving all rival alternatives and then showing that the data observed are consistent with the hypothesis which is thus, not so much 'proved', as shown to be the most probable. This is especially true of factor analysis.

Critics of the general factor commonly point out that correlation tables exhibiting patterns like that shown in Table 2.6 can usually be explained in terms of group factors only, provided these are allowed to overlap with each other and (in most cases) to be correlated with each other. Such an interpretation is indeed nearly always *possible*; but what the critic generally overlooks is the need to show, not only that his particular scheme is possible, but also that it is *more probable* than the simpler and more obvious general factor hypothesis. To do this, he must first devise a situation in which his group factors will appear as uncorrelated factors, otherwise he cannot claim that they are really distinct and so free from any common factor underlying them all, since a general factor hypothesis proves to be a *possible* explanation in practically every correlation table hitherto obtained with cognitive tests applied to *unselected* populations. Secondly, he ought also to show that his particular set of factors, postulated for this or that table, reappears in other contexts. Thirdly, it should be remembered that the notion of a general factor does not rest solely or even primarily on the statistical evidence. Biological evidence, every-day observation (the frequency of all round geniuses and all round dullards), and above all the neurological evidence combine to make it highly probable antecedently to any statistical comfirmation.

The nature of the commoner group factors so far established is in keeping with what one might expect from neurological evidence. Unfortunately nowadays most investigators appear content to name their group factors after the nature of the tests for which they have high loadings; and the nature of the tests is usually inferred from the names given to them and the purposes for which each was constructed. Earlier investigators, particularly in Britain, nearly always checked their inferences about the nature of their tests and their factors by picking out the individuals who obtained the highest scores for each and then asking for introspective descriptions of their mental processes when carrying out the tests. (This was sometimes supplemented by independent reports on their efficiency in relevant respects.) Unfortunately, with the advent of behaviouristic principles, introspection has fallen into disuse. It is, however, urgently to be hoped that it will once again be revived as an essential part of factorial and test research.

III

Problem-solving and concept attainment

TWO KINDS OF PSYCHOLOGICAL APPROACH

No account of human intelligence would be complete without some attempt to review experimental work on problem solving. It is unfortunate that in the past the study of intelligence, thought and cognition has been remarkably fragmented. Books on intelligence and abilities have been published which deal solely with evidence from correlations between tests, whereas others on thinking contain no reference at all to research of that kind. Works of one kind or the other have in fact formed not the exception but the general rule, and psychologists have, until quite recently, confined themselves to one field, either to the study of individual differences and practical applications, or to that of basic principles. Eysenck (1966) has put forward a strong case for the need to consider both general laws of behaviour and individual differences in conjunction, and quotes convincing instances in which the interpretation of experiments has been largely obscured by a failure to do so. His own work has been notable for putting this precept into practice, both in taking into account the effect of personality differences on conditioning and learning, and also in attempting to find regularities governing differences in general ability (see p. 35). By and large, very few other psychologists have been able even to attempt this necessary synthesis. Hunt (1962), reviewing studies of concept formation comments:

> It is a bit puzzling (at least to this author) why studies of individual differences in intellectual functioning have not made more use of concept-learning tasks in preference to vaguely defined 'problem-solving' tasks. However, they have not, and the field of individual differences in concept learning is largely unexplored.

This excessive specialisation in the study of thinking, between the experimental psychologist seeking laws of behaviour (and often concerned to derive higher mental processes from simpler non-cognitive

72

ones) and the psychologist of individual differences or 'psychometrist', mainly concerned with statistical norms, prediction and selection has been doubly restrictive, impoverishing both areas. It has certainly obscured results in experimental psychology in the way indicated by Eysenck, and the effect on the study of abilities has probably been even more detrimental. Firstly, the range of procedures and mental processes sampled in commonly used intelligence tests has been unduly narrow and unadventurous. Admittedly this has widened in recent years with the addition of tests of 'creativity', but one can whole-heartedly endorse Hunt's point that the study of individual differences in the broad field of concept learning is 'largely unexplored'. It is quite possible that standardised tests could be constructed with this kind of material that would supplement or improve on conventional tests in many respects. Tests of this kind have, it is true, been developed to some extent for diagnostic and clinical purposes (Semeonoff and Trist, 1958), but it is hard to believe that they would not also yield interesting results in the normal range.

One of the relatively few studies in which an attempt has been made to study individual differences in categorising in a normal population and to relate these to other kinds of standardised test data is that of Lovell (1955), who adapted some individual tests of sorting and classification (Vinacke; Trist-Hargreaves) to serve as group tests. The main aims of his enquiry were to study the early levelling-off and drop in measured intelligence after the age of about 15, to assess the effect of continued intellectual stimulation (as the form of secondary education) in arresting this decline, and to determine which intellectual factors were more and less susceptible to early deterioration. Lovell found strong evidence that the tests of categorising and classification were assessing an ability 'not adequately measured by g, v, k tests'. He also concluded that the categorising tests discriminated more effectively than ordinary intelligence tests between the 'stimulated' and 'non-stimulated' groups. A recent study by Freyberg (1966) in New Zealand has shown that a test of concept development can significantly improve the prediction of children's attainment in arithmetic and produce a significantly higher correlation than the use of ability tests alone. In another recent study, Duncanson (1966) performed one of the relatively rare experiments in which a wide selection of learning tasks and ability tests are analysed together, and found a concept-formation factor distinct from the usual ability factors (see also Glaser, 1967, p. 5).

Another consequence for intelligence testing of the split between experimental and applied psychology is that, relative to the total amount of research on intelligence tests and their predictive power, very little consideration has been devoted to the psychological processes involved in attaining the correct answers (or in failing to attain them). There are some honourable exceptions here, such as the work of Miller (1955), Campbell (1963, 1964, 1965), Heim (1955, 1957) and Donaldson (1959, 1963), but there is certainly room for far more research of this kind. In spite of the vast literature concerned with the testing of abilities, we know remarkably little about the detailed mental processes involved, the strategy and tactics of the successful intelligence test performer, and the equally interesting processes that result in error. We also know very little about the relation in detail between performance on standardised intelligence tests and performance in the very varied 'problem-solving' situations that have been set up by experimental psychologists.

Fisher (1966) makes two points about intelligence and aptitude testing in general. Firstly, he suggests that the sequence of development should have been, (a) decide on important kinds of behaviour in 'real life' that can be characterised as intelligent, (b) choose a representative sample of actions of this kind, then (c) construct tests corresponding to each of these and look for any common elements or factors that might enable us to shorten the list. What has happened in practice, he maintains has been more like (a) pick a set of performances and kinds of behaviour, not entirely arbitrarily, but with choice influenced by un-analysed pre-conceptions or prejudices, (b) make tests to predict these, (c) decide that any factors not included in the list so obtained are not worth devising measures for.

It is probable that many users of existing tests have an uneasy and justified feeling that certain kinds have been developed, and other kinds neglected or not thought of, with the result that we have a biased and inadequate sample from the universe of all possible useful kinds of test.

Fisher's other main point is that an important aspect of intelligent behaviour (the most important or typical in his view) is being able to achieve an unchanged goal in changing conditions – in other words, to be rapidly flexible in method, to be able to re-structure the problem while it changes, to track it, so to speak, as a guided missile tracks an elusive moving target. Obviously, no existing paper-and-pencil tests can assess this kind of flexibility directly, and Fisher goes so far as to conclude that, for this reason, measures of intelligence, properly so called, do not seem to have been developed. If there is anything in these views, they reinforce the argument for closer co-operation between test constructors and experimental students of thinking. Many of the experiments to be described do very much what Fisher says an intelligence test should do, i.e. they study the ability of subjects to change tactics and methods of thinking while maintaining a constant aim and purpose. This feature is represented, though to a differing extent, in experiments of the two main kinds we shall describe, in researches such as those of Maier in which the re-structuring of the problem by the subject is a main point of interest, and particularly in the work of Bruner, Goodnow and Austin, in which the experimenter can vary the successive presentation of pieces of information in such a way as to study the subject's changing strategies.

It would be reassuring if one could summarise experimental results on problem-solving and on concept formation and attainment, and then demonstrate the incorporation of the principles discovered in currently used tests. Unfortunately no such correspondence is possible. The best that can be done is to summarise a limited selection of what appears to be the most typical and interesting experimental work, and occasionally to suggest how this might be linked with the study of individual differences in ability as revealed by standard tests.

WAYS OF STUDYING PROBLEM SOLVING AND CONCEPT ATTAINMENT

It is worth mentioning briefly why we choose to talk about 'problem-solving' instead of about 'thought' or 'thinking'. The latter terms are too broad and Protean, including fantasies, 'autistic' and other non-realistic thinking, imaging, attitudes and so on. 'Problem-solving', though broad and vague enough, reduces the area of thought to something directed and relatively formal. However, the degree of formality and control which is imposed by the kind of experiment on the problem-solving activity may vary a great deal. Sometimes this dimension resembles a 'real-life' versus 'artificial' dimension. Not only will the results of experiments on thinking and problem-solving depend upon the kind of problem, the setting and the conditions imposed, but they will also be strongly influenced by the theoretical pre-suppositions of the experimenter. This has been shown quite clearly even in the relatively restricted field of habit learning by rats, where an assumption that learning could be fully explained in terms of stimulus-response connections sometimes gave results that conflicted with those of other workers who believed that the animals formed 'cognitive maps' or 'hypotheses'. Similarly it has often been pointed out that the contrasting results and interpretations offered by Thorndike, on the one hand, in his early experiments on trial-and-error problem solving by cats, and on the other by Köhler in his famous account of 'insightful' problem-solving by apes, probably owed almost as much to the theoretical outlook of the investigators as to inter-species differences.

In the case of human problem-solving it can well be imagined that there is scope for a much wider range of theoretical approaches, to such an extent that work in this field is by no means easy to classify and summarise. One broad distinction is fairly obvious, somewhat similar to the one just described in the case of animal learning. Theoretical approaches to human problem-solving can be divided into those that treat it as a particularly complex and highly developed kind of learning, and therefore attempt to make use of the extensive research findings concerned with simpler forms of learning, including classical and operant conditioning. The other approach assumes that human thinking, at least in many of its most important aspects, is different enough from the simpler processes typically studied by learning theorists to justify different methods of study and different explanatory concepts.

The former viewpoint has the advantage of greater scientific economy. Learning and thinking can be represented in all their forms as constituting a continuous spectrum of complexity, with the ultimate aim of linking the mental processes of Voltaire or Keynes with those of the earthworm in the T-maze and of deriving the two performances from identical principles. This aim is at present a long way from being fulfilled. A recent book by Berlyne (1965) represents a determined attempt to advance a step or two on this path and to describe a wide range of cognitive activities in stimulus-response terms. Gagné (1964, 1965) also charts some of the degrees of complexity in the suggested continuum between simple response learning and problem solving, suggesting that intermediate stages (in ascending order of complexity) are represented by simple verbal learning (paired-associates), concept learning, and principle learning. H. H. Kendler (1964), in Gagné's symposium, and Hunt (1962, Ch. 3) also provide thoughtful summaries of the similarities and differences between relatively simple forms of learning and concept attainment.

The second approach, which treats human problem-solving in relative isolation from simpler processes, and in particular from classical learning theory, is naturally less unified. In the period 1930–1950, or thereabouts, many of the best-known and most important studies, such as those of Duncker (1945), Katona (1940), Maier (1930, 1933, 1937) and Wertheimer (1959) were strongly influenced by the principles of

Gestalt psychology. These researches are mostly characterised by the use of real-life problems (or of laboratory problems employing familiar, everyday materials and operations), and often by an emphasis on the importance of initial attitude, 'set' or direction of thinking. Typically, also, they are concerned with the *quality* of solutions more than with speed or quantity of output, and often with a distinction between 'good' (sensible, insightful) and 'bad' (blind, routine) errors. Similarly, as part of the 'Gestalt' influence, emphasis was placed on interpreting and structuring the problem as a whole rather than on an analytical, elementaristic or trial-and-error method of solution. This general view-point can be seen influencing both the kinds of problem devised and the interpretations of results during that period.

Since about 1950, several other kinds of theoretical influence have become increasingly important as supplements to or as substitutes for the stimulus-response framework. Information and communication theory, that is to say the systematic and mathematical study of the amount of information and redundancy conveyed in messages, have illuminated many aspects of problem-solving, especially the kind of experiment where the subject receives successive partial confirmations (or dis-confirmations) of his hypotheses. Games theory (for a simple and easily intelligible introduction see Williams, 1965) and the formal study of strategies in situations of uncertainty also have obvious relevance. Most importantly of all, the development of data-processing by electronic computer, and the possibility of simulating human problem-solving processes have transformed the outlook of many psychologists.

A joint effect of these new developments is that recent studies of problem-solving, compared with those in the period 1930–1950 have become more formalised, less naturalistic, in some ways narrower in scope, more quantitative and rigorous. This is not to say that they have necessarily become more concerned with mathematical and logical abstractions at the expense of human beings. T. S. Kendler (1964) points out, a little wrily and ironically, that the humanistic viewpoint of the Gestalt theorists is exemplified in its contemporary form by theorists who draw upon the programme of the electronic computer as a source of inspiration. Certainly, as we shall see, a humanistic approach to thinking and an interest in entire functioning human beings are by no means incompatible with a viewpoint that employs many computer analogies (Miller, Galanter and Pribram, 1960) or with one that borrows concepts and methods from games theory (Bruner, Goodnow and Austin, 1956).

One consequence of these trends has been a relative decline in experiments designed to study problem-solving in a broad, general sense, and an increased concentration and volume of research concerned with concept attainment. In this latter kind of experiment a number of cards, each of which bears a symbol, can be presented to the subject successively or simultaneously. The symbols differ in a number of ways, and the task of the subject may be, for example, to discover the common feature in a subset of them (Hull, 1920) or to match them in as few trials as possible against locations pre-determined by the experimenter (Whitfield, 1951). Many other variations are possible in kind of material used, method of presentation and experimental design; some of these will be described in Section 4 of this chapter. Terminology tends to vary according to the design of the experiment and the theoretical orientation of the experimenter, and rather similar processes are variously described as concept learning, concept identification, concept attainment, concept formation. 'Concept learning' best describes those experiments (e.g. Hull, 1920) in which the experimental design emphasises the similarity of the mental processes employed to those required in discrimination learning, and where the subject may recognise examples of a concept without being able explicitly to formulate it. Concept attainment and concept identification seem to be practically synonymous and describe the results of experiments in which the subject is required to 'attain' or identify a concept or category predetermined by the experimenter. 'Concept formation' is rather a misleading phrase as applied to most of the experiments with adults and might be applied more accurately to the kind of work done on children's thinking by Piaget and his associates.

In a short account it will be impossible to explore many of these experimental approaches in detail. Firstly it will be necessary to confine ourselves to the second of the two main orientations distinguished, that is to the one which treats human problem-solving as basically *sui generis* and not as a more complex kind of stimulus-response learning. The next two sections will describe respectively some of the older research in problem-solving and some of the more recent work on concept attainment. In both of these areas it will be necessary to restrict discussion virtually to one worker or team of workers chosen as representative, if any detail is to be provided.

SOME EXPERIMENTAL WORK ON PROBLEM SOLVING

Maier (1930, 1933) carried out a series of experiments which we may take as illustrative of the kind of research outlined on page 76 (top).

These were conducted with adult subjects and the problems and materials used were 'real-life' problems adapted to the laboratory and to experimental control. Like other Gestalt and Gestalt-influenced psychologists, Maier was particularly interested in the structuring and re-structuring of the problems in the minds of the subjects and the extent to which this depended on attitude and expectation.

The first problem required the subjects to construct two pendulums so that they would swing over two marks several feet apart on the floor of the laboratory. They were provided with materials as follows: three poles, large and small clamps, lengths of wire, pieces of chalk. The solution required was to clamp two poles together, making a pole long enough to reach from floor to ceiling, with this to wedge the third pole (whose length was exactly the distance between the marks on the floor) against the ceiling, and from the two ends of this horizontal pole to suspend plumb lines. At the end of each plumb line one of the smaller clamps could be used to hold a piece of chalk.

Five groups of subjects tackled this problem, each group working under slightly different experimental conditions. One (the control group) worked without any preliminary practice or special briefing. Groups two and three were briefed to varying degrees on the constituent operations in the required solution, such as making a plumb line, joining two poles, and wedging a pole (but against a doorpost, not against the ceiling). Group four received 'direction'. Group five received briefing on constituent operations *and* 'direction'.

Maier's (1930) description of the 'direction' is as follows: 'I should like to have you appreciate how simple this problem would be if we could just hang the pendulums from a nail in the ceiling. Of course, that is not a possible solution, but I want you to appreciate how simple the problem would be if that were possible. Now that it is not possible, the problem is, as you may find, really quite difficult.' This was demonstrated by holding one of the wires against the ceiling.

It was found that the group receiving both briefing on partial solutions *and* 'direction' did far better than any of the other groups, including those that had had briefing. Maier interpreted this result as indicating the importance of 'direction' in helping the subjects to start thinking along the right lines, and argued that the subjects who had been briefed on the three constituent operations possessed all the knowledge that was required but lacked the ability to combine the operations by seeing the problem in the right way.

Weaver and Madden (1949) repeated this experiment with only minor modifications, such as a more careful matching of groups for intelligence. The results were fairly similar, although a smaller proportion of subjects attained the required solution. The most important point of agreement was that in this situation neither briefing on constituent operations nor 'direction' was sufficient in itself (except for a very few subjects) but that both were required. Weaver and Madden, however, sounded a note of scepticism as to whether the idea of 'direction' of thought was as simple and clear-cut as had been suggested by Maier and the Gestalt psychologists.

Besides the 'two pendulum' problem, Maier (1933) devised other problems of a rather similar kind. These included: (1) The 'string' problem, in which subjects were required to join two strings hanging from the ceiling which were too far apart to take hold of simultaneously. The required solution was to convert one of the strings into a pendulum. (2) The 'hat-rack' problem which involved clamping poles together so that they could be wedged between floor and ceiling, and using the clamp as a hook. (3) The 'candle' problem, in which a candle had to be blown out from a distance of eight feet. Short lengths of glass and rubber tubing, putty, poles and clamps were available. The required solution was to construct a long tube by joining short lengths suspended on a pole. In all these three problems, some irrelevant materials were also displayed.

For these experiments Maier again employed a control and an experimental group. The first received no specific preparation, the second attended a lecture on problem-solving, with particular reference to the need for flexibility in direction of thinking and for keeping the mind open to new combinations and new ways of structuring. Markedly better results were obtained by the experimental group, particularly on problems (2) and (3).

Saugstad (1955, 1957), a Norwegian psychologist, was not entirely convinced by Maier's interpretation, and repeated the experiments with some variations. He argued firstly that the briefing on constituent operations had been inadequate, in that the possible functions of the clamps, poles, tubes, etc. had not been adequately demonstrated, and secondly that, if such briefing were made adequate, the importance of 'direction' might be diminished.

This indeed is very much what he found. In a repetition of the 'two pendulum' problem, Saugstad demonstrated that if subjects thoroughly grasped the constituent operations and the principles involved in them, and if they were practised in them instead of being merely briefed, a much higher proportion of subjects solved the problem without 'direction', the effect of which became negligible. He makes it clear, however, that he does not discount the importance of initial attitude or 'set' in general, but claims to have demonstrated that 're-structuring', 'direction' and so forth were not essential in the solution of this particular kind of problem. Saugstad also (1955) repeated the 'candle' problem, and again came to rather similar conclusions. The main modification to knowledge about problem solving suggested by Saugstad's work is that greater account needs to be taken of 'availability of function' depending upon the previous experience of the subject. A rather similar modification of opinion has taken place in the study of problem solving by animals, in which the conclusions arrived at by Wolfgang Köhler (in his classic work with apes in Tenerife) are now seen as sometimes having taken insufficient account of the animals' early experience.

One of the most thorough (but in parts, difficult) accounts of this kind of approach to problem-solving is provided by Duncker (1945). This is mainly theoretical, but describes some experimental work, and includes many ingenious problems such as the following:

(a) 'Given a human being with an inoperable stomach tumour, and rays which destroy organic tissue at sufficient intensity, by what procedure can one free him of the tumour by these rays and at the same time avoid destroying the healthy tissue which surrounds it?'

(b) 'Why is it that all six-place numbers of the type abcabc, for example 276276, are divisible by thirteen?'

(c) 'The duration of a pendulum's swing depends, among other things, on its length, and this of course in turn on the temperature. Warming produces expansion and cooling produces contraction, although to a different degree in different materials. Thus every temperature change would change the length of the pendulum. But the clock should go with absolute regularity. How can this be brought about?'

Like Maier, Duncker was especially interested in the effects of initial 'set' and in how these could be controlled by the experimenter. He interprets Maier's emphasis on the importance of 'direction' as showing the need, in solving all problems of this kind, for *re-structuring* or *reformulation*. As evidence of the great importance of this re-formulating process, even when it appears unimportant or even trivial, he quotes the problem of proving that there is an infinite number of prime numbers. A step that is absolutely crucial in solving this problem, although it may not appear so at first, is to re-structure the problem so that it takes the form 'I must prove that, for any prime number X there exists a greater one'.

Duncker analyses in considerable detail kinds of false starts and unsuccessful attempts to solve the problems described above, and groups these attempts into 'family trees'. He also discusses extensively the 'functional fixedness' or insufficiently flexible attitude that frequently impairs performance in problem solving and describes experiments (similar in some respects to those of Maier) to illustrate this point.

The kinds of experiment so far reviewed demonstrate clearly that in all studies of problem-solving, and particularly in the relatively informal experiments employing 'real-life' problems and material, very careful specification of the conditions and instructions given is required. Small alterations in these may greatly affect the results. Secondly, the theoretical preconceptions of the experimenter about the complex processes involved may affect both the design of the experiment and its interpretation. Thirdly, it is particularly difficult in the case of 'real-life' problems (and of formal mathematical problems, such as those requiring proofs) to discount or effectively allow for the subjects' varying previous experience and 'availability of function'. For all these reasons the modern tendency is therefore to use simpler material, often rather more artificial types of experiment, and especially to design investigations so that conditions can be varied in clearly defined ways by the experimenter and so that results are suitable for mathematical analysis.

STRATEGIES IN CONCEPT ATTAINMENT

An important aspect of both problem-solving and concept attainment concerns the strategy or strategies adopted by the solver. This idea of strategy in problem-solving is not quite so general as the idea of initial 'set' or attitude to a problem, nor so specific as the testing of a particular hypothesis. Initial 'set' is most important when the method of solving a problem is still obscure, whereas the formation and testing of a particular hypothesis is the terminal stage in solving the problem – if the hypothesis works. Intermediate between these stages in many types of problem there arises the necessity to consider alternative plans of action, to foresee how unsatisfactory hypotheses can be most effectively eliminated, and to put into action what seems the best available procedure. The experiments of Maier and of Duncker illustrated (among other things) the effect on problem-solving of 'set' and of preconceptions about how objects and materials are used in real life; the kind of experiment that has most effectively shown the importance of *strategies* in thinking and concept attainment has been described by Bruner, Goodnow and Austin (1956).

A 'concept' as studied in these experiments, is a grouping of things into a single category. Clearly this is a basic feature of thinking, both in formal problem-solving and in real-life situations, since the nature of our thinking is dictated to a considerable extent by the categories we habitually employ. To quote the authors, 'the Navaho had best learn to make distinction between events that occur naturally and those traceable to witchcraft, and the Englishman becomes adept indeed in placing a man by the stripes on his tie'. Productive and original categorisation also form an important part of scientific research. 'The neutrino in nuclear physics was postulated first as an empty category on logical grounds, and only when appropriate measures became available was it "found" '.

Categories may be broadly classified as affective, functional and formal. We place together in affective categories the people, books, music, landscapes, philosophies that produce in us a similar kind of emotional response. Functional categories, on the other hand, are those that group together people, materials, and courses of action, that are equivalent for a given purpose. The problem situations of Maier (and one might add, most of the famous experiments of Köhler with apes) are primarily concerned with functional categories and functional equivalence. The third kind, formal categories, are employed in the most abstract thinking, particularly in philosophy and mathematics, but also to a large degree in all scientific work. All these types of categorisation are of enormous interest to psychologists, and for some purposes need not be distinguished. Thus the techniques of G. A. Kelly (1955), which aim to plot the pattern of an individual's characteristic attitudes and modes of thought, invite the respondent to categorise in any or all of these ways. The work under review, on the other hand, is concerned only with formal categorisation and the attainment of formal concepts.

This work of Bruner, Goodnow and Austin is further limited to concept attainment as distinct from concept formation. That is to say, the material presented to the subjects is not such that they are required to impose their own categories or to invent new categories, but, rather as in the game 'Twenty Questions', to arrive at a particular category predetermined by the experimenter. Within these limitations the strategies of search and hypothesis elimination can be systematically and exhaustively studied.

In a typical experiment of this kind, an array of figures is presented to the subject (see Fig. 3.1). These are clearly classifiable by four attributes, shape, number, (e.g. one, two or three circles), colour, and border. Each attribute has three values. The experimenter has already decided on a particular category or concept, such as 'red circles', 'crosses' or 'black crosses with single border'. The task of the subject is to identify this pre-determined concept with as few questions as possible. He is instructed to proceed by asking if any particular figure is an example of the concept. If the answer from the experimenter is 'yes',

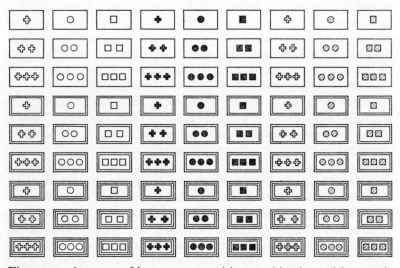

Figure 3.1. An array of instances comprising combinations of four attributes, each exhibiting three values. Plain figures are in green, striped figures in red, solid figures in black. From Bruner, Goodnow and Austin, (1956)

this is referred to as a 'positive instance'; if 'no', as a negative instance. It is thus possible to study both the ideal strategies from the point of view of efficiency and the strategies actually adopted, the relative efficiencies of the latter, and the possible factors, such as variations in the complexity of the material and individual differences among the subjects which affect choice of strategy.

Bruner, Goodnow and Austin describe four ideal strategies – ideal in the sense of forming one general plan and sticking to it. These are called simultaneous scanning, successive scanning, conservative-focusing, and focus-gambling. As soon as one guess has been made and the subject has been told that the instance is positive or negative, a large number of possibilities are at once eliminated. Thus, if the subject picks a red cross with single border and is told that this is a positive instance, it is clear that the pre-determined concept cannot be 'circles', or 'squares', or 'crosses with two borders'. The ideal simultaneous-scanning strategy assimilates all this information and successively rejects all the impossible hypotheses. Clearly, this requires enormous mental powers to carry out successfully if the array is at all complex. Successive scanning, on the other hand, tests only one hypothesis at a time. In the example quoted, the subject might start by adopting the hypothesis that the correct concept was 'red' and test this by picking a card showing a red square with double border; if this proved negative, he could then adopt a new hypothesis, that the concept was 'single border', for example. Compared with simultaneous scanning, this is clearly less efficient in theory, but less stressful in practice.

The two focusing strategies are rather different from the scanning strategies as follows. In conservative focusing, the subject systematically changes one attribute at a time, starting from a positive instance. If the new card provides a positive instance, the attribute changed is clearly not relevant and does not form part of the concept. Focus gambling again involves starting from a positive instance in the same way, but changing more than one attribute at a time. This *may* produce better results than conservative focusing, but involves much more risk, and does not guarantee (as conservative focusing does) that redundant instances will be avoided. The main distinction between the scanning and the focusing strategies is that in the former the subject successively eliminates *hypotheses*, in the latter *attributes*.

It can hardly be hoped that this highly condensed account will have made the differences between types of strategy fully clear. The interested reader is referred to the account by the original authors, or to a fairly full summary and explanation by Thomson (1959, Ch. 4). The main point is that strategies of these kinds (and possibly others) can be distinguished, their advantages and disadvantages theoretically assessed their frequency of employment studied experimentally, and their relevance to intelligent behaviour in a wider context discussed.

The advantage of adopting *some* relatively systematic strategy is intuitively obvious, but is clarified by the listing of particular gains. Bruner and his associates summarise three of these. Firstly, a strategy (as distinct from a random or haphazard selection) can ensure that appropriate information relative to the information already received will be forthcoming. One may wish to ensure that one encounters, for instance, a positive instance within a certain number of choices. Secondly, the degree of cognitive strain can be controlled. Thus we have already seen that successive scanning is much less onerous in this respect than simultaneous scanning. Thirdly, the degree of risk involved can be controlled. Some strategies will prove relatively slow but sure (e.g. conservative focusing); others may be quicker, but involve the risk of being slower still (focus gambling).

A series of experiments showed that the kind of strategy adopted and its relative success was indeed linked to considerations of this kind. In one experiment, for instance, the variable of cognitive strain was manipulated by requiring one group to operate without the array of instances in front of them. One would expect that the strategies imposing least cognitive strain would come into their own and be particularly effective relative to the more ambitious strategies, and this was clearly established. Focusing strategies in this and other experiments were found to yield more successful results in high-strain situations, and this advantage was relative to the degree of cognitive strain imposed by the experimental conditions.

Very briefly, one or two other variations and distinctions require mention. Firstly, according to the experimental arrangement, either *selection strategies* or *reception strategies* can be investigated. Selection strategies are those in which the subject sees the whole array of cards, and is instructed to select instances as he pleases. The experiments just described fall into this class (even those in which the array was not visually present, since the subject still knew the extent of the array and what it contained). In the other kind of experiment, designed to investigate reception strategies, it is the investigator, not the subject, who selects the instances, presenting a selection of cards to the subject and in each case telling him whether the instance is positive or negative. All sorts of variations are possible, but a common procedure is to present just sufficient instances, without redundant information, for the subject to be able in theory to identify the concept. It was found that, in general, the strategies available and the results of using them were fairly similar to those employed in the 'selection' situation. They could again be divided into 'scanning' and 'focusing' strategies, and the 'focusing' method, eliminating dimensions rather than hypotheses, was again usually more successful, and this relative superiority was more evident in situations where cognitive strain was greater.

In a sense, these experiments involving reception strategies, although at first sight appearing more artificial, since the situation is more closely controlled by the experimenter, are more analogous to real-life problems, or at least to problems in many scientific fields. The scientist typically does not have the whole array of relevant information spread before him, as in the 'selection strategy' experiments, but very often has to make inferences from what is available or what turns up.

Another important distinction refers to the nature of the concept or category to be attained. Three kinds are commonly distinguished, conjunctive, disjunctive and relational. A *conjunctive category* is one defined by the joint presence of several attributes, such as 'red', 'single border' and so on, as in all the examples so far discussed. A *disjunctive category* (Bruner, Goodnow and Austin, 1956, p. 41) is exemplified in terms of the array in figure 3.1 as 'that class of cards that possess three red circles, *or* any constituent thereof: three figures, red figures, circles, three red figures, red circles, or three circles'. This kind of categorisation, however, is much more easily grasped when one looks at analogous 'real-life' categories. Categorisation of the population for market research purposes by socio-economic level, or categorisation of people into those eligible and not eligible for membership, say, of the British Psychological Society illustrate disjunctive categories. Whereas the conjunctive category is based on 'and', the disjunctive one is based on 'or'. Thus the market researcher may class someone in socio-economic category A if he has an income of over £3,000 a year, *or* if his father is an earl; similarly someone may be accepted as a full member of the B.P.S. if he became one before a certain date *or* if he has obtained an honours degree in psychology, *or* if he has obtained a M.Ed. degree with specialisation in a psychological area, and so on. The third kind of category, the *relational category* is illustrated by Bruner et al. in terms of their array as 'one defined by a specifiable relationship between defining attributes. Thus in the universe [of Figure 3.1], we may define as a class all those instances containing the *same* number of figures and borders, or those cards with fewer figures than borders.' This kind of category has been much less commonly used in experiments, though it was employed in the pioneer study by Smoke (1932).

To many people's way of thinking, there is something untidy, arbitrary and unsatisfactory about disjunctive categories (cf. Hunt and Hovland, 1960). Bruner suggests that this feeling of arbitrariness may be one cause of dissatisfaction with the typical categories used by clinical psychologists, such as 'stable personality' or 'serious disturbance'. The point is highly relevant to the whole theme of this book, since 'intelligent behaviour' must be admitted to be a splendid example of a disjunctive concept. If a man is a senior wrangler, or an international bridge player, or scores very highly on an intelligence test, or efficiently manages an intricate business, or is a successful barrister or newspaper editor, it is hard to deny him the status of 'highly intelligent', but the signs or criteria which we can adopt with more or less justification are almost innumerable. It is not surprising, therefore, that experiments involving disjunctive concepts have shown that they present particular difficulties when subjects attempt to identify them. The subjects, in fact, in the Bruner experiments very often tried to attain these concepts by strategies which were clearly more appropriate to *conjunctive* concepts, even though the nature of the pre-determined disjunctive concepts had been carefully explained. One of the detailed reasons for this greater difficulty in attaining disjunctive concepts was the greater need to make use of negative instances. It can be shown (Bruner et al., p. 165) that in general far more information is conveyed and far more possible hypotheses are eliminated by a negative instance than by a positive one when the concept to be attained is disjunctive. Now it has often been noted that people have more difficulty in making inferences from negative instances (Wason, 1959; Huttenlocher, 1962) and this is true even when the two kinds of instances convey equal amounts of information (Hovland and Weiss, 1953). Analogous effects have been demonstrated in matching tasks and in the deciphering of codes (Donaldson, 1959; Campbell, 1965). This difficulty in handling negative instances is certainly part of the explanation of most subjects' lesser ability to solve problems involving disjunctive categories, and another part may be, as Bruner suggests, the general feeling that such categories are untidy and arbitrary. He also puts forward a third suggestion, that the difficulty is also related to habitual, scientific ways of thinking in our Western culture, by which we expect common effects to have common causes. This suggestion is more speculative, and would provide an interesting hypothesis to test in cross-cultural studies.

RECENT RESEARCH ON CONCEPT ATTAINMENT

The scope and insight of the Bruner, Goodnow and Austin work have rather tended to dwarf other, subsequent studies of this kind of problem solving. Increasingly, too, particularly in the last five years, studies of problem solving have involved attempts to develop computer programmes to simulate human thinking processes, as will be described in Chapter 5. An obvious extension of the Bruner work, however, is the developmental study of how problem-solving strategies evolve in children. The researches of Forrest (1961) and of Boote (1967) throw some light on this. As might be expected, few systematic strategies of the kind described were found at age 7, but their frequency increased quite rapidly with increasing age. Forrest found problem-solving success in this kind of task quite highly related to IQ as well as age, but in many cases, even with the older and more intelligent children, he was unable to identify and classify kinds of strategy so readily as Bruner, Goodnow and Austin. Boote found some perfectly consistent strategies applied at age 15 in the attainment of conjunctive concepts. Findings in this area are, however, scanty, and further research would be welcome.

The difficulty encountered by Forrest in distinguishing the kinds of strategy described by Bruner et al. was probably only intensified and not entirely caused by the fact that he was working with children. Eifermann (1965a; 1965b) found similar difficulties with adults. She shows, in fact, that it is frequently impossible, in a repetition of the Bruner experiments, to distinguish even in principle between, for instance, simultaneous scanning and conservative focusing from the actual sequence of choices. Further information is necessary and Eifermann obtained this by requiring subjects to describe their strategies in verbal reports.

A particularly useful paper extending this kind of work on concept attainment is that of Glanzer, Huttenlocher and Clark (1963), and their work represents an advance on that of Bruner and his associates in several respects. Firstly, they provide a useful, systematic summary of the experimental variations possible in studies of concept attainment. They also vary the conditions (e.g. complexity of array, timing, amount of redundant information etc.) more systematically than in earlier studies, and analyse the separate and joint effects of these varying conditions by complex analysis of variance. Thirdly, they go some way towards providing an answer to what has already been pointed out as a possible source of weakness in the Bruner experiments. This is that the strategies adopted by subjects can only be determined by the investigator's inference (unless the subjects' introspective reports are also canvassed, as by Eifermann). Both these sources are to some degree subjective, and there is a margin of error in classification. It is possible that some of the tables of Bruner et al. showing percentages of scanners, focusers and so on, are too neat, reflecting the wish of the investigators to obtain a clear classification of strategies. Glanzer et al. found an interesting non-linear relationship between concept complexity and success in attainment which they claimed to provide a new, objective kind of evidence that focusing rather than scanning procedures were being used. Finally, the Glanzer et al. research relied on a large number of problems in each experiment, since it was soon found that even with over a hundred subjects the effects of major factors such as exposure time were hardly significant when only one or two problems were given. This research was therefore a welcome continuation, with greatly improved methods of analysis, of the brilliant but largely impressionistic work of Bruner, Goodnow and Austin.

Dienes and Jeeves (1965) describe a series of experiments rather similar in nature and aim to those of Bruner, Goodnow and Austin. The hypotheses they were designed to test were in fact influenced by the ideas of Bruner and Bartlett. An ingenious aspect of these experiments was the use of mathematical groups to determine the presentation of the material, in particular a group with two elements (the two-group) and groups with four elements (the Cyclic and Klein groups).

In the simplest task, based on the two-group, subjects were presented with a stack of blue and yellow cards. A blue or yellow card appeared in the window of the experimental apparatus, and the subject was instructed to play either a blue or a yellow card in response. A third card, either blue or yellow, then appeared in the window. The subject was informed that the kind of third card appearing depended on the card first shown and on the card played, according to a constant set of principles, and it was his task to discover these principles. They were (based on the two-group):

> Blue followed by blue produces blue
> Yellow followed by blue produces yellow
> Blue followed by yellow produces yellow
> Yellow followed by yellow produces blue

Similar, but more complex and difficult tasks, were based on the groups of four elements.

This experimental technique is undoubtedly promising and suggests many further interesting possibilities. Like Bruner's work, the research of Dienes and Jeeves makes one want to repeat and extend it. Unfortunately, the report is idiosyncratic and tantalising in the extreme. Firstly, the tables of results are hard to interpret. Percentages of subjects in various categories, tests of significance of correlations and so on are presented without any statement of the numbers of subjects in the groups! Practically nothing is said about the age, educational level or other highly relevant characteristics of the subjects, who included both children and adults. The last quarter of the book is devoted to 'educational implications' and to 'some extrapolations and generalisations', yet no information is given (except that the adults were first year students) about the sample (or about the method of sampling) from which these extrapolations, generalisations and implications for educational policy are derived. One must agree with Bartlett's foreword or imprimatur to the effect that the research 'effects a bold and new step forward in the investigation of thinking activities', but suspend judgment about any new substantive findings until work of this kind has been repeated and extended and an adequate analysis provided of the results.

TRENDS TOWARDS UNIFICATION

In the first section of this chapter it was stated that *until very recently* the study of individual differences in ability on the one hand and that of problem solving, concept attainment and similar processes on the other, had remained very distinct fields of enquiry. During the last year or so, in addition to the important article by Eysenck already quoted, two American collections of papers have been published which describe and summarise most of the work that attempts to bridge this gap. The two symposia are edited by Klausmeier and Harris (1966) and by Gagné (1967).

The contributors write from quite varied theoretical viewpoints, but most agree, particularly in the Gagné volume, that concept learning, concept attainment and problem solving should and can be related to simpler forms of learning. Equally there is general agreement that individual differences have not been adequately studied nor their effect sufficiently taken into account in work on learning ranging from classical conditioning to classroom learning. In the case of the latter, for instance, which one would suppose to be a thoroughly explored field, it is remarkable to hear Cronbach saying, no doubt perfectly correctly, that there are no well-established interactions of instructional method with mental age. In other words, there is no instructional method, for instance, which has been convincingly shown to be relatively more suitable to bright than to dull children of the same age or vice versa.

These two books are unfortunately too recent and cover too wide a field for me to review them here in any detail. They are useful, however, in describing bridging operations across the gap between the study of individual differences and that of basic processes, particularly in the field of learning. Early in this chapter a few researches were listed which attempted to bridge the gap by starting from individual differences and interpreting them in terms acceptable to experimental psychologists, (e.g. the work of Heim and of Donaldson). The collections of Klausmeier and Harris and of Gagné describe pioneering work from the other side of the gap, carried out by learning theorists coming to grips with individual differences.

Suggested Additional Reading (Chapter 3)

THOMSON, R., *The Psychology of Thinking*. London: Penguin Books (1959).

BRUNER, J. S., GOODNOW, J. J., and AUSTIN, G. A., *A Study of Thinking*. New York: Wiley (1956).

DAVIS, G. A., 'The current status of research and theory in human problem-solving'. *Psychol. Bull.* 66, 36–54 (1966).

GAGNÉ, R. M. (Ed.) *Learning and Individual Differences*. Columbus, Ohio: Merrill (1967).

KLAUSMEIER, H. J., and HARRIS, C. W. (Eds.) *Analyses of Concept Learning*. New York and London: Academic Press (1966).

EYSENCK, H. J., 'Personality and experimental psychology'. *Bull. Brit. Psychol. Society*. 19, 1–28 (1966).

IV

Creativity and Intelligence

THE RECENT INCREASE OF INTEREST IN CREATIVITY

Fifteen years ago a book about intelligence would have been unlikely to deal with this subject at all. 'Creativity', however defined, was considered, except by a few brash pioneers, to be on the fringe of psychology and hardly capable of being investigated by empirical methods. Books had been written about the genealogy and estimated intelligence of men and women of genius (e.g. Galton, 1870; Havelock Ellis, 1904; Cox, 1926), but few attempts had been made to investigate creative abilities and their correlates as manifested at a more humdrum level in the general population. The common opinion among psychologists was probably that anything describable as 'creativity', except at the level of genius or in particular specialised fields, was largely accounted for by known and measurable abilities. This was certainly the dogmatically expressed opinion of Spearman, and the view is still tenable (Burt, 1962; Vernon, 1964b) that much of what passes for 'creativity' is ascribable to general intelligence, (though a recent paper by Vernon (1967) recognises that 'creativity tests' may represent a common factor other than general intelligence and may be useful in cross-cultural comparisons). Apart from opinions of this kind, one must recognise an understandable repugnance, particularly among people most involved in and responsive to the arts, against the crude effects of a young science to drag into the market-place and explain away consummate artistic achievements. The gulf between 'arts' and 'science' viewpoints is made especially apparent in experimental and statistical studies of creativity. But, by and large, humanists have little reason to be alarmed for many years yet, since the mysteries of artistic creation are at present a long way from being reduced to explanation in behaviouristic terms. During the last decade or so, there has however been a great increase both in theoretical speculation and in empirical work in the general area of creative abilities, particularly in the USA, and many leading workers in the field believe that these can be usefully distinguished from general intelligence both

93

conceptually and in terms of measurement or assessment. A great flood of articles has appeared on the topic. Parnes and Brunelle (1967) report that some 1,250 had been published in the preceding eighteen months, and provide a useful first instalment (running to some 60 pages) of a comprehensive annotated bibliography including summaries of recent theses in American Universities.

Various circumstances have favoured this growth of interest. During the early fifties the climate of opinion in the USA was particularly favourable to any new suggestions for diagnosing, encouraging and using original scientific talent. This appreciation of the national value of scientific creativity and originality was intensified when the first Russian satellite was launched.

Secondly, both in Britain and the USA, the development of new ways of assessing ability was seen to have been unenterprising and unsatisfactory between about 1920 and 1950. Multiple-choice tests had proliferated, and had been more widely standardised and refined, but their disadvantages were sometimes too readily discounted by applied psychologists. Cognitive tests in general use have been limited and narrow in the kinds of ability they tap and in the sort of item they employ. This has been true both of general intelligence tests and of tests of special abilities and aptitudes. Both the kind of material employed and the usual multiple-choice type of item direct the subject's thinking along rather narrowly prescribed lines if he is to find the correct answer. If he *does* find an original and justifiable answer that the test constructor has not thought of, he will be penalised by being scored wrong. Admittedly this will be rare (though not impossible) in an adequately constructed test such as is normally used in selection procedures, but the design of multiple-choice, objectively scored, tests tends by its very nature to exclude original thinking.

There is a plausible commonsense case that originality and the power of achieving new, personal syntheses will never be detected in performance on the conventional kind of test, and may even prove an actual handicap. This is a case that has often been put forward by parents and teachers, but has usually been rejected by educationists, partly on account of the considerable operational success achieved by tests of the accepted type, and partly because of the difficulty of assessing objectively such intangible and elusive qualities as originality or creativity. The quite reasonable public distrust of the limitations of multiple-choice tests has also been the main reason for the retention of 'essay-type' rather than 'new-type' or objectively scored answers in examinations, but again this view has carried less weight with psychologists than with parents or teachers because of the demonstrated subjectivity and un-reliability typical of much examination marking (Hartog, Rhodes and Burt, 1936) and because of the many other defects in current examination procedures that have long been suspected but are only beginning to receive due attention (Cox, 1967; Jahoda, 1967; Pilliner, 1968). Also, of course, there is no guarantee that an 'essay-type' question will automatically give scope for originality and creative thinking. It may be phrased and marked so as to discourage or penalise them.

Another line of criticism that might be directed against both established tests of ability and school examinations is that they have often failed to detect people whose subsequent careers have given proof of remarkable talent. Jan Masaryk, during a childhood stay in America, was briefly confined in an institute for the mentally deficient as the result of his performance on an intelligence test (Cronbach, 1960). Einstein was not a particularly good student at school, *'unless he did productive work on his own account'* (Wertheimer, 1959). At a somewhat lower level also, MacKinnon (1962) has shown that distinguished architects and outstanding figures in other professions were often rather mediocre students.

It might be argued that illustrations of this kind, which could be multiplied, constitute no criticism of tests of ability or attainment as such, but merely indicate that factors of temperament, motivation and interest need also to be taken into account if one is to have any hope of predicting success in later life. This is certainly true, and, as we shall see, creativity appears to lie as much in the temperamental-motivational field as in the cognitive. The distinction between cognitive and temperamental traits is a useful one conceptually, but it is possible that the line has often been too rigidly drawn to have healthy effects on applied psychology and educational selection or allocation. Cattell has been unusually wise in always including a measure of intelligence in his general personality questionnaires. Barron (1963) expresses a complementary view when he writes, 'Intelligence is a complex set of inter-related aptitudes and abilities, some verging closely on the temperamental'. In the case of intelligence, this is a very arguable statement but if applied to creativity it would win wide acceptance.

The studies which originally stimulated much of this recent interest in creativity were concentrated on its cognitive aspects. J. P. Guilford, whose scheme for the classification of abilities has been described in Chapter 2, chose the topic of creativity for his presidential address to the American Psychological Association (Guilford, 1950), and it was the work of his laboratory that aroused much of the new wave of enthusiasm for the subject. In particular, the distinction between convergent and divergent thinking, which had much earlier been suggested by (among others) William James, Sully and Stout, was subjected by Guilford and his associates to careful experimental investigation. The distinction is an important one. Briefly, convergent thinking is the kind required to solve a problem which has one definite right answer, whereas divergent thinking is more open-ended, less analytical, the kind of thinking needed to tackle a problem where there may be any number of more or less right answers or no right answer at all. Furthermore, Guilford's laboratory has been the main source of the open-ended psychological tests used by other investigators both in the USA and in this country when they try to assess divergent thinking abilities. Many of these tests appear crude, and the intelligent layman will no doubt be quite sceptical about any relation between, for example, finding as many uses as possible for a brick and anything he is accustomed to regard as original thinking. This is inevitable at the present stage. On the whole, it is a sign of the vigorous and healthy development of psychology that its practitioners are increasingly willing to apply empirical methods, at first necessarily rough and ready, to the study of such elusive and complex aspects of behaviour.

The word 'creativity' is not a very elegant one and its use begs a number of questions. The application of one word to an enormous variety of performances implies, probably wrongly, a broad unitary trait. Are artistic and scientific creation fundamentally examples of the same psychological process? Even within the scientific sphere, are the mental processes of Einstein and the man who invents a new kind of clothes peg similar enough to justify the same description? They may be, but no one has proved so. If there is reason to cavil at the idea of intelligence as a unitary trait – and, as we have seen, there have been plenty of cavillers – there is even more reason to suspect that creative abilities are diverse and related in a subtle and complex manner. Moreover it has not been demonstrated so conclusively as many suppose that tests of divergent thinking are properly describable as tests of creativity. There is some evidence that scientists are better at convergent thinking and arts specialists at divergent thinking (Hudson, 1966), and that, quite apart from this distinction, either kind of specialist may in his own way be 'creative'. Eysenck (1967) has supported this view, suggesting that the divergent thinking of arts specialists largely consists of verbal fluency and is associated with extraversion. But in spite of these objections, 'creativity' is a useful word for the time being, which avoids clumsy periphrases about the largely unknown and debatable inter-relationship of hypothetical abilities and motivational processes. Until the area is plotted in more detail, it serves a purpose. It implies a high degree of ability at divergent-type thinking (probably allied to a particular kind of temperament and motivation), enabling us to reserve 'intelligence' as a description of the convergent thinking exemplified in the eduction of relations and correlates (in Spearman's language).

DIFFERENCES BETWEEN 'HIGHLY INTELLIGENT' AND 'HIGHLY CREATIVE' CHILDREN. THE GETZELS AND JACKSON STUDY

The study that has attracted most attention and that has been most often quoted in this connection is that of Getzels and Jackson (1962), who explain their starting point and aims as follows:

> Our argument then is this. Giftedness in children has most fre-
> quently been defined as a score on an intelligence test, and typically
> the study of the so-called gifted child has been equated with the study
> of the single IQ variable. Involved in this definition of giftedness are
> several types of confusion, if not of outright error. First, there is the
> limitation of the single metric itself, which not only restricts our
> perspective of the more general phenomenon, but places on the one
> concept a greater theoretical and predictive burden than it was
> intended to carry. For all practical purposes, the term 'gifted child'
> has become synonymous with the expression 'child with a high IQ',
> thus blinding us to other forms of excellence. And second, within the
> universe of intellectual functions themselves, we have most often
> behaved as if the intelligence test represented an adequate sampling of
> all mental abilities and cognitive processes. Despite the already sub-
> stantial and increasing literature regarding the intellectual functions
> closely allied to creativity, we still treat the latter concept as applicable
> only to performance in one or more of the arts to the exclusion of other
> types of achievement requiring inventiveness, originality, and perfec-
> tion. The term 'creative child', in becoming synonymous with the
> expression 'child with artistic talents,' has limited our attempts to
> identify and foster cognitive abilities related to creative functioning
> in areas other than the arts.
>
> Despite its longevity there is after all nothing inevitable about the
> use of IQ in defining giftedness. Indeed we might argue that in many
> ways this definition is only a historical accident – a consequence of the
> fact that early inquiries in the field had as their context the classroom
> and its attendant concern with academic abilities and achievement. If
> we were to move the focus of inquiry from the classroom setting, we

D

might identify cognitive qualities defining giftedness for other situations just as the IQ did in the classroom. Should we change only the original criteria of learning, we might change the cognitive qualities defining giftedness even in the classroom. For example, if we recognize that learning involves the production of novelty as well as the remembrance of course content – *discovering* as well as *recalling* – measures of creativity as well as IQ become appropriate defining characteristics of giftedness.

The issues we have raised are, of course, not new or unique to us. The American Association for Gifted Children some time ago argued that qualities other than IQ be included in the conception of giftedness, and defined the gifted individual as 'a person whose performance in any line of socially useful endeavor is consistently superior. This definition includes those talented in art, music, drama, and mathematics, as well as those who possess mechanical and social skills and those with high abstract verbal intelligence.' Despite such calls for freeing the concept of giftedness from its one-sided attachment to the IQ metric and for broadening the base for examining intellectual and social excellence in children, the essential point remains: in research as in educational practice, the IQ metric has continued to be the predominant and often exclusive criterion of giftedness. Accordingly, we undertook to examine empirically the consequences of applying other conceptions of giftedness as well as 'high IQ' to the study of children.

The school studied by Getzels and Jackson was an atypical one, being a private school in which a large proportion of the pupils came from the families of lecturers at the University of Chicago, and only a negligible proportion from the families of semi-skilled or unskilled workers. The mean IQ of the children was 132.

The method adopted was to form two contrasting groups, one of pupils who scored very high on measures of intelligence (even compared with the general level in the school) and relatively low on tests of creativity, and the other of those who scored, vice versa, high on the tests of creativity and relatively low on the tests of intelligence. There were five creativity measures, some of which were taken or adapted from tests made up by Guilford and by Cattell, and others specially constructed by the authors. The five measures were, briefly, as follows:

1. *Word association.* Meanings and uses required of common words with multiple meanings e.g. 'bolt', 'sack'. Scored both for number of definitions, and number of radically different meanings.

2. *Uses for things.* As many different uses as possible to be given for objects such as 'brick', 'paper-clip'. Scored for number of uses and originality of uses.

3. *Hidden shapes* (part of Cattell's Objective-Analytic Test Battery). 18 simple geometrical figures, each followed by four complex figures. Subject required to find the geometric figure hidden in the more complex pattern.

4. *Fables.* Four fables were presented in which the last lines were missing. The subject was required to provide three different endings to each story, one moralistic, one humorous and one sad.

5. *Make-up Problems.* Four complex paragraphs containing many numerical statements were presented. Subject required to make up as many mathematical problems as possible from them (but no need to *solve* them). Scored on number, complexity, appropriateness and originality of problems.

Correlations between these measures and of each measure with IQ were calculated for 292 boys and 241 girls separately. All correlation coefficients were positive, and of moderate size, between $+\cdot1$ and $+\cdot5$, those for the girls being slightly higher. The matrix of intercorrelations for boys has already been reproduced in this book, as Table 2.1 on page 41. It appears that the five separate measures were then combined into one composite measure of creativity, though this is not made at all clear in the report. At least, performance on these five measures of creativity was one criterion and IQ the other, by which the contrasting groups were formed, one high creativity group (all in top-scoring 20% on creativity, but below top-scoring 20% in IQ) and one high IQ group (vice versa.) Because it is not made clear how the five creativity measures were combined into a single criterion, it is also not quite clear in detail how the contrasting groups were formed. They were at any rate reduced in number because some of the subjects were required for other aspects of the study, with the result that out of 533 original subjects, the 'high creativity' group contained 26 and the 'high IQ' group 28 children.

Interesting and important similarities and differences were found by Getzels and Jackson between the 'high creativity' and 'high IQ' groups. Most striking, perhaps was the finding that the high creativity group equalled the high IQ group in scholastic achievement (assessed by a composite score on several standardised tests) in spite of having an average IQ 23 points lower (127 against 150). This result suggests the possibility that some or all of the creativity measures might be used as predictors of scholastic achievement. Getzels and Jackson in fact report quite high positive correlations (between ·3 and ·6) between some of the individual tests and both verbal and numerical achievement for the whole sample of 533 subjects. The three tests which showed up best in this way were Word Association, Make-up Problems, and Hidden Shapes in that order. Getzels and Jackson also attempted to find out whether this unexpectedly high degree of scholastic achievement on the part of the high creativity group could be ascribed to higher strength of motivation. They found, however, no difference between the two groups on McClelland's 'need for achievement' measure, and therefore concluded that the explanation lay not in any motivational difference, but in the predictive limitations of the conventional intelligence test.

Another striking finding in this study was that teachers appeared to approve more strongly of the high IQ group than of the high creativity group. The average rating for 'desirability as a student' was slightly higher for the former group, even though it was made clear in the rating instructions that 'brightness' was not to be taken specifically into account. Getzels and Jackson comment that the reverse should have been true, since the high IQ group were only doing scholastically what was expected of them, whereas the high creativity group (as shown by the achievement results) were doing relatively more than might have been expected of them. Getzels and Jackson have been criticised (Dunnette, 1964) for making too much of this result. The difference in average rating was apparently not statistically significant, so that the claim should only have been that the high creativity group were rated *no higher* than the high IQ group in spite of their apparent 'overachievement'.

A third respect in which the groups were found to differ was in their attitudes to success in adult life. In the high IQ group the correspondence between the qualities they valued for themselves and the qualities which they thought would be conducive to success in adult life was quite close. Similarly, there was quite a close correspondence between qualities they said they would like to possess themselves and qualities they thought teachers tended to approve of. Neither of these correspondences held to nearly the same degree in the 'high creativity' group. In other words, although the 'high creativity' children agreed in general with the 'high IQ' children both about the qualities making for success in adult life and the qualities in pupils that teachers approved of, unlike the 'high IQ' group they were not very interested in these qualities for themselves. One of the qualities the 'creative' group valued considerably *more highly* than did the 'high IQ' group was a sense of humour.

Getzels and Jackson suggest that the undervaluation of creative

children by their teachers was partly accounted for by the less con-
formist values held by these children, as just described. They also
describe other differences between the groups besides those reviewed
here, and their book includes a great deal of interesting material about
these gifted children, such as reproductions of their drawings and
extracts from their essays, responses to T.A.T. pictures and autobio-
graphical sketches. Many of these certainly suggest creative talent, and
quite a few are skilfully written to amuse. Here are two short extracts,
the first from a boy's T.A.T. response, the second from a girl's
'autobiography'.

Freddie Jones was a nice boy. If you don't believe it just ask him.
Freddie came from a theatrical family and wanted to be in show
business somehow. However, the only talent he had was a nice
smile. He posed for tooth-paste ads on T.V. You may think this is
kind of low-brow, but I see nothing wrong with it. Freddie wanted to
satisfy an ambition and he did it the best way in which he could.
Freddie will never amount to much but he will be happy. How are
you doing?

A shriek rang through the hall of the hospital. It was the nurse. In
the process of being born, I had kicked her in the stomach. I was little
and round and red. I am no longer red or round, but I am still little.
As a nursery-school child I was bashful. While the other children
romped and played I hung back in the corner. The teacher tried to
make me join the happy throng and I took a bite out of her ankle.
Ah, my carefree childhood.

RECENT STUDIES OF CREATIVITY AND INTELLIGENCE

The research of Getzels and Jackson deservedly attracted a great deal of
interest and aroused some controversy. De Mille and Merrifield (1962)
criticised it quite severely as being ill-designed and inadequately
reported (cf. Dunnette, 1964). This criticism is largely justified. Often
Getzels and Jackson appear only to be reporting what favours their own
viewpoint and to be omitting crucial information, such as the characteristics of the children who scored highly in both 'intelligence' and
'creativity'. Their statistical treatment is so sketchy as sometimes to be
positively misleading. Furthermore, their contrasting 'high IQ' and
'high creativity' groups were at the extremes in these directions in a
sample of children already extreme. Even granted that all Getzels and
Jackson's findings were perfectly accurate and fully reported, one would

have to be very careful about attempting to generalise from these very exceptional small groups to children outside this range.

A number of writers have suggested that Getzels and Jackson's approach may not be so novel as might be supposed, and that the tests of creativity would, as Burt (1962) put it, 'form very satisfactory additions to any ordinary battery for testing the general factor of intelligence'. The creativity tests in Getzels and Jackson's research did not correlate with each other to a much higher degree than they correlated with IQ, and it is therefore possible to analyse their results further and to show that the creativity tests can be interpreted as partly assessing a factor of general intelligence (Marsh, 1964; Thorndike, 1963).

There have also been several attempts to repeat Getzels and Jackson's work, but with more typical and representative groups of children. These have produced conflicting results. Several of these repetitions have been carried out by Torrance and his associates at the University of Minnesota, and have lent partial support to the Getzels and Jackson finding that 'creative' children were more successful in school work than could be expected from their IQ. Extensive work into other aspects of creativity has been reported by the Minnesota group (Torrance, 1960, 1962, 1964, 1965; Yamamoto, 1964 a, b and c, 1965 a and b). The tests devised by Torrance and his associates have been described and evaluated by Goldman (1964) who is using them for research into the creative abilities of English primary school children (Goldman and Clarke, 1967).

Rather mixed findings have been typical also when other proposed tests of creativity have been examined in terms of validity. Mednick (1962) proposed that a test of 'remote associates' would prove effective as an indicator of creative ability. The principle of the test is that the respondent is presented with two or three stimulus words (not obviously connected in sense or association) and is required to find one further word linking them all together. Mednick himself found some positive evidence for the test's validity with two small samples of architecture and psychology students. Findings by Datta (1964a; 1964b) and by Andrews (1965), whose criterion was scientific output in terms of patents, published papers and so forth among 1,300 scientists (both academic and industrial) were predominantly negative. Shapiro, however, (1965, 1966) has developed two new tests, allied to Mednick's R.A.T., and claims that they have proved useful in identifying creative research scientists.

Several of the more recent studies in which attempts have been made to separate creativity from intelligence (e.g. Edwards and Tyler, 1965;

Hasan and Butcher, 1966) have been almost completely at variance with the more ambitious claims. Hasan and Butcher carried out a fairly close repetition of much of the Getzels and Jackson study, but with 175 Scottish children who, unlike the highly able children tested by Getzels and Jackson, were unselected for ability and approximately representative in this respect of the whole population of secondary school children. Very much more overlap between the measures of intelligence and those of creativity was found than had been reported in the Chicago study. For instance, Getzels and Jackson reported for the boys in their sample a correlation of $+\cdot131$ between score on the 'tables' test and IQ. The corresponding correlation found by Hasan and Butcher was $+\cdot726$. Not all the discrepancies were so large as this, but they were all in the same direction and all substantial. An important additional point is that, although one might suppose the greater overlap between intelligence and creativity in the Scottish study to be a purely statistical effect due to a wider range of ability, this was not the case since there was an equal range of variation in Getzels and Jackson's sample, although the average level was some 25 IQ points higher. Moreover the large overlap found by Hasan and Butcher was striking. IQ correlated more highly with total 'creativity' score than did 9 out of 10 of the separate 'creativity' tests, even though the latter correlations were part-whole correlations.

When contrasting groups were formed of children scoring high respectively in IQ and on the battery of 10 tests of creativity, those of high IQ scored significantly more highly on two tests of attainment. The Getzels and Jackson finding of teacher preference for intelligent (rather than creative) children was partly confirmed, but it seemed evident in the Scottish survey that it was not the higher 'creativity' as such that resulted in more adverse teacher ratings of desirability as a pupil, but primarily the lower level of intelligence.

Two possible explanations were suggested for these discrepancies. Firstly, there is the plausible 'threshold' suggestion about the relation between general intelligence and creative ability, which suggests that up to a level of about IQ 120 general intelligence is the most important factor, particularly in predicting school achievement, but that at levels about this creative abilities begin to assume more importance (Barron, 1963; McClelland, 1958; Mackinnon, 1962; Meer and Stein, 1955; Yamamoto, 1964b; Moore, 1966). This could partly account for the negative findings in the two studies quoted, which both included children in a wide range of ability in non-selective schools. A recent report suggests that new evidence supporting this theory has been amassed by Fuqua (1967). Secondly, Torrance (1965) has found some evidence in his own studies to suggest that differences in school atmosphere and methods of teaching may account for the discrepant results; according to this suggestion the more creative children would be relatively favoured by the more permissive, flexible kind of school environment. It seems unlikely, however, from a consideration of all these researches that a general factor of creativity, if established, will be uncorrelated with general intelligence. It is much more likely to be oblique or correlated, as found by Cropley (1966).

Further light on these conflicting findings has also been thrown by a recent extensive research reported by Wallach and Kogan (1965). They begin by reviewing earlier reports of the distinction between creativity and intelligence, including the Getzels and Jackson book and papers by Cline, Richards and Needham (1963), Cline, Richards and Abe (1962), Flescher (1963), Torrance (1960), Yamamoto (1964 a, b, c), and Guilford (1956, 1959, 1963). Their main conclusion from this survey is that the distinction between creativity and intelligence has not been adequately supported by empirical evidence and that the correlations between measures of 'creativity' are generally lower than those between a typical test of 'creativity' and one of 'intelligence'. They admit to having been disappointed by this general conclusion, but suggest that all the earlier researches reviewed suffered from one particular methodological failing, and that if this is remedied, there may still be hope of maintaining a legitimate distraction between creativity and intelligence. The failing stressed by Wallach and Kogan is the reliance of earlier investigations on group tests administered in a 'psychometric' and usually competitive situation. In contrast, therefore, they took especial trouble in their own research to make sure that all the psychological measures were obtained in situations designed to minimise 'test anxiety'. The subjects were 10–11-year-old children, and the 'experimenters' were teachers who had established close rapport with the children and who derived the required data from 'games' and 'lessons' without appearing to upset the normal school programme.

The tests used owed something to Guilford's conceptions. They were measures of associative fluency in response to both verbal and nonverbal stimuli, and were given untimed. There were five of these measures, each being scored separately for number and uniqueness of responses. Wallach and Kogan comment that very few bizarre or inappropriate responses were forthcoming.

Two of the sets of non-verbal patterns to which the children were required to produce associations are shown in figures 4.1a and 4.1b below. Of these two rather similar tasks, it appears from Wallach and

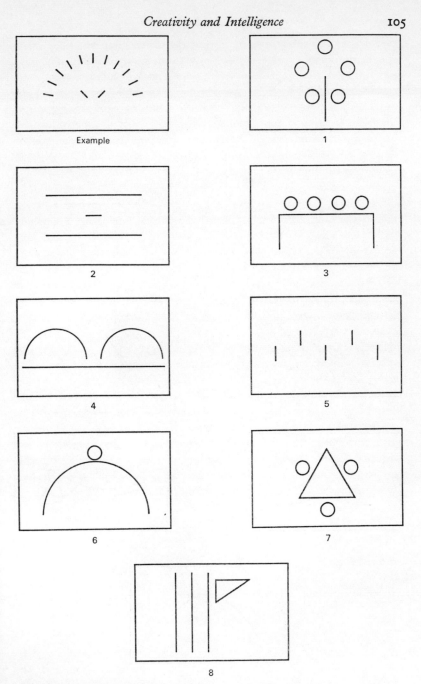

Figure 4.1a. Stimulus materials for the Pattern Meanings procedure. (Original cards, 4 in. × 6in.) Wallach and Kogan (1965)

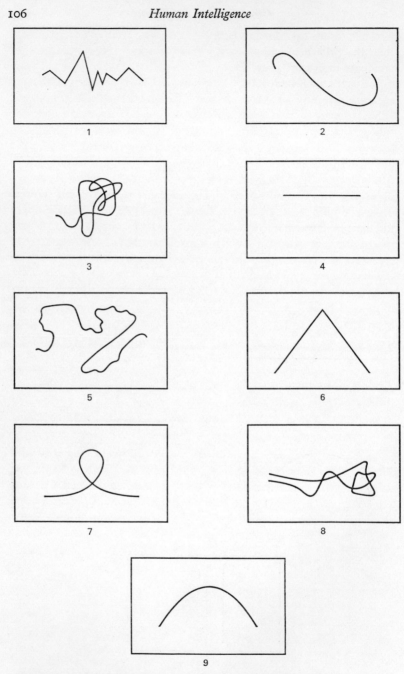

Figure 4.1b. Stimulus materials for the Line Meanings procedure. (Original cards, 4 in. × 6 in.) Wallach and Kogan (1965)

Kogan's results that the line-meanings task was a rather better measure than the pattern-meanings one, at least in correlating with the other creativity measures.

Wallach and Kogan report a fair degree of success in establishing separate measures of creativity and intelligence in these conditions. What is more, one can assess this progress adequately, as they provide full details, for instance, of the reliabilities and inter-correlations of their measures; they also, where necessary, carry out tests of significance and again provide enough detail for one to see what these are worth. Methodologically their work is far less crude than that of their predecessors. One can therefore put more trust in their claim to have achieved quite a satisfactory practical separation of creativity from intelligence. The extent of this separation is shown in Table 4.1 below, where it can be seen that the average correlation between measures of creativity was about $+\cdot41$, but the average correlation of those with intelligence measures only about $+\cdot1$.

TABLE 4.1 *Average Intercorrelations among Creativity Measures, among Intelligence Measures, and between Creativity and Intelligence Measures*

	Total sample ($N = 151$)	Boys ($N = 70$)	Girls ($N = 81$)
Among creativity measures	·41	·34	·50
Among intelligence measures	·51	·50	·55
Between creativity and intelligence measures	·09	·05	·13

Contrasting groups of children were then formed as in the Getzels and Jackson study (but including also groups who were high in both creativity and intelligence or low in both) and were compared on a variety of aspects, including for instance attitude to study, degree of social adjustment, level of anxiety and so forth. Wallach and Kogan summarise the main differences between these groups as follows (p. 303).

High creativity–high intelligence: These children can exercise within themselves both control and freedom, both adult-like and childlike kinds of behavior.

High creativity–low intelligence: These children are in angry conflict with themselves and with their school environment and are beset by feelings of unworthiness and inadequacy. In a stress-free context, however, they can blossom forth cognitively.

Low creativity–high intelligence: These children can be described

as 'addicted' to school achievement. Academic failure would be per-
ceived by them as catastrophic, so that they must continually strive
for academic excellence in order to avoid the possibility of pain.

Low creativity–low intelligence: Basically bewildered, these children engage in various defensive maneuvers ranging from useful
adaptations such as intensive social activity to regressions such as
passivity or psychosomatic symptoms.

Thus, our work progressed from the definition and operationaliza-
tion of two types of cognitive activity to an investigation of their
correlates in such areas as observable social and achievement-relevant
behaviors, ways of forming concepts, physiognomic sensitivities, and
self-described levels of general anxiety, test anxiety, and defensive-
ness. From the findings obtained, it seems fair to conclude that the
present definition of creativity denotes a mode of cognitive functioning that matters a great deal in the life of the child. Furthermore, consideration of the child's *joint* status with regard to the conventional
concept of general intelligence and creativity as here defined is
evidently of critical importance in the search for new knowledge concerning children's thinking.

These summaries, although containing in very condensed form the
gist of Wallach and Kogan's findings, hardly do justice to the scope of
their work. Many aspects of temperament and personality in this group
of children were discussed, and interesting suggestions made about
differing types of conceptualisation and classification corresponding to
the four groups distinguished. One finding, for instance, was that the
high-intelligence, low-creativity group strongly preferred abstract,
formal bases of classification. This was not due to inability to use other
kinds of category, as Wallach and Kogan showed experimentally, but
was interpreted as a kind of defence-mechanism. Similar interesting
hypotheses and speculations were advanced about the other three
groups. Wallach and Kogan quite correctly point out, however, that
even if the findings about creativity in children are valid and come to be
generally accepted, there is a particularly large gulf of ignorance about
the relation of creativity in children to performance in later life. What is
needed, perhaps, is a team like that of Terman and his associates to
carry out a large-scale longitudinal study much as he did in the case of
intelligence.

Hudson (1966), in a lively and provocative book, has maintained that
the distinction between divergent and convergent thinking is a fundamental one, but that it is hardly related to creative ability. In his view it

is much more closely related to the differences between scientists and specialists in 'arts' or literary subjects. His work with English Public School and Grammar School boys showed a close connection between specialisation in arts subjects and divergent thinking and between work in scientific subjects and convergent thinking. Hudson argues this case persuasively, but the selected nature of the sample of subjects with which he worked makes it uncertain how far his results are generalisable. It is very possible that the degree of specialisation in the upper forms of selective English schools was the cause rather than the result of the marked distinction in modes of thought. His work clearly merits replication in other kinds of school and at other levels of ability. Cameron (1967) has found partial confirmation of Hudson's views in a study of Aberdeen University undergraduates, and two further researches (by Mollison and Amour) are at present being carried out with Edinburgh school-children.

There are two further lines of research that seem to have been relatively neglected and that should help to clarify the confused picture of individual differences in creativity. First, processes of thinking have been too rigidly classified as convergent or divergent, and tests have been constructed either with one 'correct' answer or with an infinite number of 'correct' answers to each item. It might be more instructive to treat the distinction between divergent and convergent thinking not as a dichotomy but as a continuum and to construct tests accordingly. Items might be framed so as to have a finite number, small or large, of acceptable solutions, and the continuum might thus be treated as an experimental or independent variable. Anagrams and numerical data could readily be adapted for this purpose.

The second profitable field of research is suggested by the predominance of verbal problems in tests of divergent thinking. This predominance is such that the assessment of creativity has often amounted to the assessment of verbal fluency and that scientific, mathematical and other forms of creativity have eluded investigation. Although the Wallach and Kogan research included two tests based on non-verbal stimuli (those illustrated in Figures 4.1a and 4.1b), the responses still depended on verbal skills. The Hasan and Butcher study included one test (the 'circles' test devised by Torrance) in which the responses required were non-verbal. An unpublished factor analysis of these data reveals that this test has a uniquely high loading on a factor orthogonal to that of verbal fluency and interpretable as divergent thinking applied to graphic or diagrammatic material.

These two lines of research, the one involving intermediate kinds of

item between 'multiple-choice' and 'open-ended', and the other concerned with allowing for non-verbal responses to tests of divergent
thinking, are currently being explored by Christie at the University of
Manchester and by Aharoni in Israel.

CREATIVE ABILITY AND ENVIRONMENTAL INFLUENCES

This is a lively area of research, particularly in the USA, where much of
the recent interest in creative talent has been concerned with detecting
and making the most of the nation's human resources.

The Getzels and Jackson study already discussed in some detail suggested certain systematic differences between the 'high creativity' and
'high intelligence' groups in respect of home background and atmosphere. The conclusions, which were admittedly based on a rather small
number of parents, were that the fathers of the 'high IQ' group tended
to be professional people in intellectual occupations, whereas those of
the 'high creativity' group were more often in business. They found the
mothers of the 'high IQ' group to be less secure and at ease with themselves than those of the 'high creativity' group; in the 'high IQ' group,
they found both parents tended to be more worried about money problems, more critical of their children, and more worried in general about
the dangers of the world. The overall impression of the 'high IQ'
family was that it was one 'in which individual divergence is limited and
risks minimised', and that of the 'high creativity' family that it was one
'in which individual divergence is permitted and risks are accepted'.
Getzels and Jackson also provide two family case-histories as illustration
of the contrasting atmospheres which they found.

One must remember that much of the work described in this chapter
is new, exploratory and provisional, and many of the conclusions drawn
are quite speculative. Little is known about the effects of home influence
and early training on creative ability. Rather more, though again little
enough, has been discovered about the effects of schooling, and especially about the effects of pressures and restraints both from teachers and
fellow-pupils. There is some agreement that the primary school years
are particularly important in determining whether creative potential
will come to fruition. A great deal of interesting work on the developmental aspects of creative ability and the influence of schooling has been
done by Torrance and his associates at the University of Minnesota.

Torrance (1963, 1964) claims to have found rather regular trends in
the development of creativity in schoolchildren, which are quite consistent and marked in one country, but vary from culture to culture. In

the USA, about which there is most information available, he finds that one peak of development is reached at age $4\frac{1}{2}$, only to be followed by a sharp drop soon after the child enters kindergarten. He finds similar drops at the ages of about 9 and about 12, with periods of slow recovery in between. He interprets the drops as occurring where cultural discontinuities coincide with discontinuities in development. There is also some evidence that sex differences and urban-rural differences interact with these changes. Torrance has found differences in favour of girls on tests of divergent thinking at some ages, and this question has been studied in some detail by Klausmeier and Wiersma (1964).

Torrance also provides a useful summary and discussion of research findings about the circumstances that inhibit and facilitate creative ability in schoolchildren. A few of these circumstances are peculiar to the USA, but most seem to have quite general application. Among the adverse factors he includes an excessive success-orientation, suggesting that the education process, in the USA at least, prepares only for success and hardly at all for coping with frustration and failure, and that risk-taking is too much discouraged. Another factor, which is particularly noticeable in the USA but almost certainly has wide application, and which undoubtedly seems often to inhibit creative ability, is the pressure towards conformity from other children, from what sociologists call the 'peer-group'. Torrance's own studies at Minnesota suggest strongly that many harmless deviations from the behavioural norm or mild eccentricities are often considered by both teachers and 'peer-group' to be indications of something abnormal, unhealthy or immoral that must be corrected at all costs. British Public Schools are not unique in this respect! Allied to this pressure to conform is an overemphasis on sex roles. Primary school girls studied by Torrance were reluctant to work with scientific toys, protesting 'I'm a girl; I'm not supposed to know anything about things like that.' To many boys, also, the very atmosphere and standards in primary schools may set up some degree of role-conflict. Kagan (1964, 1966) has shown, in an ingenious experiment, that American boys label the school situation as feminine. He has also pointed out the probable connection between this fact and the much higher proportion of reading difficulties among boys than girls in the United States and Western European countries. In Japan, by contrast, where half the primary school teachers are male, there is no excess of boys with reading problems.

Yet another factor is an exaggerated work-play dichotomy. In many, if not most schools, the child soon has the feeling that he is supposed to like play and dislike work and that there is something a little odd about him if he doesn't. Children who take a creative delight in their school work may even make their teachers uneasy. Teachers may unwittingly inhibit creative abilities in many ways, as for instance by telling a child what is 'best' in order to 'save time', by being unready to accept unexpected and original solutions when they are prepared for more prosaic and plodding ones, or by evading questions they find it difficult to answer.

Bruner (1961), in an influential book, particularly stresses the importance of guessing. 'The shrewd guess, the fertile hypothesis, the courageous leap to a tentative conclusion – these are the most valuable coin of the thinker at work, whatever his line of work. Can schoolchildren be led to master this gift?' Only too often, he fears, the influence is in the opposite direction and guessing is discouraged as a form of laziness, so that the child is induced to keep quiet if he does not know the full and exact answer. Admittedly, of course, there is guessing and guessing, some silly, some brilliant, and children should also be encouraged to learn that even a brilliant guess needs to be followed up and verified. But the general point is an important one and underlines the need for teachers to recognise the 'good error' and the bold intuitive leap if they wish to encourage creativity in children.

Dienes and Jeeves have re-iterated the same point in a different context (1965, p. 104). 'How can we train scientists if we tell them never to guess?' Scientific hypotheses are very often inspired (or even uninspired) guesses. 'Intuition' sounds more impressive, but is frequently a polite word for 'guessing'.

In addition to the kind of research so far described, which has been concerned with the origins and development of creativity in childhood, there has been much interest and some research in the USA concerned with environmental conditions affecting the creativity of the adult scientist. A series of three conferences on the identification of creative scientific talent was held at the University of Utah between 1955 and 1959. A selection of papers read at these conferences has been made by Taylor and Barron (1963) and includes some useful contributions on this topic.

PERSONALITY TRAITS RELATED TO CREATIVE ABILITY

Considering the very varied kinds of research in this area, employing all sorts of measurement technique and numerous different criteria of creativity, there is a tolerable amount of agreement about the personality traits that seem commonly to be associated with creative ability.

One of the most frequent observations is that creative people, and perhaps especially creative scientists, tend to display (and very likely require) a stubborn intellectual autonomy and independence of judgment, which makes them less willing than most to be influenced by group opinions and pressures. Anne Roe (1953) has found something of the kind in her careful and detailed studies of scientists; so also have Barron (1955) and Cattell (1957). This seems a plausible finding. One thinks of Einstein worrying away for seven years from the age of 16 at one basic paradox that disturbed few other people (Wertheimer, 1959); also of the probably apocryphal but significant story of Galileo's 'eppur si muove'!

Barron (1963) describes some experiments on independence of judgment and associated features of personality that have some relevance. The technique for determining independence of judgment was the well-known and rather unethical one devised by Asch, in which the subject is a member of an experimental group, all of whom except himself are, unknown to him, previously briefed by the experimenter to defend unanimously some indefensible or erroneous proposition. Usually about 25% of subjects stick firmly to their own opinions, and about 75% agree with what is apparently an overwhelming majority opinion. Barron investigated some of the ways in which 'independents' and 'yielders' differed, and one was that the 'independents' rated themselves significantly more often as 'artistic', 'emotional' and 'original'. These in fact were the three qualities on which there was the biggest difference between the self-ratings of the 'independents' and the 'yielders'. This would be shaky evidence in itself, but fits in quite neatly with the other observations quoted.

Cattell and Drevdahl (1955) compared the scores of 140 eminent research scientists in American universities, when tested with Cattell's 16 Personality Factor questionnaire, with those of university teachers and administrators and also with the average scores of the general population. The research scientists and the presumably less 'creative' university group showed a family resemblance in personality profile when compared with the general population norms, but interesting differences were also found. The research scientists were significantly more 'schizothyme' (withdrawn, unsociable), less emotionally stable, more intellectually self-sufficient and more radical. The same differences in schizothymia, self-sufficiency and radicalism were found when Drevdahl (1956) compared 'creative' and 'non-creative' students in science and arts subjects.

Cross, Cattell and Butcher (1967) have shown that the 16 P.F. discriminates clearly between artists (art teachers and professional painters) and a control group matched for age and level of education. The artists differed significantly on 12 out of 15 factors (intelligence excluded), particularly in being more dominant and intellectually self-sufficient, but lower on ego-strength or emotional stability and on super-ego strength or conscientiousness. One of the largest differences was on factor M (Autistic or bohemian tendency, 'hysterical unconcern'), perhaps the artistic factor of temperament par excellence, in which the difference between artists and controls was more than a standard deviation. An especially convincing finding in this research was that on eleven of the twelve factors a group of craftsmen (potters, silversmiths, dress designers, and so forth) obtained average scores intermediate between those of the artists and controls.

What of the commonly held opinion that 'great wits are sure to madness near allied'? Or of the Shakespearian grouping in the well-known lines 'The lunatic, the lover and the poet are of imagination all compact'? (*A Midsummer Night's Dream*, V, 1). This view in its most extreme form, that artists as such are degenerate neurotics was, or should have been, dispelled once for all by G. B. Shaw (1911) in one of his most devastating essays. Is there any support from scientific studies of personality for the belief in weaker form, i.e. for the existence of a correlation between creative talent and nervous disorder? A few psychologists have thought so, such as Kretschmer (1931), who, in a study of the psychology of men of genius, found evidence in many cases of 'warring heredities' or of creative tension arising from conflict and internal compatibilities. Cattell (1963c) has reviewed the evidence about scientists of genius and comes to the conclusion that their level of ego strength and emotional stability is certainly higher than the average of the general population, but may be lower than that of other very able but less creative men. He further suggests that Kretschmer may well have been right in observing signs of high anxiety in many very creative people, 'There are innumerable evidences in biography of a high anxiety level in productive researchers, as in the high irritability and excitability frequently recorded in the behavior of such men as Mayer, Priestley, Darwin, Kepler, and several of our leading physicists.' Cattell, however, makes a sharp distinction between anxiety and neurosis, and concludes from an extensive survey of the biographies of major scientists that overt neurotic disorder is relatively rare. The fullest and most lucid account of Cattell's very interesting work on the role of personality factors in scientific creativity is to be found in Cattell and Butcher (1968, Chapters 14 and 15).

There is stronger reason for believing in quite a high rate of neurosis and psychosis among artists, writers and composers. Evelyn Waugh described his alter ego, Mr Pinfold, as 'despite his dangerous trade' seeming 'to himself and others unusually free of the fashionable agonies of angst', but even Mr Pinfold suffered from disturbing auditory hallucinations. Certainly it seems quite possible, from the most cursory reading of the lives of artists and writers, that these trades may be statistically dangerous ones in terms of mental health. It may be, as Barron (1963) has suggested, that 'the effectively original person may be characterised above all by an ability to regress very far *for the moment* while being able quite rapidly to return to a high degree of rationality, bringing with him the fruits of his regression to primitive and fantastic modes of thought', and that this regression has its dangers. A rather different attempt to describe and explain artistic creation in psychoanalytic terminology has been made by Kubie (1958), who sees preconscious processes (those near the level of consciousness) as key ones, and as hampered from both sides, so to speak, by conscious and by deeply unconscious functions.

This is territory virtually unpenetrated – some would say impenetrable – by scientific enquiry, though speculation has been copious. Only small beginnings have been made in the more modest task of finding the correlates of creativity at less exceptional levels. Considering the limited amount of research that has been done, the findings are fairly consistent and promising. Taylor and Holland (1964) sum them up as follows.

There is some evidence that creative persons are more autonomous than others, more self-sufficient, more independent in judgment (they go against group opinion if they feel it is incorrect), more open to the irrational in themselves, more stable, more feminine in interests and characteristics (especially in awareness of their impulses), more dominant and self-assertive, more complex, more self-accepting, more resourceful and adventurous, more radical (Bohemian), more self-controlled, and possibly more emotionally sensitive, and more introverted but bold. R. B. Cattell warns that exuberance, which decreases with maturity, should *not* be confused with creativity.

Creative scientists rate themselves high in professional self-confidence, self-sufficiency, independence, and emotional restraint, and low in aggressiveness, assertion, social desirability, sociability, and masculine vigor.

THE PROCESS OF SCIENTIFIC AND ARTISTIC CREATION

So far we have been concerned with the pioneering attempts of psychologists to distinguish an ill-defined group of abilities and temperamental qualities that fall under the heading of creativity from the more easily recognised ability involved in what Guilford has called convergent thinking. These attempts have been mainly concerned with the assessment of individual differences among talented but not uniquely talented people. No account of this topic, however, would be complete without an outline of what little is known about the operation of creative thought at full stretch in exceptionally talented men and women. Here we necessarily move from the sphere of painstaking testing procedures and the calculation and comparison of correlation coefficients to the more subjective and perhaps more exciting realm of introspective accounts and sympathetic insight.

In this section I shall present one or two first-hand accounts of the process of creative thought, chosen more for their vividness, clarity and power of conviction than for their typicality, since systematic knowledge is scanty, to say the least, about what is typical at this level. These examples will cover both scientific and artistic creation. Secondly, we shall consider some accounts that have been given of the phases or stages that always seem to be necessary for the production of a symphony, a poem or a scientific theory. Thirdly, something will need to be said about the differences in character and operation between scientific and artistic creativity.

The three first-hand descriptions by men of genius of their creative processes (by Mozart, A. E. Housman and Poincaré) refer to music, poetry and mathematics respectively. They have been frequently and deservedly quoted and discussed, as by Hadamard (1945), by Ghiselin (1952) and by Bartlett (1958). The passages by Mozart and Housman need no preliminary explanation.

Henri Poincaré's mathematical work in the early part of this century was of the first importance and was of great value to Einstein as a stepping-stone to his own discoveries.

When I am, as it were, completely myself, entirely alone, and of good cheer – say, travelling in a carriage, or walking after a good meal, or during the night when I cannot sleep; it is on such occasions that my ideas flow best and most abundantly. *Whence* and *how* they come, I know not; nor can I force them. Those ideas that please me I retain in memory, and am accustomed, as I have been told, to hum them to myself. If I continue in this way, it soon occurs to me how

I may turn this or that morsel to account, so as to make a good dish of it, that is to say, agreeably to the rules of counterpoint, to the peculiarities of the various instruments, etc.

All this fires my soul, and, provided I am not disturbed, my subject enlarges itself, becomes methodised and defined, and the whole, though it be long, stands almost complete and finished in my mind, so that I can survey it, like a fine picture or a beautiful statue, at a glance. Nor do I hear in my imagination the parts *successively*, but I hear them, as it were, all at once (gleich alles zusammen). What a delight this is I cannot tell! All this inventing, this producing, takes place in a pleasing lively dream. Still the actual hearing of the *tout ensemble* is after all the best. What has been thus produced I do not easily forget, and this is perhaps the best gift I have my Divine Maker to thank for.

When I proceed to write down my ideas, I take out of the bag of my memory, if I may use that phrase, what has been previously collected into it in the way I have mentioned. For this reason the committing to paper is done quickly enough, for everything is, as I said before, already finished; and it rarely differs on paper from what it was in my imagination. At this occupation I can therefore suffer myself to be disturbed; for whatever may be going on around me, I write, and even talk, but only of fowls and geese, or of Gretel or Barbel, or some such matters. But why my productions take from my hand that particular form and style that makes them *Mozartish*, and different from the works of other composers, is probably owing to the same cause which renders my nose so large or so aquiline, or, in short, makes it Mozart's, and different from those of other people. For I really do not study or aim at any originality.

Having drunk a pint of beer at luncheon – beer is a sedative to the brain, and my afternoons are the least intellectual portion of my life – I would go out for a walk of two or three hours. As I went along, thinking of nothing in particular, only looking at things around me and following the progress of the seasons, there would flow into my mind, with sudden and unaccountable emotion, sometimes a line or two of verse, sometimes a whole stanza at once, accompanied, not preceded, by a vague notion of the poem which they were destined to form part of. Then there would usually be a lull of an hour or so, then perhaps the spring would bubble up again. I say bubble up, because, so far as I could make out, the source of the suggestions thus proffered to the brain was an abyss which have I already had occasion to mention, the pit of the stomach. When I got home I wrote them down, leaving gaps, and hoping that further inspiration might be forthcoming another day. Sometimes it was, if I took my walks in a receptive and expectant frame of mind; but sometimes the poem had to be taken in hand and completed by the brain, which was apt to be a matter of trouble and anxiety, involving trial and disappointment, and sometimes ending in failure. I happen to remember distinctly the genesis of the piece which stands last in my first volume. Two of the stanzas, I do not say which, came into my head, just as they are printed, while I was crossing the corner of Hampstead Heath between the Spaniard's Inn and the footpath to Temple Fortune. A third stanza came with a little coaxing after tea. One more was needed, but it did not come: I had to turn to and compose it myself, and that was a laborious business. I wrote it thirteen times, and it was more than a twelvemonth before I got it right.

It is time to penetrate deeper and to see what goes on in the very soul of the mathematician. For this, I believe, I can do best by recalling memories of my own. But I shall limit myself to telling how I wrote my first memoir on Fuchsian functions. I beg the reader's pardon; I am about to use some technical expressions, but they need not frighten him, for he is not obliged to understand them. I shall say, for example, that I have found the demonstration of such a theorem under such circumstances. This theorem will have a barbarous name, unfamiliar to many, but that is unimportant; what is of interest for the psychologist is not the theorem but the circumstances.

For fifteen days I strove to prove that there could not be any functions like those I have since called Fuchsian functions. I was then very ignorant; every day I seated myself at my work table, stayed an hour or two, tried a great number of combinations and reached no results. One evening, contrary to my custom, I drank black coffee and could not sleep. Ideas rose in crowds; I felt them collide until pairs interlocked, so to speak, making a stable combination. By the next morning I had established the existence of a class of Fuchsian functions, those which come from the hypergeometric series; I had only to write out the results, which took but a few hours.

Then I wanted to represent these functions by the quotient of two series; this idea was perfectly conscious and deliberate, the analogy with elliptic functions guided me. I asked myself what properties these series must have if they existed, and I succeeded without difficulty in forming the series I have called theta-Fuchsian.

Just at this time I left Caen, where I was then living, to go on a geologic excursion under the auspices of the school of mines. The changes of travel made me forget my mathematical work. Having reached Coutances, we entered an omnibus to go some place or other. At the moment when I put my foot on the step the idea came to me, without anything in my former thoughts seeming to have paved the way for it, that the transformations I had used to define the Fuchsian functions were identical with those of non-Euclidean geometry. I did not verify the idea; I should not have had time, as, upon taking my seat in the omnibus, I went on with a conversation already commenced, but I felt a perfect certainty. On my return to Caen, for conscience' sake I verified the result at my leisure.

Then I turned my attention to the study of some arithmetical questions apparently without much success and without a suspicion of any connection with my preceding researches. Disgusted with my failure, I went to spend a few days at the seaside, and thought of something else. One morning, walking on the bluff, the idea came to me, with just the same characteristics of brevity, suddenness and immediate certainty, that the arithmetic transformations of indeterminate ternary quadratic forms were identical with those of non-Euclidean geometry.

Returned to Caen, I meditated on this result and deduced the consequences. The example of quadratic forms showed me that there were Fuchsian groups other than those corresponding to the hypergeometric series; I saw that I could apply to them the theory of theta-Fuchsian series and that consequently there existed Fuchsian functions other than those from the hypergeometric series, the ones I then knew. Naturally I set myself to form all these functions. I made a systematic attack upon them and carried all the outworks, one after another. There was one however that still held out, whose fall would involve that of the whole place. But all my efforts only served at first the better to show me the difficulty, which indeed was something. All this work was perfectly conscious.

Thereupon I left for Mont-Valérien, where I was to go through my military service; so I was very differently occupied. One day, going along the street, the solution of the difficulty which had stopped me suddenly appeared to me. I did not try to go deep into it immediately, and only after my service did I again take up the question. I had all the elements and had only to arrange them and put them together. So I wrote out my final memoir at a single stroke and without difficulty.

These three accounts of the process of creation in quite different fields are interesting in their similarities. One striking point is the unpredictability of when the solution or the theme or the poem will arrive; they cannot be forced, but must bubble up like a spring of water. Haefele (1962) quotes a variety of occasions for the occurrence of original ideas to research chemists, 'Sunday in church as the preacher was announcing the text', 'in the morning when shaving', 'just before and just after an attack of gout', 'while resting and loafing on the beach', and so on. Writers have tried to facilitate the process in all kinds of personal and idiosyncratic ways. Balzac was dependent on large quantities of strong coffee, Proust had his room lined with cork, several writers have worked best in bed. Other examples are discussed by McKellar (1957). But even with these aids, the almost universal experience of creative artists, and particularly perhaps of poets, has been that the occurrence of brilliant solutions or happy inspirations is rarely subject to conscious control.

This unpredictability must not be exaggerated. Implicit in the accounts of sudden inspiration, there is always an earlier period of intense involvement in the problem or the theme, supported by a long and devoted technical apprenticeship.

'Ars [or scientia] longa, vita brevis.' Mozart, Housman and Poincaré do not dwell on this point, but a study of their lives would amply confirm it.

Besides the suddenness and unpredictability, one often finds a kind of fleeting, ephemeral quality in these moments of insight. If the idea is not quickly and firmly grasped, and perhaps put down on paper, it may be lost. Mozart writes 'provided I am not disturbed'. The classical instance of losing the finished product by being disturbed is Coleridge's account of composing 'not less than from two to three hundred lines of "Kubla Khan" ', only to be 'unfortunately called out by a person on business from Porlock' and to find on his return 'that though he still retained some vague and dim recollection of the general purport of the vision, yet, with the exception of some eight or ten scattered lines and images, all the rest had passed away like the images on the surface of a stream into which a stone has been cast'.

Another interesting point in the quoted accounts, one that is often reported and is of great psychological interest, is the calm certainty with which a solution is seen to work, even before all the details have been consciously examined, or equally the certainty with which a stanza is known to be right as soon as the words have fallen into place. It may be that some such conviction is necessary, and that, if it were not present, the frail early creation might be obliterated by premature self-criticism. Kelly (1965) suggests something of the kind when he describes 'vague, unexpected and dream-like constructions . . . gently lifted from the miasma of incoherence and sensitively shaped to definition without being subjected to prematurely harsh tests of consistency'. This early conviction of rightness is perhaps a matter of degree, and one would suppose there must often be occasions when a poet produces a verse that seems to him *fairly* right, that approximates to what he is trying to convey but still requires to be improved and polished. There must be differences here between solving a particular mathematical problem, and writing, say, a long narrative poem, and probably also considerable individual differences within one medium. Even though Shakespeare was said never to have blotted a line, some first-rate poets have regularly produced 10 or 20 successive drafts. But even if many creative workers achieve their finished product by slow degrees and with less spectacular leaps than in the quoted passages, the common experience seems to be that there is a clearly definable point at which the creator relaxes and the critic within him is satisfied (Renoir said of his paintings of women that he knew this point had been reached when he felt inclined to smack their buttocks). To anticipate our future analysis, there are clear similarities between the processes of mathematical or scientific innovation and those of artistic creation; the differences are most marked and most affected by the nature of the material at the stage of completion and appraisal.

Accounts by psychologists of the creative process both in art and science have not always agreed in their analysis of the successive stages, some employing a finer breakdown than others, but there has been fairly general acceptance, with some qualifications, of the scheme suggested by Wallas (1926). Variations on and modifications of Wallas' scheme are conveniently summarised by Haefele (1962) and by Kneller (1965, Ch. 3). The four stages suggested by Wallas were:

(1) Preparation
(2) Incubation
(3) Illumination
(4) Verification.

These stages form only a rough-and-ready framework and suggest many further questions. Preparation must include, for example, (a) an immersion in the subject-matter (b) an application of all the relevant skills derived from past experience (c) in particular, a sufficiently flexible approach to achieve any required re-structuring of habitual sets and attitudes (as was described in our survey of experimental work on problem-solving in the last chapter). Nor will any of these be sufficient without (d) a high level of motivation and of confidence in one's own ability to achieve the task. Obviously, too, the nature of the preparatory stage will be quite different for scientific and for artistic work. It will normally be more specific, direct and purposeful for the former. Compare, for instance, Poincaré's preliminary struggles with Housman's afternoon walk. In the latter example the stages of preparation and incubation appear indistinguishable.

The stage of incubation raises even more questions, most of them as yet unanswerable. Here the stream of thought dives underground and is lost to sight, and discussions of unconscious and preconscious processes are at present largely confessions of ignorance. Work such as that of Lowes on the scraps of information and associations from which Coleridge built his poems throw a little light on some of the kinds of transmutation of material that can occur, but less on *how* it is done. Similarly, studies such as Freud's ingenious and imaginative but highly debatable account of unconscious elements in the work of Leonardo da Vinci do very little to clarify the workings of genius or to distinguish them from those of less talented men with similar fixations. All we can say with any certainty is that in creative work in many very different fields the frequent necessity for one or more periods of apparent inactivity and unconscious digestion and processing of the material before the theory emerges or the work of art takes shape is everywhere acknowledged. Even more difficult to predict, and in some sense essentially unpredictable, is the mode of occurrence (if it ever occurs) and nature of the eventual insight or illumination. Some tentative generalisations have already been attempted in the earlier discussion of the first-hand accounts quoted.

These first three stages provide a scheme that, although inadequate, is about the best we can do to summarise the aspects of the creative process common to scientific and artistic work. The names of the stages are largely self-explanatory, even if they vaguely describe rather than account in detail for the actual phenomena. The stage of verification is less happily named, and has been used to cover every kind of further activity from the verification proper of a scientific hypothesis to the actual writing of Gibbon's *Decline and Fall of the Roman Empire* after sketching out the idea on a visit to Rome (Haefele, 1962). At this stage the similarities between artistic and scientific thinking seem much less evident. One very important difference, for example, is that scientific theories, however much inspired by considerations of logic and elegance, are expected to have testable empirical consequences, in other words to *work*. Their verification and falsification are or should be taken literally, whereas to apply these terms to a work of art is at best metaphorical. Mathematical discovery, such as that described in the passage by Poincaré, stands nearer to scientific in this respect, that it too may require 'verification', but the verification will be a check on logical consistency and an examination of logical consequences, not an empirical one.

There is vast scope for further work by psychologists in this difficult and exciting field. The similarities and differences between the processes of thinking in the various kinds of mathematical and scientific discovery and of artistic production require both further logical analysis and further empirical research.

Suggested additional reading

TAYLOR, C. W. (Ed.), *Creativity: Progress and Potential*. New York: McGraw Hill (1964).

GHISELIN, B. (Ed.), *The Creative Process*. London: Cambridge Univ. Press (1952).

BUTCHER, H. J., 'Creativity'. *In Multivariate Personality Research: Contributions to the understanding of personality in honour of R. B. Cattell.* (Ed. R. M. Dreger). (1968).

HAEFELE, J. W., *Creativity and Innovation*. London: Chapman and Hall (1962).

MCKELLAR, P., *Imagination and Thinking*. London: Cohen and West (1957).

WALLACH, M. A., and KOGAN, N., *Modes of Thinking in Young Children*. New York: Holt, Rinehart and Winston (1965).

TAYLOR, C. W., and BARRON, F. (Eds.), *Scientific Creativity: Its Recognition and Development*. New York: Wiley (1963).

V

Brains and Machines

Diverse aspects of intelligence have already been discussed, but so far the organism supposed to be behaving intelligently has to a large extent been taken for granted. The approach has been molar, not molecular, and a normally functioning human being has been assumed, without considering in neurological detail how the brain works. This remained true even in Chapter 2, where the structure of intelligence was analysed and possible components at various levels were described, but where the work reviewed was still entirely correlational, depending on the observed statistical relations (in effect averaged over large groups of people) between different kinds of intelligent performance. Although findings of this kind are of importance in showing what kinds of ability hang together and resemble one another in their effects, there is no direct evidence that any of the numerous factors identified corresponds to any biological or functional unity. Even if evidence of this kind were found, it would presumably relate to large areas or systems in the central nervous system, since the factors discussed operate at a general level. One would still wish to ask, 'How does the brain work *in detail*? What are the neurological units involved? What kind of functional organisation exists in the entire human brain?'

Questions of this kind are more easily asked than answered. The short answer is that no one knows, but that interesting guesses of various kinds have been made, some of which have a good probability of being partly true. Much of this work is physiological rather than psychological, but is of vital interest to psychologists. Psychological theories of thinking and intelligence must obviously not run counter to established facts about the central nervous system. This should not, however, be taken to imply that psychology is merely a kind of appendage or superstructure to physiology since any advance in physiological knowledge that can at present be imagined would still leave room for an independent science of psychology.

Current theories of how the brain works depend on recent advances in two very different fields, not only in neurology and the physiology of the brain, but also in computer design and operation. Developments in both these fields have been rapid and have far-reaching implications that demand non-technical dissemination in their own right and are particularly relevant to any discussion of intelligence. Indeed, early in the development of computers, scientists such as von Neumann and Norbert Wiener saw, some 20 years ago, striking parallels between the computer and the nervous system, such as the apparent similarity of neurones and relays (Wiener, 1948).

The advances in neurology and in computer science have been expressed in different kinds of language and have different degrees of immediate relevance to our topic. The break-through in biological knowledge of how the human brain works has not yet occurred, although it might occur in five or fifty years' time, and what we have is a collection of tantalising hints, which are extremely difficult to synthesise into anything like a unitary theory. The cybernetic revolution, on the other hand, has already taken place, and it is possible to summarise its main consequences for the psychology of human intelligence. Much more of this chapter, therefore, will be concerned with electronic computers than with details of the central nervous system, although this certainly reverses the *ultimate* importance of the two areas to the study of human thinking. Descriptions in this chapter of neurological findings and speculations will be limited to (a) those that can be easily stated in non-technical language, and (b) those that fit in with analogies from the functioning of computers. It may seem surprising that analogies between machines and living organisms should be taken so seriously. Some of the reasons are summarised as follows by Galanter (1966) in his interesting and original textbook.

Many scientists fear the invention of invisible mechanisms. The reason for this fear is well-founded and fairly obvious. It is always possible to invent a mechanism of sufficient complexity to explain anything. As a result, many organization theorists who would like to talk about such internal representations of the actions and ideas of the organism attempt to alleviate whatever guilt they feel about their inventions by couching the description of the mechanisms in the fleshy terms of physiology and anatomy. If there is some organization behind the temporal string of actions that we observe, then this organization must be represented, so the argument goes, by the internal organization of neural activity or anatomical structure.

The historical fact of the matter seems to be, however, that the physiologists are able to find physiological machinery that conforms to almost whatever psychological theory happens to impress them most. Thus, we may be assured by physiological knowledge that the basic mechanisms necessary for the exploitation of choice theory can be found in the connection pattern and electrical activity of the nervous system. It is, however, a quite reasonable conjecture to presume that if organization theory provides a coherent description of certain forms of behaviour, then physiologists may discover mechanisms appropriate to represent organization theory within the subject matter that is their province. Thus, if hierarchical organizations are shown to be needed by an organization theorist, then there is little doubt that they will be discovered in the anatomical and physiological structure of the nervous system. As a consequence, we shall here eschew the use of neurological and physiological terminology to describe the nature of the organizational mechanisms that guide behavior. Instead we shall use terms more common in the field of electrical engineering, on the assumption that there will be less tendency to believe in the existential reality of the proposed mechanisms if they are characterized as made of metal and glass than if they are presumed to be made of flesh and blood.

The development of computers has had the following effects, none perhaps astonishing in itself, but in sum amounting to an enforced change in attitude to human intelligence.

(1) Any problem at all that has a solution and that can be unambiguously formulated in logical or mathematical terms can in theory be solved by a computer.

(2) The programming of computers is not limited to 'convergent' operations of the kind implied in the last sentence. Programs exist, by which computers find proofs for geometrical theorems or play a first-class game of draughts.

(3) The often-voiced opinion (already formulated by Lady Lovelace in the first half of the nineteenth century) that a computer can only do what it is instructed to do by its program, while technically correct, is misleading. It certainly does not imply, for instance, that the computer will not play a better game of draughts than its programmer.

(4) None of the preceding statements implies any kind of random element in the computer program. If a random element is introduced, new possibilities of 'creative' activity arise. It is quite possible in principle for a computer to 'discover' a theorem, or 'write' a poem, or

'compose' a piece of music which will fulfil all the criteria of a human creative product, in particular those of being new, surprising, and logically-cum-emotionally satisfying. It may be objected that while the product appears indistinguishable, the process is altogether different. This objection is much weaker than it appears. The history of both art and science is replete with examples of 'lucky accidents'. (Cf. Campbell, 1960.)

The impact of the electronic computer is therefore two-pronged. The first aspect, which needs less emphasis, is its power to carry out very quickly and systematically all kinds of specified operations which would require a lifetime or longer from a human mathematician or logician. The second aspect, often designated 'computer simulation' as distinct from 'artificial intelligence', is the use of computers not as powerful aids in computation and reasoning, but as tools of psychological experiment. They may be used to solve problems not in the most efficient way, but in a way that appears to reflect human procedures. Interesting experiments have been performed comparing the performance of a computer programmed to solve problems in symbolic logic with that of a human subject. Quite a close correspondence may be found between the sequence of computer operations and the corresponding stages of human reasoning as revealed in the 'protocol' or introspective account. (Newell and Simon, 1963a).

The operations of even the most elaborate and powerful computer are extremely simple, and amount essentially to copying and adding, but thanks to the machine's design and to its fantastically high speed of operation one can instruct it to combine these operations so as to perform virtually any mathematical or logical task, however complex, a million or more times faster than could a human being.

It is the quality of extreme flexibility that makes a computer a 'general purpose' machine. 'General purpose' computers are normally 'digital', not 'analogue', which means, to put it crudely, that they add by counting 'one-and-one-and-one', where each 'one' may be represented by the movement of a switch or by current passing through a valve. Analogue computers, on the other hand, represent numbers as physical quantities, rather as does a slide-rule, though they may use the voltage of an electric current rather than the length of a bar to represent the size of a number; although it may be versatile, a machine of this kind does not possess the almost unlimited flexibility of the digital computers. It is interesting to note in passing that this 'general purpose' feature was clearly envisaged and planned by Charles Babbage (1792–1871) in his project for an 'analytical engine' although this was never actually constructed.

The organisation of an electronic digital computer is thus very simple in conception and very complex in detail. Assuming for the moment a means of getting data into and out of the machine, the three essential parts required are a store (or 'memory'), an arithmetical or operating unit, and a control unit. The first is used both for receiving and storing the incoming data, and also for storing any data that may be required in the course of the calculation. The arithmetic unit performs the simple, basic arithmetical operations required, and the control unit, as its name implies, controls the whole sequence of operations.

The operation of digital computers is made a great deal simpler by the use of what is called the binary system of arithmetic. Normally, using the familiar decimal system, we employ ten numerical symbols, representing each successive whole number by a different symbol up to nine, and then starting again. It is often supposed that the adopting of this system is dependent on the accident of our possessing 10 fingers.

The binary system of arithmetic employs exactly the same method, reduced to its simplest possible form. It uses only two symbols 0 and 1, and therefore has to start again after one, using the same conventions of order and position. The principle can quickly be grasped by inspection of the following table.

Decimal representation	Binary representation
1	0001
2	0010
3	0011
4	0100
5	0101
6	0110
7	0111
8	1000

and so on.

The great gain that accrues from using this apparently laborious and cumbersome notation is that, since only two symbols are required to represent any number, one of these can be represented in the machine by e.g. a switch being open, or by current passing through a valve, and the other by the opposite state. Thus any number or logical unit can be coded into a simple notation that is capable of being handled (e.g. counted) in the machine as fast as a valve can go on or off. This principle is equally convenient for the handling of logical, as distinct from numerical problems. Boolean algebra, the calculus of logical operations, is based on the fundamental binary classification of something being in a particular class or not.

The speed of elementary operations in modern computers (using transistors) is very high indeed. The number of operations per second has increased during the twenty years of their existence from about 1000 to about 1,000,000. The raising of the speed of the elementary arithmetical-logical operations by such an enormous factor would not be a great help unless other parts of the procedure were equally accelerated. A major problem has been to ensure rapid access to any specified part of the memory store, so that a number or element could be forthcoming when needed without slowing up the whole procedure. For this reason, computers have usually incorporated a special quick-access store. In the earlier computers these quick-access stores were quite small, but technical advances have resulted in their capacity growing fast enough to keep pace with other developments. Whereas the earlier computers could store less than 1000 binary digits in their high-speed store, some modern ones can store several million and still achieve selective access to any one address (i.e. part of the store) in a fraction of a milli-second.

Nothing has been said so far about programming, i.e. about preparing and feeding into the machine instructions so that it does what is required. This is a skilled and complicated business, in which the most important point to remember is that the machine is an idiot and may not perform as you intend it to, but *exactly*, in the minutest detail, as instructed. Preparing a complex new programme is a lengthy business, and to talk of the enormous speed of operation of computers without taking this preliminary programming into account may be misleading Machine speeds are already so fantastically high, but programming procedures still often so inconvenient and unstandardised, that progress in the computer field in the next decade or so is likely to depend very largely on new developments in programming.

Borko (1962) provides a useful summary of the successive stages involved, from which the following account is condensed. Four such stages can be distinguished; analysis, programme design, coding, testing. Analysis involves the preliminary clarification of the problem. The programmer cannot get down to work until he knows *exactly*, in operational detail, what is required. This point is vividly made by Ross Ashby (Ch. 19 in Borko, 1962), who says 'The same problem confronts the would-be programmer of a machine to play chess, or to write music like Bach's . . . "What do I mean by music like Bach's?" is the essential problem to be solved. This is difficult; once the answer is known, making a machine to do it is today a mere matter of routine.' Programme

E

design refers to establishing the main pattern of the programme instructions, having particular reference to the efficient use of time (programmer's time as well as machine time) and of the characteristics of the machine. The general design, but not all the details, is represented in a flow chart. The facetious flow chart in fig. 5.1 shows the general idea.

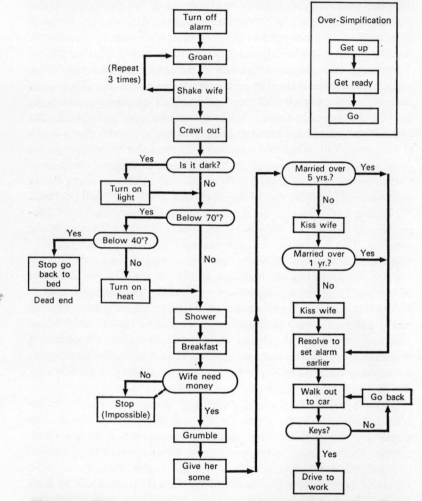

Figure 5.1. Flow chart: How to get to work in the morning. (From Borko, 1962, p. 116).

The third stage, coding, involves changing each of the still relatively large steps represented by each box in the flow chart into a set of very precise and detailed instructions couched in the right notation for the machine to handle. It is at this stage that the fact of the machine requiring *everything* to be reduced to its ultimate level of discreteness, simplicity and unambiguity must constantly be borne in mind. Finally the programme must be checked to see if it works as it should, and amended ('debugged' in programmers' argot) if it fails. A thorough checking may be difficult, since the programme may work correctly on a trial set of data, and only have its weak spot found out by the peculiarities of the thousandth lot of data on which it is employed. Hence a correct result is not an absolute assurance of a correctly functioning programme, and other, supplementary methods of checking have also to be used. This problem of whether a programme is working absolutely correctly is a major one. Where many new programmes are used, up to 30% of the total computing time may be spent on programme checking (Hollingdale and Tootill, Ch. 10).

INTELLIGENT PERFORMANCES BY COMPUTERS

It will be possible here to pick out only a few applications which exemplify what would beyond any doubt be classified as highly intelligent behaviour if it originated from a human being instead of from a machine. There will be no need to consider any metaphysical or linguistic problems of the kind 'Can machines think?' or 'Is the human mind a machine?', nor will it be necessary to review the very varied applications that are of mainly practical importance, such as the use of computers to plan railway timetables, to analyse the investment market, to assist in medical diagnosis, to carry out textual analyses, and so on. One particularly important application, however, that may be briefly mentioned is the development of teaching machines and methods of programmed instruction (Bitzer and Braunfeld, 1965; Schurdak, 1967). In the last four or five years projects called PLATO and SOCRATES have been carried out in the University of Illinois. These code-names stand respectively for Programmed Logic for Automatic Teaching Operations, and System for Organising Content to Review and Teach Educational Subjects. (Since someone christened a computer MANIAC computer scientists have delighted in literary ingenuity of this kind, fitting the function to the name rather than vice versa). The great advantage of a computerised teaching machine is that, whereas ordinary machines, even with elaborate branching variations to allow for different wrong responses, take into account only the student's last single response to a multiple-choice question, the computer can take into account *all* the previous responses and, in principle, diagnose the student's general difficulties. A second advantage is that one such system can attend simultaneously to many students. SOCRATES, for instance, employing an IBM 1620, attends to 13 people at once. Nor is this kind of individual supervision limited to work at university level. Suppes (1966) describes similar instructional programmes for children from first-grade onwards and predicts that 'in a few more years millions of school-children will have access to what Philip of Macedon's son Alexander enjoyed as a royal prerogative: the personal services of a tutor as well-informed and responsive as Aristotle'.

The most valuable source-book for important articles on both artificial intelligence and computer simulation is by Feigenbaum and Feldman (1963), from which some of the following illustrations will be summarised. Useful supplementary accounts can be found in Tomkins and Messick (1962), Carne (1965), Sass and Wilkinson (1965) and Collins and Michie (1967).

One of the more impressive achievements of the computer (or, if you like, of the computer programmer) would be to play draughts or chess well. This has already been achieved in the case of draughts, and is quite possible in principle in the case of chess. In fact it is probably true that the only obstacle that prevents the development of a programme which would make a computer the world chess champion within a few years is that the money and effort would be disproportionate to the importance of the result.

Botvinnik, himself a former world champion, is on record as saying that the time will come when computers will be awarded the title of international grand master, and that a separate league will have to be formed for them. These developments would only be rather spectacular extensions of what has already been achieved. Very recently a game of chess has been reported, played between a computer in the Moscow Institute of Experimental Physics and one in Stanford University, California, which induced C. H. O'D. Alexander, the chess correspondent of the *Sunday Times*, to renounce his scepticism about such performances. In his comments on the game, he says that if he had not known who the 'players' were, he would have supposed it to be a game between a player of good club standard and a beginner. (No political conclusions should be drawn.) The game, with notes, is reproduced in the appendix to this chapter. An electronic computer is apparently already world champion at a lesser-known board game called Kalah, in which it is possible to analyse exhaustively the branching tree of alternatives some 10 moves ahead, and which is therefore particularly well suited to programming (Selfridge, 1965). Another board game well suited to programming, and one in which the learning process can be effectively simulated, will be familiar to some middle-aged readers as having been marketed in the thirties under the commercial name of 'Peggotty', but is now generally known as Go-Moku. An instructive account of the programming of this game is given by Elcock and Murray (1967). Moreover, as far back as 1959, Samuel showed that a computer can be programmed so that it will learn to play a better game of checkers (draughts) than the person who wrote the programme. 'Furthermore it can learn to do this in a remarkably short period of time (8 or 10 hours of machine-playing time) when given only the rules of the game, a sense of direction, and a redundant and incomplete list of parameters which are thought to have something to do with the game, but whose correct signs and relative weights are unknown and unspecified'.

The computer's performance was evidently not exaggerated in this quotation. One of its opponents, a player of very high calibre, confirmed that 'in the matter of the end game, I have not had such opposition from any human being since 1954, when I lost my last game'.

A performance of this kind is very interesting for several reasons. Firstly, draughts-playing may be taken as quite a good measure of intelligence, and as one that is not heavily weighted in favour of the machine. If not a paradigm of high-level intelligent human behaviour, it is by no means untypical. Secondly, the machine's performance was not achieved by taking advantage of its incomparably superior ability to explore a large number of possibilities in simple routine fashion. It is surprising to many people at first hearing that even with the fantastic speed of operation of modern computers, the number of possible combinations of moves in a game of draughts, and still more in a game of chess, is such that a 'brute-force' attempt to compute all the possibilities would be quite hopeless. It has been estimated that the number of such permissible combinations in chess is 10^{120}. Thirdly, the fact of the machine having 'learned' to play so well, with relatively unspecific guidance, is perhaps the most impressive feature of Samuel's account, and suggests extraordinary possibilities. In a classic article, Turing (1950), writing as a pioneer in the development of computers, and from a severely mechanistic point of view, discusses half-seriously the idea of a computer being deliberately exposed to a wide variety of data and 'experience', being 'sent to school', as it were, to acquire a number of skills by learning. This still sounds absurd, but the gap between 'absurdities' of this kind and what is actually taking place has narrowed very appreciably in the 17 years since the appearance of his article.

One of the most ambitious and important developments, and one that is much more general than the games-playing programmes, interesting as they are, is the General Problem Solver of Newell, Shaw and Simon. Useful summaries of their work, more accessible than the original papers, are to be found in Beloff (1962) and Hilgard and Bower (1966). Newell, Shaw and Simon aimed to produce a versatile programme that would solve a variety of logical problems, including the discovery of proofs in trigonometrical problems. The starting-point or original data and the intended end-point or theorem to be proved must be stated in the same language. The programme then initiates a systematic search from both ends for logical connections between starting-point (A) and end-point (B). It examines differences between A and B, selects them in order of apparent importance, and applies permissible transformations until the differences are lessened. Each time a transformation is applied, a whole new set of possibilities comes into view, and the programme again selects the most promising to reduce remaining differences, and so on. Newell and his associates have compared the performance of this programme with the performance of human beings faced with the same problems. The subjects have been asked to think aloud and the successive stages of their problem-solving compared with those adopted by the machine. In many cases a close correspondence is claimed, though it is hard to formulate objective criteria for such correspondence.

Other programmes can cope with some kinds of items that occur in intelligence tests. Simon and Kotovsky (1963) describe one that simulates human performance on tests such as the Thurstone Letter Series Completion. The nature of the test and the instructions given to human beings taking it are shown in Table 5.1.

As an approximate indication of the difficulty of the 15 items, Simon and Kotovsky found that in a group of 67 High School Seniors, the easiest series was correctly extended by 65 subjects, the hardest by 27. In contrast, the machine programme in its most efficient version (several alternative versions were tried) solved 13 out of the 15 problems correctly. One of the two in which it failed was no. 7, which was also the most difficult for the human subjects. Examination of the whole pattern of human responses suggested that failure was particularly associated with difficulty in keeping two distinct lists (e.g. alphabet forwards and alphabet backwards) in immediate memory.

Minsky (1966) describes a programme devised by Thomas Evans in a

TABLE 5.1 *Letter Series Completion Problems**

Training problems	Test problems
Your task is to write the correct letter in the blank.	1. cdcdcd—
	2. aaabbbcccdd—
Read the row of letters below	3. atbataatbat—
A. abababab—	4. abmcdmefmghm—
The next letter in this series would be a.	5. defgefghfghi—
Write the letter a in the blank.	6. qxapxbqxa—
Now read the next row of letters and	7. aduacuaeuabuafua—
decide what the next letter should be.	8. mabmbcmcdm—
Write that letter in the blank.	9. urtustuttu—
B. cadaeafa—	10. abyabxabwab—
You should have written the letter g.	11. rscdstdetuef—
Now read the series of letters below and	12. npaoqapraqsa—
fill in each blank with a letter.	13. wxaxybyzczadab—
C. aabbccdd—	14. jkqrklrslmst—
D. abxcdxefxghx—	15. pononmnmlmlk—
E. axbyaxbyaxb—	

You will now be told what your answers should have been.
Now work the following problems for practice. Write the correct letter in each blank.

F. rsrtrurvr—

G. abcdabceabcfabc—

H. mnlnknjn—

I. mnomoompom—

J. cegedeheeeiefe—
You will now be told the correct answers.

doctoral thesis at Massachusetts Institute of Technology. This solves problems based on analogies between geometrical figures, problems that were in fact taken from a test of high-level intelligence used in student selection. Some of these are shown in Figure 5.2.

The way the programme is devised to solve problems of this kind bears some resemblance to the procedure just described in connection with the General Problem Solver. The differences between figures A and B and the transformations required to convert one to the other are analysed. Secondly, common features between figures A and C are sought. Thirdly, the five possible answers to the problem, D^2 to D_5, are

* From Simon and Kotovsky 1963, p. 536.

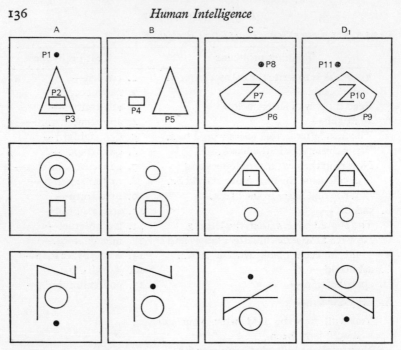

Figure 5.2. Analogical reasoning is exhibited in a program developed by Thomas Evans in an M.I.T. doctoral thesis for answering a class of problems frequently included in intelligence tests: '*A* is to *B* as *C* is to (D_1, D_2, D_3, D_4 or D_5?).' Three such problems are illustrated here. A

scanned and the differences between each and C are compared with the already-analysed differences between A and B. To describe this procedure in detail would require a great deal of space, and the interested reader must be referred to the fuller account of Minsky or to the original thesis.

Minsky's general conclusions about progress in this field and about likely developments in the near future deserve quotation and supplement the remarks made earlier in this chapter (in the description of Samuel's draughts-playing programme) about the extent to which computers can 'learn'.

The questions people most often ask are: Can the programs learn through experience and thus improve themselves? Is this not the obvious path to making them intelligent? The answer to each is both yes and no. Even at this early stage the programs use many kinds of processes that might be called learning; they remember and use the methods that solved other problems; they adjust some of their

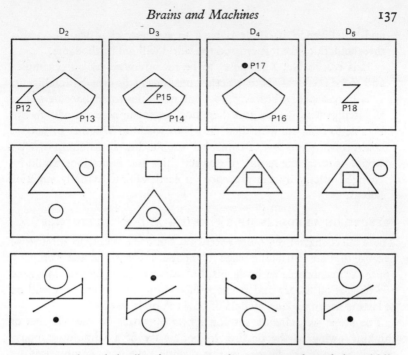

computer selected the 'best' answer to the top example and the middle one but missed on the bottom one because the program is weak in assessing relations among more than two objects. From Minsky (1966)

internal characteristics for the best performance; they 'associate' symbols that have been correlated in the past. No program today, however, can work any genuinely important change in its own basic structure. . . .

In order for a program to improve itself substantially it would have to have at least a rudimentary understanding of its own problem-solving process and some ability to recognize an improvement when it found one. There is no inherent reason why this should be impossible for a machine. Given a model of its own workings, it could use its problem-solving power to work on the problem of self-improvement. The present programs are not quite smart enough for this purpose; they can only deal with the improvement of programs much simpler than themselves.

Once we have devised programs with a genuine capacity for self-improvement a rapid evolutionary process will begin. As the machine improves both itself and its model of itself, we shall begin to see all the phenomena associated with the terms 'consciousness,' 'intuition' and 'intelligence' itself. It is hard to say how close we are to this threshold, but once it is crossed the world will not be the same.

It is reasonable, I suppose, to be unconvinced by our examples and to be skeptical about whether machines will ever be intelligent. It is unreasonable, however, to think machines could become *nearly* as intelligent as we are and then stop, or to suppose we will always be able to compete with them in wit or wisdom. Whether or not we could retain some sort of control of the machines, assuming that we would want to, the nature of our activities and aspirations would be changed utterly by the presence on earth of intellectually superior beings.

EFFECTS ON THEORIES OF THINKING AND INTELLIGENCE

These effects have been quite extensive, but are not easy to summarise because they are still taking place. It is possible that some will eventually appear as fashionable enthusiasms, but very probable that the language of information theory and perhaps of computer programming will be of lasting use in making models of how the brain works.

The scene was already set for a new approach to mechanisms of thinking owing to the decline in popularity of a stimulus-response model. Some of the factors in this decline have been summarised by Hunt (1961). Lorenz (1966) also forcibly expresses the change in opinion away from the view that the central nervous system primarily reacts to stimuli.

The completely erroneous view that animal and human behaviour is predominantly reactive and that, even if it contains any innate elements at all, it can be altered to an unlimited extent by learning, comes from a radical misunderstanding of certain democratic principles: it is utterly at variance with these principles to admit that human beings are not born equal and that not all have equal chances of becoming ideal citizens. Moreover, for many decades the reaction, the 'reflex' represented the only element of behaviour which was studied by serious psychologists, while all 'spontaneity' of animal behaviour was left to the 'vitalists', the mystically inclined observers of nature.

The fact that the central nervous system does not need to wait for stimuli, like an electric bell with a push-button, before it can respond, but that it can itself produce stimuli which give a natural, physiological explanation for the 'spontaneous' behaviour of animals and humans, has found recognition only in the last decades, through the work of Adrian, Paul Weiss, Kenneth Roeder, and above all Erich von Holst. The strength of the ideological prejudices involved was plainly shown by the heated and emotional debates that took place before the endogenous production of stimuli within the central nervous system became a fact generally recognized by the science of physiology.

The idea of the brain as an inert telephone exchange coming to life only when messages are delivered from the outside world is in fact obsolete. The picture is now one of a normal state of continuous activity, modified and influenced by signals from the environment. Similarly the picture of three main areas in the cerebral cortex, called projection, association and motor, and responsible respectively for the receipt of stimuli, selection of an appropriate response and initiation of the response has undergone considerable modification. The position is complicated by links between, on the one hand, incoming paths and motor areas of the brain, and, on the other between outgoing paths and projection areas. The reaction against a simple stimulus-response conception should not, however, be carried too far in consequence of arguments such as those quoted from Lorenz. Although the existence of autonomous or semi-autonomous brain processes has been well established, the work of Hebb and his associates at McGill university has been equally important in showing the necessity of external stimulation, if the human organism is to function normally. Their studies of sensory deprivation have amply demonstrated how rapidly abnormality, cognitive inefficiency and derangement can ensue when the usual range of sensory stimulation is experimentally reduced.

The most accessible account of the changing view of brain structure as related to function is the important review article of Pribram (1960). Pribram makes the following points, among others. The traditional view of a hierarchy of higher and lower centres in the brain, with the cerebral cortex (and particularly the association areas) as director and all sub-cortical areas as comparatively uninvolved in high-level thinking, is also undergoing modification. Of course, even in the earlier view, it was not supposed that thinking could take place *without* intact sub-cortical centres, any more than we could think without an adequate blood supply to the brain, but the newer viewpoint ascribes to some of these areas, particularly in the thalamus and the limbic system, an altogether more direct participation in 'higher' mental activity. Pribram also introduces a distinction between 'intrinsic' and 'extrinsic' areas of the brain, which he links with function in a way strongly influenced by the computer model.

A word of warning must be interposed, however, in case the reader supposes that intelligence, or even any quite specific kind of thinking, has been or ever will be firmly localised in a particular area of the brain. For a hundred years this has been a question for lively dispute, with the battle swaying to and fro as new pieces of evidence became available (see the review by Krech, 1962). The whole question of localisation of function in the brain is one that is particularly full of traps. Zangwill (1963) points out that because a certain area of brain, when damaged or cut out, results in a particular loss of function, one is by no means entitled to assume without further evidence that the function is localised in that area. 'The removal of any of several resistors in a radio set may cause the emission of strange sounds', as Gregory has pointed out, 'but it cannot therefore be concluded that the function of the resistors is to inhibit howling.' Similarly, 'the southern section of British Railways is a complex system of railway lines, signal boxes, stations and control systems. A breakdown on a section of the line, a power failure, or a slip in the central control room at Waterloo may disrupt traffic over a wide area. But we cannot therefore say that the function of the system is localised in the permanent way, the power station, the central control room, or for that matter in the brain of Dr Beeching! All are essential to its smooth working but none could appropriately be entitled its seat. And much the same is true of the nervous system, except in that we do not yet know precisely how the system is organised.'

Bearing in mind this warning, it is still interesting to note that certain modes of mental functioning are associated not only with particular parts of the cerebral cortex, as has been known for a century and more, but also with certain sub-cortical structures in the central nervous system, and particularly with what is known as the limbic system, which comprises parts of the hypothalamus and thalamus and also areas known as the amygdala and hippocampus, all these being situated in the border area between midbrain and forebrain.

There is considerable evidence that the hippocampus, for instance, is intimately involved in some way with fairly short-term memory. It is not known, however, whether it actually provides the machinery for laying down memory traces or functions as a temporary memory store (McCleary and Moore, 1965, Ch. 6).

These authors also summarise the apparent necessary participation of another part of the limbic system, the amygdala, in complex reasoning.

The amygdala contributes to psychological abilities that are more complex than flight and defense response or the facilitation of avoidance behavior. For instance, monkeys with bilateral damage to the amygdala have trouble solving complicated visual problems when required to solve them in order to receive a small reward of food. These animals can solve simple visual problems as well as normal animals can, but they are deficient when they must generalize what they have learned to new visual patterns that are similar, but not identical, to the original patterns they learned to distinguish. These brain-damaged monkeys also have difficulty when they must reverse a learned habit and select a visual pattern that previously was not the correct choice. Following lesions of the amygdala, these animals may have difficulty when a visual problem is altered in some way simply because they cannot habituate themselves easily to any kind of novel situation. This possibility is suggested by the fact that such brain-damaged monkeys persist in exploring and re-exploring new surroundings and accordingly remain hyperactive long after normal monkeys have become calm and well adapted to the same novel environment.

Our interest in such accounts is not, however, primarily in the question of localisation, but (in the context of the present section) in the analogies drawn between the operation of the human brain and that of an electronic computer. This is made fully explicit by Miller, Galanter and Pribram (1960).

In their account, two of the principal theoretical concepts are the 'image' and the 'plan'. The 'image' is the information, subjective and objective, with which one starts, including one's self-picture and picture of the world. The 'plan', corresponding in many respects to a computer program, is a formalisation of how one achieves or attempts to achieve an objective, or, to define it more generally and precisely in the authors' own words, it is 'any hierarchical process in the organism that can control the order in which a sequence of operations is to be performed'. The basic unit in this formulation is the feedback loop, described as operating according to a sequence which the authors call TOTE (test-operate-test-exit). This scheme is intended largely to supersede the older reflex-arc picture. The basic features of a TOTE unit are shown in Figure 5.3.

These TOTE units or feedback loops are conceived as forming elaborate hierarchies, so that the 'operate' part in a higher-order TOTE will itself be a TOTE, just as computer programs contain frequent loops within loops. Thus the complexity of human thinking is construed to arise out of complex hierarchical chains of essentially simple units, in the same way as a complex computer programme is constructed from very simple operations.

What is more, the authors (and Pribram, 1960) advance plausible speculations, for which they adduce experimental evidence, about the actual role of various parts of the brain in carrying out these computer-like operations.

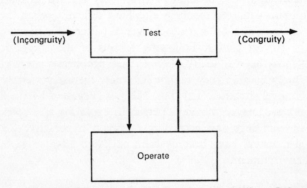

Figure 5.3. The TOTE unit. Reproduced from Miller, Galanter and Pribram (1960)

'The relation of a Plan to the mind is analogous to the relation of a program to a computer, and both are analogous to the relation of X to the brain. What is X?'

What parts of the brain correspond to the basic parts of the computer on this theory, i.e. to the parts such as memory store and arithmetic unit as described earlier in this chapter?

The authors' general conclusion, which they admit to be highly speculative, is that the internal core of the forebrain, (i.e. the intrinsic system mentioned earlier in this section) consisting of the limbic systems and of a frontal 'association' area of the cortex, is intimately concerned with the operation of Plans in the sense described. Also that an analogy can be drawn between the 'arithmetic' or operating unit of a computer and the limbic portions of the internal core; whereas the frontal association area is more analogous to the memory-store, and particularly to the working memory-store, i.e. to the part that stores data temporarily while calculations are in progress.

In the last few years there has been a great deal of experimental work done both in Britain and in the USA on how human beings retrieve recently memorised material and (by inference) on how this material is classified and stored in the mind. An interesting and lucid paper by

Broadbent (1966) summarises much of this work, particularly that being done at Cambridge, and uses computer analogies. One of the important experimental findings he describes is as follows.

If a series of items (e.g. letters of the alphabet) is presented to a subject through one earphone, and another series simultaneously through another earphone, when he is asked to recall the total series, he will find it much easier to do so by recalling separately the sequence fed to one ear, and then the sequence fed to the other. Suppose, however, that each ear receives, say, two letters and one number. It has been confirmed by several independent experiments that the subject will have no difficulty in recalling the total series of numbers or the total series of letters, although each of these series was divided between the two earphones.

It seems therefore as though in both reception and recall the items are given, where possible, a kind of identifying tag whereby they can be assigned to separate short-term stores. Broadbent discusses these and similar experiments, which obviously have important consequences for theories of thinking in general and of information retrieval in particular. Some of the experiments reviewed throw light on acoustic cues in recall. In trying to remember series of letters presented visually, subjects tend when they make mistakes, to suggest letters that *sound* like the correct ones. Differences have been found between British and American subjects when the letter Z is involved, because the latter call it 'Zee'. Clearly the subjects in these experiments have been influenced in the way they store the sequences in memory by the acoustics of the letters' names, i.e. by 'saying them to themselves'. The commonly experienced 'tip-of-the-tongue' phenomenon, in which a word or name hovers just outside recall, and in which one is sometimes fixated on a wrong but similarly sounding name perhaps suggests that similar factors operate also in long-term memory, though probably less powerfully. This phenomenon has tended to be ignored by experimentalists until very recently, but Brown and McNeill (1966) have attempted to investigate it. Their results tended to confirm the popular impression. Although some of the words that came to mind, while the sought-for word still remained elusive, were allied in *meaning* to the correct response, most were similar in sound, initial letter, number of syllables or pattern of stress.

In interpreting some of these experiments, Broadbent draws analogies between the way information is stored and retrieved in the mind and information storage in libraries and computers. If comparison is to be made with library cataloguing, the analogy is not so close with traditional, hierarchical systems of cataloguing such as the Dewey Decimal System as with some recent developments. Where a library possesses only one copy of a book, a fairly rigid classificatory system is needed to determine its physical location. But any such system is inadequate for information retrieval if it is the only method of cataloguing. As Broadbent points out, all sorts of hierarchies are possible, and no single one is unarbitrary or suitable for all purposes. 'One might have a hierarchy in which one first decided if a book was psychological or not, and then divided those books which were psychological into those which were fact and those which were fiction, rather than doing it the other way round.' Modern and more ingenious information retrieval systems need to employ complex-cross classifications, while retaining some restrictions such as, perhaps, that in a given library there are no books classifiable as both 'science' and 'fiction'. Such systems provide a slightly closer analogy to the operation of human memory.

It seems likely, though, that the operation of computers will provide closer analogies still. The 'library catalogue' model is much too static to serve as anything more than a crude expository simile. It makes no allowance for such features of human remembering and thinking as random and systematic decay and interference, whereas the only obstacle in principle to the simulation of such processes on computers is the difficulty of forming hypotheses which will be at the same time sufficiently specific and sufficiently complex to account for the mass of observed phenomena.

What becomes of the traditional picture of mind and intelligence, if these computer analogies are taken seriously, as indeed they are meant to be? Many, perhaps most, cyberneticians (e.g. Turing, Mackay) are quite happy to see mind essentially reduced to machinery. Miller, Galanter and Pribram do not think this is a necessary consequence of their theory; or at least, if it is, they sugar the pill.

'Most scientific advances have reduced man's dignity, moved him out of the centre of the universe, given him apes for cousins, subjected his brain to the fickle endocrines and his mind to the unconscious forces of lust – the reduction of his cognitive processes to machine operations would seem to be the final, crushing blow. At least we can take comfort in the fact that we are too complicated to reduce to simple machines. Thus far the human brain seems to be the most amazing computing machine ever devised – nothing else we know even approaches it. The more carefully we analyse the information-processing that must go on in order to solve even the simplest problems, the more respect we gain for this beautiful piece of biological equipment.'

In general, however, cyberneticians have tended to be tough-minded, not only about commonsense (or philosophical) concepts such as 'mind' itself, as may be seen in the interesting controversy between Beloff and Mackay (Smythies, 1965) but also about such psychological abstractions from behaviour as 'intelligence'.

'Should we ask what intelligence "really is"? My own view is that this is more of an aesthetic question, or one of a sense of dignity, than a technical matter! To me "intelligence" seems to denote little more than the complex of performances which we happen to respect but do not understand.' (Minsky, 1963). Similarly, in the introduction we quoted the expression of a related view held by another computer expert, to the effect that intelligence is a slippery concept and that in explaining it one necessarily explains it away.

One has much sympathy with the impatience of those who are developing interesting new technologies, but such conclusions still seem premature. Firstly, *all* psychological concepts are slippery ones, and, from one point of view, inhabit a not too clearly defined territory between physiology and cybernetics on the one hand and philosophy on the other, and from time to time border-raids are made from either direction. It is noticeable, however, that few present-day philosophers denigrate psychology as a science as unreservedly as, say, Collingwood (1940). To return to the criticism of the concept of intelligence, one might urge that the difference between 'explaining' and 'explaining away' raises more questions than it settles. A great deal is known about the mechanics of conditioning. In so far as many phenomena of learning are accounted for, are they explained or explained away?

But behind these viewpoints lies a real problem, which may be represented as follows. Granted that these new machines display such prodigious skills, and that with further development they will encroach much further on areas thought of as essentially human is there any scrap of territory we can preserve as exclusive to human thinking? This is still an open question.

One can perhaps argue that the man programming the machine is always displaying a higher order of skill or intelligence than the machine, because he is one step higher in the hierarchy of plans. And this, it may be maintained, will still be true even with the increasing development of largely self-programming computers. The same argument may be used even when machines have become much more capable of 'heuristic' or 'divergent' or 'creative' operations than they are at present (and this advance is already taking place). This is Beloff's view (1962, p. 124).

It should follow, from our previous discussion about formal systems and their informal components, that there must be an unspecifiable component in the very process of formulating computer-programmes; since any attempt to specify it would require skill of a still higher order which would itself have either to remain unspecified or else involve us in a sort of Godelian regress . . . it looks as if there may be logical reasons why the attempt to produce an exhaustive account of Mind must necessarily fail, if only because the human intellect must always be one jump ahead in richness and complexity, over anything it can itself create.

This is an effective argument, difficult to *disprove*, and generally in accord with the view of human intelligence advocated in this book, that it is the most general and far-reaching of human skills and is characterised principally by the complexity or hierarchical order of Plans that can be put into operation. This idea of a hierarchy, supported by evidence and provisional conclusions from such diverse kinds of enquiry offers circumstantial support for the views of Burt on the structure of abilities, in contrast with those of Thurstone or Guilford, although, as we saw in Chapter 2, any of these is *mathematically* defensible.

There is more than an accidental similarity between (a) the hierarchical system of abilities resulting from the factor analytic studies of Burt, (b) the hierarchy of Plans, analogous to the assembling of computer programs from sub-routines, sub-sub routines and so on, put forward by Miller, Galanter and Pribram as a paradigm of human thinking, and (c) the hierarchy of accumulating schemata culminating in general intelligence as described by Piaget (see Chapter 7).

The correspondence is not exact, since the hierarchy of Plans is a logico-practical hierarchy, indicating how a job such as that of solving a problem can be most effectively broken down into simple units and then put together again. The hierarchy of abilities revealed by factor analysis, on the other hand, is one of psychological dispositions; it is more empirically based in that it starts from measured real-life performances, but the classificatory principles it produces remain a little abstract and shadowy. The Piagetian framework, as we shall see, is different again, being a developmental hierarchy, of which the main point is that many conceptual and other skills depend on earlier developments different in kind, and that if the earlier skills and ways of looking at things are retarded or impeded, it is impossible for the later, more abstract skills to develop.

There are other kinds of impact on thinking about thinking that may be felt as consequences of the computer revolution. It is quite likely that individual differences in ability may come to be described in something more like computer-language. If the analogies described in this chapter between machine and human intelligence are not entirely misleading – and they appear plausible enough to most cyberneticians and many psychologists – the appropriate components into which human intelligence should be analysed and most effectively described will be such variables as capacity of working store, speed of basic operations, speed of access to store, sophistication of programming language, number and variety of standard programmes on file, and so on. It is not difficult to think of findings and claims among research results which would readily translate into such terms. Thus Eysenck (1967), as we saw in Chapter 1, has maintained that speed is a basic, probably *the* basic factor in measured intelligence (number of basic operations per second). Valentine found that students with training in symbolic logic obtained markedly higher scores on his intelligence test (superior programming language available).

One difference, however, between a human being and a machine, even if both are considered as data processing mechanisms, was pointed out by Wiener (1948), but is not always taken into account. After any operation, the computer can be completely cleared, and become a tabula rasa, with no trace of previous experience. Only if the computer were 'sent to school', as suggested by Turing, and programmed from the start to retain all its experience, or at least a representative selection, should we have anything like a parallel to the human situation. Even then, some simplifying or filtering mechanism would presumably have to be incorporated to be analogous to the selectivity of human memorising. In other words, an analysis of the kind just outlined would be completely static, taking no account of stages of development or of learning, both efficient and faulty. In the analysis of human abilities this is one great advantage of the Piagetian approach in contrast both to the factor-analytic one and to the cybernetic one outlined in this chapter. This point will be further taken up in Chapter 7.

Suggested additional reading

MICHIE, D., 'Machine intelligence' in *Penguin Science Survey B*. 1965. Penguin Books.

BELOFF, J. R., *The Existence of Mind*. London: MacGibbon and Kee (1962). Ch. 4.

GREEN, B. F., 'Current trends in problem-solving'. In *Problem-solving*. (Ed. B. Kleinmuntz). New York: Wiley (1966).

WOOLDRIDGE, D. E., *The Machinery of the Brain*. New York: McGraw Hill (1963).

MILLER, G. A., GALANTER, E., and PRIBRAM, K. H., *Plans and the Structure of Behavior*. New York: Holt (1960).

BORKO, H. (Ed.), *Computer Applications in the Behavioral Sciences*. Englewood Cliffs, N.J.: Prentice-Hall (1962).

Appendix to chapter 5

Game of chess played between two electronic computers (notes by C. H. O'D. Alexander).

1 P-K4, P-K4; 2 Kt-KB3, Kt-QB3; 3 Kt-B3, B-B4; ? (better 3...Kt - B3); 4 Kt x P!, Kt x Kt; 5 P-Q4, B-Q3; 6 P x Kt, B x P; 7 P - B4, B x Kt ch; 8 P x B, Kt - B3 (too risky) 9 P-K5!, Kt-K5; 10 Q -Q3? (White's only inaccuracy 10 Q -Q5, Q-R5ch; 11 P-Kt3 is stronger and should win), Kt - B4; 11 Q-Q5, Kt-K3? (11...P-Q3!); 12 P-B5, Kt-Kt4? (A blunder, but after 11...Kt-B1; 12 B-QB4 White is clearly winning) 13 P-KR4, P-KB3; 14 P x Kt, P x Kt P; 15 R x P! ; R-B1; 16 R x P, P-B3; 17 Q -Q6, R x P; 18 R-Kt8 ch, R-B1 (18...K-B2; 19 B-B4 mate); 19 Q x R mate

VI

The Influence of Heredity and some Related Questions

INTRODUCTION

A large amount of research has been devoted to investigating the relative effects of heredity and environment on human intelligence but no final conclusions have yet been reached. The question is one, to judge by the emotional and dogmatic tone of much that is written, about which it is particularly difficult to retain a cool head and to divest oneself of prejudices, preconceptions and ideologies. Thoughtful and balanced accounts of what has come to be known as behaviour genetics include the book by Fuller and Thompson (1960) and a chapter in Hilgard and Atkinson (1967). For a more advanced discussion of recent developments see Vandenberg (1965).

A useful distinction can be drawn between strictly hereditary effects, that is those arising directly from the transmission of parental genes, and other pre-natal influences. Cattell (1965a) provides a diagram in which he interprets the meaning of several commonly used terms.

As an example of the distinction between hereditary and innate qualities Cattell suggests that the haemophilia which affected several descendants of Queen Victoria was innate but not hereditary, since it

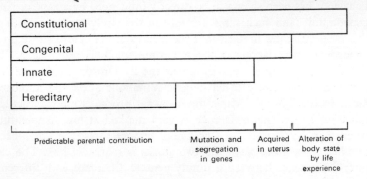

Figure 6.1. Definitions of contributions to personality commonly considered 'non-environmental'. From Cattell (1965a, p. 34)

had apparently appeared as a mutation and not as inherited from her ancestors. The second distinction, that between 'innate' and 'congenital', is also important. Identical (one-egg, monozygotic) twins are described as having identical heredity because they result from the splitting of one fertilised ovum, yet there are often observable differences between them at birth which can therefore be legitimately called congenital. These differences are largely due, it would appear, to differences in intra-uterine environment, though they may also be due to the asymmetrical splitting of the egg (Darlington, 1963).

It is worth while to bear these distinctions in mind when reading research reports. As we shall see, twin studies, and in particular comparisons between identical and non-identical twins, have very often been quoted as crucial to the determination of the extent of hereditary and environmental influences. The assumption of identical heredity in identical twins may be justified, but must not be extended to an assumption that no congenital differences exist.

Generally speaking, however, the most important division is between heredity in the sense of genetic characteristics demonstrably transmitted by the parents, and, on the other hand, variation due to any other sources from the moment of fertilisation onwards. It may be of practical concern to learn about modifications to the developing organism resulting from the intra-uterine environment, but the questions of greatest theoretical importance are about what is inherited (in the narrower sense) and the mechanisms by which this transmission of potentialities is accomplished.

It should be realised at once that hardly any observable quality, physical or mental, can be ascribed to the influence of heredity alone or of environment alone. Even where a particular observable aspect of behaviour has been shown to be directly influenced by a gene or single genetic unit (and such cases are rare in the study of human beings), this is no guarantee in itself that the behaviour is not also substantially dependent on variations in the environment. This principle is illustrated by a finding of Hogben about the fly Drosophila, in which he established that two distinct genetic mutations affect the number of facets in the fly's eye. Mutation A always produces more facets than mutation B, but this difference is very marked at low temperatures, whereas if the flies are bred at higher temperatures, the difference in number of facets between the two stocks is markedly less. The close inter-dependence between a purely genetic difference and differences in the environment could hardly be more neatly demonstrated.

If, therefore, even in the most favourable circumstances genetic and environmental effects cannot at least in man be entirely separated by experiment and observation, what can we do about assessing the relative importance of these two kinds of influence? Some psychologists and geneticists would say that the question is not very meaningful as it stands, or at least that it is better to ask how the two interact rather than which is the major influence (Anastasi, 1958b). Others (Fuller, 1960) would grant that the question cannot reasonably be posed about an individual, but may be meaningful and useful when asked about a population. Others again (Burt and Howard, 1957; Cattell, 1963a), maintain that it is possible by statistical analysis to split up the total variation in test performance in a group into three main categories, the proportion due to genetic factors, that due to environmental influences, and a third due to interaction between the two. At best, however, such allocation is approximate, and any statement that $x\%$ is due to genetic factors and $y\%$ due to environmental ones must be treated with reservation.

The main reason for this reservation is that, even if such a statement about proportions is justified, it can only apply to a particular, defined population of people in a constant and stable environment. Even within one culture environmental conditions such as standard of affluence and nutrition, child-rearing practices and availability of educational opportunities are all changing quite rapidly, often with demonstrable effect on measured intelligence. When other, future developments are taken into account, and when one considers the enormous variations in environmental conditions between different nations, cultures and civilisations, the need to qualify any simple statement about the proportionate influences of heredity and environment becomes clearer still. Even the question whether an increased similarity in environmental conditions will lead to a greater or lesser influence of genetic differences is apparently open to argument. J. McV. Hunt (1961) maintains that an increased equality of environmental stimulation will *diminish* the effect of genetic differences, but this appears to be a personal view, not shared by geneticists (e.g. Carter 1962, p. 136).

The issues are obviously complex and have been further obscured by social, political and humanitarian *idées fixes*. It is often assumed, consciously or unconsciously, that the admission of genetic differences in mental ability opens the door to all kinds of undemocratic and socially unjust practices; or, conversely, that a recognition of the importance of environmental factors implies a rigidly egalitarian society. In fact the interaction is subtle enough to make any such conclusions quite unacceptable except to the simple-minded.

Over the last 60 or 70 years, as new evidence has constantly accumulated, accepted opinion on this issue has oscillated or rotated in a kind of dialectical spiral. In this chapter it is possible only to sketch some of the major trends.

TWIN STUDIES

Nature has provided a convenient means of partly disentangling the contributions of heredity and environment to behaviour by ensuring that approximately once in ninety times a human birth produces twins, and that among these sets of twins from about a quarter to two-fifths are identical (Penrose, 1963; Burt, 1966). Galton appears to have been first (as in so many other areas of biology and psychology) to appreciate the scientific possibilities suggested by the existence of monozyotic twins, and by the fact of their virtually identical hereditary endowment.

That both identical and non-identical twins occur is fortunate from the point of view of research, because the non-identical twins serve to a large extent as a control group. It cannot be assumed, if identical twins are extremely similar on a certain characteristic, that the characteristic is thereby shown to be inherited. It is perfectly possible that fraternal (non-identical) twins may also be very alike in this respect, in which case the evidence for hereditary determination is greatly weakened. But if fraternal twins differ quite widely and identical twins do not, the variation among fraternals can serve as a baseline against which to measure the degree of similarity, and if the difference or ratio is large enough, one can conclude that there is good evidence for genetic influence on the trait in question. The baseline is, however, a relative not an absolute one, because fraternal twins are much more alike than randomly selected individuals; the correlation for measured intelligence, for instance, is about $+\cdot5$. It is on this difference in extent of correlation between fraternal and identical twins that numerical and percentage estimates of genetic influence are usually based.

Such comparisons are not ideal, because they only contrast the similarity of fraternal twins with that of identical twins *within the same family*, where each member of a pair, whether fraternal or identical, is reared under much the same environmental conditions as his fellow. Valuable additional information has been derived from a few studies in which the rare cases of identical twins reared apart have been examined.

So far it has been assumed that identical and non-identical twins can be easily distinguished. This is far from being the case, and in many of the earlier studies it is probable that there was an appreciable degree of misclassification. Even at present, although methods of classification have become more objective and thorough, there is usually no single reliable criterion of zygosity. But when a large number of characteristics are taken into account, including, for instance, superficial appearance, eye colour, blood group, fingerprints, ability to taste phenylthiocarbamide, it appears that from a large number of indicators, each of which discriminates at a high level of probability, the final likelihood of misclassification is very low and indeed almost negligible relative to other possible sources of error (Shields, 1962).

The most general finding has been, in practically all studies of intelligence test results in identical and fraternal twins, that identical twins are much more alike than fraternal and that a high degree of similarity persists even when they are reared apart.

The following results were reported by Burt (1955), who includes some of the earlier findings by Newman, Freeman and Holzinger for comparison; they were presented again in slightly revised form in his (1966) paper, from which table 6.1 is reproduced.

Burt comments that the most notable feature of these results is the high correlation between the assessments of identical twins even when they have been reared apart, which approaches the correlation between successive testings from the same individual. The resemblances between non-identical twins are much lower and scarcely more marked than between ordinary brothers and sisters. The trends in the physical data are rather similar.

In Burt's table, both the American figures and his own show that the picture in the case of scholastic attainment is quite different. The correlations for siblings and dizygotic twins reared together, for instance, are higher than those for monozygotic twins reared apart. It appears therefore that environmental factors, in these studies at least, have a much more substantial influence on attainment than on intelligence, and also that this influence is particularly marked on verbal and literary attainment.

These figures presented by Burt from his own and the American studies have generally been supported by similar, more recent findings. Until quite recently, studies of identical twins brought up apart were, as might be expected, rather scanty. Apart from the two studies summarised in the table overleaf, reports were generally confined to detailed accounts of only one or two pairs of such twins. Shields' (1962) report is an important addition to the list, giving a detailed account of the tests for zygosity employed and containing many summarised case histories. It describes one of the largest groups of identical

TABLE 6.1 *Correlations for mental, educational, and physical characteristics*

	A. Burt et al.						B. Newman et al.		
	Monozygotic twins reared together	Monozygotic twins reared apart	Dizygotic twins reared together	Siblings reared together	Siblings reared apart	Unrelated children reared together	Monozygotic twins reared together	Monozygotic twins reared apart	Dizygotic twins reared together
Number of pairs*	95	53	127	264	151	136	50	19	51
Intelligence									
Group test	·944	·771	·552	·545	·412	·281	·922	·727	·621
Individual test	·918	·863	·527	·498	·423	·252	·881	·767	·631
Final assessment	·925	·874	·543	·531	·438	·267	—	—	—
Educational									
Reading and spelling	·951	·597	·919	·842	·490	·545	—	—	—
Arithmetic	·862	·705	·748	·754	·563	·478	—	—	—
General attainments	·983	·623	·831	·803	·526	·537	·892	·583	·696
Physical									
Height	·962	·943	·472	·501	·536	-·069	·932	·969	·645
Weight	·929	·884	·586	·568	·427	·243	·917	·886	·631
Head length	·961	·958	·495	·481	·506	·110	·910	·917	·691
Head breadth	·977	·960	·541	·510	·492	·082	·908	·880	·654
Eye colour	1·000	1·000	·516	·554	·524	·104	—	—	—

* Figures for boys and girls have been calculated separately and then averaged. In columns 3, 4, 5 and 6 the correlations for head-length, head-breadth and eye colour were based on samples of 100 only.

twins reared apart that has yet been studied (forty-four pairs) and contrasts these with another forty-four pairs reared together. Comparisons were made of height, weight, and personality, as well as of intelligence. Tests of the latter consisted of the Dominoes test (a 20-minute, non-verbal test) and the Synonyms section (Set A) of the Mill Hill Vocabulary Scale (Form B, 1948). The results were striking in one respect. The identical twins reared apart were slightly more similar in terms of intra-class correlation on total score than those reared together ($+\cdot77$ compared with $+\cdot76$). It seems likely that the size of the correlation for twins reared apart has in this study been inflated by sampling error or by the fact that many of the separated twins were brought up in rather similar environments, but the result, even when such allowance has been made still appears to lend substantial support to the hereditarian point of view.

Huntley (1966) has reported a study of monozygotic and dizygotic twins in London (85 MZ pairs, 235 DZ) that leads to similar conclusions. He derived estimates of heritability by three methods for each of four variables – finger-print ridge counts, height, intelligence and social maturity. The finger-print count provided a useful criterion of an unlimited characteristic with which to compare the other estimates, being known to produce figures approximating closely (in fact better than any other human characteristic) to the theoretical ones expected on the basis of a simple model of polygenic inheritance. 'Intelligence' (although it was perhaps rather attainment that was being measured, by the use of a vocabulary test) was found to produce estimates closer to those derived from the fingerprint data than to those from the social maturity scale, scores on which were clearly very largely determined by environmental factors.

Two other recent twin studies did not employ identical twins reared apart, but are of interest for other reasons. Gottesman's (1963) research was mainly concerned with the effects of heredity and environment on personality factors, but his battery included the Otis intelligence test, and his results consequently throw light on the relative heritability of personality and intelligence. His conclusion was that '62% of the within-family intelligence variance measured by the Otis is accounted for by hereditary factors in this sample'. Of the parallel estimates made for 31 personality factors assessed by the MMPI and Cattell's HSPQ, only one was higher (MMPI social introversion).

Vandenberg's (1962) study was concerned with the relative effects of heredity and environment on 'primary mental abilities' as defined by Thurstone. Earlier studies by Thurstone, Thurstone and Strandskov

(1953) and Blewett (1954) had suggested that verbal ability was most highly influenced by heredity. An incidental finding in Blewett's work was that when the Nufferno intelligence tests, designed to assess 'speed' and 'power' in intelligence quite independently, were administered, 'power' was found to be appreciably determined by genetic factors (although to a lesser degree than scores on most of the primary mental abilities), but 'speed' not at all.

It is natural to speculate on the connection between genes and 'mental factors' of the kind discussed in Chapter 2. Most factorists would expect the influence of either heredity or environmental conditions to be clearer on factors and factor scores than on factorially complex test scores. Royce (1957) suggests a conceptual scheme of their relations, and urges psychologists to think in the more specific terminology of 'genes' and 'patterns of behaviour' rather than of nature-nurture or heredity-environment.

Diagrams such as that of Royce in Figure 6.2, although they represent a very desirable conceptual synthesis of allied areas of research,

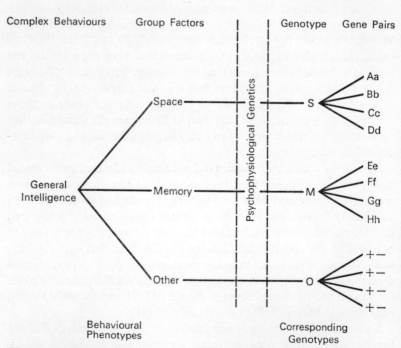

Figure 6.2. Royce's Concept of the Paths between Genes and Behavior. From Royce (1957)

must be drastic oversimplifications. In addition there are big differences in the assessed heritability of primary mental abilities (Blewett, 1954; Vandenberg, 1962) that must make one doubt if they are useful concepts at all for this purpose. The findings about general intelligence are on the whole much more consistent. Thompson (1966) points out the many kinds of covariation that may result in factors. He distinguishes, for instance (p. 721) genetic communality, chromosomal communality, gametic communality and environmental communality. Observed correlations may depend on complex combinations of these.

What can be concluded from all these studies? The field is a complex and difficult one, where the non-expert is well advised to tread warily. As Penrose (1963, p. 91) puts it, 'the study of twins, from being regarded as one of the easiest and most reliable kinds of researches in human genetics, must now be considered as one of the most treacherous'. The general opinion of most authorities, however, seems to be that a substantial degree of genetic determination of measured intelligence can hardly be denied. Halsey (1959), for instance, many of whose publications have been concerned to stress the importance of social and environmental factors, suggests that the fraction of variance in test

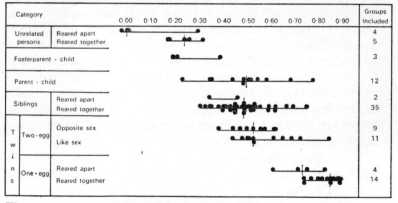

Figure 6.3. Correlation coefficients for 'intelligence' test scores from 52 studies. Some studies reported data for more than one relationship category; some included more than one sample per category, giving a total of 99 groups. Over two-thirds of the correlation coefficients were derived from IQ's, the remainder from special tests (for example, Primary Mental Abilities). Midparent-child correlation was used when available, otherwise mother-child correlation. Correlation coefficients obtained in each study are indicated by dark circles; medians are shown by vertical lines intersecting the horizontal lines which represent the ranges. From Erlenmeyer, Kimling and Jarvik (1963)

scores attributable to inheritance is between a half and three-quarters. Some would go further, and maintain (Darlington, 1963) that the findings in many of the twin studies *underestimate* the effects of heredity.

Another related line of attack on these problems must be briefly mentioned, which compares the varying degrees of correlation in measured intelligence between relatives of different degrees of closeness, and which estimates the extent to which these observed correlations parallel the theoretical ones that would occur if measured intelligence were genetically determined. Erlenmeyer-Kimling and Jarvik (1963) have produced a diagram (see Figure 6.3) summarising some of these findings in relation to the twin studies.

This diagram contains the correlations found in 52 studies which remained after the authors had weeded out a number that they found to be methodologically unsatisfactory. They interpret the whole picture as follows:

> Taken individually, many of the 52 studies reviewed here are subject to various types of criticism (for example, methodological). Nevertheless, the overall orderliness of the results is particularly impressive if one considers that the investigators had different backgrounds and contrasting views regarding the importance of heredity. Not all of them used the same measures of intelligence (see caption to figure) and they derived their data from samples which were unequal in size, age structure, ethnic composition, and socio-economic stratification; the data were collected in eight countries in four continents during a time span covering more than two generations of individuals. Against this pronounced heterogeneity, which should have clouded the picture, and which is reflected by the wide range of correlations, a clearly definitive consistency emerges from the data.
>
> The composite data are compatible with the polygenic hypothesis which is generally favoured in accounting for inherited differences in mental ability.

CATTELL'S M.A.V.A.

An ingenious method has been devised by Cattell (1953, 1960, 1963a) for analysing hereditary and environmental influences and their interaction, which he calls Multiple Abstract Variance Analysis. A simplified account is given in his recent Pelican book (1965a).

Consider first the whole range of variation in intelligence in a given population. This can be divided into variation within families and variation between families (fuller insight into this idea will be available to those familiar with the technique of analysis of variance, but the basic idea is simple enough). Each of these two kinds of variation can in its turn be divided into a hereditary and an environmental component, so that the whole range of variation in the population is theoretically split up into four components as follows:

1. $Var._{we}$ = variation within families due to environment.
2. $Var._{wh}$ = „ „ „ „ „ heredity.
3. $Var._{be}$ = „ between „ „ „ environment.
4. $Var._{bh}$ = „ „ „ „ „ heredity.

So far so good, in theory. But critics of the usual kind of attempt to split up variation into a proportion due to heredity and another due to environment have often rightly pointed out that in real life the two are correlated. Bright children tend to be brought up by bright parents, which may mean that components 1 and 2 above will not be independent but correlated. In fact, to analyse the total variation in the population, not four but ten components will be required, the four already listed and six more representing the six possible correlations between these four (r_{12}, r_{13}, r_{14}, r_{23}, r_{24}, r_{34}). Some of these correlations may be of negligible importance, but this cannot be safely assumed.

The nature of these correlations may be more clearly seen by examination of Figure 6.4. A systematic study of their existence or non-existence,

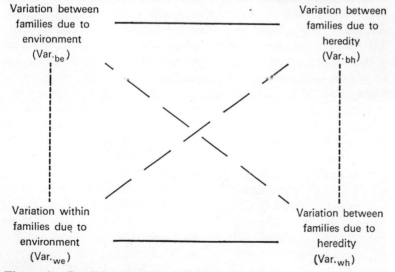

Figure 6.4. Possible correlations between hereditary and environmental effects on intelligence. Adapted from R. B. Cattell (1965a)

and of their relative importance to particular psychological traits, as suggested and started by Cattell, goes far to answer the commonly heard criticism that attempts to distinguish hereditary and environmental influences ignore the vital fact that they are usually not independent.

How may such correlations arise and how are they to be interpreted? To consider first two of the correlations between heredity and environment, those linked by solid lines in Figure 6.4, we have already mentioned the possibility of the two factors reinforcing each other as between families, in that intelligent parents, besides passing on genes that tend towards high intelligence in the children, may also provide an environment particularly favourable to its development. Within families, too, there may be positive correlations between hereditary and environmental factors, caused by greater encouragement of the abler children, or by giving them harder intellectual nuts to crack. This kind of correlation, however, is only hypothetical, and might be tempered or reversed by the tendency in many families to give more encouragement to the *less* able. The two other kinds of possible correlation between heredity and environment, shown by the diagonal dashed lines in Figure 6.4, are less easy to interpret in practical terms, but cannot be assumed to be negligible. Cattell suggests for instance that a correlation between hereditary within-family variance and environmental between-family variance might arise as follows. 'Genetically less assortative matings [e.g. those in which the parents are not closely matched in intelligence] will tend to yield greater within-family variance in the children. Since differences of the parents are part of the common family environment of the children, a child more deviant from his family hereditary mean is likely to be brought up in a family in which the environmental effects of having more "discordant" parents are greater.' (1963a, p. 197).

Some of these possibilities are frankly speculative (it must be remembered too that Cattell is not speaking only of intelligence, but of possible effects on other personality traits), but the main point to be made is that this model enables us to investigate empirically the existence and extent of such possible effects. The account given here is only a sketch of the possibilities considered in the original papers, which discuss the effects, for instance, of non-linear correlations and also of non-additive, interactional (as distinct from correlational) effects. Many speculations have been made by other writers about possible correlational and interactive effects, but Cattell's technique, which adapts procedures originated by Sir Ronald Fisher, is probably the first to assess them so effectively in practice. The method is in principle far superior to the study of identical and non-identical twins, since the latter typically gives no information about the correlation between hereditary and environmental influences. In addition, as has already been pointed out, the environmental differences between non-identical twins, which serve as a kind of baseline in such studies, are not typical of differences between siblings in general.

By suitable choice of a large sample containing sibs reared together, sibs reared apart, identical twins reared together, identical twins reared apart, half-sibs, unrelated children and so on, it is possible to analyse the total variation into the 10 components (four kinds of variation and the six possible correlations between them) *and* to determine their relative size and importance. The method is an extension of one already developed by geneticists in animal husbandry, the extension being needed because, as Cattell says, 'we cannot control independent genetic and environmental influences in human beings, and because the latter produce social as well as biological families, whereas cows do not' (or at least are not encouraged to in dairy farming).

The technique seems extremely promising in principle and some applications of it have been attempted (Cattell, Blewett and Beloff, 1955; Cattell, Kristy and Stice, 1957).

From the observed test variance between, for instance, siblings brought up together, an equation is formed with the observed figure on the left, and, on the right the hypothetical components and correlational terms which logically should be involved, as below.

$$\sigma^2_{(\text{siblings together})} = \sigma_{\text{wh}}^2 + \sigma_{\text{we}}^2 + 2r_{\text{wh.we}}\, \sigma_{\text{wh}}\, \sigma_{\text{we}}$$

Similar equations are formed for siblings brought up apart, and so on; the whole set of simultaneous equations can be solved, and the components on the right evaluated.

Difficulties, both theoretical and practical, however, are not lacking. It is possible that the analysis of variance model may be too restrictive in making variance due to heredity and environment independent *by definition*, and in therefore making the correlation terms cancel each other out (see discussion at end of Cattell, 1965b). There is also the practical difficulty that the full version of the model is over-elaborate in the sense that it makes difficult demands in terms of sampling rare groups for the sake of possibly insignificant components, yet it is difficult to know which of many alternative simplifying assumptions to adopt. A salient difficulty in putting the technique into practice is that even for the simpler versions large and carefully selected samples are needed for the estimates of the various components to be at all reliable. A full-scale application requires about 5,000 subjects, but would probably justify the work and expenditure involved. Among Cattell's many original and brilliant contributions to psychological method, this is perhaps the most promising and the most neglected.

HEREDITY AND THE DISTRIBUTION OF INTELLIGENCE

The 'distribution of intelligence' treated in this section refers not to its distribution among various classes and subgroups of the population, which will be discussed later, but to the statistical distribution in the whole population and the kind of curve which best describes it.

It is widely believed that this distribution is best represented by the 'normal' or Gaussian curve, which is symmetrical, tapering off from the centre at first sharply and then gradually (dotted line in Figure 6.5). There is no doubt that standardised tests, as generally used at present, when administered to a large and unselected group of people, tend to produce a distribution that fits this theoretical curve fairly closely. This is due at least in part, however, to the fact that it has become almost an article of faith that intelligence is normally distributed, and a test that produced any other kind of distribution of scores might even be criticised as poorly constructed. Since it has not been possible so far to produce tests with anything but arbitrary units of measurement, the 'true' distribution of intelligence is unknown – or it would be better to say that no satisfactory criterion exists for determining it. Quotients derived by the original formula Binet tests, for instance, are less directly forced into a particular kind of distribution by the test construction than are the 'deviation' quotients from group tests, but even the distribution of the former is to a large extent arbitrary and influenced by accidents of item selection.

But although we have no absolute criterion, there are good reasons for thinking that an approximately normal distribution fits the facts better than any other. Given a large and fairly representative sample of people, practically any measure, provided its range of difficulty is sufficient for it to stretch the able and to discriminate among the least able, tends to produce a clustering of scores in the middle and a gradual, approximately symmetrical tapering off at the extremes. The reasons why this general finding has been developed into a working assumption that the distribution of intelligence is fitted quite well by the mathematical Gaussian distribution are both practical and theoretical. The practical reason is that the normal distribution has convenient properties that have been tabulated. Once a distribution of scores is known to be normal, one only needs to know the mean and standard deviation of scores to describe the whole distribution in detail. This is true of few other kinds of distribution. The score of any individual can be related to the whole population and to know what percentages of people will score higher and lower.

A theoretical reason for the assumption is that, given a large number of independent (chance) factors, their joint influence will tend to produce such a distribution. There are good reasons for supposing that intelligence, as affected by heredity, is determined by the joint effect of a large number of genes (Burt and Howard, 1956).

For many decades, however, there have been scattered indications that the normal curve model is only an approximation. The clearest discrepancies between model and observed data have been at the lower end, where the number of individuals had been clearly in excess of what would be expected. But to a lesser extent at the top end also an excess of observed over predicted numbers has been noted. Many psychologists have suspected, half consciously, that exceptionally talented people are not quite so rare as the normal curve model would prescribe. In the 1932 Scottish survey of the intelligence of an entire national age-group (the first of the two described in the next section of this chapter), a carefully chosen representative sub-sample of 1,000 children was tested individually with the Stanford-Binet, and the investigators comment on the unexpectedly large number of children with IQ of less than 70. Burt (1955, 1963) has discussed the evidence for the actual distribution of intelligence very thoroughly and has produced a model which, although not universally accepted, seems to fit the known facts better than any alternative account. He considers four main possibilities that have been suggested by various authors, which are (a) a normal (Gaussian) distribution, (b) a distribution slightly negatively skewed, i.e. with a rather longer 'tail' at the lower end, resulting in larger numbers of very low IQs than would occur on the 'normal' hypothesis, (c) a more definitely negatively skewed distribution, (d) a positively skewed one.

The second of these, according to Burt, best fits both theoretical expectations and observed results. The actual model is technically known as a type IV distribution (from the classification devised by Karl Pearson) and is shown, in comparison with a normal curve, in Figure 6.5.

As can be seen, the discrepancy between the two curves is not very great, but the type IV one allows for a markedly larger number of very low IQs and a slightly larger number of very high ones. The histogram,

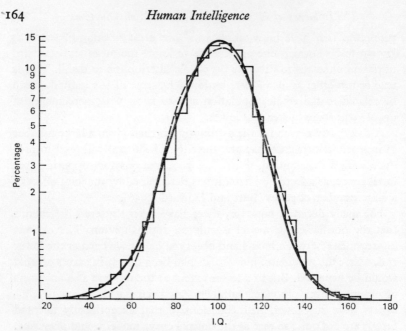

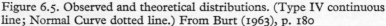

Figure 6.5. Observed and theoretical distributions. (Type IV continuous line; Normal Curve dotted line.) From Burt (1963), p. 180

or stepped distribution curve in the diagram represents the distribution of quotients found by Burt among about 4,500 children who formed the standardisation sample for an English adaptation of the Stanford-Binet scales. This obtained distribution apparently is fitted very closely by the theoretical type IV curve. Burt's theory of why the distribution of quotients should be slightly skewed in this way is as follows. He believes intelligence to be genetically controlled by two distinct mechanisms. multifactorial and unifactorial. Firstly the operation of a large number of genes would tend to produce a normal distribution. This is to ignore certain complications such as assortative mating (like tending to mate with like) and the existence of dominant and recessive and of sex-linked genes, but it appears that these additional factors would not greatly alter the picture. In addition to the numerous small influences combining to constitute the multifactorial mechanism, Burt suggests that intelligence is also affected by a few major genes, each of which may produce a large effect. It is these latter that produce the discrepancies from the normal distribution. Since the genetic constitution of man consists of a delicate balance, the effect of these few major genes, or of the mutations that produce them, is more likely to be unfavourable than favourable. Hence the asymmetrical distribution.

IS NATIONAL INTELLIGENCE DECLINING IN BRITAIN OR THE USA?

It is well known that in Western industrial societies for some generations past until quite a recent date the birth rate has usually been higher among the 'lower' than among the 'higher' socio-economic classes. Since many studies have also shown that measured intelligence is positively correlated with socio-economic level, the fear has often been expressed (from Galton 1892 to Cattell, 1937) that in such societies there may be a long-term tendency for the average level of innate intelligence to decline. Furthermore, even within particular social classes there has been evidence of a negative correlation between measured intelligence and family size which might be thought to make such a decline even more plausible. A decline of this kind, if it were in fact taking place, would be particularly alarming, in that, being a kind of detrimental natural selection, it would be irreversible without some deliberate, enforced eugenic measures, whereas improvements in nutrition, child-rearing, educational methods and so forth would fail to raise the basic average level of innate capacity. Some writers have feared that such a decline may have been sharply accelerated in the last generation or two owing to improved hygiene and medical technique, which would prevent the higher reproduction rate of the less intelligent from being offset by a higher death rate.

The opinion of most psychologists working in this field is that these fears have been largely dispelled by the results of several studies in which no such decline has appeared when corresponding samples of the population have been tested at the interval of about a generation. Four such studies are those of Burt (1946), Tuddenham (1948) in America, Cattell (1950) and the Scottish Council for Research in Education (1949, 1953).

Burt reviewed the evidence up to the end of the Second World War and concluded that on theoretical grounds, a decrease of about two IQ points per generation seemed likely. He also reported direct comparisons of the average score obtained by London schoolchildren on selected items from the Binet scales between 1913 and 1939. These data were obtained when three successive versions of the scales (with some items common to all three) were standardised; the versions were the original Binet, the Stanford revision, and the pre-war Terman-Merrill. These comparisons suggested a decline of rather more than half what was theoretically expected, but Burt points out that this result was provisional and tentative in view of disturbing factors such as population movements into and out of the LCC area.

Tuddenham administered the Army Alpha test (which had been given to tens of thousands of American recruits in the First World War) to a sample of 768 American enlisted men in the second. He ensured that this sample was representative of all recruits in 1943 and that the test, although a revised version, was scaled so as to yield comparable scores. He found that the average performance of the 1943 soldiers was greatly superior to that of the 1917 ones, to such an extent that 80% of the former exceeded the average (median) performance of the latter. An obvious and crucial question, of course, is whether the two groups of soldiers reflected equally the standards of the whole national population at the two dates. No satisfactory information was available on this point. Tuddenham advanced three possible explanations for the apparent improvement: (a) greater test sophistication, (b) improved nutrition and health, (c) higher educational standards.

Cattell tested a whole age-group of children aged 10 in Leicester in 1936 and a corresponding group in 1949. He had expected an average drop of about one IQ point per decade, but found an average rise of rather more than one point. Cattell suggested three possible explanations, as follows; (a) a genetic decline masked by educational improvements, (b) no genetic decline, because the differential birth-rate between intelligent and less intelligent groups had been offset by the contrary effect of differential death-rate, celibacy rate, and so on, (c) no genetic decline because the original data to be explained depended only upon educational differences and not differences in inherited intelligence. He rejected this last possibility as too opposed to the evidence, and reserved judgment as between the first two, though inclining towards (a). Cattell also emphasised the need to explore possibility (b) in more detail. This has now been done in studies which we shall review (e.g. Higgins et al. 1962; Bajema, 1963). They show that in certain US communities these other factors have indeed had a counter-acting effect on any tendency for average IQ to decline. Whether or not they accounted for the Leicester findings cannot, however, be determined.

The most thorough and comprehensive of these studies was that organised by the Scottish Council for Research in Education and carried out by Sir Godfrey Thomson and his associates. Almost complete national age-groups of children aged 11 years were tested in 1932 and 1947 with a group test, and samples of about 1,000 on each occasion with an individual (Binet) test. In the 1947 survey fairly extensive data about home circumstances (e.g. parents' age and occupation, living space, birth order) were obtained for a 10% sub-sample. No evidence of decline in average intelligence among Scottish children was found, and some suggestion of improvement, particularly in performance on the group test. A negative correlation of about −0·3 was found between family size and intelligence, whether measured by the group or the individual test. This relationship corresponded closely to the findings of many other studies, both British and American (Anastasi, 1956). There is considerable evidence that at least a substantial part of this relationship is due to environmental influences such as relative deficiency in parental care in larger families. Douglas (1964) found a lower correlation in social classes I and II, where such deficiency would presumably be less likely. Nisbet and Entwistle (1967) report a higher correlation in the case of verbal than of non-verbal tests, and a probable cumulative environmental effect up to the age of about 12.

The last three of these surveys all point in the same direction, to an increase rather than a decrease in average measured intelligence in the populations of Britain and the United States among both children and adults. How are they to be interpreted and what bearing do they have on the relative effects of heredity and environment?

It is possible, but not very satisfactory, to explain them in terms of a real decline in average innate capacity masked and more than offset by gains due to greater test sophistication and to improved standards of health and education. Such might be the view of the convinced hereditarian, but there is no direct evidence for the supposed decline in the innate capacity. At best there is a faint hint in the Scottish results that test sophistication might have accounted for the slight improvement on the group test and the lack of it on the individual test. On the other hand, there is evidence (Templin, 1957) that children of a given age are more competent in some language skills than corresponding children 20 years earlier, a gain that cannot be ascribed to test sophistication, though it has been suggested that it may be due to the impact of television programmes. Against the idea of a 'real' decline masked by an apparent rise, a number of writers have made a telling comparison between measured intelligence and measured height (Maxwell, 1954; Anastasi, 1956; Hunt, 1961; Penrose, 1963). The same paradox or a very similar one is evident. Physical height is correlated positively with socio-economic level and very probably is correlated negatively with family size. It might have been predicted, as for intelligence, that average height would be declining, but there is no trace of evidence that this has occurred. As Maxwell puts it, 'Though the environmental influences affecting height may not be the same as those affecting test score, it is not easy to conceive of a situation where the relationship of two variables with fertility and social class are closely parallel, and yet where for one (intelligence test score) the relationship is accompanied by a decline and for the other it is not. The model for height does not, by analogy, suggest a decline in average intelligence.'

The change over the generations is not confined to physical height. It is very clear that physical maturation in general has speeded up over the last 100 years or so, and there is no sign that this trend has ceased or even slackened (Tanner, 1961). Children are born larger and mature earlier in practically all the countries where reliable records are available. These changes are not of the kind that require minute statistical analysis to demonstrate their significance, nor are they confined to one social class. It would be easily understandable that improved nutrition should accelerate development among the under-privileged, but there have been almost equally striking gains among the upper classes. Tanner quotes, for instance, the average height of boys aged 16½ at Marlborough College (who were, presumably, not grossly undernourished in the nineteenth century).

It therefore seems fairly clear that the inference from the differential birthrate to a decline in measured intelligence (and very probably to a decline in the hereditary component of intelligence) is mistaken. The studies quoted strongly suggest that environmental changes such as improvements in health and education have a decided effect on measured intelligence. One would expect this effect to be much more evident in societies and cultural groups where such improvements have been particularly rapid, and Hunt (1961) cites a number of further investigations which suggest that this is so. There are other points, too, that must be mentioned even in a rapid survey of these important issues. It seems at first sight reasonable enough to suppose, if (a) certain groups in society are on the average more intelligent, and (b) they produce less children on the average, that the average level of intelligence in the whole society will decline. But this is an inadequate analysis. Higgins, Reed and Reed (1962) point out that when single or non-reproducing individuals are taken into account, the picture may change. If the population is divided into groups of high and low IQ, it will be found that those in the lower IQ groups *who are parents* have a higher reproductive rate, but this is offset by the higher proportion of people in these groups who never become parents at all. This has not been demonstrated for the whole population of a country, but Higgins et al. found that it applied to a large sample of about 4,000 people. It is not very clear from the report how far this result can be generalised to a whole country, but at least a very possible resolution of the paradox might be along these lines.

Bajema (1963) comes to rather similar conclusions. He shows that natural selection in relation to intelligence cannot be properly assessed without taking into account all of the following.

1. Number of offspring per fertile individual.
2. Proportion of non-reproductive individuals.
3. Mortality rates up to the end of the childbearing period.
4. Generation length.

He reports a survey which is claimed to be the first to take account of all these variables in relation to the trend of intelligence. Bajema's study confirmed the results of Higgins et al. and again found that the relative proportions of non-reproductive individuals in high- and low-intelligence groups played a crucial part in explaining how the negative correlation between intelligence and family size was misleading He found the overall percentage of non-reproductive people to be about 20, and to be twice as high among those with IQ less than 80 as among those with IQ over 120. In addition, the relation itself between IQ and number of offspring appeared to have reversed in recent years among people who did have children. Bajema concluded that fertility at the present time probably showed a higher positive correlation with intelligence than at any time during the past 75 years. As with the Higgins study, one cannot be certain that the results were generalisable even to the whole of the USA, let alone to other countries, but the combined effect of these two researches is most important in explaining what have previously appeared to be contradictory findings.

Two papers given at a recent symposium in England are also relevant (Benjamin, 1966; Carter, 1966). In these the corresponding trends in this country are discussed, and, although much of the evidence is rather old, depending largely upon the 1951 census, unfortunately the most recent available, it appears that the differences in fertility between social groups, which had been at their largest in the second half of the nineteenth century, had markedly declined from about 1930 onwards. The latest information tended to show that the gap was still narrowing, and particularly that fertility was increasing among professional and managerial people relative to the average of the whole population. It was not yet known however whether the trend had actually gone into reverse, although this seemed quite possible.

Finally, it is possible to question whether the universally observed differences in average measured intelligence between social classes are due *in any degree* to the hereditary component. A spirited and highly technical discussion of this issue took place between Halsey (1958, 1959), Conway (1959) and Burt (1959). Halsey's case was that differences in measured intelligence might be due only to social and environmental differences and that innate intelligence is distributed randomly among social classes. This is indeed possible, but not very probable. It is hard to see how, on this view, some generally accepted research results could be explained at all. Skodak and Skeels (1949), in their longitudinal study of adopted children, reported an increasing correlation, as the children grew older, with the intelligence of their *true* parents who had placed them for adoption in the first few months of life with foster-parents of generally different social status. Similarly, Lawrence (1931) had earlier demonstrated for children who had never lived with their father at all a correlation between the children's intelligence and the father's social class. This finding was replicated in a number of different groups. There seems therefore to be enough empirical evidence available to make Halsey's hypothesis an unlikely description of the facts.

Suggested additional reading

CARTER, C. O., *Human Heredity*. London: Penguin Books (1962).

BURT, SIR CYRIL, 'The inheritance of mental ability'. *Amer. Psychologist*, 13, 1–15 (1958).

HILGARD, E. R., and ATKINSON, R. C., *Introduction to Psychology*. 4th edn. New York: Harcourt, Brace (1967). Ch. on genetics.

FULLER, J. L., and THOMSON, W. R. B., *Behaviour Genetics*. New York (1960).

BURT, SIR CYRIL, 'The genetic determination of difference in intelligence: a study of monozygotic twins reared together and apart'. *Brit. J. Psychol*. 57 (1966).

CATTELL, R. B., *The Scientific Analysis of Personality*. Penguin Books (1966).

MEADE, J. E., and PARKES, A. S. (Eds.), *Genetic and Environmental Factors in Human Ability*. Edinburgh: Oliver and Boyd (1966).

VII

Normal Stages in the
Development of Intelligence

INTRODUCTION

Many fields of research which could reasonably be reviewed in this chapter will have to be omitted, and even those included can be treated only sketchily. Much of the space available will be given to the work of Jean Piaget and his associates, and only a brief description can be provided of some more 'behaviouristic' work in the USA and USSR (represented by one or two examples). Equally brief reference will be made to one or two of the relatively few longitudinal studies of intellectual development.

A field that can be mentioned only in passing is described in the title of Griffiths' (1954) book, *The Abilities of Babies*. Gesell (1925; 1940) was a pioneer in making the study of young children's development more objective by drawing up schedules of progress (motor, adaptive, language and personal-social) which incorporated approximate norms based on extensive observation of the earliest ages at which infants achieved various kinds of behaviour. Some of these were natural indications of development such as crawling or walking; others were reactions to semi-standardised material and situations (e.g. dangling rings, cubes, form board). Building on this work, Psyche Cattell (1940) in the USA and Ruth Griffiths in England developed schedules that were more akin to tests or scales. These are admirable for many observational and diagnostic purposes, but it is nonetheless generally accepted that no reliable or accurately predictive estimate of future ability can be made before about two years (the 1960 revision of the Stanford-Binet test extends downwards to age two, the WISC only to age five). Stott and Ball (1965) have written a very thorough review of work in this area. From the age of about four, ability can be assessed, however, with fair reliability. Bloom (1964), for instance, in a careful survey of the main longitudinal studies of the growth of intelligence, concludes that, on the average, 50% of the variation at age 17 is already predictable at age four.

Another flourishing field of research that can only be mentioned in passing is concerned with early language development, with how young children learn to acquire the rules of grammatical structure in their native language, with the relation of speech to thought, and so on. Two interesting and relevant books have recently been published (Smith and Miller, 1966; Lyons and Wales, 1967), reporting the proceedings of conferences on psycholinguistics in Virginia, USA and in Edinburgh respectively. Some of the recent work on the acquisition of language, such as Weir's (1962) very detailed analysis of the bedtime talking-to-himself of her two-and-a-half-year-old son, describes phenomena which are hard to account for in terms of conditioning, and attempts such as that of Skinner (1957) to explain language learning in these terms seem already outdated. Many of the recent findings seem even to indicate an innate or 'prewired' structure of the central nervous system specifically organised to handle the acquisition of languages, with the result that many linguists now believe the structure of *all* languages to be influenced by certain complex features of the human cerebral cortex. 'Linguistic universals' are therefore a great deal more acceptable than they were only about 15 years ago. This is one of the most striking examples of the current reaction against over-simple, behaviouristic explanations of complex human activities. (C. F. Lenneberg, 1967)

COGNITIVE DEVELOPMENT AS SHOWN BY STANDARDISED TESTS

It is generally agreed that intelligence increases up to adolescence and declines in old age, but apart from these very general trends little is known with sufficient certainty to be widely accepted. The technical and theoretical difficulties in obtaining a reliable curve of growth and decline are considerable. Two of the most fundamental are (a) that intelligence at age five is very different from intelligence at age 15 or 55 and that appropriate tests for different age-groups can only be said to be comparable in a rather general sense, and (b) that cross-sectional studies, i.e. those that report the results of different age-groups tested at one time, often produce results that differ markedly from those of longitudinal or follow-up studies, in which the same individuals are tested at successive ages.

This latter difficulty is particularly evident if one attempts to describe the general trend of intelligence through the whole life-span from childhood to old age. The extent to which intelligence declines in middle age is still an open question. Although many surveys have shown a decline beginning in the middle or late teens, Bayley (1955) has argued that, if appropriate tests were available, intelligence could be shown to increase up to age 50. But in both longitudinal and cross-sectional studies as so far carried out there are almost always serious methodological failings that are by no means easy to overcome. Cross-sectional studies in general tend to show a considerable and relatively early decline, but are biased by the fact that the older subjects have usually had a lower average level of education; the longitudinal studies, on the other hand, show little or no decline up to quite an advanced age, but tend to be biased by a selective dropping-out of subjects, with the more able tending to remain more available to study. It is clear, however, that the longitudinal studies are much more valuable in principle, though much more difficult and expensive in practice. This is true not only of psychological studies, but equally, for instance, of physical ones (Damon, 1965). Only in the longitudinal researches is it possible to see the actual course of development. In cross-sectional ones it has to be inferred, and the inference involves all kinds of dubious assumptions.

Besides the difficulties already mentioned, there are peculiar and technical difficulties involved in studies of change and growth of any kind (Lord, 1958; McNemar, 1958; Kodlin and Thompson, 1958; Davis, 1964, Ch. 10; Schaie, 1965; Thorndike, 1966). Thorndike points out, for instance, that measures of gain (even from adequately reliable tests) are inherently unreliable, that they are typically almost unrelated to initial score, that the required assumption of equal units of measurement is rarely met, and that there are particular dangers in correlating initial *quotient* and gain in quotient. Schaie attacks the problem even more fundamentally, maintaining that the interaction between age and the variable under consideration, such as intelligence, will produce discrepancies between cross-sectional and longitudinal studies even if compensations are made for the factors already mentioned, and that a full understanding of development requires an experimental design combining both kinds of approach. Unfortunately, taking into account the maximum human life-span, a complete study of this kind, in which 'cohorts' (i.e. age-groups) were followed through and compared with other cohorts throughout the age range would take 200 years! Schaie describes experimental designs which overcome this difficulty in part, and refers to an application of the suggested technique (Schaie and Strother, 1964).

One of the most thorough earlier cross-sectional studies designed to plot the trend of intelligence through most of adult life was that of Jones and Conrad (1933). They administered the Army Alpha test to some

1,200 subjects in New England aged between 10 and 60, taking pains to ensure that the sample was relatively homogeneous in economic status and educational opportunity, and also entirely native-born and of native-born stock. 'To develop community co-operation and insure reasonable completeness of sampling, a carefully elaborated administrative technique was employed. This technique involved the use of a free motion-picture show and supplementary house-to-house (or farm-to-farm) testing' (p. 232). Good co-operation was received from over 95% of people under 40. Over the age of 40, however, more difficulties were experienced, and in spite of efforts, the authors suspected that an above-average sample resulted, owing to the selective effect of refusals. It did not prove practicable to include a satisfactory sample of people over 60.

The curve of growth and decline found when results were plotted showed a sharp, straight-line increase in score from age 10 to about age 16, then an abrupt inflection, and a slow, steady decline involving a recession by age 55 to the 14-year level. Jones and Conrad suggested that the rate of average decline was perhaps rather under-estimated by this result, which was mainly based on subjects who were sufficiently energetic and motivated to attend meetings in village halls and so on. A comparison of this majority with the minority tested in their own homes suggested that the sample of older adults on which results were based was a slightly superior one.

Quite marked differences, which have been generally confirmed in more recent work, were found between rates of decline on sub-tests of the Army Alpha test. The trends on 'general information' and 'vocabulary' were practically level from age 20 to 60, with the highest point at about age 40. There was a fairly sharp decline in score on numerical problems, particularly those involving non-routine procedures, and the sharpest decline of all was on 'analogies'. In this last sub-test, the average score at age 55 was hardly above that at age 10. There was some evidence that, although the Army Alpha was a moderately speeded test, the decline was as much in 'power' as in 'speed'. (Many other studies, however, have adduced evidence for a greater decline in 'speed' than in power, e.g. Miles, 1934). Finally, Jones and Conrad pointed out that the trends described must be interpreted only as averages, and that there were very many individuals in the group to whom they did not apply. Individual differences at any one age were generally greater than differences between age-groups.

These findings have been generally confirmed in later cross-sectional researches, such as those of Foulds and Raven (1948) and of Wechsler (1958), and are summarised by Vernon (1960, pp. 171–3). Vernon also adduces evidence to show that the rate of decline is slowest among those who score high and is sharpest among low scorers, so that the declining curves fan out. The graphs of results obtained by Raven and Wechsler are shown in Figures 7.1, 7.1a and 7.1b. Wechsler's graphs start at age 16, and are therefore not comparable with all the data in Raven's diagrams but only with the right-hand three-quarters or so of the 50% curve. Marked similarities can be seen in the trends, both overall and

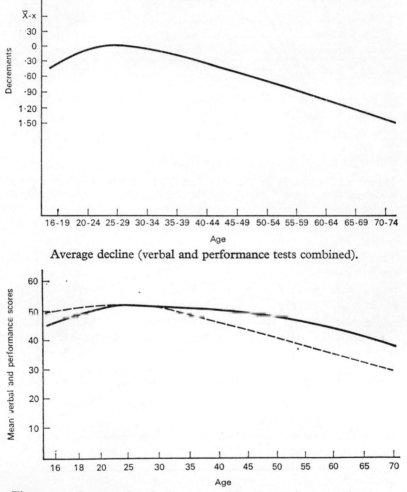

Average decline (verbal and performance tests combined).

Figure 7.1. Comparative decline of verbal and performance subtests on WAIS with age. Ages 16–75 and over (2052 cases). *Solid line,* Verbal. *Dash line,* Performance. From Wechsler (1958), p. 202

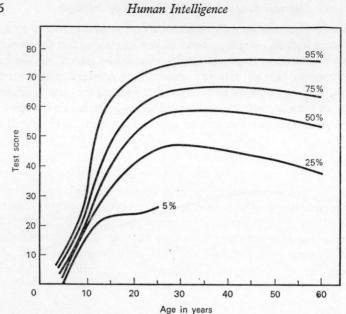

Figure 7.1a. Changes in the Matrices Test percentile points as age advances

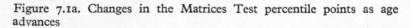

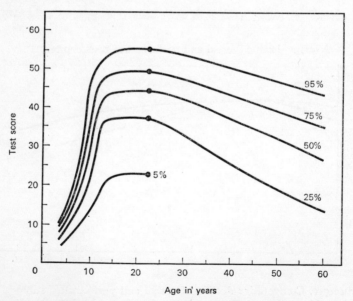

Figure 7.1b. Changes in the Vocabulary Test percentile points as age advances. From Raven (1948)

in the different trends for verbal and non-verbal measures. There is also some support for the popular view that those who 'exercise their brains' best preserve their effectiveness in functioning (cf. the research by Lovell, discussed in Ch. 3). Support for this belief can be found in the research of Nisbet (1957) who retested in 1955 a group of about 140 graduates previously tested with the Simplex group test in 1930–4. Their average age on the first occasion was $22\frac{1}{2}$, and on the second, 47, and their average score increased during this period by 11·9 or about ·8 standard deviations in terms of the whole adult population. Nisbet points out that some of this gain, but certainly not all, may have been due to the difference in conditions of testing on the two occasions and also to increased test sophistication. He compares these findings with those of a number of similar American investigations and concludes that people of superior ability show no decline in measured intelligence at least up to their late forties. Burns (1966) has now reported a further testing of the same subjects at the age of 56. Their average score was still well above that of the first testing, but had decreased compared with that of nine years earlier. Much of this decline was due to lower scores on the numerical sub-tests. These studies suggest a slow decline of ability among people following intellectual pursuits and a more rapid one among those whose daily life involves less intellectual stimulation. There is even some neurological evidence for a lesser deterioration in brain cells among old people who have maintained a high level of activity (Vogt, 1951).

Owens (1966) has reported results that agree with those of Nisbet as just outlined. Owens' findings are of particular interest for several reasons, firstly that his longitudinal study covered a period of 42 years, with the first testing in 1919 and the latest in 1961, secondly that the test used was the Army Alpha (with the result that his research can be compared with several others, including the cross-sectional one of Jones and Conrad), and finally because he attempted to apply a correction to discount the general improvement in standards between 1919 and 1961.

The uncorrected figures showed *gains* on nearly all the sub-tests between mean age 19, and mean age 61, in striking contrast to the cross-sectional studies such as that of Jones and Conrad. But the pattern of change was parallel; for example, the tests which produced the smallest decline in performance with age (Jones and Conrad) such as informational and verbal sub-tests, showed the greatest gain (Owens); similarly those showing the greatest decline in the earlier study showed the smallest gain, or even a slight decline, in Owens' survey.

Owens produced evidence to show that these results were probably not due to selective dropping-out from the sample, but he believed the gains were partly due to general improvement in cultural and educational standards over the 40 years. When a correction was applied to try to discount this change (based on a comparison of 19-year-olds in 1919 with others in 1961 on the same test), many of the gains disappeared. The net changes in the sample over 40 years of their life span were estimated to be (a) a slight gain in the verbal and informational sub-tests, (b) a slighter loss in the numerical sections, (c) a more substantial loss in the 'reasoning' sub-tests (e.g. analogies). These findings confirm those of several other studies. Maxwell (1961) found that high performance on intelligence tests in old age depended greatly and increasingly on verbal comprehension, and Birren and Morrison (1961) found increases in score on Wechsler's verbal comprehension scale up to age 65.

Welford (1958) summarises in an excellent book the experimental studies carried out at Cambridge under his direction by the Nuffield Unit for research into problems of ageing. His main conclusion, particularly with regard to problem-solving by elderly people, is that the most readily detectable decline occurs in two associated functions, and that most of the known results can be explained in these terms. These two are channel capacity and short-term memory. Welford concludes that there is no evidence for any limitation with increasing age, at least far into later life, in the basic ability to make intellectual leaps and to attain 'insights'. The decline is rather in the prerequisite processes necessary for their attainment and is noticeable mainly in situations where span of intake and immediate memory capacity are stretched and strained. This applies both to problem-solving and to learning in general.

The serious student should not consider the preceding account as more than a lightning sketch of what has been discovered about age-trends in measured intelligence. A comprehensive account of the evidence about changes in maturity and old age is given by Jones (1959), and another, more up-to-date and accessible survey of psychological (including cognitive) changes with age is provided by Bromley (1966).

THE BEHAVIOURISTIC APPROACH

Wallace (1965) in an extensive review of work on children's cognitive development, points out that nearly all the researches reviewed fall into one or other of two main categories, 'studies in the behaviourist mould' and those in the 'main stream'. In the present account, we shall be able to do little more than briefly indicate the nature of a few investigations 'in the behaviourist mould', in the hope of doing rather more justice to some of those 'in the main stream'.

In the USSR the name of Pavlov and the principles of classical conditioning are unanimously and frequently invoked (Berlyne, 1963) although the frequency of reference to Pavlov has been decreasing recently since the peak around 1930, when at a joint meeting of the Academy of Sciences and the Academy of Medical Sciences it was decreed that Pavlov's theories and techniques should be carefully adhered to. Secondly, even when this precept was being urged most strongly, it was not so restrictive as might be feared; as Berlyne points out, Pavlov's writings, like the Bible and many other holy works, can be used to justify almost any point of view. Thirdly, much has been made of one or two references by Pavlov to 'the second signal system', with the implication that the functioning of that part of the central nervous system which produces and responds to language requires additional principles of explanation besides those of classical conditioning as derived from experiments with animals. Finally, the study of children's cognitive development has been strongly encouraged in the USSR for both practical and philosophical reasons, with the result, as Berlyne puts it, that 'the child is, in other words, the rat of Russian psychology'. The consequence of all these circumstances is that Russian work in child psychology, although certainly falling within the 'behaviourist mould', is *not* narrowly reductionist, but comparable to liberal and elastic interpretations of stimulus-response theory in the USA.

Some interesting work has been concerned with the generalisation of verbal stimuli in children (e.g. if a child has been classically conditioned to respond involuntarily to the stimulus 'eight', will a response be forthcoming to the stimulus 'four plus four'?) A readily available paper which describes the tracing of semantic connections by conditioning procedures is that of Luria and Vinogradova (1959). A second important area of Russian research is concerned with differences between younger and older children in the relative importance of verbal mediation, with young children up to the age of five or six displaying behaviour in a problem situation that can be accounted for fairly well by simple principles of conditioning, but with older children clearly making use of internal, unspoken verbal responses.

Experimental and theoretical analyses of the child's cognitive development in the USA have also, more often than not, been framed in terms of behaviourist, and particularly of stimulus-response concepts. But there, as in the USSR, the trend has been steadily in the direction of liberalising the S-R framework, of recognising more explicitly the crucial importance of implicit verbal processes, and of putting more emphasis on autonomous central nervous functioning (and correspondingly less on external and peripheral factors).

The work of the Kendlers (e.g. Kendler, T. S., 1963; Kendler and Kendler, 1959) on mediating responses appears in several ways to be quite similar to some of the Russian work reviewed by Berlyne. Much of the Kendlers' work has been concerned with 'reversal shifts' and 'non-reversal shifts'. The experimental design of these studies has usually been as follows. The subjects are presented with objects that differ on two dimensions; the dimensions might be colour (black or white) and size (large or small), with four possible kinds of presentation (large white; small white . . . etc.). Discriminations in one of these dimensions (e.g. response to black) are rewarded, and the other dimension is treated as irrelevant by the experimenter until subjects are trained; then, without warning, the 'correct' response is changed in one of two ways. Substituting 'white' as the response to be rewarded is a reversal shift, and substituting one value of the previously irrelevant dimension (size) is a non-reversal shift.

On pure conditioning principles, re-training to respond to the previously irrelevant stimulus (non-reversal shift) should occur more quickly; if verbal or conceptual mediation is taking place, the reversal shift (responding to white instead of black) should come more easily. It has often been shown that rats find the non-reversal shift easier, but that the opposite is true of college students. One of the questions the Kendlers attempted to answer was whether, at this rather simple level, children's problem-solving like that of the rats, but unlike that of the college students, could be explained in terms of conditioning. The interesting result they obtained was that it can only up to the age of about six (see Figure 7.2). Children between five and seven years of age split fairly evenly, around 50% apparently making use of mediating processes and 50% not, but at later ages 'reversal' shifts begin to be made much more readily than 'non-reversal' ones. Similar results have been obtained by O'Connor, working with mentally defective children, who found 'reversal' shifts to be easier above a certain level of IQ, and we have already briefly mentioned somewhat similar findings by Russian child psychologists. Also Kuenne (1946), experimenting with children of mental age between three and six, convincingly demonstrated a marked dependence of 'transposition' (ability to generalise a relation such as greater/smaller) on verbalisation, and an increase in its occurrence from 50 to 100% between these age levels. The literature on the relation between children's age and extent of verbal mediation has been usefully reviewed by Reese (1962). Piaget, as we shall see, has for a long time suggested that a major new period of cognitive development typically begins at age six–seven. There are therefore converging lines of research that indicate an important step in mental functioning in normal children at about that age.

As we have already seen, to describe all Russian research on early cognitive development as based on Pavlovian principles is something of an over-simplification; to suggest that all American research has been done in a simple S–R framework is to over-simplify enormously. Until fairly recently, however, this has been a major trend in the USA. In the

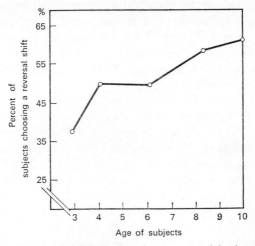

Figure 7.2. Percentage of children choosing a reversal (rather than a non-reversal) shift at various ages. From Kendler and Kendler (1962)

last few years, what Wallace describes as 'main-stream' research, based either on the methods and findings of the Swiss psychologist Jean Piaget or on a similar general approach, has made rapid headway. Most European research has always been of this kind, since, as Berlyne points out, the sheer bulk of empirical study carried out in the last 30 or 40 years by Piaget and his associates is greater than that of all other research in cognitive development put together. This would not in itself, of course, be sufficient justification for devoting most of this account to Piagetian formulations and experiments, but in fact their importance is commensurate with their volume.

Some indication of the recent delayed impact in the USA of Piaget's work is the suggestion by Roger Brown (1965) that Piaget, after Freud, is the greatest figure to emerge in the young science of psychology.

PIAGET'S MAIN THEORETICAL IDEAS

Even Piaget's most devoted followers rarely claim that he is a very lucid expositor of his own ideas. It is therefore surprising at first sight that until about five years ago there were hardly any satisfactory summaries or secondary accounts of his system (in English, at least). In part this was due to the delayed translation of his more recent books and articles, and partly also to the sheer difficulty of compressing and elucidating his highly complex theoretical system. Flavell, for instance, confesses that his original intention was to write one chapter about Piaget's work in a textbook on theories of child development. 'All was smooth sailing at first, and I judged that the project would be completed within a year. . . . One very important theory of child development – Piaget's – turned out to be in a state so utterly recalcitrant to this plan that the plan itself finally unravelled.' Eight years later Flavell's book of 450 pages on Piaget alone was published.

Lucid secondary accounts are therefore particularly valuable and the present writer can testify to the difficulty of acquiring a satisfactory total view of the system from a sampling of Piaget's huge and complex series of publications. During the last five or six years, there has been a welcome spate of summaries and interpretations. The following articles and books, listed in roughly ascending order of length and amount of detail, from Nathan Isaacs' useful pamphlet to Flavell's definitive summary, will afford the student a comprehensive but by no means an exhaustive account (Isaacs, 1963; Tuddenham, 1966; Brown, 1965; Inhelder, 1953; Berlyne, 1957; Brearly and Hitchfield, 1966; Wallace, 1965; Lunzer, 1968; Maier, 1965; Hunt, 1961; Flavell, 1963). Biggs (1959) has provided a useful introductory discussion of Piaget's work on the child's conception of number, and Lovell (1964; 1966) a more extended discussion, including details of his own continuation of Piaget's work in this area. Holloway (1967a, b) has recently added two further useful introductory summaries.

A more fundamental reason, perhaps, for the difficulty many have had in understanding Piaget's ideas is his unusual and powerful integration of two viewpoints, that of the biologist and that of the logician-epistemologist. From this two-fold approach comes Piaget's own description of his field of study as 'genetic epistemology', a phrase coined by J. M. Baldwin, but one that admirably embodies Piaget's dual interest both in biological adaptation and development and in the study of knowledge. Grize (1965) summarises the status of 'genetic epistemology' as a discipline, maintaining that it is scientific in its use of the methods of psychological investigation, but more closely related to philosophy in the kinds of question it asks.

These two aspects continually recur in Piaget's work, and their synthesis has been a large part of his achievement. In the first paragraph of his (1950) book, *The Psychology of Intelligence*, he states, in his dense and aphoristic style, the apparent conflict (or at least lack of contact) between the two disciplines, both of which have to be taken into account in providing a comprehensive theory of thought. Konrad Lorenz is on record as having believed for a long time that Piaget was 'one of those tiresome empiricists'. Far from it! In spite of his enormous production of empirical findings, he can be formidably theoretical.

Every psychological explanation comes sooner or later to lean either on biology or on logic (or on sociology, but this in turn leads to the same alternatives). For some writers mental phenomena become intelligible only when related to the organism. This view is of course inescapable when we study the elementary functions (perception, motor functions, etc.) in which intelligence originates. But we can hardly see neurology explaining why 2 and 2 make 4, or why the laws of deduction are forced on the mind of necessity. Thus arises the second tendency, which consists in regarding logical and mathematical relations as irreducible, and in making an analysis of the higher intellectual functions depend on an analysis of them. But it is questionable whether logic, regarded as something eluding the attempts of experimental psychology to explain it, can in its turn legitimately explain anything in psychological experience. Formal logic, or logistics, is simply the axiomatics of states of equilibrium of thought, and the positive science corresponding to this axiomatics is none other than the psychology of thought. With the tasks thus allotted, the psychology of intelligence must assuredly continue to take account of logistic discoveries, but these will never go so far as to dictate to psychology its own solutions; they will merely raise problems for it.

So we must start from this dual nature of intelligence as something both biological and logical. The two chapters that follow aim to define these preliminary questions and, in particular, will attempt to reduce to the greatest unity possible in the present state of knowledge these two fundamental but at first sight irreducible aspects of human thought.

Piaget attempts to attain this unity somewhat as follows:

Throughout the development of intelligence in any human being, the main *functions*, analogous in many ways to other biological functions, are said to remain unchanged. But the *structures*, by which Piaget means both the logical processes available and the way these are organised, are frequently changing, at least up to adolescence.

The contrast is peculiarly Piagetian and requires further explanation. One might expect the contrast to operate the other way round, since a biological function sounds in some respects more changeable than a 'structure'. Piaget, however, sees intelligence as operating by means of two basic functions, each of which forms one aspect of adaptation to the environment. These two functions, called 'assimilation' and 'accommodation' are complementary, like two sides of a coin, and represent the two basic unchanging aspects of intelligence throughout life. The young infant, investigating his immediate surroundings, grasps, sucks, explores, probes, shakes, absorbs, *assimilates*. But the environment, whether of inert objects or of living people, resists, moves, hurts, eludes, rewards and punishes, compelling the infant to *accommodate*. The distinction between assimilation and accommodation bears some resemblance to that of Freud between the 'pleasure-principle' and the 'reality-principle', but is by no means identical, since Piaget's distinction between these two kinds of adaptation appears to cut across the Freudian one. Assimilation and accommodation alike *may* yield pleasure but the main point is that they are *combined* to ensure realistic adaptation. It may be clear therefore how these key terms are readily applicable to the development of infants, but less evident how they apply to mature intelligence.

Consider the situation of Copernicus, attempting to re-interpret and to synthesise parsimoniously data that made it increasingly difficult to preserve the ancient Ptolemaic theory of the movements of the planets and the sun. Two courses were open to him if realistic adaptation was to take place, *assimilation* of the data to the traditional theory, and *accommodation* of theory to the new data. Both processes had to be attempted, and the weight to be given to each is a constant dilemma in scientific work, particularly when observations are known to contain a generous component of error.

The discussion so far leads us to some further points about Piaget's use of the two concepts. Firstly, both are normally involved in any intellectual task; secondly, the relative preponderance will vary according to the kind of task and the kind of intellectual operation; thirdly, assimilation is in a sense the more conservative process, at least in the illustration just given, and it is also probably the dominant function in most people at most ages; fourthly, the reader familiar with G. A. Kelly's increasingly popular interpretation of personality differences in terms of personal constructs (Kelly, 1955; Bonarius, 1965; Bannister, 1962) will see some similarity between Kelly's idea of how people construe reality and Piaget's concept of assimilation.

The idea that assimilation and accommodation may both be involved in a mental task, but in different proportions according to the kind of task and method of performance, leads us to another important cluster of Piagetian concepts centering round that of *equilibrium*. In some mental states (dreaming, autistic thinking) accommodation may play little part; to others, involving for instance close imitation of an external performance or rigid adherence to a schedule, assimilation may contribute very little. In all intelligent behaviour properly so called there will, according to Piaget, be this state of equilibrium between the two functions, 'a functional state in which potentially slavish and naively realistic (in the epistemological sense) accommodations to reality are effectively held in check by an assimilatory process which can organise and direct accommodations, and in which assimilation is kept from being riotously autistic by a sufficiency of continuing accommodatory adjustments to the real world. In short, intelligent functioning, when equilibrium obtains, is made up of a balanced recipe of about equal parts of assimilation and accommodation. Through this fine balance, a both realistic (accommodation) and meaningful (assimilation) rapport between subject and object is secured' (Flavell, p. 65).

Piaget not only lays stress on this need for an appropriate balance between these two adaptive functions, but also appears to use it as a kind of definition or criterion of a new stage of reasoning having been fully achieved. In this sense it refers approximately to the assimilation and mastery of an entire set (a 'group' or quasi-group in the mathematical sense) of logical operations. 'From the psychological standpoint, a system is in equilibrium when a perturbation which modifies the state of the system has its counterpart in a spontaneous action which compensates it' (Inhelder and Piaget 1958, p. 243). This extended use of 'equilibrium' as a technical psychological term is not entirely easy to grasp, although it is an important part of Piaget's theoretical system. It implies that a degree of reversibility has been attained, so that alternatives can be considered and if necessary rejected without the thinker wandering off into a blind alley. When a hypothesis has been formulated and negated, equilibrium is restored. Piaget certainly does not think of equilibrium between functions as being attained once for all, but rather that much of cognitive development is a process of equilibration, of successively achieving equilibrium between more complex functions. Children below the age of about 11 for instance, when attempting to solve a combinatorial problem, cannot generally grasp the idea of a complete set or population of possible combinations, but form some *ad hoc* hypothesis which disturbs the equilibrium.

MAIN PERIODS OF COGNITIVE DEVELOPMENT, ACCORDING TO PIAGET

Something has been said about the permanent intellectual *functions* as described by Piaget, but nothing as yet about the changing *structures*. These 'structures' or 'organisations' of intelligence are thought of as changing qualitatively in several main periods from birth to adolescence. Each successive structure develops from and incorporates the preceding one, producing a kind of hierarchical development. At each stage new kinds of concept are attained, and each of the qualitative changes between the periods opens up the possibility of many new problem-solving capabilities. Piaget has devoted a very large amount of observation and experiment to establishing these successive stages, which he believes always occur in the same order, though with a fair amount of variation in actual chronological age, and it is for these that he is best known to teachers and educationists.

Piaget distinguishes four main periods: (1) the period of sensory-motor operations, extending from birth to 18 months or two years; (2) the period of preoperational representations, lasting until the age of about seven; (3) the period of concrete operations extending to age 11 or 12; (4) the period of formal operations beginning at 11 or 12 and typically complete at about 15. Sub-periods and sub-sub-periods are recognised within these three main periods of development; sometimes the first two main periods are grouped together, despite the important change generally occurring at age six or seven.

Relatively little need be said about the sensory-motor period, which ends around the age of two. Although Piaget's observations, based very largely on his own three children, are fascinating, the scope of this present book excludes very early development. On Piaget's own account, sensory-motor intelligence is rather a base for the development of intelligence in the adult sense than a primitive form of it, or, if describable as intelligence, is an intelligence of the limbs, so to speak, of the co-ordination of movement, of the differentiation of self from environment. 'Penser, c'est opérer' is a key doctrine of Piaget, by which he means among other things that the most abstract and abstruse kinds of formal thinking have evolved from simpler manipulations of ideas, and that these simpler manipulations have in their turn evolved eventually from physical manipulations in the sensory-motor period. It might perhaps be supposed that this general conception of intellectual development would also involve the theory, particularly favoured in the past by a number of American psychologists (such as J. B. Watson, and in a less extreme form by the psychiatrist H. S. Sullivan) that speech necessarily precedes symbolic thought, and that the latter depends upon the former. All Piaget's observations, however, tend to support the opposite view. Flavell (p. 155) concisely summarises his conclusions on this important question:

> Piaget makes two important points. First, he asserts very strongly that representational thought does not begin with and result from the incorporation of verbal signs from the social environment (1954, pp. 52–54). Rather, the first signifiers are the private, nonverbal symbols which emerge towards the end of sensory-motor development and whose evolution we have described in terms of the internalization of imitation in the form of image-signifiers. The very first signifiers are not linguistic signs but things like the piece of cloth which Jacqueline used to represent a pillow in pretended going-to-sleep actions, the piece of paper she playfully treated as a food symbol, and so on. It is not the acquisition of language which gives rise to the symbolic function. Quite the contrary, the symbolic function is a very general and basic acquisition which makes possible the acquisition of both private symbols and social signs. Piaget of course admits, in fact, stresses, the enormous role which a codified and socially shared linguistic system plays in the development of conceptual thinking. Language is the vehicle par excellence of symbolization, without which thought could never become really socialized and thereby logical. But thought is nonetheless far from being a purely verbal affair, neither in its fully formed state nor, above all, in its developmental origins. In essence, what happens is that language, first acquired through the auspices of a symbolic function which has arisen earlier, will reflexively lend tremendous assistance to the subsequent development of the latter.

Any student at all interested in this important topic should also read the brilliant and lucid short book by Vygotsky (1966), written over 30 years ago, but translated into English only recently.

The second main period, that of pre-operational representations, lasting approximately from age two to age seven, covers an enormous span of development, and in particular the child makes the great advance from mainly sensory-motor manipulation to the first manifestations of inner, symbolic, abstract representation. Piaget suggests that sensori-motor intelligence, in the earlier period, is analogous to a series of still photographs that can be projected only one at a time and in a given order. Representational and symbolic intelligence, on the other hand, is analogous to a film that can be projected at high speed, stopped and started, and reversed. In the pre-operational period, the child is gradually advancing from one of these modes to the other, and in the latter stages, at the age of six or seven, there is a particularly interesting state of development when the child hesitates, so to speak, between two kinds of thinking (cf. the experiments of the Kendlers described in the second section of this chapter).

The Geneva group has accumulated a large amount of information about the latter part of the pre-operational period, and the transition to the period of concrete operations proper, partly because it is only from the age of about five onwards (as conventional intelligence testers also have found) that the child is readily testable.

Beginning at about this transitional period and continuing through the remaining period of concrete operations, important changes are taking place in the child's conception of causality, time, space, quantity, chance, morality, and of numerous other basic categories and constructs. The weight of documentation Piaget and his associates have produced to describe the nature of these changes, and the extent to which children's reasoning regularly shows characteristics which would be denied by 'common sense' (and which appear implausible until one has seen them experimentally demonstrated) have together made a great impact, greater perhaps than that of Piaget's theoretical ideas.

Much of Piaget's early work was concerned with the developing ideas of children (particularly of children in the pre-operational period and in the early part of the period of concrete operations proper) about the nature of the world, and about cause and effect in nature. He described various modes of 'pre-causal' thinking, to which he gave names such as 'animism', 'realism', and 'artificialism', and traced their gradual supersession by more objective and scientific modes of thought. Piaget himself in recent years has been a little scornful of this early work, (rather as Beethoven in later years spoke disparagingly of his delightful early septet), going so far as to call it jocularly his pre-operational period of research. While it is true that most of this work depended on verbal enquiry, and that Piaget had not yet developed many of his ingenious experimental methods, much of it is extremely interesting and suggestive. It will be discussed in detail in the next section of this chapter, in connection with recent related research.

The experimental work of Piaget and his associates on cognitive development during the middle years of childhood up to the onset of the final period of formal operations constitutes his best-known work and contains many of its most striking findings. Very numerous and inventive techniques were developed, particularly for the study of the child's concepts of length, volume and number. Many of these experiments, e.g. those with balls of clay or plasticine (conservation of amount), one-to-one correspondence of beads or matchsticks (concept of cardinal number), with building houses of the same 'size' on different bases with wooden blocks, and so on, have become well-known to most students of psychology and education. For this reason, and because whole books can and have been written on each of these aspects, it is not possible to describe them in this summary.

THE RANGE OF APPLICATION OF PIAGET'S FINDINGS

Enough has already been said to suggest the effect on psychology of Piaget's thinking. It is necessary also to consider how widely his findings can be generalised and to describe some of the attempts to repeat his work. The Geneva workers have often been criticised for ignoring considerations of sampling and for basing very wide generalisations on the observation of a small and perhaps unrepresentative sample of children. In this respect 'genetic epistemology' has often appeared to be out of step with the general practice of psychological research, particularly of research in Britain and the USA, although it is likely that these criticisms may have been exaggerated. Piaget has produced a volume of interesting work that would take most men several lifetimes, and it would be absurd to say that he and his associates should have done it *differently*, but until very recently their findings have urgently required repetition and confirmation by other psychologists.

In some ways also (Kessen and Kuhlman 1962, p. 165), Piaget has narrowly escaped the fate of Freud – an uncritical veneration, the status of a cult and a widespread conviction that many of his propositions are essentially unverifiable in principle. It has sometimes seemed only a matter of time before books were written on 'Piaget and the existential self' or 'Piaget and psychological man'. As with Freud, it is difficult to say to what extent Piaget has devised a highly abstract, *a priori* framework, and has then suited his techniques of observation to this very personal formulation.

Obviously many of the same questions about cultural and environmental effects will arise about children's development as assessed by Piaget's methods as have been raised about conventional intelligence tests. How far does the attainment of a stage depend upon stimulation, nationality, cultural and educational opportunity and so on? To what extent are the Piagetian measures 'culture-free' or 'culture-fair'? In the last few years, however, there has been quite a spate of research in a number of countries designed to repeat and extend Piaget's findings. It will not be possible to review these in detail, but a fairly full account will be given of one Canadian survey, which was on a larger scale than most and which will also provide an opportunity of outlining some of Piaget's early results not yet mentioned.

In attempting to assess the general validity of the best-known of all the main Piagetian ideas, that of inevitable successive stages of cognitive development, a distinction must first be made between the order of the stages and the age of reaching them (if in fact they are all reached). Piaget and his associates firmly believe that the order of at least the main stages will be constant in almost any society, though it may be that in some primitive and isolated societies the stage of formal operations will typically not be attained or only imperfectly attained.

Brown (1965), reviewing the evidence for the cultural determination of Piaget's findings, concludes that development in the sensory-motor period as described by the Geneva school is likely to apply very generally in most societies. Conservation of the object, for instance, and first conceptions of space and time are likely to follow a similar course under widely differing conditions. Similarly (p. 235) 'among the progressions described by Piaget there may be others that are universal; for example the occurrence of non-conservation answers before conservation answers and, among the conservations, a progression from quantity to space and still later to volume.'

Brown also believes, although he admits that full evidence is not available, that the ordering of the four main periods, sensory-motor, pre-operational, concretely operational and formally operational will stand up well to cross-cultural testing.

As regards the age at which a stage is reached in different countries or in different social groups within a country, it seems that cognitive development as judged by Piaget's criteria is markedly affected by social and environmental conditions.

Inhelder (1956) gave some indication of the variation in age to be expected within one town when she stated that in one of the conservation problems solved by 75% of the children at the age of six and a half, she did not find any cases of success until the age of exactly five years and no failure after seven-and-a-half. These were all 'normal' children in day nurseries and primary schools in Geneva. There is thus admittedly a fair range of ages at which a particular stage is reached even in one society. In the same discussion in which Inhelder was taking part, Zazzo (p. 88) concludes that the conventional kind of intelligence test is a more precise instrument in indicating level of cognitive development than the Piagetian procedures (though without giving much information about the cognitive mechanism employed) whereas, vice versa, the Piagetian procedure has the opposite strength and weakness. Piaget himself, however, who was also present in the discussion, suggests (p. 90) that Inhelder has rather over-emphasised the effect of environmental factors on the age at which a stage is reached, and suggests that 'if you take our tests on space, here is a field where one can find all the operations which can be presented relatively independently of language by a system of drawings, by comparison between a given concrete situation and drawings among which the subject can choose the true and the false. . . . As long as no systematic comparison has been made between different cultural environments with these spatial tests, one has great difficulty in separating the part played by language, with all its cultural significance, and the part played by operations'. In other words, Piaget here seems to be suggesting that the non-verbal parts of his procedure might be relatively culture-free, rather as has been claimed for some non-verbal intelligence tests.

The fullest and most systematic attempt to repeat and validate Piaget's work in a different country has been that of Laurendeau and Pinard (1962) in Montreal. Their book describes a large-scale experiment designed to test the validity of some of Piaget's early work (Piaget 1925; 1927; 1955, Ch. 3) on the child's conception of the world and in particular his conception of physical causality.

The main theme of Piaget's account is that the child progresses from an egocentric to an objective view of the world and of causation. In this progress a kind of naive 'realism', in which the child's immediate perceptions and individual perspective are assumed by him without question to give the one true picture, is gradually superseded by an ability to discount or to stand outside these immediate impressions and to distinguish between the self and external reality. Complete objectivity is rarely or never reached, since there are 'adherences' surviving from earlier stages, but the development of intelligence is intimately connected with this increase in objectivity.

Five characteristics or sub-stages are distinguished within the earlier stage of 'precausality' and in some respects Piaget's classification reminds one of Sullivan's description of the early stages of thinking as 'prototaxic' and 'parataxic' (Hall and Lindzey 1957, Ch. 4). In Piaget's system the five kinds of thinking are described as phenomenism, finalism, artificialism, animism and dynamism. 'Phenomenism is the most primitive form the child uses in his representation of reality. It is the establishment of a causal connection between phenomena which are contiguous either in space or time, or between facts which, for the subject, bear some resemblance or relation . . . For instance, the colour of an object may explain its floating, the heat of the sun may be the reason why it is classified as a living object etc. . . .' (Laurendeau and Pinard, p. 11). 'Finalism' describes the child's tendency to see natural phenomena as serving a human purpose. 'Artificialism' is rather similar in representing the tendency to see the explicit action of a maker, and again natural phenomena are thought to imply a purposeful design analogous to human industry. (Paley's celebrated argument for the existence of God, on the analogy that the existence of a watch implies a watchmaker, comes to mind.) 'Animism' describes the belief that inanimate objects possess some sort of soul or consciousness, and 'dynamism' that they possess a power of voluntary motion.

In the Piagetian formulation, progress towards objective thinking occurs through several successive processes of 'decentration' or decrease of egocentricity. In the early, sensory-motor stage, the child learns to distinguish between self and external environment in terms of movement and manipulation of objects. A second decrease in egocentricity (at a different level) occurs at the concrete operational stage of thinking, when an increasing awareness develops of the difference in viewpoint, literal and metaphorical, between different individuals. Finally, at the stage of formal thinking, a third decentration occurs. The adolescent learns to consider the form of an argument as conceptually separable from its content and, in the social sphere, becomes more capable of distinguishing his own ways of thinking and views from those of society in general and from those held by the sub-group within society to which he most requires to adapt. Laurendeau and Pinard's children in Montreal were chosen so as to range in age from four to 12 years, since they were attempting to survey the decline of 'pre-causal' modes of thought throughout the second main stage.

Both the details of these stages, and, more fundamentally, the very existence or occurrence of the 'pre-causal' modes of thought as described by Piaget have been subjects of considerable controversy. Laurendeau and Pinard therefore begin their account by reviewing the conflicting results of research studies designed to confirm or disprove the existence in children of these kinds of thinking. Susan Isaacs (1930), Deutsche (1937), Huang (1943) found little evidence to support this Piagetian formulation. Several studies by Dennis and Russell, on the other hand, tended strongly to confirm its applicability to both US and American Indian children (e.g. Dennis and Russell, 1940; Dennis, 1943).

A number of factors probably accounted for these discrepancies, prominent among them being (a) age of children tested, (b) form and objectivity of questionnaire or set of questions used, (c) method of tabulating and categorising kinds of response, (d) methods of analysis. Laurendeau and Pinard suggest fairly convincingly, with only a little special pleading, that many of the studies in which Piaget's findings were not replicated were of children too old to show pre-causal thinking very clearly, or that the children's answers were tabulated and analysed in too automatic and superficial a way.

There is also the point to be disposed of that many studies of adults have revealed 'pre-causal' thinking to occur at least on occasion or on certain topics in a remarkably high proportion of the people studied. Animistic thinking, or ascribing life to lifeless objects, was found, for instance, to occur in some 75% of old people in a study by Dennis and Mallenger (1949). While this finding might be accounted for in terms of regression in old age to early modes of thinking, such an explanation was hardly possible when similar effects were found even in students. Various ad hoc arguments could be advanced to show that these adults were not 'really' thinking animistically, but perhaps misunderstood the questions. Inevitably, however, such explanations lend support to those who argue that evidence for animistic and other forms of pre-causal thinking in children may also be partly ascribed to artifacts arising from misunderstanding, from the form of the questionnaire employed, and so on.

Laurendeau and Pinard provide a thorough discussion of such problems and a copious mass of evidence for the occurrence of the various forms of pre-causal thinking in their large, stratified sample of Montreal children. They found, for instance, that of all these children (aged 4–12) nearly 70% used artificialistic terms in their replies, and substantial (though rather less high) proportions gave indications of the other forms of pre-causal thinking. As expected, the general trend of occurrence was downwards with increasing age; at four and four-and-a-half, all the children capable of responding to the questions used pre-causal modes of thought at least part of the time. By the age of twelve, recourse to these modes was exceptional, except in cases of general retardation. In addition, as in Piaget's early work, considerable variation in incidence was found in different areas of enquiry. For instance, two of the five questionnaires used were concerned respectively with the concept of life and the movement of clouds. In responses to the latter, all five kinds of pre-causal thinking were frequently displayed, though animism and artificialism were the most common. In responses to the former, however, only examples of animism occurred (198 times) and the other four possible modes never occurred at all. Obviously, therefore, the area of enquiry makes a very important, indeed crucial, contribution to the occurrence of the phenomena forecast.

There is another point to be borne in mind when one attempts the tricky task of assessing the extent to which such findings are generalisable and of resolving the contradictory results of various earlier investigations already mentioned. One may suspect that the method of investigation used by the Piagetian school, and particularly by Laurendeau and Pinard, will have disadvantages as well as advantages when compared with more 'objective' or 'psychometric' techniques. One doubt that may strike the non-Piagetian critic is concerned with the possibility of 'leading questions'. For instance, one of the questions in the questionnaire about the movement of clouds is: 'Do the clouds know it's we who make them move, when we are walking?' Another is 'Can the clouds go where they want?' A third 'Does the wind know it makes the clouds move?' and so on. Admittedly, not every question is put to every child, since some are only presented as 'follow-up' questions in case of particular responses, but an inspection of the kind of questions put suggests a *possibility* that some of the examples of 'animism' and so forth were elicited by the wording of the questions. No wonder, perhaps, that one eight-year-old subject asked 'Is it catechism or geography we are now doing?' (p. 185).

On the whole, however, Laurendeau and Pinard's study is a useful demonstration of the validity and cross-cultural robustness of part of Piaget's system. Their moderate and sensible views (pp. 47–8) on the way in which Piaget-type assessment and conventional intelligence testing can usefully supplement each other are also worth quotation but fall more readily within the scope of the next section. Thérèse Décarie, another member of the Montreal group, has also recently published an account of an experimental and statistical research, in which she tested a hypothesis of Piaget that intellectual structures and emotional maturity develop in close conjunction and parallel one another in successive stages.

PIAGET'S WORK AND THE TRADITIONAL CONCEPT OF INTELLIGENCE

How does Piaget's work fit in with statistical studies and with the extensive results of intelligence testing? A contrast somewhat similar to that between his clinical-experimental approach, which aims at establishing general laws of functioning, and the study of individual differences, which emphasises prediction and in general lacks any firm theoretical basis, has already been discussed in Chapter 3. The gulf between these two kinds of research is equally wide in the field of developmental psychology.

One first point is that Piaget does not scorn the use of the word intelligence. This fact might seem hardly worth pointing out, except that his followers or summarisers sometimes object to other people using it (Wallace, 1965). Also, Moyra Williams (1965), discussing definitions of intelligence, oddly states (p. 3) that 'Piaget himself gets over the difficulties of defining the word intelligence by simply not using it.' In fact he not only uses it, but quite often includes it in the titles of his books and articles (e.g. Piaget, 1936, 1937, 1950, 1953, 1954, 1955, 1956).

There are one or two respects in which the Piagetian results confirm those of applied psychology and support administrative practice. The age at which primary schooling ends and secondary schooling begins (11 in England, 12 in Scotland, but the Plowden Committee has now recommended that England should adopt the Scottish practice) tallies with the major change from concrete to formal operations, which is supposed typically to occur at age 11–12. Secondly, there is agreement between the psychometric and Piagetian viewpoints about the age at which mental development is complete in most individuals, that is about 15. This agreement is the more convincing in that it flies in the face of normal 'common sense', which would generally hold that intelligence may go on developing for another 30 years.

It seems very possible that Piaget-type observation and intelligence testing have both independently and almost accidentally hit upon the completion of biological or neurological development. There are other lines of evidence pointing in the same direction. Channel capacity for intake of information (in the technical, 'information theory' sense of the word) increases rapidly and almost linearly from ages 10 to 14, and then much more slowly, reaching an asymptotic value between 14 and 18 (Pont, 1963). What increases after 15, as observed by common sense, is attainment, and perhaps, if one accepts Cattell's distinction, crystallised intelligence. Depressing as it may seem, the capacity to handle new problems and the plasticity and flexibility of intellect so evident in bright 14- and 15-year-olds will probably never be quite the same again, though the decline is fortunately very slow and masked by increased maturity and experience.

Many psychologists would accept the fact that attainment may go on increasing after age 15, but question Cattell's distinction between attainment and crystallised intelligence (Cattell and Butcher, 1968). A case can be made, however, for cognitive development beyond adolescence which is not simply attainment, or at least not specific attainment in one direction. Bruner (1959), for instance, has questioned the view often ascribed to Piaget that the stage of formal operations fully attained in adolescence is the terminus of cognitive development, and has argued that to be intelligent about intelligent behaviour (as Piaget himself certainly has been) represents a further, uncharted stage. This illustration perhaps hardly does justice to the case. Being intelligent about intelligence is one very specialised form of further cognitive development, though one particularly likely to impress psychologists. It is more to the point that Piaget's devotion to the study of children has apparently set an arbitrary bound on the full development of intelligence – not entirely arbitrary, since, as already suggested, it may quite possibly coincide with the peak of neurological development – but arbitrary in terms of complexity and creativity. Hebron (1966, p. 154) has estimated that nearly 90% of the population attain or are capable of attaining Piaget's stage of formal operations, and also (p. 178) quotes a finding by Goldman that, in the study of the Bible, a chronological age of approximately $16\frac{1}{2}$ years and a mental age of 19 years is usually needed before the concept of Israel as the future cradle of Christianity can be fully grasped! Suggestive as the Piagetian scheme is, it hardly accounts for all the phenomena of cognitive development, and complements rather than supplants the use of standardised tests.

Laurendeau and Pinard (1962, p. 47), describing a finding by Russell that mental age was correlated to the extent of +·59 with stage of animism, comment:

So even under these conditions, there is a noticeable overlapping: children of the same mental age do not all give the same type of answers. Would one, then, be justified in concluding that stages are not a good indication of intellectual maturity, or that they do not correspond to the various phases of mental development? A person who accepted such a conclusion without reservations would have to have a rather blind faith in the value of the mental ages provided by intelligence tests. This is not the place to question the validity of these commonly used measurements. Their analytic and artificial character has been emphasized too often to require further reiteration. As Piaget and Inhelder, for instance, pointed out on several occasions, these tests measure only the end product of intellectual activity, but they completely disregard the internal dynamics of mental operation. One would be ill-advised to draw definite conclusions, on the basis of test results, about the quality of the reasoning process or about the fundamental nature of intellectual maturity. Therefore, the comparison of the mental age of children, as determined by the usual type of psychometric test, with the various stages to which they belong according to a diagnostic examination such as that of Piaget, should not be expected to yield a very high correlation. Those two types of instruments explore partial, and also very different, aspects of the child's mental activity, and neither instrument can by itself form the basis for valid conclusions regarding the totality of what is conventionally called, by a term very difficult to define, the level of intellectual maturity. Briefly, it is unwarranted to make the *a priori* assumption that results formulated in terms of mental ages rather than in terms of stages of development yield more information about the maturity of a child.

There do not appear to be many studies which directly relate in detail results obtained by Piaget's clinical-experimental method and those obtained by group tests of intelligence. Yet, as Lunzer (1965) points out, there should clearly be a direct and detectable change in the performance of children on certain kinds of item according as they have or have not attained a particular Piagetian stage. Different kinds of analogy item (both verbal and numerical) were constructed by Lunzer on the hypothesis that certain types would clearly demand reasoning at the stage of formal operations to answer them successfully. The items were administered to groups of children (numbers in groups ranging from 6 to 28) and adolescents of age 9, 10, 11 etc. up to 17. In general the hypotheses were fairly well confirmed, although the numbers in each age-group were small, so that differences between proportions of children successful at different ages would not be very reliable.

Studies such as Lunzer's represent a welcome development and further research on these lines would appear to be well worth while. It would be an interesting confirmation of Piaget's hypotheses if proportion of success at certain kinds of items which theory suggested could be solved only at a certain stage of development suddenly increased by a discrete jump. This would be in contrast to other kinds of item (those not relevant to a Piagetian stage), on which success increases smoothly from year to year, and indeed from month to month. This is clearly revealed when one prepares a conversion table and age allowance for, say, a Moray House test administered to a large number of children varying in age over a range of two years or more. The smooth increase in average score, both on tests and on individual items, that is normally found when such large numbers of children are involved is to some degree at variance with the Piagetian findings in which, as Inhelder (1956) has stated, the dispersion of ability within a stage has been found to be relatively small compared with the wide differences between one stage and another. To demonstrate such a hypothesised jump convincingly would, however, require evidence of the stage each child had reached in Piagetian terms in addition to evidence from the test itself, and this would be a large undertaking. Admittedly, if different children advance from one Piagetian stage to another at different ages, the anticipated effect will be considerably blurred, and one would not expect a marked jump in average score. If relevant material is being used, however, and if the Piagetian claims are valid, some discontinuity should be detectable. The preparation of objectively presented and objectively scored tests designed to assess the 'Piagetian' stage a child has reached in a particular area should make the testing of such hypotheses considerably easier. Inhelder (1956) announced that tests of this kind were being developed by Vinh-Bang and other members of the Geneva group, but these do not appear to have been published. Similarly, Tuddenham (1966) reports the construction and use of such tests by his own associates, and Warburton (1966), in his account of the development of the new British Intelligence Test, describes the inclusion of material designed (at least in part) to facilitate assessment in Piagetian terms.

Suggested additional reading

MAIER, H. W., *Three Theories of Child Development*. New York and London: Harper and Row (1965).

INHELDER, BARBEL, 'Criteria of the stages of mental development'. In *Discussions on Child Development*, Vol. I (Eds. J. M. Tanner and B. Inhelder). London: Tavistock (1953).

STOTT, L. H., and BALL, R. S., 'Infant and pre-school mental tests: review and evaluation'. *Monogr. Soc. Res. Child Developm.*, Vol. 30, No. 3. Serial 101 (1965).

WALLACE, J. G., *Concept Growth and the Education of the Child*. Slough, Bucks., Nat. Foundation for Educ. Research in England and Wales (occasional publication No. 12) (1965).

LUNZER, E. A., 'Children's Thinking'. In *Educational Research in Britain*. (Ed. H. J. Butcher). London: Univ. of London Press (1968).

FLAVELL, J. H., *The Developmental Psychology of Jean Piaget.* Princeton, N.J.: Van Nostrand (1963).

WELFORD, A. T., *Ageing and Human Skill.* Oxford: Oxford Univ. Press (1958).

VIII

Principles of Psychological Measurement and Test Evaluation

THE POSSIBILITY OF 'MENTAL MEASUREMENT'

The first reaction of many people to the idea of 'measuring' intelligence is one of scepticism, perhaps of antipathy. The scepticism is justified, if measurement is thought of as similar to the physical measurement of length or volume, but there are *degrees* of measurement, and although many qualities, even physical ones, cannot be put against a yardstick, they may still be capable of being ordered and given a numerical value. Actual antipathy to psychological measurement may arise from many different causes. Some may think that too much emphasis is placed in our society on competition and 'meritocratic' selection and may even sympathise with Lord Melbourne's reported comment on being made a Knight of the Garter – 'at least there's no dam' merit about it'. Radicals may fear that social stratification and inequality of opportunity are being perpetuated by means of the selection procedures with which the idea of intelligence testing is often associated. We have already seen, however, that these two issues are quite distinct.

Leaving the social implications of intelligence testing for the next chapter, we shall here be concerned with what is meant by the 'measurement' or 'assessment' or 'appraisal' of intelligence. These three terms form in fact a kind of descending scale of confidence about the precision obtainable; psychometricians or specialists in test theory talk quite happily about measuring cognitive and other traits, neutralists talk of assessing them, psychologists who are most conscious of the defects in mental testing prefer to speak of appraisal. In what sense, then, is 'measurement' applicable to psychological qualities?

The common objections to any claim to be able to measure intelligence are as follows: (1) Intelligence is a broad concept, incorporating many kinds of high-level skill. How can one believe that a numerical score on a restricted and standardised set of miniature problems reasonably represents such a concept? (2) Is the quality stable enough to be assessed at one or a few sittings? The same people sometimes behave intelligently and sometimes unintelligently. And even if the trait is stable, may not the scores be affected by irrelevant circumstances? (3) Even if the first two objections can be answered, is the resulting assessment sufficiently analogous to physical measurement to justify the implied similarity when one talks of psychological measurement?

These three questions are concerned respectively with *test validity*, with *test reliability* and with *scales of measurement*. They will be dealt with in this and the next two sections, but it will be convenient to take them in reverse order.

Measurement, whether in the physical sciences or in psychology, is certainly not an all-or-nothing affair. On the one hand, such an apparently simple example as applying a yardstick to a physical object ultimately raises difficult questions. The complexities involved in obtaining a completely objective and standardised measurement even of a property such as physical length are well brought out in a passage from Bertrand Russell, quoted by Eysenck (1952), and already discussed in Chapter 1. On the other hand, intelligence quotients and similar scores are certainly not the crudest examples of 'measurement' as broadly interpreted.

Faced with the problem of classifying degrees of precision in measurement, psychologists have distinguished four main categories, which are differentiated according to the nature and properties of the kind of measuring scale involved (Stevens, 1951). Another way of describing these scales is as 'strong' or 'weak', and they will be described in ascending order of strength.

The simplest kind of measurement, which hardly deserves the title except for the sake of logical completeness, is the assignment of things or people to separate and clearly defined categories. These categories may be given in nature, such as the categories 'man' and 'woman', they may be rather more arbitrary such as 'town-dweller' and 'country-dweller', or they may be thoroughly arbitrary, as in the distinction between different schedules of income tax or between officers and other ranks. A set of categories of this kind is sometimes called a *nominal scale*.

Even this kind of crude classification permits useful analysis. In particular, it permits analysis of the degree of independence or association between two bases of classification (as by the chi-square technique). If for instance one classifies people into smokers and non-smokers, and as sufferers or non-sufferers from a particular disease, the relation can be expressed quantitatively.

With the second kind of scale, the *ordinal scale*, we enter more definitely the area of usage commonly associated with the word 'measurement'. This second kind is measurement by ranking. Wherever we can assign things or people or sensations or properties to a particular order in some one respect, we have this kind of measurement, which is still fairly crude but may be extremely useful. We may be ranking concrete objects in terms of a definable physical quality, as when we grade eggs by size, or as when we say that diamond is harder than iron and iron than tin, or we may be in the position of a teacher trying to assign an order of suitability for some kind of further education to his various pupils.

Even the hardness of metals was for a long time determined on a scale of this type, being assessed by the transitive, non-reversible effect that metal *a* was found to scratch metal *b* but not to be scratched by it, metal *b* to scratch metal *c*, and so forth. To take a more homely example, Jane may well show that she prefers Tom to Stephen and Stephen to Eric; this rank ordering in personal preference may show the same consistency as in the example of the three metals; it may also be of great importance to the people concerned.

The disadvantage of this kind of ordering measurement is that it tells us nothing about the relative distances between the objects or people ordered. One would like to know whether the difference in hardness between diamond and iron was greater than that between iron and tin or whether Jane liked Stephen very nearly as much as Tom but loathed Eric. Much, perhaps the majority, of psychological measurement cannot be confidently assigned to any higher category. A reliable rank-ordering tells us a good deal, and a variety of statistical methods have been devised to handle ordered data of this kind and to correlate the results. But where possible the aim must be to develop a stronger scale of measurement such as the two types to be described.

The *interval scale* yields measurements as commonly understood, including differences of equal size between units. An example of an interval scale is the scale of temperature on a thermometer. An increase in temperature of one degree may be taken as meaning the same thing whether it is from 90 to 91 degrees fahrenheit or from 100 degrees to 101. But there is some relativity, since different scales of temperature are possible, as in the Fahrenheit, Centigrade and Réaumur systems. It is not possible to say that 100 degrees fahrenheit is twice as hot as 50 degrees because if these temperatures were translated into one of the other systems the two to one ratio would no longer hold. This becomes ever clearer when one recalls that the boiling and freezing points of water in the Fahrenheit scale are 232 and 32 degrees, suggesting that boiling water is about seven times as hot as freezing water, whereas in the Centigrade scale the corresponding figures are 100 and 0 and the relative factor is infinite.

Despite this disadvantage one can hardly cavil at the use of the term 'measurement' for the appraisal of temperature by a thermometer. It is probable (although debatable) that many psychological measurements, including those of IQ, approximate to an interval scale. This classification of types of measurement is over-simplified and to some degree arbitrary, so that mixed or intermediate types are probably the most common in practice. Thus the assessment of intelligence from a good intelligence test properly used and correctly interpreted certainly yields something more than a mere rank order, but something less strong than a physical measure of temperature.

The disadvantage of interval scales, that ratios are not meaningful, is equivalent to saying that such scales have an arbitrary zero point. The fourth type of scale, the ratio scale, has a meaningful zero, such as absolute zero temperature. Given such an absolute zero, ratios between different points on the scale become meaningful. A ratio scale of intelligence would be very desirable, but it is unlikely that it can ever be attained. E. L. Thorndike and L. L. Thurstone have independently attempted to establish ratio scales of intelligence, using different principles and assumptions, but few psychologists would maintain that either had been entirely successful.

Some writers distinguish a fifth 'absolute scale' which is stronger than a ratio scale. 'On the absolute scale, numbers have already been ascribed to all the magnitudes. Such are the ratios themselves on the ratio scale; also, the results of counting objects, events, and the like. An important example of quantities measured on the absolute scale are probabilities. Probabilities are absolute numbers, because they are not measured in special units.' (Rapoport, 1964).

Classifying scales in this way is not only a useful reminder of the relativity of 'measurement', but is also a necessary preliminary to the selection of appropriate statistical techniques. However one cannot automatically assume that a ratio scale is always better than an interval scale, an interval scale better than an ordinal scale, and so on. Many psychological qualities can be expressed in terms of physical results, such as the number of pages of writing produced in a given time, deflection of a galvanometer (in measurement of the galvanic skin response), time taken to perform a particular task, and so on. Such results provide objective measurements on a ratio scale, but it may be misleading to treat them as ratio measurements of the psychological variable.

An analogy with athletic performance will make this point clearer. The time taken to run a mile is an example of objective measurement on a ratio scale, but it may not be, in fact almost certainly is not, a ratio scale of the athletic ability required. One can hardly say that a man running a mile in four minutes displays twice as much ability as one who takes eight minutes. It would be more realistic to guess that he shows twenty or a hundred times greater ability. In assessing athletic ability, we implicitly make comparisons with a norm.

The same point applies even more strongly to mental measurement. By all means let us improve our measuring scales, progressing from 'weak' to 'strong' instruments. Any improvement in this respect is greatly to be welcomed, and makes for more accurate comparisons between groups. But it looks as if comparisons of intelligence will always remain relative rather than absolute, and be related to a given population and to the kinds of test used.

TEST RELIABILITY

This is a topic of which excellent and detailed accounts are readily available (e.g. Cronbach, 1960; Guilford, 1965). The present summary will therefore be condensed but will briefly mention some new suggestions and developments.

'Reliability' refers to at least two distinct features of measurement. The usage is not ideal, and Cronbach (1960) has urged that the two aspects should be given separate names, suggesting 'consistency' and 'stability'. The former would refer to the internal consistency or homogeneity of the test, the extent to which the parts or items are similar and inter-correlate; the latter would describe the stability of the test over time, that is the extent to which similar results are produced in successive administrations. Unfortunately the present usage, in which reliability refers to both aspects, is firmly established, so that to be quite clear one has to specify 'internal-consistency reliability' or 'test-retest reliability'. The justification for grouping these two aspects under a common name lies in the fundamental assumption behind reliability theory that a person's score is made up of two parts, a true score and an error component. According to this model the internal consistency of a test will gradually increase as the test is lengthened (other things being equal) because random errors will gradually cancel out, and the true score component will become predominant. Similarly, if a test is administered several times to the same group of people (other things being equal again), random errors peculiar to particular occasions will neutralise each other, and the true score component will predominate. The assumptions and consequences of this kind of approach to test reliability have been analysed in great detail by Gulliksen (1950).

In practice, a test that has high internal consistency will usually tend also to have high test-retest reliability and vice versa, but this is not a logical necessity. A test composed of heterogeneous items (such as a well-constructed questionnaire covering many different topics) may produce stable results from one administration to another. The reverse case, in which a highly homogeneous test possesses low test-retest reliability, is less common but is sometimes found.

(a) *Determining internal-consistency reliability.* The most familiar method is known as the 'split-half'. One divides the test into two halves containing approximately equal numbers of items, scores each half-test separately for each person, and correlates the two sets of scores. The reliability of a test can be thought of as its correlation with itself or with a parallel test of equal length. Using the split-half technique, we are correlating two sub-tests each only half as long as the original test. Since, as we have seen, lengthening a test increases its reliability, the resulting correlation coefficient will underestimate the test's reliability, and will require an upward adjustment or 'boosting'. This adjustment is made by the Spearman-Brown correction (Guilford, 1965, p. 457). The corrected correlation is the coefficient of reliability.

Although this is the procedure most commonly used, it has some disadvantages. In particular, the value of the reliability coefficient will vary according to how one splits the test. It will generally not be satisfactory to divide the whole test into a first half and second half, using the order in which the items were answered, because of practice effects, fatigue effects and so on. It is better (though more laborious) to form two halves of odd-numbered and even-numbered items respectively. Even this method remains rather arbitrary since other divisions might have produced different values.

This arbitrariness is avoided if one uses what is known as the Kuder-Richardson method. A formula, or rather a family of formulas (incorporating slightly different assumptions) is available (Guilford, 1965, p. 458), which in effect give the average coefficient that would be obtained if the test were split in every possible way. The Kuder-Richardson formulas are quite straightforward to apply, but are applicable only when each item is scored dichotomously, e.g. right or wrong. This is no great disadvantage in the case of ability and intelligence tests, which are almost universally scored in this way, and in any case the same method may be generalised to items which involve more complicated scoring (Cronbach, 1951). Results equivalent to those provided by the Kuder-Richardson technique can be obtained by the employment of analysis of variance (Burt, 1966.)

Sometimes 'parallel' forms of a test are available. What constitutes 'parallelism' merits further analysis (Cronbach, Rajaratnam and Gleser, 1963; Lord, 1964), but if we accept the two forms as equivalent and administer them at one session, we have in effect one test of double length. We can correlate scores on the two tests (without needing to apply any correction) and obtain what is in principle similar to the split-half reliability coefficient but is known as the coefficient of equivalence.

(b) *Determining test-retest reliability.* Little needs to be said under this heading, since the purpose and the procedure are both straightforward. The aim is to discover whether a test will discriminate between people in the same way on successive occasions, or, in other words, whether the results obtained by testing a particular group of people are stable over a period of time. The usual method is to administer the same test to the same people twice, and to correlate the two sets of scores.

Attention needs to be given to the length of time between the two testing sessions. If this is too short, the subjects will remember the items, their own thought processes and perhaps their answers. The second testing will not be serving its intended purpose of repeating the original test situation, and one might expect the resulting reliability coefficient to be artificially high. If, on the other hand, the interval is too long, the capacity or ability that is being assessed may change, with the result that the reliability of the test may be under-estimated. Fortunately this latter danger is relatively unimportant in intelligence testing, where the trait is fairly stable, but it can be a serious problem in other kinds of psychological testing. In intelligence testing, an interval of three or four weeks between administrations should usually be long enough.

If parallel forms of the test are available, the second administration will be with an alternative form. The coefficient then obtained is sometimes called the coefficient of equivalence and stability, and may be expected to be rather lower than those previously mentioned, since it will incorporate error variance both from change during time and from difference between the two forms.

The four main kinds of reliability can therefore be summarised in a fourfold table, as in Figure 8.1 opposite.

FIGURE 8.1 *Main kinds of reliability*

	Single test, A	Parallel forms, A and B
One administration only	Coefficient of homogeneity or consistency measured by 'boosted' split-half correlation or Kuder–Richardson method.	Coefficient of equivalence measured by AB
Two administrations 1 and 2	Coefficient of equivalence measured by A_1A_2	Coefficient of equivalence and stability measured by AB (but with longer interval)

(*c*) *The interpretation of reliability coefficients.* The most important point to bear in mind when reading research reports or test handbooks is that reliability, of whatever kind, is a relative concept. A test in itself has no single reliability, whether this refers to internal consistency or to stability. Its reliability is a function not only of the constituent items, but of the people answering it and of the circumstances in which it is administered. We have already seen, too, that reliability is a function of test length. If one test is twice as long as another, one will expect it to be more reliable – not twice as reliable, but the expected increase can be calculated by the Spearman-Brown formula. A new short test, therefore, may have a relatively low reliability, but may be quite promising if it can be lengthened by the addition of similar material.

It is crucial in evaluating any test's reported reliability to consider the sample of people on which it was based, since the size of any correlation coefficient is affected by the range of variation in the sample. If this variation is restricted (in either or both of the variables being correlated) the size of the correlation will be reduced. If the reliability of an intelligence test has been based on a sample of people covering the whole range of intelligence in Britain, this will tend to be higher than one that has been obtained from a sample of university students. If, however, one knows the ratio between the two ranges of variation (e.g. if one knows the standard deviation of scores to be expected in both the restricted sample and in the whole population), it is possible to apply a correction and to estimate the expected reliability in the population from the obtained reliability in the restricted sample or vice versa (Guilford, 1965, p. 343).

Many other kinds of coefficient can be usefully distinguished (Cattell,

1963d; Cattell and Butcher, 1968). The most important point is that no test has one single reliability, and that a reported coefficient may mean very little unless the circumstances in which it was obtained are fully described. Moreover reliability, although an important property of a test, is in some respects only a means to an end. The second main technical requirement, test validity, is of more far-reaching importance.

TEST VALIDITY

Whereas reliability may be compared to the precision of an instrument validity is a measure of the extent to which that instrument is fulfilling its purpose. One might construct a test which was intended to be a test of intelligence, and which yielded a high reliability coefficient, but it might subsequently appear that the test was assessing some limited knack, and was of little use in predicting any other kind of performance. The test would then have low validity *as an intelligence test*.

Everything said in the last section about reliability being a relative concept applies even more to validity. Test validity will be dependent on most or all of the factors affecting reliability and is also relative in a further sense, in that it depends on the purpose or purposes for which the test was constructed and for which it is used. The most important point about test validity (even more than with reliability) is that one would do much better to talk about 'test validities', since almost any useful test will be usable for more than one purpose, and there will commonly be no single criterion by which its general usefulness can be measured.

Establishing the validities of a test is therefore no easy matter. The more useful the test in predicting successfully a wide range of behaviour, the more difficult it will be to assign a single estimate of validity. If a test is designed to fulfil a limited purpose, such as predicting success at typewriting, it will be easy to validate; but a test of intelligence, which we have already seen to be a multi-faceted concept, cannot be satis-factorily validated against one simple criterion. Several kinds of validity are clearly required. One widely accepted classification is that suggested by a committee of the American Psychological Association (1954). This will serve as a starting-point for our discussion.

Before discussing the four kinds of test validity distinguished in the APA report, there is one kind of pseudo-validity to be briefly mentioned. This is *face validity* and refers not to a test *being* valid for any par-ticular purpose but to its *seeming* so, particularly to the person taking it. In the general context of test theory, this is not important and often not desirable, as in many situations disguised tests are more effective than overt ones, nor does it bear much relation to validity proper, since one test may appear more valid than another but prove less so. But there is some place for 'face validity' in the testing of intelligence and abilities, principally to ensure an adequate level of motivation among the respondents. If one knows, from the situation or from having been told so, that one is taking a test of ability, one may legitimately expect it to seem like one. If the questions appear stupid or ambiguous or suggest faulty construction, the likely and reasonable response is to shrug one's shoulders and economise one's efforts.

The four main kinds of validity described in the APA report are *content validity*, *concurrent validity*, *predictive validity* and *construct* validity.

Content validity is more directly applicable to examinations and to tests of attainment than to psychological tests, and is a measure of the extent to which the test or examination has adequately sampled the curriculum or the subject-matter concerned. It could very possibly be expressed as a quantitative index, but this is rarely, if ever, attempted.

Concurrent validity and predictive validity have much wider applications, and are generally expressed in the form of correlation coefficients. Both imply the comparison of scores on the test with performance or score on some definite criterion, or with the judgment of an experienced observer. The only difference is that, as the names imply, concurrent validity refers to simultaneous comparison (or comparison of scores registered within a brief period), whereas predictive validity refers to the capacity of a test to predict future behaviour, possibly after an interval of years. Obviously, within each of these categories, very many 'validity coefficients' will be possible according to the criteria selected.

Construct validity is a measure of the extent to which a test actually represents the intended construct, such as intelligence. It is the most important kind and the most difficult to establish; the most important because it is, at least in principle, free from the arbitrariness that applies to the other types, and because it is closest in conception to the intuitive idea of validity as the degree to which the test fulfils its purpose. It is just this that makes construct validity difficult to establish. The detailed discussion in chapter 1 of operational and open-ended definitions of intelligence is relevant. One can chart a kind of spectrum of possible views, from those on the one hand that define intelligence as score on a particular test or measure or combination of measures; in this case validation is no problem and is assumed in the definition. At the other extreme, a very 'open-ended' view of intelligence will insist that no test can be satisfactorily validated against a single criterion or even a few criteria; it will be much more satisfactory if the test predicts a wide range of performances to a moderate extent than one or two almost perfectly. All intermediate gradations are possible.

In general the notion of construct validity implies an 'open-ended' view. Construct validity is a kind of second-order concept in which the evidence, for instance, of concurrent and predictive validities may be taken into account. A quantitative measure of construct validity again is not easy to obtain, except by factor analysis. This is an important exception, however, since if one makes the required assumptions, factor analysis provides the only kind of validation that is not tied to a particular arbitrary criterion. The limitations and indeterminacies involved in factor analysis, particularly in the sampling of variables and the criteria of rotation, have been described in the latter part of Chapter 2, but in spite of these it remains in principle the most powerful if not the only method of determining how far a supposed measure of some psychological trait is representative of the whole domain of relevant behaviour.

The validation of intelligence tests, like the definition of intelligence, therefore takes us straight into difficult and disputable issues in the philosophy of science. But in practice test constructors, with the confidence of practitioners in a well-charted area, are generally content with specific criteria, such as correlation with a well-established test or adequate prediction of scholastic attainment. These criteria are satisfactory for most purposes, but it is well to bear in mind their rather limited and circular nature from a theoretical point of view.

GENERAL PRINCIPLES OF TEST CONSTRUCTION

Anyone requiring a primer of test construction will have to read some of the fuller descriptions such as those of Lindquist (1951) and Anstey (1966) or at least the useful shorter account by Wood (1961). The most that can be attempted here is a sketch of the main principles. The kinds of test referred to will usually be paper-and-pencil tests for group administration, since the construction of individual tests raises differen problems, which will be considered in Chapter 9.

The first step in constructing any psychological test (including an examination paper) should be to define clearly its purpose and scope. This sounds obvious enough, but the purpose and functions of tests may be more various than is usually realised. Tests of ability or of educational attainment may be designed primarily to put students or pupils into an order which reflects their *present* level. On the other hand, the aim may be to predict *future* potentialities or suitability for a particular kind of education. Tests constructed with one or other of these aims are perhaps the most familiar, but other objectives are possible. There may be a greater need for diagnosis and for information about particular strengths and weaknesses than for general classification and prediction.

The constructor should define the kinds of item he intends to use, first of all broadly and then more specifically, and consider particular items as being sampled from a large or infinite population of items of the same kind. He may have decided to make a 'verbal reasoning' rather than a non-verbal kind of intelligence test, and may then decide to include four kinds of item, known from previous research to have good validities, such as 'series', 'analogies', 'codes', 'absurdities'. It will be useful to consider what kind of selection the verbal analogies he uses for his items form from the imagined population of all possible verbal analogies. It is of course unlikely that they will form anything like a random or a 'representative' sample, nor is it necessary that they should. But the idea of sampling provides a useful frame of reference for the constructor, in that it brings home to him more clearly what he is or should be doing.

Besides thinking about the kind of material he wants to use, the test constructor must decide what kind of people the test is designed for. In practice the two aspects will often be considered together. In the case of people, the idea of defining a population and sampling from it has a more direct and obvious application than to test items. One might think a 'general-purpose' test of intelligence could be constructed for group administration which would place everyone on one scale in one operation. This is a matter of degree. If one makes up a test to cover a wide range of ability or attainment, it will discriminate less effectively at a particular level of ability than a test which has a limited range. Clearly too, a test which is good at discriminating fine degrees of difference between university graduates will not reveal many differences among ESN children, and *vice versa*.

It is therefore advisable to define the population for whom a test is intended in terms of both level and range of ability. This becomes important when the test reaches the 'try-out' stage, in which it is administered experimentally before reaching its final form, since it is desirable that the samples of people used for the 'try-out' should be as typical as possible of the population for whom the test is eventually intended.

When these preliminary decisions have been taken, the actual construction of a test falls roughly into two parts. The first stage contains the more 'creative' part of the work, the actual thinking up of the items and the expression of the ideas in words or diagrams or material. Some knowledge is needed of the kind of items that have previously proved most successful, but a flair and interest in the work are at least as important as any other factors in this stage of construction. Perhaps a test is needed to select good test constructors!

The second stage involves statistical techniques. The general aim is to assess the items one has provisionally put together, to see how well they are doing their work, and to retain the best possible set. These procedures are referred to collectively as 'item analysis'. Methods of item analysis differ principally in being very laborious or merely laborious.

The test constructor has to tread a careful path between two pitfalls. The first danger is the belief that intelligent inspection of an item is sufficient in itself to establish whether it will work effectively or not. The experienced constructor of chess problems knows that he may spend dozens of hours making a problem with a difficult and elegant solution, yet miss an unwanted but justifiable alternative. Much the same applies to the construction of test items. The opposite danger is to suppose that the blind application of statistical analysis will solve all one's problems and that once an item has been 'passed' by the approved procedures it needs no further consideration.

Items must be constructed before they can be analysed, and the statistical analysis can do no more than show which are the better and which the weaker. Item analysis cannot *improve* items, and often the best that can be done is to pick the least bad from a bad bunch. It is therefore important to exercise skill, flair, hunch and expertise *before* the stage of item analysis as well as during and after it. Since the aim is to sort out the sheep from the goats it is necessary to make up a larger number in the first place than one expects to need in the finished test. It is common practice in making a test of a well-established type to make twice as many items as will be needed, since this has the advantage of providing two roughly parallel forms for the try-out. But in the construction of a highly experimental test, it may be advisable to make up far more than twice as many.

The results of an item analysis are based on a particular sample of people, and all statistics derived from the analysis will therefore be subject to sampling error. This would be random error in the unlikely case where the test was tried out on a random sample of the population for whom it was designed, but in practice there will be unknown biasing factors. Statistics for single items are particularly prone to this kind of error. When all these cautions have been urged, the fact remains that item analysis is a desirable, if not an essential, stage in any attempt to produce a good test.

METHODS OF ITEM ANALYSIS

The two measures of efficiency obtained for each test item from a typical analysis are (1) an index of difficulty (or of its opposite, facility) and (2) an index of power to discriminate.

The difficulty of an item is, superficially and for practical purposes, a simple enough concept if expressed in terms of a particular group of people. Only if one aspires to establish any sort of absolute measure of difficulty do real problems arise.

It is doubtful in fact whether an absolute level of difficulty is even meaningful. The work of Heim (1955, 1957) has theoretical implications that are relevant here. She showed that adaptation to level of difficulty constantly takes place and that a group of people who have just taken a difficult test will do better on a second test of moderate difficulty than if they have started by taking an easy one. This will presumably only apply within a certain zone of difficulty. If the pre-test were too difficult, it might well fail to have this effect of causing beneficial adaptation. Nor does this finding invalidate the ordering of people on a scale, except in so far as their adaptation in this respect may vary. These are points that would be well worth further investigation.

In practice these effects are probably not large; we are concerned only with relative difficulty and can express it as the percentage of people failing to obtain a correct answer. For many purposes we can group together those who selected a wrong alternative, those who were pressed for time and did not reach the item, and those who reached the item but did not attempt it. Often it is more convenient to operate with an index of 'facility' than of 'difficulty', i.e. with the percentage of people who *did* obtain the correct answer to an item.

If we want our test to be equally effective throughout its range, the average difficulty should be about 50%. If, however, it is important to discriminate mainly towards the top end, we shall aim at greater average difficulty. If the most important discrimination we have to make is between the top 10% and the remaining 90%, then our average item facility should be around 10%, but this would be uncommon in practice. More often the aim is to have good discrimination over the whole range.

The second measure of item efficiency, the index of discrimination, raises much more complicated problems. If the whole test is designed to assess reasoning power, each item should be doing the same thing to some degree. How is this degree to be estimated? What we want is some measure of correspondence between each item and the test as a whole.

Sometimes it may seem preferable to use as criterion not total score on the test but some outside measure. Whether one chooses an internal or external criterion (or a combination of the two) will mainly depend on the nature of the test and is also related to the questions of reliability and validity already discussed. The use of an internal criterion will, broadly speaking, ensure item reliability, the use of an external one will ensure item validity in terms of the particular external criterion.

If one is working in a field with which one is familiar, if the material is of a well-tried kind, and if the test is designed to measure a single trait or psychological factor, the internal criterion is fairly satisfactory. It will still be necessary, of course, to obtain evidence about the external validity of the whole test. These conditions are usually satisfied in the construction of intelligence tests.

Two useful articles on item analysis, and in particular about the various measures of discrimination available and their respective advantages and disadvantages, are those of Vernon (1948) and of Anstey (1948) in the same volume of the British Journal of Psychology (Statistical Section). Vernon's paper is the more general, offering a survey of all the methods available, whereas Anstey's goes into more detail about one class of methods. A more recent and easily available survey is that of Helmstadter (1966, Ch. 7).

The main distinction made by Vernon is between 'grouping' methods and 'distribution' methods. In the former methods the people taking the test are divided into two or more groups according to score on the criterion (whether internal or external). Thus, if one is using the internal criterion of score on the whole test, people might be divided into top, middle and bottom groups containing equal numbers. Each item is then examined in turn, and the performance of the three groups compared. If it is a satisfactory item and discriminating well, one will expect a steady decline in the number of people obtaining the correct answer from the top down to the bottom group. One can plot this trend as a graph, and the slope of the line will indicate the sharpness of discrimination achieved by the item. This slope may vary, being for instance steep between top and middle groups and gentle between middle and bottom ones, and it is therefore possible to see not only the overall discriminative power of the item but its effectiveness in discriminating at various levels of ability.

The 'distribution' methods omit the preliminary grouping of people by total score. In these methods each item is considered in turn, and people are sorted either into two categories, those passing and those failing the item, or preferably into five categories (in the case of a multiple-choice item with five possible answers) according to which answer they gave. The average score on the whole test is then computed for each of the two (or five) categories. Anstey's (1948) paper gives a detailed description of the fuller procedure, in which a separate category is made for each of the multiple-choice responses. This method, which he calls the '*d*-method', has the advantage that the effectiveness of the wrong answers or 'distractors' can be accurately assessed. If, for instance, the average score on the whole test is higher for those people who gave a particular wrong answer than for those who gave the intended right one, this suggests that there were good reasons, to some extent overlooked by the test constructor, for choosing that 'wrong' alternative, and that the item is in need of amendment. This is a powerful aspect of the technique, especially as it does not depend on a crude all-or-nothing indication. It will be a danger sign if the average score on the whole test of those giving a particular 'wrong' answer approaches that obtained by those giving the intended right one. There is much scope for imaginative interpretation of statistics of this kind, and this is a practical illustration of the general precept already stated that statistical methods of item analysis are no substitute for intelligent inspection *after* as well as before early drafts of the test have been tried out. Anstey's paper and his (1966) book give copious illustrations of how items may be improved by these means.

What are the respective merits and disadvantages of these two kinds of item analysis? The 'grouping' methods are certainly less laborious and much less time-consuming. In experiments reported by Vernon the full *d*-method was found to take about twice as many man-hours as one of the grouping methods. In addition, if both internal and external criteria are to be used, as we have already seen to be often desirable, the amount of time required for the grouping methods is increased by only a small factor, but for the distribution methods it is doubled. Another advantage of the grouping methods, though a more doubtful one, is that it is easier to apply a correction for guessing. On the other hand, the distribution methods make fuller use of the information available, and are therefore likely to produce more reliable indices of discrimination. Where the number of subjects available for the try-out of a test is necessarily small, this is an important advantage.

It is not always realised that the most obviously attractive feature of the *d*-method, that is the possibility of analysing each alternative response separately and thus of evaluating the effectiveness of the wrong answers or 'distractors', can be incorporated into the grouping methods, which are in other ways more convenient. When the results of tabulating by the grouping method are plotted, it will be remembered, the simplest kind of graph shows the respective numbers of correct answers in the three (or six, etc.) criterion groups. Fuller information can be obtained by making similar plots for each of the wrong answers. Whereas one hopes for a steepish declining trend in the plot of correct answers, one will hope for a level or reverse trend in the case of wrong ones. This fuller version of a grouping method is probably the best for most purposes, and is regularly employed in the construction, for instance, of Moray House verbal reasoning and attainment tests.

Suggested additional reading

WOOD, DOROTHY A., *Test Construction*. Columbus, Ohio: Merrill (1961).

CRONBACH, L. J., *Essentials of Psychological Testing*. 2nd edn. New York: Harper (1960). Chs. 2–6.

ANSTEY, E., *Psychological Tests*. London: Nelson (1966).

GUILFORD, J. P., *Fundamental Statistics in Education and Psychology*. 4th edn. New York: McGraw Hill (1965). Chs. 17 and 18.

LINDQUIST, E. F. (Ed.), *Educational Measurement*. Washington, D.C.: American Council on Education (1951).

VERNON, P. E., 'Indices of item consistency and validity'. *Brit. J. Psychol.* (statist. sect.) (1948).

CATTELL, R. B., 'Validity and reliability: a proposed more basic set of concepts'. *J. educ. Psychol.*, 55, 1–22 (1963).

IX

A Selective Survey of Intelligence Tests

THE CLASSIFICATION OF TESTS OF INTELLIGENCE AND ABILITIES

Tests of intelligence and ability can be classified in many ways. One may divide them, for instance, into (a) those that are administered to groups and those which have to be given to one individual at a time, (b) 'pencil-and-paper' tests and performance tests (the former being further divisible into verbal and non-verbal), (c) tests for children and tests for adults, with finer distinctions of age also possible, (d) wide-range tests and tests suitable for specialised groups, such as people of particularly high ability, (e) tests that give a single measure of general intelligence and those that yield measures of particular abilities.

The most radical of these differences is perhaps that between individual and group tests, at least as regards the theories and purposes of their users. Individual tests, such as the successive versions of the Binet and the Wechsler, are time-consuming, demand training and skill on the part of the tester, and involve a certain amount of apparatus; they are in fact batteries of tests rather than single instruments, sample a range of ability and attainment, and in theory provide a more complete and rounded picture of the subject's ability than can be obtained from any group test. Individual tests, therefore, have been more widely used for clinical diagnosis than for classification and selection. In the past also, they have been most commonly used as measures of children's mental development and have been interpreted in terms of 'mental age' and of intelligence quotient based on the well-known formula

$$IQ = 100 \times \frac{\text{mental age}}{\text{chronological age}}$$

The calculation of quotients by this method has given rise to great difficulty (Pinneau, 1961), particularly that of achieving an equal spread or dispersion of quotients at different ages (and is also clearly inapplicable to adults). Terman and Merrill, therefore, incorporated in their latest (1960) revision of the Stanford-Binet the principle of 'deviation' IQs. The 'classical' IQ originated in the work of Stern and Terman, and has always been closely associated with results obtained on the Binet tests. Now that these have been rivalled or supplemented by the Wechsler tests (which provide deviation IQs), and now that deviation IQs are also available on the latest version of the Binet, it is unlikely that quotients as originally calculated will be used much in the future. Deviation IQs, of course, are really a misnomer, and not quotients at all but scores scaled to give a particular mean and deviation, generally a mean of 100 and a standard deviation of 15. The usual method of scaling also ensures a normal distribution of deviation quotients at each age.

We shall give most space to the two main sets of individual tests, the Binet and the Wechsler, which merit a fairly full account for several reasons. The first reason is historical, that Binet's early work is interesting in its own right, and not always fully appreciated by modern writers. Secondly, at least in theory, individual tests fulfil the main purposes of group tests and other purposes as well. They have been shown to be capable of predicting scholastic achievement fairly adequately, and most of their users feel that they yield an overall picture of a person's cognitive development that is more informative than any provided by group tests. To some extent they aid clinical insight into, for instance, causes and circumstances of backwardness and retardation in children. Perhaps their biggest drawback (apart from the time needed to administer them and the skill and training involved in giving them) has been their excessive reliance on verbal factors. With the development of the Wechsler tests, which include sets both of 'performance' and of 'verbal' tests and yield a 'performance' and a 'verbal' as well as a total IQ, this criticism has less force. Finally, the sheer multiplicity of existing group tests makes it virtually impossible in part of a chapter to do more than outline the characteristics of a few that appear particularly interesting or valuable.

THE BINET SCALES AND THEIR LATER DEVELOPMENTS

To many students of psychology and education Alfred Binet (1857–1911) is familiar only as the author of an intelligence test that, in its later versions, has become the best known of all. He was however a highly talented and inquisitive general psychologist and a prolific writer on diverse psychological topics. Goddard (1916) had to persuade his readers that Binet's Measuring Scale of Intelligence was his magnum opus, since in those days many supposed it to be a mere incidental chapter in his work. Today the boot is on the other foot and it is necessary to stress that Binet was far from being only a test constructor. A survey of his contributions to psychology was made by Varon (1935) and a recent ably written chapter by Reeves (1965) summarises the development and change in his approach to thinking from an almost entirely mechanical associationism to a view whereby thinking appeared 'in some degree the activity of a whole personality, in which action, feeling and unconscious mental attitudes play a vital (though not an exclusive) role'. Reeves also includes interesting accounts of some of Binet's work that is untranslated or not easily accessible, including his pioneering investigations of the psychology of chess masters and the reasoning and imaging processes involved in simultaneous blindfold displays; also of the methods of work of a number of well-known writers including Alphonse Daudet, Sardou, Edmond de Goncourt and the younger Dumas; and of certain celebrated arithmetical prodigies, including a convincing demonstration that their results were obtained by very different methods.

In 1904, the French Minister of Public Instruction formed a committee (at Binet's suggestion, and including him as a member), whose task was to study how mentally defective and severely retarded children could best be taught. Among its recommendations was that no child should be removed from an ordinary to a special school without first undergoing both a medical and a psychological examination to determine his ability to profit from instruction in the ordinary school.

This recommendation was the starting point for the development by Binet and Simon first of a set of tests, published in 1905 and, three years later, of the first Binet-Simon intelligence scale, designed for children aged between three and 12. The 1905 tests were extensively tried out and graded for difficulty, but had not yet been formed into an age-scale. They included diverse kinds of clinical observations and reasoning problems. The first, for instance, 'le regard', was designed to discover if head and eyes were properly co-ordinated for vision, and consisted of the examiner moving a lighted match slowly across the subject's field of view. In the last, 'without preliminaries, one asks of the subject, "What difference is there between esteem and affection? What difference is there between weariness and sadness?" Often the subject does not reply. He sometimes gives an absurd or nonsensical answer.'

Between 1905 and 1908 Binet and Simon made the first systematic study of *norms* in the development of children's intelligence, having been unable, in a search of the literature, to find anything of this kind except a few scattered anecdotes and useful pointers. They now found after systematic research that normal three-year-olds could point to their eyes, nose and mouth, and also name parts of the body and many familiar objects in a picture, but could not repeat a sequence of three figures. The normal five-year-old, in contrast, could repeat three figures; he could also compare two lines, compare two weights (after being shown how) and so on.

Binet and Simon's (1908) paper begins with the kind of defence of mental measurement and rejection of armchair criticism that has had to be repeated many times since.

'Some psychologists affirm that intelligence can be measured; others declare that it is impossible to measure intelligence. But there are still others, better informed, who ignore these theoretical discussions and apply themselves to the actual solving of the problem', and 'We have sometimes been accused of being opposed with blind infatuation to all theory and to the *a priori* method. . . . What we strongly reject, are theoretical discussions which are intended to take the place of an exploration of facts.'

It then describes the incorporation of their new knowledge of average development at a particular age into a standardised age-scale, so that in thirty minutes' testing time a more scientific estimate than had previously been possible could be made of the level of intellectual development reached by a particular child relative to the average of his age-group. The practical importance of what may seem in 1968 a fairly obvious enquiry, but which was then unprecedented, is shown by Binet and Simon's study of 25 children confined in institutions. Five of these were of average intelligence or above, but, of these five, four had been classified as feeble-minded, and one as 'enfant idiot'.

Most of the features that have become well-known in subsequent modifications and revisions of the Binet test are already evident in these early accounts. Binet and Simon were concerned to sample broadly the intellectual performances of which typical children at particular ages would be capable, including as little as possible that was distinctively scholastic, but taking equal pains to retain a broad conception of intellectual progress and, above all, to tie down the items to what children actually were found able to perform as distinct from any purely theoretical ideas of what they ought to be able to. They also developed the idea of tabulating statistically the degree of overlap between different ages, and the possibility of assessing degree of retardation or advancement in terms of what came to be known as mental age.

Binet and Simon produced a revision of their scale in 1911, shortly before Binet's premature death, and it was rapidly taken up in other countries, translated into many languages, and modified and further revised. The revision which became accepted as the most useful one, and as the standard individual general-purpose test of intelligence, was Terman's 1916 Standard version, which was superseded only after 21 years by his 1937 Terman-Merrill revision.

In the 1916 version, the concepts of mental age and intelligence quotient, implicit in the Binet-Simon scales, were more fully worked out. The 'classical' quotient, first suggested by Stern, and based on the ratio of mental age to chronological age, had its heyday in the twenties and thirties, depending very much on the success of the revised Binet scales. It is now obsolescent, however, for reasons that have already been mentioned briefly in the first section of this chapter.

The 1937 Terman-Merrill revision is the one with which most psychologists are familiar, and which essentially is the one still in use today, since the latest (1960) version introduced comparatively slight changes. It consisted of two forms, L and M, L being the more commonly used one, with M often reserved for a second testing.

The development of these two forms required many years of patient work by Terman and his associates. The basic criterion for the inclusion of items, many of which were new, was that they should show a steadily increasing proportion of success with increasing age, but an internal criterion was also used, i.e. it was ensured that each item should show a reasonable degree of correlation with total score on the two forms. Careful efforts were also made to see that the test should not yield systematically higher scores for either boys or girls. Considerable attention was paid to sampling of the whole white American population in the standardisation, but the coverage was not entirely satisfactory (Anastasi, 1961, p. 194). The sample was above average in socio-economic level and included too many urban children. In general the 1937 version of the Stanford-Binet seems to have represented a considerable improvement over all earlier batteries of this kind. As compared with the 1916 version, it provided better measurement at extremes of age and ability, rather more objective instructions for scoring, and had the advantage of providing parallel forms.

The factorial structure of the battery was examined in considerable detail by McNemar (1942, Ch. 9). The general aim had been that the whole scale should tend to measure one massive common factor, on the grounds that the presence of large group factors would make the scores of individuals less comparable, since a given score might then represent several possible combinations of ability. This was apparently fairly well achieved. McNemar considers two main questions, overlapping but distinct. Does the battery of tests appropriate to any one age adequately combine to assess one common factor ? Secondly, if this is found to be satisfactorily achieved, to what extent is the common factor measured at one age similar to that at another ? McNemar was fairly satisfied with what he found, with a few reservations. An overall view of these extensive analyses is given in Table 9.1 opposite.

In interpreting Table 9.1, one can obtain an answer to the first question, about extent of a common factor at a particular age, by look-ing down the columns, each of which represents a separate analysis. The second question can be partially answered by looking across the rows. Any row (representing a particular test) will contain a number of loadings on the general factor obtained from different analyses. To the extent that they are reasonably constant along a row, we have some evidence that the test was probably assessing a similar function at different ages and had a fairly constant degree of importance in the battery. If, over the whole table, the figures vary relatively little along the rows, there is a presumption that the general factor at one age is interpretable in much the same psychological terms as at another. Some trends are detectable, however, in the relatively increasing or decreasing loadings of particular tests with change in age. There is some sign of the increasing importance of verbal tests with increasing age, paralleling findings already mentioned in Chapters 2 and 7.

The third and latest revision of the Stanford-Binet was published in 1960. This consists mainly of selected and particularly satisfactory items from the 1937 forms L and M, brought up to date (many were looking and sounding decidedly old-fashioned) and compressed into one form. Rather more of these came from the L form, which was in fact always more popular with test users than form M. Another way in which the battery was adapted to present-day needs was in re-ordering items, which for various reasons had changed in relative difficulty during the intervening 23 years. Yet another change was the provision of deviation IQs, as already described, based upon a mean of 100 and standard deviation of 16 at each age level. No complete restandardisation on the scale of the 1937 one was undertaken, with the result that norms are to some extent still based on the 1937 sampling, although readjusted in the light of more recent information.

Himelstein (1966) has reviewed research carried out with this latest revision, summarising some 30 studies. In general, it appears to have had a favourable reception, and the selection of items seems satisfactory. One or two defects suggested in recent studies are (a) a still hardly adequate 'ceiling' for gifted adolescents, although the new version

TABLE 9.1 *The Stanford-Binet (1937) and the general factor**

First Factor Loadings (Averages) for Overlapping and Recurring Tests and for Recurring Test Situations

Experimental age	2	2½	3	3½	4	4½	5	6	7	9	11	13	15	18
Obey. simple commands	·61	·59	·58	·78										
Picture vocabulary	·76	·76	·77	·69	·68	·66								·56
Identify obj. by use	·73	·66	·53	·69			·67							
Repeating digits	·69	·70	·70		·57	·64		·50	·56	·45	·48			
String. beads	·66	·44	·48	·24	·40									
Patience: pictures			·65	·54	·56	·55								
Response to pictures			·75	·66			·52				·68	·58		
Comprehension			·63	·72	·78	·71	·63	·51	·70	·67				
Discrim. animal pict.			·60	·67	·50	·44		·61						
Picture completion: man				·54	·50	·63	·43							
Opposite analogies				·70	·77	·80	·62	·63	·67	·44			·66	·61
Memory for sentences				·66	·67	·57	·57	·72	·62	·49	·58	·52	·70	·37
Pictorial like. and diff.					·47	·58	·61	·73						
Repeat. digits reversed								·72	·70		·52	·41	·57	·59
Vocabulary								·59	·65	·74	·84	·85	·85	·91
Picture absurdities								·51	·58	·39	·52	·69	·61	
Verbal absurdities									·76	·73	·73	·70		
Memory for stories										·54	·73	·40		
Abstract words											·82	·83	·84	
Minkus completion										·60	·62	·50	·73	·64

* From Q. McNemar (1942).

includes tables up to age 18, in place of age 16 in the 1937 version; (b) the appearance of abstract verbal items at too low a level in the test, and of rote memory items at too high a level; (c) significant differences in score resulting from differences among testers, with women testers tending to give higher scores (Cieutat, 1965). Himelstein comments, too, on the lack of systematic research on the validity of the new version, excepting only a series of studies by Kennedy and his associates (e.g. Tiber and Kennedy, 1964).

THE WECHSLER INTELLIGENCE SCALES (general)

The first intelligence test published by David Wechsler (in 1939) was known as the Wechsler-Bellevue, after the large New York hospital at which he was working. This was designed primarily as a test for adults, though it could also be used with older children. More recently he has produced the Wechsler Intelligence Scale for Children (WISC), in 1949, and the Wechsler Adult Intelligence Scale (WAIS), in 1955. These two latter tests have between them largely superseded the original Wechsler-Bellevue.

Wechsler has given a detailed account of his views on intelligence and of the rationale of his tests in successive editions of his book *The Measurement of Adult Intelligence* (latest edition published in 1958). Anastasi (1961, Ch. 12) also provides an excellent description and evaluation of the Wechsler Scales. These tests have been very widely used for a multitude of purposes in diverse countries, and review articles summarising the main findings have been published about the WISC (Littell, 1960) and about the adult scales (Rabin and Guertin, 1951; Guertin et al. 1955, 1962, 1966). These last four articles cover successive five-year periods from 1945 to 1965. The following summary will mainly be based on these sources, with an occasional reference to particular researches.

In constructing the Wechsler-Bellevue, Wechsler was keenly aware of the fact that intelligence testing had mainly been directed at children, and that certain features had become traditional in individual testing that were inappropriate to adults. Adults were frequently being tested with material that was unlikely fully to deploy their interest and might in extreme cases seem frankly puerile. Often this material was presented in too highly speeded a form to elicit adults' full potential. Moreover, tests such as the Stanford-Binet had been constructed to yield mental ages, and thence classical IQs, which were not applicable to adults.

Wechsler also saw advantages in having his test (really a battery of 10 tests) divided into two main parts, a set of predominantly verbal and a set of 'performance' scales. Each of these 10 scales was made to contribute an equal amount to total score, and each to be comparable with the others, so that a meaningful profile could be derived. Each set of five produced a total score, so that a 'verbal IQ', a 'performance IQ' and a 'total IQ' could be derived. This general principle applies to the original Wechsler–Bellevue, and also to the WAIS and WISC. It was also hoped that comparison of various sub-scores would yield patterns that would prove typical of particular clinical groups and thus be of use in diagnosis. The general approach might be summarised as trying to put into operation Galton's famous description of ability testing as the exploratory sinking of shafts at carefully chosen points (as in drilling for oil). The characteristics of these tests follow logically from Wechsler's views on the nature of intelligence and from his appreciation of the possible uses of individual tests, particularly for use with adults. His definition is; 'Intelligence is the aggregate or global capacity of the individual to act purposefully, to think rationally and to deal effectively with his environment.' Although open to criticism (Miles, 1957) this definition provides a reasonable starting-point for someone embarking on the construction of a battery of tests planned to assess a broad variety of cognitive and adaptive functions and to assist in diagnosing numerous kinds of retardation, pathological states and general malfunctioning. If one imagines a kind of spectrum, with at one extreme a narrow conception of intelligence as power of formal abstract reasoning, and at the other a broad conception involving general adaptation and evidenced by social skills as well as by formal reasoning, Wechsler's position is far out towards the latter 'broad' end. Many of his statements about the nature of intelligence can produce a slight shock of reaction, as when he says 'Every reader will be able to recall persons of high intellectual ability in some particular field, whom they would unhesitatingly characterise as below average in general intelligence' or 'it would seem that so far as general intelligence is concerned, intellectual ability as such merely enters as a necessary minimum'. Similarly, Wechsler lays stress on non-cognitive components contributing to measured intelligence, quoting, for instance, the study of Alexander (1935), who found two such temperamental or motivational factors (which he called 'X' and 'Z') involved in intelligence test scores. Wechsler does not see such factors as supplementing intelligence, but speaks quite readily of 'the non-intellective factors in general intelligence'. This approach is at the opposite end of the continuum from that of, say, R. B. Cattell. Both might be in approximate agreement, perhaps, about the concepts of fluid and crystallised intelligence, and about most existing tests measuring a mixture of the two, since the conception of intelligence adopted by Wechsler and other constructors of individual tests emphasises the total adaptive power. The latter equate 'intelligence' more closely with 'common sense' than with 'reasoning power' and are therefore uninterested in disentangling from intelligence either temperamental factors or factors characteristic of attainment rather than of reasoning. Cattell, following Spearman, is much more concerned with paralleling the methods of other sciences and with specifying logically and empirically satisfactory dimensions. The contrast is, among other things, one between the attitude of the research scientist and that of the practising clinician. Such then is Wechsler's general approach. How it has been put into practice and how useful the tests have proved both as clinical instruments and research tools will become more apparent in the following sections.

THE WECHSLER ADULT INTELLIGENCE SCALE

This battery is largely based on the earlier Wechsler-Bellevue one, but represents a technical improvement, being more satisfactorily standardised, and tending to produce rather more reliable scores on some of the sub-scales, particularly the verbal ones, and consequently more reliable total IQs. (Guertin et al., 1962). It contains eleven sub-tests, as described below, the first six contributing to 'verbal IQ' and the remaining five to 'performance IQ.'

1. *General Information.* Contains items of the type 'Who is the President of the US?' but this is an easy, 'lead-in' item, not actually scored.

2. *General Comprehension.* Items typically ask 'What would you do if. . . .?' 'Why do we usually. . . .?' tapping 'common sense' and knowledge of social mores. These items cause more difficulty in scoring than those of sub-test 1. Detailed instructions for the tester are given.

3. *Arithmetical Reasoning.* Simple problems in mental arithmetic.

4. *Digits Forward and Backward.* Series of digits (one-figure numbers) are read out. In the first part, subject is required to repeat series, in second part to repeat it backwards.

5. *Similarities.* Pairs of words are read out. In each case, subject has to say in what way the two things are alike.

6. *Vocabulary.* Subject is required to explain meaning of words, presented in increasing order of difficulty. Examples are provided to help tester in scoring doubtful definitions.

7. *Digit Symbol.* This was originally adapted from the Army Performance Scale, used by the US Army in the First World War. Symbols and numbers are presented as paired and the subject must continue pairing symbols against appropriate numbers.

8. *Picture completion.* Pictures are presented from which a part is missing (e.g. nose missing from face). Subject required to name missing part.

9. *Block design.* Similar to Kohs Block Design.

10. *Picture Arrangement.* Sets of cards are presented, one set at a time, in which each set contains pictures which in correct order make a story. Subject has to put each set in right order.

11. *Object Assembly.* Subject has to form objects (e.g. human being) by placing pieces in right position in manner of a jig-saw.

Findings about the reliability and validity of the scale and about its diagnostic value and usefulness in research are summarised in the four papers by Guertin and his associates. The first two of these were concerned with the older Wechsler-Bellevue version, and were generally quite favourable about its general usefulness as a test, but ended with a note of warning or a verdict of 'not proven' about its ability to diagnose clinical syndromes. In particular (1956, p. 251) 'our somewhat jaundiced eye, continues to reject the assumption of unique subtest performances by schizophrenics', and more generally 'when one looks at the work done with various psychiatric populations by means of scatter and patterning methods, one can readily conclude that "nothing new has been added" either in methodology or in definite findings'.

An interesting fact about the WAIS, and a respect in which it differs somewhat from the earlier W-B, is that in the standardisation sample, which appears to have been fairly representative of white American adults, the best overall scores occurred in the 25–29 year-old age group, as compared with the 20–24 age group in the older test. Similarly, the rate of decline with age is slower for the newer test at least up to age 50.

Although tests such as the W-B and WAIS are commonly thought of as primarily more for clinical and individual use than, say, for statistical predictions of academic success, a research by Frandsen (1950) shows that, with care and and favourable circumstances, the predictive value of the W-B against a scholastic criterion was at least as high as, and probably higher than, that of most group tests. This predictive power, against a criterion of grade point average and with a sample of 16–19 year-old High School students (mean IQ 119), was concentrated in the verbal subtests. Addition of the performance IQ to the verbal one slightly lowered the validity coefficient, from ·69 to ·685, and of the sub-tests in the performance section, only block design came near to being as effective as most of the verbal subtests. Frandsen noticed that all the most successful students did well on the block design test, and concluded that the performance involved was necessary for high academic achievement but did not guarantee it.

In the most recent of their review articles, Guertin (1966) and his collaborators cover the literature of the preceding five or six years. By this time the literature on Wechsler's tests had become enormous, as is shown by their reference to a 1961 bibliography containing over 1,000 items and their own survey of about 200 more recent publications on the adult scales alone, which they describe as selective rather than exhaustive.

A number of the studies reviewed were concerned with the comparability of the WAIS with the WB and the WISC. In general, there was a high degree of correspondence. Guertin et al. quote, for instance, a study by Webb (1963) in which WAIS scores of negro retardates were compared with their scores on the WISC obtained two years earlier. The correlations between verbal IQs, performance IQs and total IQs were respectively ·80, ·91 and ·84. Considering both the time interval, the restricted nature of the sample, and the fact of two different test batteries, these correlations seem to provide good evidence of the continuity and approximate equivalence of the two instruments. It was found in this study, as in several others, however, that the WAIS tends to produce appreciably higher IQs, particularly perhaps performance IQs. Comparisons between Wechsler adult batteries and other intelligence tests were also summarised, and, although the figures varied fairly widely between different studies, typical correlations with such tests as the Stanford-Binet and the Henmon-Nelson seemed to be around ·75 or ·80. Studies were also quoted showing little difference between the Stanford-Binet and the WAIS as predictors of academic ability.

The division of the Wechsler batteries into the two main groups of 'verbal' and 'performance' sub-scales appears on the whole to have been a useful one. Most of the factor-analytic studies confirm this a priori grouping (e.g. Cropley, 1964) and many of the diagnostic and clinical studies continue to find the difference between verbal and performance IQ of importance. Patients with various kinds of cerebral pathology and damage have generally been found to have a verbal IQ significantly higher than performance IQ. The survey by Guertin et al. of a large number of clinical studies indicates that this usually holds good, but with numerous exceptions and modifications. Terms such as 'cerebral pathology', 'brain damage', 'organic' and so forth are of course much too general. The pattern of behaviour will be affected according to which cerebral hemisphere is impaired. If it is the right, the pattern just described (of higher verbal IQ) will often be exhibited; if it is the left (generally playing a larger part in the control of speech), this pattern may be absent or less evident. In general, too, the length of affliction interacts with this pattern. The longer the condition has existed, the less differentiation by means of test performance between left- and right-hemisphere cases will be possible.

As regards more specific diagnostic clues from the patterning of scores on particular subtests, the writers are in general rather pessimistic. 'Wechsler's paradigms for different diagnostic groups, his Mental Deterioration and Masculinity-Feminity Indices, thus far have also produced interest but little else of practical value. . . . The apparent basis of work with the WAIS has often been "it would be nice if a highly reliable and valid sign could be discovered". Thus far, this has not happened, but if it did, the discovered sign would probably identify only a small percentage of the subjects possessing a given trait or symptom.'

THE WECHSLER INTELLIGENCE SCALE FOR CHILDREN (WISC)

The WISC covers the age-range 5–16, and was constructed partly from the easier items of the Wechsler-Bellevue, particularly from form II. It consists of 10 basic subtests, five 'verbal' and five 'performance'. There is one optional extra verbal subtest, and one extra performance test (Mazes, similar to the Porteus Maze test described in a later section of this chapter) that may be substituted for Coding. The 10 basic subtests are as below. All these follow similar principles to the corresponding sub-tests in the adult batteries. The apparent exception (coding) is similar to 'digit symbol'.

Verbal Scale	*Performance Scale*
General Information	Picture Completion
General Comprehension	Picture Arrangement
Arithmetic	Block Design
Similarities	Object Assembly
Vocabulary	Coding

The test was carefully standardised on a sample of 100 boys and 100 girls for each year of age, i.e. aged approximately $5\frac{1}{2}$, $6\frac{1}{2}$ . . . $15\frac{1}{2}$. The sample was closely representative of all white children in the USA in respect of geographical area, urban-rural location, and father's occupation. This standardisation is generally agreed to have been satisfactory apart from the omission of negroes, and the norms are consequently not applicable to minority racial groups.

The reliability of the whole test was found to be excellently high, but that of some of the subtests naturally considerably lower, with the result that they are better used for group than for individual comparisons, and the standard error of score for individuals on these particular subtests must be excessively large. Validity, and particularly predictive validity, of the test is much more uncertain; Littell (1960) comments, in his review of 10 years' research with the WISC and of about 80 studies,

> If the use of the term predictive validity is restricted to correlation between the WISC and some nontest measure of predicted behavior obtained at some time subsequent to the administration of the WISC, there are no relevant studies in the literature reviewed. This is very surprising, as it is difficult to conceive of any situation in which the WISC might be used that would not involve the prediction of behavior. As it stands, this lack of explicit evidence of the value of the WISC in the prediction of subsequent behavior must be viewed as a major weakness of the test.

Or perhaps of the researchers concerned. But if studies of predictive validity were lacking in the first 10 years after the publication of the WISC, studies of concurrent validity were super-abundant. Many of these were comparisons with the Stanford-Binet. Littell summarises 21 such researches, in which correlations were calculated between total WISC IQ and the Stanford-Binet, form L. The range of these correlations was between ·49 and ·94, and the median ·82. This is undoubtedly an underestimate of the correspondence between the two tests for two reasons. Firstly, the distribution is skewed; seven of the correlations are ·88 or over, and only one is below ·6; secondly, about three-quarters of them are based on samples severely restricted in range of ability. It seems likely that, without this restriction, the two tests would have about 80% of variance in common. Although these correlations are high, comparisons of results obtained on the two tests in terms of actual scores are more complex and tricky. In some investigations, Stanford-Binet IQs have been found to be systematically higher throughout the age range up to adolescence. In addition, the WISC has less 'top' for very exceptional children, with norms allowing for a maximum IQ of 154. Finally, deviation IQs, when calculated for the 1937 Stanford-Binet were based on a standard deviation of 16 (Pinneau, 1961), but those of the WISC on the more familiar figure of 15.

The lack of negroes in the standardisation sample has resulted in norms of the test not being applicable to them, particularly to those in southern USA. Studies are quoted in which negro children 'not retarded, by socio-economic criteria or by the judgment of observers' (Littell, 1960) averaged an IQ of under 70 on the whole scale. Similarly, immigrant groups would require special norms. The size of these discrepancies perhaps suggests a particularly strong modification of WISC test scores by cultural and social factors. On the other hand, some studies have shown that although there is a marked correlation (in the USA) between socio-economic status and WISC score on entering school, this tends to drop within a few years, presumably because of the levelling effect of the school environment. There is also some indication that performance IQ on the WISC is rather less susceptible than verbal IQ to social factors.

In general, however, there is little evidence for the valid use of WISC difference scores (e.g. verbal IQ minus performance IQ) or of more detailed patterned or profile scores based on the subtests. In fact, the adoption of the particular pattern of the WISC seems in a sense paradoxical, as Anastasi notes, in that a particular style of battery was developed specifically to fulfil the needs of adult testing, and then re-adapted to form a battery for children.

Littell's (1960) summary stresses both the promising nature of the WISC and the lack of valid evidence about it.

> The WISC does not have an adequate rationale. Much more thought and effort need to be devoted to putting the WISC on a firm theoretical foundation. ... The lack of investigations of the test's predictive validity is appalling. At present the test's construct and content validities are not strong enough to support the use of the test without this criterion – oriented validation. ... There appear to be strong reasons to suspect that WISC scores are affected systematically by many variables other than intelligence, but little information about the exact nature of these variables and the relationships involved is available. ... On the other hand, the WISC appear to be a relatively well-standardized test with many virtues. It correlates consistently well with other measures of intelligence, appears to be widely accepted and used, and, in general, seems to merit further research and development.

THE BRITISH INTELLIGENCE TEST

An ambitious project to produce a new individual test of general ability in Britain has been under way for two or three years, under the direction of Professor F. W. Warburton of the Department of Education at Manchester University, and should be complete, with the test in operational use, early in the 1970s.

It will be primarily designed for the testing of children between ages five and 12, but will also cover a wider age range upwards and downwards. The test will yield a measure of general ability, and six sub-scores. There are 12 scales in all, more than one being used in several cases to produce a sub-score. The sub-scores are similar in conception and nomenclature to Thurstone's Primary Mental Abilities, being as follows: (i) R (Reasoning), from the Matrices, Induction and Operational Thinking scales; (ii) V (Verbal), from the Vocabulary, Information and Comprehension scales; (iii) S (Spatial), from Kohs Blocks and Visual-Spatial scales; (iv) N (Number), from the Numerical scale; (v) M (Memory), from the Visual Memory and Auditory Memory scales; (vi) F (Fluency), from the Creativity scale. Each of the scales will probably contain about 25 items in the final version. The score for general ability will be on a 9-point scale, corresponding to deviation quotients (as distinct from mental age ones) of 135 and over, 125–34, 115–24, 105–114, 95–104, 85–94, 75–84, 65–74, 64 and under.

An interesting feature of the test will be the attempt in at least three of the scales (Reasoning, Numerical and Information) to include items based on Piaget's work that will yield information in standardised form about the child's stage of cognitive development. As a simple example, one item for younger children might contain two rows of cats (shown in a drawing), with one row more widely spaced than the other but containing the same number, and the child might be asked which row had more cats in it. The Numerical scale is also designed to lay much less emphasis on mechanical and computational operations than have many earlier tests (such as Thurstone's) and much more on the development of concepts as encouraged by the 'New Mathematics' that has recently been adopted in most primary schools (Skemp, 1964; Fletcher, 1964). The Information scale will attempt to afford insight into the child's self-concept and understanding of the world, and some items designed for the younger children will probably elicit relatively primitive ideas of causality (as described in the latter part of Chapter 7).

The development, try-out and standardisation of such a test involve a great deal of thought and planning, particularly about the sampling designs at successive stages. The sample for the first main try-out of items, before the calculation of item difficulties and indices of discrimination, is stratified (a) by country, including children from England, Scotland, Ireland and Wales, (b) by sex, (c) by urban or rural background, (d) by socio-economic level. At a later stage, when items have been selected for the final version, even more careful sampling will be required to achieve satisfactory standardisation, with attention being paid to the range of variation in sub-categories as well as to average levels.

This project is an exciting one, and many of the kinds of item employed are novel and promising, but cannot be described in detail here or reproduced, for reasons of security. Rather more detail about the progress and present stage of development of this test can be found in the paper by Warburton (1966).

SOME PERFORMANCE TESTS OF INTELLIGENCE

It was recognised quite early that for many purposes tests such as the various forms of the Binet, depended too highly on verbal material and were too conspicuously influenced by schooling and social experience. In the spectrum between 'Intelligence A' and 'Intelligence B', or between 'fluid' and 'crystallised' intelligence, the Binet test was seen to be at the 'B' or 'crystallised' end in giving heavy weight to educational attainment. For this reason, it generally proved a satisfactory predictor of educational progress, but perhaps less adequate where the need was to discount learned material. Hebb's starting-point in formulating the two kinds of intelligence 'A' and 'B', was the remarkable observation that even the removal of large sections of cerebral cortex in an adult often resulted in hardly detectable losses in intelligence as assessed by many tests. Similarly, in the period from about 1935 to 1950, when the drastic surgical procedures of pre-frontal leucotomy and lobotomy, were widely practised for the relief of psychoses and very acute neuroses, observed losses in performance on many tests including the Binet were often surprisingly slight.

In contrast, appreciable deterioration was observed on certain 'performance' tests, including, for instance the Porteus maze test. Many of these results were far from clear, being complicated by the special nature of the sample of people and by such factors as post-operative shock, but Porteus (1966, Ch. 3) has assembled evidence that his test was quite sensitive to deterioration that could not easily be detected by other tests. This test, first constructed in 1914, has remained essentially unchanged, though with the addition of supplementary forms known as the 'Extension' and the 'Supplement' (Porteus, 1955, 1959a). The subject is required to trace a path through a maze (after inspection and thought) without taking his pencil from the paper and without entering any blind alleys. A certain number of unsuccessful attempts are allowed for in the scoring. Tables are provided for ages 4 to 14 which provide an approximate conversion of test score to quotient.

The most useful contribution of the Maze Test has probably been its sensitivity to brain damage. But it has also been used quite extensively

TABLE 9.2 *Maze Scores: Illiterate Adults*

N	Group	Locality	Maze Mean Years	SD	Investigator
50	Rural Bhil	Central India	7·44	1·2	Ray
25	Bushmen	Kalahari, S. Africa	7·56	2·17	Porteus
29	Sakai Jeram	Coastal Malaya	7·88	2·49	Stewart
100	Abor, Upper Padam	N.E. India	8·3	1·25	Chowdhury & De
100	Abor, Lower Padam	N.E. India	8·34	1·61	Chowdhury & De
28	Mchopi	Port. E Africa	8·34	2·45	Porteus
29	Urban Bhil	Central India	8·36	1·8	Ray
50	Santal	India	8·55	1·79	Chowdhury & De
22	Negrito	Luzon, Philippine Is.	8·86	2·76	Stewart
145	Pasi (Minyong)	Upper Assam, India	8·9	2·24	Chowdhury & De
100	Kanikkar	S. India	9·27	2·19	Ray
25	Shangaans	Port. E. Africa	9·3	2·66	Porteus
36	Bengali	W. Bengal	9·42	2·44	Vicary
59	Santal	N. Bengal	9·52	—	Vicary
27	Pasi (Adi)	Upper Assam, India	9·63	1·63	Chowdhury & De
50	Wailbri	C. Australia	10·4	2·63	Gregor
56	Senoi	Mts., Malaya	10·43	2·73	Stewart
56	Keidja-Nyul	N.W. Australia	10·48	2·34	Porteus
24	Karadjeri	N.W. Australia	10·52	2·6	Piddington
27	Chinese	Peiping, China	10·52	2·67	Stewart
22	Bajou	N. Borneo	10·61	2·56	Stewart
25	Amaxosa	Cape Prov., S.E. Africa	10·78	2·76	Porteus
21	Ghurkas*	Malaya	11·33	2·71	Stewart
50	Chinese Coolies	Peiping, China	11·68	2·74	Stewart
20	Tamils*	Malaya	13·18	2·32	Stewart

* Ghurkas and Tamils were immigrants working on Malayan plantations. From Porteus 1965, p. 212

Table 9.2 is reproduced from Porteus (1965), p. 212

with primitive peoples, particularly in detailed studies of Australian aboriginals and of African pygmies and bushmen. The range of these studies is indicated in Table 9.2 on p. 234.

The great variation in average score, apparently ranging from a European IQ equivalent of below 70 to over 100, is striking. Porteus adduces evidence that degree of contact with urban civilisation, although it can affect scores, cannot possibly account for all this variation, but explains some part of the differences in terms of diet deficiency and proneness to debilitating diseases.

In some respects the Maze Test has therefore been shown to be less dependent than many on learning and education, but this difference is only relative, and it certainly cannot be placed with confidence very far down the spectrum from Intelligence B to Intelligence A. According to Porteus (1966), scores show less decline with age than on most tests and men score higher than women (in 99 out of 105 studies). Both of these facts tend to suggest (in contrast to the brain damage experiments) a considerable degree of educational and social influence.

The Porteus tests were one of the earliest kinds of performance tests. In contrast we now turn to quite a recent development, again a maze test, but of a rather special kind.

Elithorn's perceptual maze test, which can be administered to groups, and which has been shown to be an aid in the diagnosis of brain damage in the frontal and temporal lobes, consists of a series of triangular lattices, with dots at some of the junctions. Two such lattices are shown in Figure 9.1.

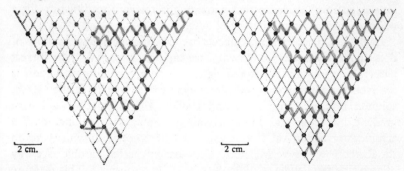

Figure 9.1
Examples of items in Elithorn's perceptual maze test
(reproduced from Elithorn *et al.*, 1964).

The task required of the subject is to trace a path along the lines of the maze from bottom to top so as to pass through as many dots as possible. At each junction of lines encountered, he has only two choices, left or right; he is not allowed to turn backwards towards the bottom again. The group version of this test is described by Elithorn *et al.* (1960).

The mazes presented in the complete version vary in two main respects, that may be called size (or rank) and 'saturation'. The size is simply the number of rows in the maze. Those in the diagram have 16, but could be extended upwards to have 20 or more. The 'saturation' is a measure of the density of dots in the maze, expressed by the ratio of dots to junctions (or, for a maze of given size, simply by the number of dots). One would suppose that both large size and high saturation would make the mazes more difficult, and this has been shown to be so (Elithorn *et al.*, 1964). Size proved to have the clearest relation to difficulty in this experiment; a high density of dots added relatively little to difficulty in the smaller mazes, but much more in the larger ones. Inspection of Figure 9.1 in detail makes one suspect that size of maze and density of dots might not be the only, or necessarily the main factors contributing to degree of difficulty. Some patterns might be more difficult than others, even with these two factors held constant. For instance, in the right-hand maze, the eye is caught by a run of 5 consecutive dots up the right-hand edge. If, however, one takes a path straight up the right-hand edge through the run of five, it is not possible to attain an optimum solution, but by branching left at the third dot in the run this can be attained. This kind of feature in the pattern was not deliberately introduced, since the dots were placed at random, but Elithorn *et al.* (1960) found statistical evidence that *patterning* is relevant to difficulty for a maze of given size and density of dots.

In the standard version, subjects are told the maximum number of dots that can be traversed in each maze and only have to find the correct path. Their solution is marked right or wrong, and no more credit is received for managing to include 11 dots rather than 1, if the correct solution involves 12. Davies and Davies (1965) experimented with graduated scoring and found certain advantages in it, including a significantly higher validity as expressed by correlation with score on the Raven Progressive Matrices. They also suggested an objective way of assessing the degree of difficulty caused by patterning. This measure was based on the ratio between number of possible correct solutions and total of possible paths through the maze, and correlated $+ \cdot 77$ with observed difficulty as obtained from subjects performance. The index of theoretical difficulty so far described did not take into account dots that were 'irrelevant' in the following sense. The optimum solution might involve traversing 3 dots (in a simple maze) and there might be, say, four different paths by which this could be achieved. Now imagine the addition of further, 'irrelevant' dots, such that the four possible correct solutions remained unaffected. When an improved index was devised 'which took into account irrelevant information of this kind (and also included another slight refinement) the correlation between theoretical and observed difficulty was raised to $+\cdot94$.

Some features of this test have been described in detail to indicate the promise, apart from its diagnostic and clinical uses, that it appears to hold for research purposes. The fact that level of difficulty can be readily varied, objectively assessed, and approximately calculated in advance, may be a step forward compared with the usual hit-and-miss procedure, checked by successive try-outs, that has been described in chapter 8, and that is only too familiar to test constructors. This objectivity in the assessment of difficulty level might be further improved and generalised by translation into the language of information theory, i.e. the factors of size, density and patterning might perhaps be summarised in terms of the 'bits' of information available to the subject, and his performance assessed in number of bits handled per unit of time. The binary nature of the mazes, whereby each choice point involves only two alternatives, appears to make such an analysis particularly appropriate. It might also be possible to convert the test from a paper-and-pencil one to a more typical 'performance' test, in which, say, a physical maze was traversed with the aid of a stylus, in which case subjects' performance could be automatically recorded and analysed.

More generally, this kind of test, whatever its merits or demerits as a practical instrument, is particularly interesting from a theoretical point of view, not least because it may well be a step forward in bridging the gap described in chapter 3, that between the study of problem-solving and the assessment of intelligence and ability. The perceptual maze test has the advantage that it can be used in the same way as other group intelligence tests (and has been shown to correlate quite highly with at least one), but can also be readily adapted to study the parameters of problem-solving, such as complexity, redundancy and amount of irrelevant information.

GROUP TESTS (VERBAL)

Tests of 'verbal intelligence' and 'verbal reasoning' have been used very extensively in '11 +' selection in England and Wales, and in the corresponding selection procedure at age 12 in Scotland. Perhaps the best known tests of this kind and the ones that have earned the highest reputation for technical excellence are the Moray House series. They received their name when Godfrey Thomson was both Principal of Moray House College of Education and Professor of Education in the University of Edinburgh. For many years they have had no connection with Moray House; Moray House tests (comprising several other kinds of tests besides selection tests) are produced by the Godfrey Thomson Unit for Educational Research, which is part of the University.

The other main supplier of verbal intelligence tests for secondary school selection has been the National Foundation for Educational Research in England and Wales. Both the N.F.E.R. and the Godfrey Thomson Unit are now concentrating to a larger extent on the production of tests for guidance and other internal purposes within schools, since the tripartite system of secondary school education has become obsolescent.

The N.F.E.R. and the Moray House tests are still used for selection purposes, though to a diminishing extent, and even with the disappearance of selection they will continue to serve a useful purpose in providing objective standards and national norms for the comparison of ability levels. The great mass of statistical information available from the past use of these tests is also extremely useful for research purposes, for the study of 'zero error' or 'cultural drift', for instance (i.e. systematic changes in performance in large populations over a period of time), and also for longitudinal studies.

Since nearly all these verbal intelligence tests are still 'closed' and subject to security restrictions, it is not possible to describe the content and composition in detail, but items of some or all of the following types are frequently included:

(*a*) *Analogies.*

EXAMPLE. Finger is to hand, as toe is to . . . . . .

(*b*) '*Odd-man-out*' (*or* '*odd-men-out*').

EXAMPLE. Underline the two words that are different and do not belong with the other four.

horse / cat / grass / goat / dog / stable

(*c*) *Codes.*

EXAMPLE. If in a secret writing or code, CAT is written as DBU and PUPPY is written as QVQQZ, write the code word for TOWEL.

(*d*) *Verbal-meaning.*

EXAMPLE. Find a word from those in the brackets that means either nearly the same as or nearly the opposite of the word in capitals.

FEW (none/many/slow/small/quantity)

(e) *Words missing from sentences.*

EXAMPLE. Underline in the bracket the word that makes most sense in the following sentence.

It was a very bumpy journey, (since/because/if/yet/hence) we all slept soundly.

Both the N.F.E.R. and the Moray House tests are carefully tried out and standardised with an age allowance on very large groups, as described in chapter 8, with the result that IQs obtained on successive tests are closely comparable, subject only to the relativity involved by slowly changing standards in the whole population.

A useful group test of a special kind has been constructed by Cornwell (1952). This is an orally administered test for junior children aged between 8 and 11, though norms are provided for a slightly wider range. Cornwell's claims for the test, as stated in the manual, are rather modest, and include 'the diagnosis of retardation, where the teacher is concerned with relatively gross discrepancies between potential and performances of the order of one and a half years'. The test has a high split-half reliability (·953) and was found to correlate highly with another intelligence test, Richardson's 'Simplex Junior Intelligence Scale' (·907).

GROUP TESTS (NON-VERBAL)

Probably the best known and most widely used test of this kind in Britain is the Progressive Matrices. The first version appeared in 1938 and was used to screen recruits to the British forces in the Second World War (Vernon and Parry, 1949). New versions appeared in 1947, consisting of sets A, Ab and B, in colour, for children aged 5 to 11 and for the diagnosis and assessment of subnormality or retardation. Sets I and II (1947) are for older children and adults of average or superior ability. Set I can be used as a preliminary classifier, and set II is difficult enough to tax superior adults. A revised version of set II was published in 1962.

Burke (1958) has reviewed published work with the Progressive Matrices up to that date. His survey reveals that correlations with a wide variety of other intelligence tests are rather lower than might be expected, being almost universally in the range ·4 to ·7. The correlations with other non-verbal tests are not in general noticeably higher than with verbal or individual tests. The concurrent and predictive validities of the Progressive Matrices against a range of criteria, including educational achievement and vocational success, are summarised by Burke as being 'fairly good but not outstandingly superior'.

The first version of the test was widely praised, both Spearman and Vernon believing it to be the purest available test of general intelligence. Burke's review, and the evidence it summarises, suggests that these opinions were perhaps too enthusiastic. The Matrices can be criticised for being narrow in content, relying essentially on one type of item. Its clinical value is also generally agreed to be rather limited. Bortner (1965) also criticises the manuals, commenting that they are both something less and something more than a test manual should be.

'Much of the information offered might better be submitted as journal articles. Some of the information might better not be offered at all. Some prospective users might be confused to learn that a "broad form" of the Coloured Progressive Matrices discussed in much detail is not commercially available, or that the working time for Set 2 of the Advanced Progressive Matrices "can be adjusted [from 15 minutes to an hour] to secure the type of score distribution one requires." Anastasi (1959) and Burke make similar comments about the inadequacy of the Matrices manuals.'

None the less the Progressive Matrices is for many purposes a very useful and serviceable test. One or two criticisms have been mentioned, mainly because it has in the past perhaps enjoyed an exaggerated reputation in this country. Norms on the test, so far as is ascertainable, apparently do not vary greatly between developed countries, and it is possibly as little affected by cultural differences as tests claimed to be 'culture-fair' or 'culture-free.'

HIGH-LEVEL INTELLIGENCE TESTS

New problems arise in the construction of tests to discriminate, say, among the most able 5% of people. It is more difficult in any kind of measurement or assessment to make fine gradations, other things being equal, than coarse ones; this causes poorer discrimination and consequently lower reliability and validity. There is also a need in the construction of this kind of test to include qualitatively different material, not only more difficult versions of problems that discriminate between broad bands of ability. Some kinds of face validity are perhaps more important, since the subjects will very likely be more critical and readier to lose motivation if the task seems unreasonable. For similar reasons there is a need to guard against plausible and arguably correct items among the 'distractors'. Anstey (1966, p. 216) also argues that multiple-choice tests are unsuitable for high-grade intelligence tests, or at least multiple-choice tests of the usual type with five alternative responses, on the grounds that they must necessarily be lacking in items of lower than 20% facility. This argument, however, is not entirely convincing, provided the try-out is with a highly selected group.

One of the most promising high-level tests is Alice Heim's A.H.5. This consists of two parts, each of 36 items, one being verbal and numerical, the other largely diagrammatic. In each part, items of various kinds are arranged cyclically, i.e. not in batches or successive sections, with the result that the subject constantly has to change his problem-solving 'set' and to tackle each item entirely afresh. Relatively easy examples of two of the *kinds* of item included in the first section are

1. Write down the number of the word that would come in the middle, if the following words were arranged in order according to their meaning.

Paragraph. Letter. Book. Sentence. Page. Chapter. Word.

2. Give the next but one number of the series:

$$3 \quad \frac{3}{2} \quad \frac{3}{4} \quad \frac{5}{4} \quad \frac{5}{6} \quad \frac{7}{6} \quad \ldots$$

Heim describes AH5 as 'a test of general intelligence, designed for use with selected, highly intelligent, subjects. It is intended for adults, such as students and research workers, and potential entrants to the university and the professions. It may be given also to senior pupils at Grammar and Technical schools and their equivalents.'

The test is not excessively speeded, 20 minutes being allowed for each part. Subjects are encouraged to attempt the items in any order. Emphasis is laid in the instructions for administration on the need to obtain rapport with the subjects, as in administering an individual test. Norms are provided for university students and for grammar-school pupils, the latter by years from age 13 to 18; these norms are for the two parts separately, as well as for total score, and are not in terms of percentiles or standard deviation units, but in bands for five broad levels of ability, graded A to E. Scores on the two halves are generally fairly close, and if a subject scores much more highly on one section than on the other, this is thought to invite further investigation. It seems quite likely, however, that systematic differences in relative score on the two parts might be found between certain groups, such as between arts and science students. The scores of engineering apprentices as summarised in the manual suggest a systematic difference of this kind, though not a very large one. Hudson (1960) has investigated this possibility, and has found quite large differences of this kind both among Cambridge undergraduates and in a sample of public and grammar-school 16-year-olds.

Heim and her associates have recently been developing another test, AH6, of the same level of difficulty as AH5. This is not yet generally available, but when published will provide users with two separate forms designed respectively for the testing of scientists, engineers and mathematicians and of arts specialists and other non-scientists. The former will yield separate scores on verbal, numerical and diagrammatic sections; the latter on verbal and numerical-plus-diagrammatic.

Suggested additional reading

VERNON, P. E., *Intelligence and Attainment Tests*. London: Univ. of London Press (1960). Chs. 4 and 5.

ANASTASI, ANNE, *Psychological Testing*. 2nd edn. New York: Macmillan (1961). Chs. 8–10 and 12.

WECHSLER, D., *The Measurement and Appraisal of Adult Intelligence*. 4th edn. London: Bailliere, Tindall and Cox (1958).

TERMAN, L. M., and MERRILL, M. A., *Measuring Intelligence*. London: Harrap.

REEVES, JOAN W., *Thinking about Thinking*. London: Secker and Warburg (1961).

PORTEUS, S. D., *Porteus Maze Test: fifty years' application*. London: Harrap (1965).

X

Social and Cultural Influences

The evidence for the effect of innate differences on measured intelligence summarised in Chapter 6 was necessarily of an indirect kind and depended on sophisticated kinds of statistical inference. Ethical considerations obviously prevent any direct experiments on the breeding of human beings. Social and environmental factors, on the other hand, act in a sense more directly, and are especially important because we can do something about them. Admittedly, ethical considerations apply here too, and we cannot simply take two groups of children and deliberately provide a favourable environment for one and an unfavourable one for the other. None the less a real distinction remains. There is not much we can do about the genes people are born with, but there is a great deal we can do about improving social conditions and educational practice.

This is an obvious point, but accounts for much of the heat generated in the familiar arguments between hereditarians and environmentalists. Even in countries self-labelled as democratic, it is hardly possible to deny that a large proportion of the population is suffering intellectual and cultural deprivation in one form or another and that very few people are able fully to develop their potential talents. Statements of this kind do not depend only on subjective impressions but are supported by a mass of evidence from research about the restrictive effects of specific deprivation, of unsatisfactory living conditions and of general inequality in educational opportunity. There is thus little wonder that many people, and particularly social and educational radicals, consider the evidence about innate differences mainly irrelevant and see social factors as overwhelmingly the most important or even as in practice the *only* determinants of school attainment and of measured intelligence.

The pervasive importance of social and cultural conditions is undeniable, but when one looks at the mass of research and tries to list what is agreed and what is still controversial, the picture becomes very blurred. The questions are so large and general that much of psychology and half of sociology are relevant. A particular difficulty is that various lines of evidence point to the crucial importance of differences in quantity and quality of experience in very early childhood, when methods of investigation are restricted by the infants' inability to communicate. Bloom (1964), for instance, suggests that the crucial effect of environmental conditions is exercised between the ages of about one and four and this suggestion would probably be acceptable to most experts. But although developmental psychology has been advancing quite fast, the problems to be solved will stretch the ingenuity of child psychologists for many generations before even the outlines of cognitive development are properly understood.

Experiments with animals throw some light on elementary and basic learning processes, but can never provide a complete substitute for the study of children. The much-investigated white rat is incapable in a lifetime of grasping abstractions that monkeys can learn to discriminate in a few hundred trials, and monkeys are readily surpassed by two-year-old children. Hunt (1961), in his book *Intelligence and Experience* has made a serious effort to integrate findings from animal experiments, from studies of deprivation in children and from the work of Piaget. His general thesis is that intelligence has in the past been thought of, quite wrongly, as largely pre-determined and capable of developing and maturing almost automatically and irrespective of environmental circumstances. He adduces a wealth of evidence that such a view is at best an over-simplification and at worst seriously wrong. But much of the evidence that deprivation of adequate early experiences cripples later development is drawn from experiments with salamanders, rats and monkeys which, although suggestive, provides only crude analogies to human functioning. Cases such as that of Helen Keller, deaf and blind from infancy, provide evidence that extremely severe deprivation of sensory experience does not *necessarily* preclude an astonishing appreciation to normal cognitive development. Another hardly less spectacular illustration of the flexibility of children's ability to learn, and the possibility of overcoming what might be supposed to be overwhelming environmental handicap, has been documented by Mason (1942). 'Isabelle' had been imprisoned from birth with her mother, who was completely mute (from the age of two) and could communicate only by crude gestures. Until the child was six-and-a-half, the two had been permanently locked in a room with the result that, apart from total lack of speech, Isabelle's legs were so bowed that she could hardly walk. Within 10 days of release and hospitalisation, however, she was attempting to vocalise; after three months she was speaking in connected phrases (and a little later, saying touchingly, 'I love you, Miss Mason'), and within two years had attained almost a normal degree of intelligence, communication and social adjustment. Such cases are of course astonishing and exceptional, but they show very vividly the dangers of extrapolating to human beings many of the findings from experiments with animals (such as those of Harlow) that early deprivation of suitable stimulation produces irremediable consequences for later development.

How human beings acquire their intelligence, and the extent to which particular kinds of experience are essential, is a central, if not *the* central, problem in psychology. Hunt's book has the merit of being one of the first knowledgeable and comprehensive attempts to give this problem its due and to synthesise a coherent account from many scattered clues.

Most of the work reviewed in this chapter will unfortunately not be nearly so basic. What is known about the effects of social and environmental factors on the growth of intelligence depends mainly on the study of groups, often of whole populations, by rough-and-ready survey methods, and relatively little on the detailed and controlled observation of individuals. The general plan adopted in this chapter is first to refer briefly to some of the largest differences reported, which arise from the most contrasting kinds of environment and social structure. These are international and inter-cultural differences. Substantial differences in measured intelligence are found also within single countries between different ethnic groups and are reviewed in the next section. Finally, the later sections contain a discussion of the less spectacular, but perhaps more important and certainly more controversial variation that arises in one country and within one ethnic group from social stratification and from socio-economic differences in opportunity. The rather conflicting evidence about how best to minimise cultural effects in testing will also be discussed in some detail.

NATIONAL AND 'RACIAL' DIFFERENCES

There are certainly striking differences between people of different countries, cultures and tribes in the way they tackle intellectual tasks and in their effectiveness in solving particular kinds of problem. The table of average performances assembled by Porteus (see p. 233) shows very marked variation, even as assessed by a test designed to give cultural factors as little weight as possible. Nor could the size and direction of these differences have easily been predicted, except perhaps by an exceptionally perceptive social anthropologist with access to very full information about the different cultures. The following extract from Warburton's account of devising ability tests for Gurkha recruits illustrates some of the difficulties involved in finding suitable instruments of assessment.

People brought up in a less competitive environment than our own do not necessarily give a true indication of their ability under testing conditions. They are not accustomed to concentrate on an abstract task. Nor are they likely to desire very strongly to succeed in it.

The most striking thing about the recruits was their lack of pep and slowness of movement. They just plodded solemnly along. The slow, deliberate manner in which they handled the apparatus made a striking contrast to the hurried scampering of the British troops. On the other hand, if they thought that speed was the main requirement of the test, as some of them did in the early stages of the experiment, they jumbled all the apparatus together in a nonsensical way and finished in record time. One man completed the Matrices test (60 questions) in 7 minutes, and scored just above chance. In general, however, they were extremely slow. For this reason the ideal intelligence test for them would have no time limit. Although this is not practicable in group testing, sufficient time was given wherever possible for a large number of the men to finish the task.

The Gurkha recruits listened to the instructions attentively but with completely motionless faces. In this respect they were markedly different from any British group, intelligent or unintelligent. Whilst performing the tests they rarely looked at one another or smiled.

Morale was high. No one appeared to sulk because he was unable to answer all the questions. No one quarrelled with his neighbour. The general attitude was one of amiable co-operation.

The recruits were not curious about being tested and had little insight into the reasons for the experiment. No one asked the officer or N.C.O. why he was expected to busy himself with building bricks and jig-saws. It was typical that, because most of the apparatus was made of wood the psychologist was known as the wood officer.

There was every indication that they were doing their best. The proportions of right and wrong answers followed the usual patterns. They were completely absorbed in the task. It was plain that, whatever the impress of their earlier environment, we were getting a measure of their maximum efficiency in answering the test questions.

In a situation like this, 'performance' tests were the only type that could be used, as most of the Gurkha recruits came from very isolated communities, had had no schooling, and did not know how to hold pen or pencil. Pictorial tests had also proved unsatisfactory, as the Gurkhas often failed to recognise pictures even of objects which they knew quite well.

Difficulties of this kind are no doubt glaringly obvious to social anthropologists, but some of the differences between 'primitive' people and people in Westernised countries are still rather novel to psychologists, who perhaps have often tended to underestimate them. It is not always realised, for instance, how far even the recognition of pictures is a complex skill that has to be learned (as was brought out in Warburton's work), even though many 'simple' pictures employ kinds of perspective that were not used by European artists before the fourteenth century. Little wonder then that isolated tribesmen are unfamiliar with these conventions. These differences indeed go very deep, affecting such apparently fundamental processes as visual perception. Recently, for instance, rather surprising results have been obtained with the well-known Muller-Lyer or ('arrowhead') visual illusion – surprising, because many of the classic visual illusions are known to operate even on animals. Gregory (1966, 1967) describes experiments which show that Zulus are less susceptible to this illusion than Europeans. They are also, and this is particularly striking, resistant to the compelling illusions produced by the well known distorted room designed by Adelbert Ames, in which a non-rectangular room, cunningly designed to appear rectangular (and to give the equivalent retinal image), produces gross apparent size anomalies. The accepted explanation is that many Africans, as Biesheuvel had stressed some 20 years ago, are less pre-occupied with linearity as compared with Europeans, who are very conscious of vertical and horizontal axes and whose habits of thought are influenced to a much greater extent than they realise by the rectangular shape of their tables, chairs, houses, books and so on. There is good evidence in other recent researches that perceptual skills vary systematically as between different tribes and cultures according to their habitat, surroundings and way of life, and that these differences are reflected in performances on standardised tests (Berry, 1966; Drever, 1967).

Other points that emerge clearly from Warburton's account are the importance of adequate motivation but also the vagueness and generality of this concept. The Gurkhas were 'doing their best', but their 'slow deliberate manner' contrasted with the rapidity of the British troops performing on the same tests. One must suppose test-taking motivation to depend on a very complex combination of previous experience, present state of cortical arousal, and appreciation of the symbolic purpose of the test and the uses to which it will be put, to mention only a few possibilities. It is possible also that motivational differences relevant to learning and intelligence are due to differences in genetic endowment, as suggested by Hayes (1962), and that such differences operate both between and within nations and races. But we have little or no solid evidence to this effect, and the massive differences that *are* clearly environmental seem to offer a more profitable field of study.

The slowness of problem-solving typical of the Gurkhas, whatever its complex causes in previous experience, is not peculiar to them, but has been commented on in many descriptions of performance on mental tests by people in non-urban societies. Even in such a relatively small, homogeneous country as Britain, predominantly urbanised and with good communications, Smith (1948), testing Hebridean children, found them disinclined to work fast, or rather unable to grasp the idea of any need for fast working, and concluded that their intellectual powers could not be fairly assessed from performance on a speeded test. (Other interesting findings also emerged, such as a particularly large practice effect due to unfamiliarity with mental tests. Smith's investigation is discussed and extended by Vernon, 1965). Moreton and Butcher (1963) found some indications of a similar outlook, though to a much lesser extent, among children living in relatively isolated parts of Cumberland and Westmorland. Biesheuvel and Liddicoat (1959) report systematic differences in performance on the Wechsler test betwen English-speaking and Afrikaans-speaking South Africans, which they interpret in a similar way. Even after matching for socio-economic status, there was a difference of five to seven points in favour of the English-speaking groups in almost every social class. This was interpreted as arising from an urban-rural cultural difference, the Afrikaner culture being supposed to have retained rural characteristics even in the cities.

All these points could be greatly elaborated, and some call for much more detailed research and more satisfactory conceptual analysis, such as the dimensions of motivation in which such striking differences have been observed. It is important to note, however, that in spite of the difficulties of assessing ability in 'primitive' cultures and in spite of the inapplicability of usual methods, the task is not impossible.

In the case of the Gurkhas, the object of attempting to test them at all had been to select potential signallers, engineers and so on, when the man-power shortage had made it difficult to provide non-Gurkha ancillaries to the infantry. Despite the initial difficulties described, testing procedures were devised which achieved this aim quite successfully.

Any hope, however, of finding a single intelligence test or battery of universal application remains illusory. This is made very clear in the extensive literature dealing with the testing of Africans and the construction of appropriate tests since the pioneering studies of Oliver (1932, 1933, 1934). Roberts (1964) summarises some of the environmental factors that have to be taken into account.

It is well known that valid measures of African intelligence are possible only when other sources of variance have been eliminated or held constant. Such variances are very great with respect to school entrance age, type of education given, environmental background and other sources of 'contamination'. These are further complicated by nutritional and other health problems, and by the fact that there is no single universal language. Cultural differences also add their own emphases. In Basutoland, for instance, education for boys in the rural areas is apparently regarded as superfluous, and even as a hindrance to cattle-herding. For girls, on the other hand, it provides parents with a welcome relief from responsibility. In Nyasaland the position is reversed, education for males being regarded as important, but almost completely unnecessary for women. Other African culture differences, such as lack of time-sense or competition, have also to be borne in mind.

A related problem has been that educational standards claimed by Africans are often unreliable, especially when high education is accompanied by high status. Furthermore, since education is in the hands of many different independent authorities, the same standard may have different meanings in various contexts. The N.I.P.R. has tried to develop tests and norms which 'predict' the actual education standard of job applicants. These have not been entirely satisfactory, as the standard error of measurement in terms of the actual standard of education is rather high, as might be expected. Time lapses of different lengths between school leaving and testing also render measurement inaccurate.

While representative intelligence test samples have been collected for Europeans, it is doubtful whether those for Africans are equally so. Nevertheless, the bias of this sampling in such tests as arithmetic and language achievement, clerical tests, the so-called 'culture-fair' tests of general intelligence, and others, is such as to reduce the actual differences of performance between the two ethnic groups. Even so, these differences are of the order of one standard deviation.

Similarly Irvine (1966), in an excellent and readily accessible review of ability and attainment testing in Africa, points out that the learning task involved simply in becoming familiar with and understanding the point of multiple-choice test items is quite a formidable one for most Africans. He summarises six sources of unwanted variance in test scores. Some of these indeed are no doubt present in lesser degree in European results, and one may also suspect that his sixth category, error variance, contains minor specific perturbations that could be analysed further.

(1) The content of the test itself.

(2) The form and style of the test.

(3) The transfer that takes place between practice items and actual test items especially when the material is unfamiliar.

(4) The particular educational or cultural bias of the test items.

(5) The motivational influence of strange testers who at present tend to be Europeans.

(6) Error variance.

STUDIES OF MINORITY GROUPS

American studies of negro intelligence will be reviewed in some detail, both because the abilities of American negroes have been frequently and thoroughly investigated, and also because they form a half-way stage between studies of different cultures and studies of socio-economic classes within one society. Negro and white sub-cultures in the USA display differences that go beyond, say, the differences between middle-class and working-class people in Britain, but the two kinds of difference overlap considerably. To a large extent, average observed discrepancies between negro and white performance contain components due to social-class and economic differences.

The literature on intellectual characteristics of the American negro is extensive. Much of the earlier research is surveyed by Klineberg (1944) and that from 1944 onwards by Dreger and Miller (1960). Klineberg, very justifiably, writes from a frankly environmentalist viewpoint, since many of the early studies reviewed were methodologically naive or unconsciously prejudiced, nearly always (as it now seems) in the direction of demonstrating the negro's probable genetic inferiority. Dreger and Miller, in their fair-minded survey, admit to being environmentalists in general, but give some consideration to the possibility of relevant genetic differences. There are now few American psychologists who adopt uncompromisingly hereditarian conclusions about the generally lower tested cognitive performance of negroes than of whites, but this kind of explanation is still a possible one, and cannot easily be proved entirely wrong. Among exponents are, for instance, Garrett, McGurk and Shuey, the last of whom has recently (1966) published a new edition of her book on the testing of negro intelligence, which is perhaps the best known statement of the evidence for lower average inherited ability in the negro.

Klineberg's review covers comparative studies going back as far as 1897, when Stetson found negro children to be superior to white in memorising lines of poetry. Intelligence tests, such as Goddard's 1911 revision of the Binet scale, were used in comparative studies as early as 1913, when it was found that of the South Carolina children tested, 29·4% of the coloured and 10·2% of the white children were markedly backward in mental development. The majority of the early findings suggested that the average IQ of the negroes tested was about 86, although such estimates varied from below 60 to over 100. This great variation no doubt reflects primarily accidents and faults in sampling, but also differing degrees of success in controlling the following variables and matching the groups on them – socio-economic background, educational opportunities, speed of response, motivation, rapport or relation to the experimenter, language facility, culturally determined attitudes and so on. As Klineberg suggests, the history of intelligence testing, particularly where minority or underprivileged groups are concerned, is largely a story of the growing appreciation of such factors, accompanied by an increasing realisation of how difficult or impossible it is fully to control them or allow for them.

Negroes were not the only ethnic group to score low on intelligence tests. Italians, Portuguese and Mexicans in the USA did no better, and American Indians appreciably worse. Most strikingly, the average measured intelligence of Northern negroes entering the army in the First World War was consistently higher than that of Southern whites (see Table 10.1 overleaf).

These figures, quoted by Klineberg and reproduced in Table 10.1 were justifiably selected to make a particular point, that in some states Negroes scored more highly on an intelligence test than whites in some other states. Two anthropologists, Benedict and Weltfish, reprinted them in 1943 in slightly more selected form, omitting the northern state in which the negroes averaged lowest and the southern state in which

TABLE 10.1 *Southern Whites and Northern Negroes, by States,* Army *Results,* 1918* *Average intelligence test scores.*

Whites		Negroes	
State	Median score	State	Median score
Mississippi	41·25	Pennsylvania	42·00
Kentucky	41·50	New York	45·00
Arkansas	41·55	Illinois	47·35
Georgia	42·12	Ohio	49·50

* From Klineberg (1944, p. 36).

the whites scored highest. The House of Representatives then declared Benedict and Weltfish's account 'unfit for US soldiers' and ensured that it was withdrawn from circulation in the army (Alper and Boring, 1944).

The contrast between the low scores almost universally found when Southern negroes were tested and the much higher ones of those in Northern states was explained by most experts in one of two ways, either as an effect of selective migration or as a consequence of better education, better opportunities and generally superior environment in the North. Some studies showed that selective migration did occur, and that the negro families moving North were higher scorers to start with (e.g. Gist and Clark, 1939), but it was also shown that this could not be the whole explanation, and probably not the most important factor (Lee, 1951). Several of the research papers about the role of improved social conditions in producing gains in measured intelligence are reprinted in the useful collection of readings edited by Jenkins and Paterson (1961).

One kind of evidence pointing towards the direct connection of IQ with social conditions was that differences in average score between whites and negroes were found to form a steady gradient, being very small in New York, not very large in Chicago, and becoming steadily larger as the surveys came from further South. A second line of evidence, even more directly convincing, was provided by Klineberg (1935) who showed that, on the whole, the longer the negroes had lived in the North, the higher was their IQ. There was a close but not perfect relationship between test score and length of residence in New York City. This trend was much clearer for verbal than for performance tests. Klineberg's study was cross-sectional, but his findings were substantiated by Lee (1951) in a longitudinal study. The increase in performance with length of residence in the North was observed not only for general intelligence, but also for each of the subtests of Primary Mental Abilities.

Another approach which was used to study the relative importance of genetic and environmental influences on difference in performance between negroes and whites has been to compare the measured intelligence of groups containing various proportions of negro blood, e.g. half-negro, quarter-negro and so on. These studies were reviewed by Witty and Jenkins (1936) who summarised their results as follows: 'One may conclude tentatively that the differences in the average test scores of American whites and Negroes are not to be attributed to differences in inheritable intelligence. Furthermore, one may conclude that the technique involving test score comparison is at present specious as a definitive single approach in racial studies.'

The more recent studies summarised by Dreger and Miller (1960) appear to add rather little either in the way of improved methods or of new substantive results, but the review is a valuable one in that it studiously avoids what the authors correctly describe as the polemical attitude of Shuey in favour of genetic differences and the rationalisation of Klineberg in the opposite direction. They also make the important point that the environmental differences between negroes and whites in the USA are not comparable with social class differences between whites. Discussing a series of studies by McGurk in which the intelligence of negroes was compared with that of whites with socio-economic status controlled, and in which the overlap of scores was 91% but differences in favour of whites were still found, Dreger and Miller reasonably maintain that equating for socio-economic status is still inadequate, since the difference is not so much one of *class* as of *caste*. 'In the state of Florida where the writers reside there are a number of Negroes whose social and economic statuses exceed those of most white persons. These Negroes, however, cannot yet sit in the same seats on public transportation (in most places), go to the same hotel, restaurant, club, school, church, social events or even restrooms.' One must agree with the writers, that while such fundamental environmental restrictions are enforced (and in addition, very different educational facilities, not mentioned in their list), equating for 'socio-economic status' is, although a step in the right direction, far from ensuring a just comparison. The surprising fact is perhaps that scores can show a 91% overlap.

Although the largest quantity of research into the abilities of 'minority groups' in the USA has been concerned with negroes, work on other races and immigrant groups has been extensive. One recent study must serve as a representative example.

Lesser, Fifer and Clark (1965) took, in effect, eight groups of six- and seven-year-old children. Four ethnic communities in New York City were sampled, Chinese, Jewish, Negro and Puerto Rican, each represented by both middle-class and lower-class children. Unlike most investigators of cultural effects, Lesser's team were interested more in the differential pattern of mental abilities than in general intelligence and expected to find different patterns characterising their eight groups. The tests used were constructed by Davis, Lesser and French and were known as Verbal, Reasoning, Number and Space Conceptualisation. Earlier studies relating performance on primary mental abilities to cultural factors were apparently rare. Lesser et al. summarise them as having indicated greater differences in favour of high-status children on the Verbal, Word-fluency and Number tests, and smaller differences on Space, Reasoning and Memory. This is very much what one would expect in view of many findings already mentioned that linguistic skills are particularly susceptible to cultural influence. The main findings about the eight groups are summarised in Tables 10.2a and 10.2b opposite.

One can see from Table 10.2b that the expected differences in favour of middle-class children were found for each test. Table 10.2a shows that considerable variations in pattern were found as between ethnic groups. What is not clear from these tables, but is amply demonstrated elsewhere in the monograph is that the differential ethnic patterns of abilities were remarkably stable irrespective of social class.

The other ethnic groups also revealed consistent patterns of ability common to both middle and lower class. Other interesting findings of a similar type are given by Lesser, Fifer and Clark, and their work deserves to be repeated and extended.

Research of the kind discussed raises the obvious question of language difficulties and of bilingualism. Again there is a considerable literature. A useful summary of the relation between bilingualism and measured intelligence is by Haugen (1961). Many of the earlier investigations found lower IQ and lower verbal ability in bilingual children, but these were apparently specious and were no longer found in better controlled studies when the bilinguals were matched with monolinguals on mental age or knowledge of English. What true differences remained applied to children entering the new culture after infancy. If brought up in it from early infancy as bilingual speakers, children appear to suffer no measurable handicap.

It must already be clear how complex is the task of assessing abilities in minority and immigrant groups, and that it is far too simple-minded to suppose that the use of non-verbal or performance tests is a sure

TABLE 10.2a *Means, Standard Deviations, Intercorrelations, and Reliability Coefficients of Scales by Ethnic Group**

Ethnic group	Verbal	Reasoning	Number	Space	Mean	Standard deviation
Chinese (N = 80):						
Verbal	·91	·42	·38	·34	71·09	14·57
Reasoning		·90	·64	·64	25·94	7·12
Number			·94	·49	27·79	9·35
Space				·83	42·51	10·09
Jewish (N = 80):						
Verbal	·87	·70	·54	·48	90·35	11·70
Reasoning		·84	·68	·49	25·21	6·67
Number			·95	·40	28·50	9·88
Space				·80	39·71	9·21
Negro (N = 80):						
Verbal	·93	·62	·58	·59	74·29	16·48
Reasoning		·85	·71	·68	20·41	9·43
Number			·96	·54	18·39	10·20
Space				·85	34·42	11·56
Puerto Rican (N = 80):						
Verbal	·90	·62	·58	·48	61·92	17·41
Reasoning		·93	·74	·49	18·90	8·62
Number			·96	·49	19·13	9·71
Space				·84	35·09	9·70

TABLE 10.2b *Means, Standard Deviations, Intercorrelations, and Reliability Coefficients of Scales by Social Class*

Social class	Verbal	Reasoning	Number	Space	Mean	Standard deviation
Middle class (N = 160):						
Verbal	·94	·52	·50	·38	82·21	16·55
Reasoning		·85	·63	·52	26·08	7·33
Number			·95	·41	27·67	9·89
Space				·80	42·12	9·33
Lower class (N = 160):						
Verbal	·89	·47	·40	·28	66·62	16·64
Reasoning		·91	·73	·57	19·15	8·35
Number			·96	·51	19·22	10·12
Space				·84	33·75	10·36

* From Lesser, Fifer and Clark (1965, p. 48).

key to the problem. This is made clearer still by the work of Ortar (1963) in Israel, who tested the assumption that the WISC performance test scores would show a smaller difference between high-status Israeli children and oriental immigrants than would the verbal scores. Her research was in fact more complex than this, including five groups of children in all, varying in status and degree of acculturation. The main, and rather surprising finding was that, whereas the verbal tests placed all five groups in the expected order, the performance tests, so far from being more 'culturally fair', produced *greater* differences in favour of the more privileged and longer-acculturated children.

Finally, an important and detailed account by Vernon (1965) of West Indian children is very relevant (see also his recent, 1966 and 1967, reports of testing Canadian, Indian, and Eskimo children). It is unfortunately impossible to consider its findings in detail, but his general conclusions, which confirm and amplify many of the points just made deserve to be quoted in full.

The major finding of the study so far is that children whose mental development is handicapped by poor socio-economic, cultural and linguistic environment, by defective education and family instability, show this to a greater extent in practical-spatial and some abstract non-verbal abilities than they do in actual educational achievements. This is borne out by the urban-rural sub-group differences within the West Indies. Even an educational system which is grossly affected by lack of funds, buildings and equipment, brief and irregular attendance, poor quality of teaching and over-formality, produces fairly good attainments, especially in the more mechanical subjects, though there is no indication that it trains a general rote-learning ability. Probably it also stimulates development in non-educational abilities when the home environment is very deprived. In the English situation, differences in regularity of schooling seem to have much less widespread effects. It must not be forgotten, however, that more able children from better homes are naturally more apt to attend school regularly, hence the causal effects of schooling as such are difficult to disentangle.

Next it is clear that the most important single factor in children's performance on *g* and verbal tests is the cultural level of the home, parental education and encouragement, reading facilities and pro- bably the speech background (though it was not possible to assess the latter aspect satisfactorily). Economic level as such is subsidiary, and among West Indian (not English) children, cultural stimulus strongly affects perceptual-practical abilities as well. Of the other factors in the home situation, suggested as relevant in an earlier publication (Vernon 1962), the most important seems to be the purposefulness and rationality of the family atmosphere. The broken home syndrome and family instability are to some extent associated with educational achievement but not at all, or even inversely, with the general ability factor. A definite connection was found in both groups between male dominance in the home or masculine identification on the part of the boy, and certain more practical abilities. Absence of a father figure is, indeed, an all too frequent characteristic of the West Indian culture.

Many psychologists and anthropologists are justifiably suspicious of the application of British or American tests in non-Western cultures, on the grounds that they may reflect different sources of variance, different background factors, effects of administration procedures, etc. In fact, the overall factor structure was extremely similar in the two groups, although certain tests differed sufficiently in their loadings to suggest that they were measuring different things. We are entitled to generalise that West Indian boys are relatively high in Education and Perceptual, lower in g and linguistic, and lowest in the Practical factor; but must, at the same time, admit that there were considerable inconsistencies in their performance on some of the tests that go to make up these factors. Particularly, was this true of the tests which, in Western cultures, may be regarded as relatively pure measures of g. Thus, the West Indians are good at a Sorting Test of Concept Formation and on some items from a battery of Piaget tests, very weak on a non-verbal Matrices and an Abstraction test, as well as on Kohs Blocks and other Piaget items – mainly those involving visualization and conservation.

It follows that the prospects for a culture-fair test or tests which might be used, for example, to test the educational potential of West Indian immigrant children in this country, are not good. Tests which yielded the best measures of g according to a factor analysis of West Indian results, were those given individually with the simplest instructions; and these tended to show as high correlations with environmental variables as any. In the writer's view, the most predictive instrument for immigrants is undoubtedly the WISC Verbal, provided the children are old enough and that it is given by a tester with some familiarity with West Indian speech. WISC Performance, Progressive Matrices and the non-verbal items of Terman-Merrill are less suitable in so far as success at these seems to depend on all sorts

I

of complex factors such as insecure, female-dominated upbringing, and lack of play and spatial experience. Of the performance tests used in this research, the most suitable seemed to be Porteus Mazes and Draw-a-Man.

DEGREES OF CULTURAL DEPRIVATION

One would not expect to find such large differences between groups of native citizens in a single Western democracy as between British soldiers and Gurkhas, or even as between urbanised Israelis and recent oriental immigrants to Israel. Nonetheless, substantial differences are often found that can be directly ascribed to cultural deprivation of one kind or another, either individual deprivation, such as suffered by orphaned and institutionalised children, or regional deprivation, such as experienced by isolated and backward communities.

Several studies of the latter have shown convincingly the direct effect of an economically and culturally impoverished community on children's measurable intelligence. A well-known early research in England by Gordon on canal-boat families and on gypsies produced particularly telling evidence. A steady and considerable decrease of IQ with age was found in both groups. The negative correlation of IQ and age in the canal-boat group was nearly ·8, but was considerably smaller in the group of gypsy children, whose environment provided more social contacts. A significant positive correlation was found between IQ and school attendance in the latter group.

Similar evidence was found in studies of isolated mountain communities in Kentucky and Tennessee, and in the hollows of the Blue Ridge Mountains (e.g. Sherman and Key, 1932; Wheeler, 1942). As with the canal-boat and gypsy children, average IQ in such communities was found to be well below national norms, and to decrease systematically with age. Some of these studies also demonstrated a steady increase in average IQ in a community, paralleling over a period of years its increasing prosperity and lessening isolation.

In this American work it was found that, in the same way as Warburton's Gurkhas, children brought up in isolated communities often failed to see the point of the questions and tasks presented. In the Sherman and Key study, most of the children were baffled by a problem that involved finding a ball in a field, because they had never seen a ball. Klineberg (1944, p. 69) quotes an account by Pressey.

He presented the familiar Binet problem: 'If you went to the store and bought six cents worth of candy and gave the clerk ten cents, what change would you receive?' One youngster replied, 'I never had ten cents and if I had I wouldn't spend it for candy, and anyway candy is what your mother makes.' The examiner made a second attempt and reformulated his questions as follows: 'If you had taken ten cows to pasture for your father and six of them strayed away, how many would you have left to drive home?' The child replied, 'We don't have ten cows, but if we did and I lost six, I wouldn't dare go home.' The examiner made one last attempt: 'If there were ten children in a school and six of them were out with measles, how many would there be in school?' The answer came even more promptly: 'None, because the rest would be afraid of catching it too.' This example, though extreme, illustrates a real difficulty in this whole field. The test situation frequently demands an ability to regard a hypothetical situation as a real one, and to react to it accordingly; lack of any previous experience or training in situations analogous to those assumed by the test may render the appropriate answer difficult, if not impossible.

Isolated communities are becoming scarcer in industrialised Western countries. In recent years psychologists have been much more concerned with individual deprivation resulting in particular from separation from the mother and institutional upbringing.

Skodak and Skeels made an extensive series of studies in the USA of children in foster homes. Skodak (1939) described 154 children, all but 14 of whom were illegitimate, and all of whom had been living with the foster parents since before the age of six months. Fairly full information was available about the status and circumstances of the natural parents, which were generally low or underprivileged, and the measured intelligence of more than half of the natural mothers was known (average IQ, 88). The social status and average intelligence of the foster parents, while covering a wide range, were in general superior to those of the natural parents. The homes were agreed by the social workers concerned to be good ones to bring children up in. The intelligence of these foster children was tested at intervals when they had lived in the foster homes for periods between two and five years, and the average IQ of the group varied between 110 and 116. This is very suggestive evidence for the effects of environment, since one can state with a high degree of confidence that such a favourable result would have been unlikely if they had been brought up by the natural parents.

Later similar studies (e.g. Skodak and Skeels, 1949; Skeels and Harms, 1948) produced similar findings. These articles included follow-up studies which showed that the above-average mental development of the children placed in good foster homes continued at least into early adolescence. Again it was made clear that children of low-IQ parents adopted and provided with a favourable home background, far exceeded their natural parents in measured intelligence. In the former study, for instance, it was found that this difference amounted on the average to between 20 and 30 points.

This evidence for the importance of environmental effects is not the whole story, however. The earlier work of Skodak and Skeels was criticised by McNemar and others for deficiencies in experimental design and method, and it is generally agreed that the effects they claimed to have shown, although genuine, were probably exaggerated. One factor which may have resulted in some degree of misinterpretation is the amount of screening or selection of children before adoption. In addition, Skodak and Skeels found a correlation of ·44 between the intelligence of the adopted children (at age 13) and that of the *natural* mothers. Moreover Honzik (1957) has shown that this correlation tends to increase with age, whereas the same is not true of the correlation with the intelligence of the foster parents, or at least is true to a markedly lesser extent.

Kellmer Pringle has carried out extensive studies of children deprived of normal family care and her collection of papers ('Deprivation and Education', 1965) suggests the following conclusions. Institutionalised children almost always score below average on tests of ability and attainment (cf. Goldfarb, 1945), and the effects of deprivation on intellectual performances seem to be directly related to the earliness of separation from the mother. Sheer length of institutionalisation is apparently of much lesser importance. Pringle's researches strongly suggest that there is a specific deleterious effect on language development, as shown for instance by a comparison of verbal and performance scores on the WISC. She also concludes that the abilities of deprived children are likely to be considerably underestimated if group tests are used. Their general emotional state and in particular the difficulties they are likely to experience in the group-test situation are such as to impair the level of motivation and sustained effort that are required. One should not, however, assume that children brought up in a communal institution without maternal care are necessarily and *permanently* retarded. The careful study by Dennis and Najarian (1957) of illegitimate and abandoned Lebanese children brought up in a well-run but understaffed creche led them to the general conclusion that early retardation does not necessarily or even typically result in permanent retardation.

TABLE 10.3 *Kinds of Items showing Unusually Large and Unusually Small Status Differences, as Found by Nine Investigators**

Investigation†	Kinds of Items Showing Largest Differences in Favour of High-Status Pupils	Kinds of Items Showing Smallest Status Differences (or Differences in Favour of Low-Status Pupils)
Binet (1911, 35) Binet-Simon (White)	Tests judged to depend on: language, 6 tests; home training, 4 tests; attention, 3 tests	Tests judged to depend on: scholastic training, 6 tests; language, 2 tests; home training 1 test; judgment, 1 test
Stern (1912, 47) Binet-Simon (White)	Items of considerably above average difficulty	Items of only average difficulty
Weintrob and Weintrob (1912, 51) Binet-Simon (White)	Items judged to involve the ability to reason	Items judged to involve the use of language
Bridges and Coler (1917, 36) Binet-Simon (White)	Absurd statements Comprehension of questions Comparison of familiar objects Concrete definitions Counting backward from 20 to 1	Arranging weights Aesthetic judgment Copying square and diamond Comparison of lines Drawing designs from memory
Burt (1922, 38) Binet-Simon (White)	Linguistic tests – wide vocabulary Scholastic tests – literary subjects Memory tests – repetition of sentences Memory tests – items of information in cultural homes	Tests with money Perceptual and drawing tests 'Practical' tests Tests of critical shrewdness
Stoke (1927, 48) Stanford-Binet (White)	Linguistic tests – original thinking	Linguistic tests– rote memory
Long (1935, 44) Kuhlmann-Anderson (Negro)	Completion Counting taps Likeness in pictures Finding of words that do not belong with others	Finding similar forms among a group of varied forms Substituting numbers for letters
Saltzman (1940, 46) Stanford-Binet (White)	Vocabulary Verbal comprehension of everyday situations Motor control	Counting and handling money Rote memory Sensory discrimination
Murray (1947, 4) Henmon-Nelson Kuhlmann-Anderson Otis Beta Chicago Tests of Primary Mental Abilities (Negro)	Items dependent on verbal ability	Items employing perception of form and space (geometric-design items)

* From Eells et al. 1951, p. 15.
† This column shows (*a*) name of investigator, (*b*) date of publication of the study, (*c*) number of reference in the Bibliography at the end of Eells' book, (*d*) test analysed, and (*e*) race of pupils studied.

Note. The references in this table are not included in the bibliography of the present book.

SOCIO-ECONOMIC STATUS AND INTELLIGENCE

Eells et. al. (1951), in their book 'Intelligence and Cultural Differences', discuss extensively the nature of social-class effects on measured intelligence, and try to isolate the particular kinds of test and item that most and least reflect social differences, with the aim of producing a test that should be culture-free or relatively so as between social classes within the USA. This book has had a rough passage from some reviewers, and the great dependence of reactions to work of this kind upon personal pre-conceptions can be seen from the unusually conflicting reviews reprinted in Buros (1965).

Eells reviews much of the earlier American work and finds that the correlations observed between measured intelligence and socio-economic status range from little above zero to almost $+\cdot6$, with typical values around $\cdot35$ for a variety of predominantly verbal tests (performance tests excluded). He also discusses the important question of the effect of age on this relationship. If environmental factors and environment-heredity interactions were predominant, one would expect the relation to increase with age. As usual, however, the matter is not so simple as that; possible influences in the opposite direction, tending to produce smaller environmental effects with increasing age, might include, for instance, the maturation of inherited characteristics and the equalising effect of a common school curriculum and relatively common environment.

Nor is the literature about what *kinds* of test and item are most sensitive or insensitive to status differences very consistent. Eells assembled this evidence (see Table 10.3, p. 261) and, while admitting some inconsistency in the findings, concluded that in general items which were mainly linguistic or scholastic favoured children from high socio-economic backgrounds, and that items primarily perceptual or practical in nature showed smaller or even reversed differences.

The main field study reported by Eells and his associates started from this point, and in general this hypothesis that 'performance' and 'perceptual' items would be more resistant to social-class influences was supported. Nine-year-olds and thirteen-year-olds in an industrial Midwest community were tested, and the expected relation between social class and measured intelligence was again found. Correlations ranged between $\cdot20$ and $\cdot43$. The differences were still very marked when the comparisons were restricted to 'Old Americans' (excluding recent immigrants) and were statistically very highly significant on all tests used, including the following:

Otis Alpha Verbal
Otis Alpha Numerical
Kuhlmann – Anderson
Henmon – Nelson
Otis Beta
Terman – McNemar
Thurstone Spatial
Thurstone Reasoning
California Mental Maturity

The conclusions about types of item are graphically summarised in Figure 10.1 below.

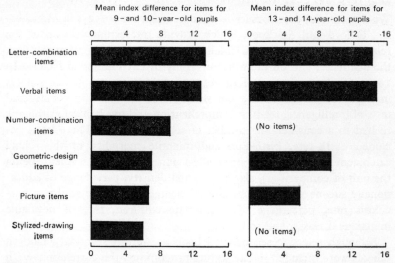

Figure 10.1. Mean status differences for items classified on the basis of symbolism used. From Eells et al. (1951), p. 212

The main suggested reason for this whole pattern of observed differences was 'variations in opportunity for familiarity with specific cultural words, objects or processes required for answering the best items' (Eells et al. p. 68).

In an attempt to take advantage of these findings, Davis and Eells developed a test designed to discount or minimise social class differences. This was called the Davis-Eells Games, since one feature of it is the presentation of the material as a game, in a relaxed and light-hearted atmosphere. It is given entirely orally, involving no reading, and the actual material is pictorial, rather in the style of a comic strip cartoon.

Praise and encouragement should be given during the admistration, to induce good motivation.

Unfortunately this praiseworthy attempt is generally agreed to have produced disappointing results, and tends to yield differences in score between social classes in the same direction and of much the same magnitude as do conventional tests (Altus, 1956; Coleman & Ward, 1955; Drake, 1959). Anastasi (1961, p. 268) comments that this test appears to have sacrified predictive validity without eliminating 'cultural bias'.

SPECIFIC EFFECTS OF HOME AND SCHOOL ENVIRONMENT

Wiseman (1964) describes in detail some extensive surveys in Manchester, Salford and Stockport which provide interesting data about the relation between measured intelligence and scholastic attainment on the one hand, and on the other a variety of environmental factors. In 1951 a whole year-group of 14-year-old children in maintained schools in Manchester was tested, and their scores on specially constructed tests of intelligence, reading comprehension and mechanical arithmetic related to a considerable number of social variables. These latter included death-rate, birth-rate and infantile mortality in the school catchment area (the ward, or smallest unit of local government, being the unit of comparison), also population density, percentage of educationally sub-normal children and of mentally defective adults, tuberculosis rate, percentage of illegitimate children, rate of notifiable infectious diseases, and so forth.

Although selective secondary schools as well as secondary modern schools were included in the testing programme, the correlations with social and environmental factors could only be calculated for the latter. The labour involved in tabulating the children's *home* addresses would have proved prohibitive, and the social data therefore apply to the area around the *school*. Comparisons of this kind between wards were thought to be satisfactory in the case of secondary modern schools, but not for selective secondary schools, which generally drew pupils from a wider area. This restriction on the completeness of the analysis, while being an unfortunate necessity, will almost certainly have had the effect of *reducing* the apparent influence of environmental factors (by restriction of range), so that conclusions drawn in this research about the extent of environmental influence will tend to be conservative ones. The correlations found in this 1951 survey are shown in Table 10.4 below.

TABLE 10.4 *Product-moment correlations between attainment and social variables. (From Wiseman, 1964)*

Variable	Backwardness			Brightness		
	Intell.	Read.	Arith.	Intell.	Read.	Arith.
Mental deficiency	·84	·64	·60	−·55	−·06	−·22
Birth-rate	·69	·37	·53	−·30	·02	−·28
Illegitimate children	·66	·48	·72	−·43	·07	−·15
T.B. rate	·63	·32	·51	−·16	·16	−·22
Neglected children	·50	·23	·57	−·23	−·25	−·21
J-index	·37	·35	·12	−·25	−·16	−·18
Death-rate	·36	·15	−·01	−·08	·14	−·20
Persons per acre	·33	·37	·51	−·19	·14	−·22
Infantile mortality	·25	·16	·14	−·20	−·17	−·09
Infectious diseases	·03	−·21	·08	·00	−·18	·00
Average correlation	·47	·29	·38	−·24	−·03	−·18

This table requires a little further explanation. 'Backwardness' refers to the number of children in the secondary modern schools of a particular ward who obtained a standard score of −1·0 or below (standardisation having been on the entire age-group, including pupils in selective schools). 'Brightness' refers to number with a standard score of +1·0 or above. The correlations are thus based in effect on the tails of the distribution only, and this may have increased their size, counter-acting the restriction mentioned in the last paragraph.

Two features of the results are immediately noticeable. The correlations with brightness are generally lower than those with backwardness. This is presumably due to the restriction of range at the top end resulting from the omission of children in selective schools. It would be interesting to know, however, whether the pattern would have been symmetrical if they had been included. (If it still showed higher correlations for backwardness, the implication would be that the deleterious effect of unfavourable environments on attainment was more marked than the beneficial effect of good ones.) The second noticeable feature is the generally larger size of the correlations with intelligence than with attainment. Wiseman suggests this may be partly due to less restriction of range in intelligence than in attainment resulting from the 11+ selection procedure, but this possibility seems unlikely to account for the whole effect.

In discussing this point (which is interesting and surprising), that intelligence is more closely related to the environmental factors than is attainment, one must be careful in arguing from correlation to causal effect, but the evidence for a strong relation between measured intelligence and social conditions is striking. When multiple correlations were calculated, the combination of social factors gave an R

for intelligence of ·963; the highest beta weight, birth-rate in a particular ward, was +·9.

Other interesting conclusions were drawn by Wiseman from this
survey. There was a striking contrast in some respects between his
results and those of Burt in London 30 years earlier. Burt had found a
correlation of ·93 between infantile mortality rate and backwardness,
whereas Wiseman's corresponding figure was ·19. Wiseman discusses
the reasons for this big difference, excludes the possibility of its being
a statistical artifact, and produces evidence to show that one consequence of improvement in welfare services is that infantile mortality
is now very much less a consequence of poverty or low economic status,
but much more clearly associated with parental neglect, relatively independent of status or income.

Interpreting the same research in a later paper, Wiseman (1966)
also makes the important point that all his findings taken in conjunction
with the results of earlier studies, such as those of Burt and of Elizabeth
Fraser, suggest strongly, almost to the point of certainty, that an adverse
environment has its greatest effects on children of above average ability.

Another survey, carried out in Salford, is described by Warburton
in the same volume. This was similar to the one just summarised in
many respects, including the necessary restriction of the group studied
to secondary modern school children. It differed, however, in taking
the school instead of the ward as the unit of comparison. As in Wiseman's research, sizeable correlations were found between environmental factors (with more emphasis this time on school variables such as size
of class) and both intelligence and attainment. Again intelligence was
found to be rather more highly correlated with these factors than was
attainment.

These results, as Warburton says, 'on every count give more weight
to the environmentalist than to the genetic viewpoint of the nature of
ability required in intelligence tests'. He adds (p. 121) that 'No doubt
in more recent times practice, coaching, habituation in the home and
school, and social attitudes to education have played a part in decreasing
the role of innate capacity. Even so, it remains surprising that tests
expressly designed to be non-teachable as distinct from reading and
arithmetic, which are essentially teachable, should give these results.'
Warburton also makes the point that, since Salford is a more homogeneous community in many respects than those studied in comparable
researches, one would expect this to have a *lowering* effect on the correlations with environmental factors.

The unexpected finding of a *higher* correlation of environmental factors with intelligence than with attainment can be partly explained, at least (see Wiseman, Chapter 8), as a consequence of selecting the ward and not the individual as the unit for correlation. This no doubt lays greater effective emphasis on the compensatory efforts of teachers in less favoured areas to instil a basic knowledge of arithmetic and reading, if necessary at the cost of being unable to devote so much time to other subjects. For the purposes of our discussion, however, what matters is not so much the relative correlations with intelligence and attainment, but the fact of high correlation between environment and intelligence. This high correlation is the more striking in being derived from a sample which was confined to secondary modern school children in one region. If selective schoolchildren and children from other parts of the country had been included, one must suppose the relation would have been higher still.

The Manchester studies have been treated at some length as being thorough, conducted with large samples, and scrupulously analysed. Other British work describing the effect of environmental factors on attainment has pointed to much the same conclusions. Joyce Morris, for instance, working in Kent, has demonstrated the relation between environmental handicap and reading difficulties, and the environmental factors found to be most important have, on the whole, paralleled those emphasised by Wiseman (Morris, 1966; Reid, 1968).

Douglas (1964) describes the results so far of a large longitudinal study of ability and attainment (among other things) carried out under the auspices of the Population Investigation Committee. This book has been an influential one, although some of the methods of analysis and of reporting results are rough-and-ready, as Burt (1965) has no difficulty in showing. Probably the most important findings are (a) the increasing difference in average IQ between socio-economic groups with increasing age, (b) confirmation of the fact that, at a given intelligence level, near the borderline, far more middle-class children enter grammar schools, (c) the crucial importance of parental interest and encouragement, which is shown to be a more important influence than, say, housing conditions, family size or academic record of school, though these too correlate with entry to grammar school.

Shortly before going to press, a great abundance of new information about mathematical attainment in 12 countries and about the effects of social and organisational factors has been presented by Husén (1967), editing the report of the International Project for the Evaluation of Educational Achievement. The conclusions of this report are complex, subject to numerous provisos about differences between national educational systems, and by no means easy to digest and interpret at short notice. One or two general conclusions, nevertheless, are very apposite to the present discussion. For instance, it was found that there were very considerable differences between countries in the extent of relationship between parental level of education and the chances of children staying in secondary school to the sixth form and (in all probability) proceeding to university. The degree of selection in this respect varied markedly, with West Germany showing the highest degree of 'élite selection', England a high degree, and the USA the lowest (Vol. 2, p. 302). Another general conclusion, with obvious relevance to the merits of comprehensive education, was that in general, over the twelve countries, pupils of low socio-economic status were found to profit better from instruction in schools with a large spread in socio-economic background than in more socially homogeneous schools.

The same conflicting evidence that was found in the case of different ethnic groups as to whether non-verbal and performance tests are fairer in discounting cultural handicap is also found in comparisons between social classes. On the one hand, we have the careful analysis of Eells and his associates, showing that test items revealed greater class differences in proportion as they involved verbal skills (and this analysis is not invalidated by the unsuccess of the Davis-Eells test). There is also the evidence produced by Kellmer Pringle that deprivation and lack of cultural stimulation affects language skills in particular and that of Nisbet and Entwistle (1967) that the negative correlation of IQ and family size is more marked with verbal tests. Finally, Bernstein, in a series of articles (1959, 1960, 1961a, 1961b, 1962; Bernstein and Young, 1966) has (a) reported much bigger differences on verbal than on non-verbal tests between children of different classes, (b) adumbrated a persuasive and influential theory to explain why this should be so, of which the gist is that working-class children possess command only of a 'public' language, lacking the 'formal' language employed by the middle class. This theory of Bernstein's, however, rests on fairly slender evidence, and in addition is not easy to confirm or disprove conclusively. Several recent studies reviewed by McDade (1967) appear to throw some doubt on the validity of Bernstein's hypothesis. Another protagonist of non-verbal tests is R. B. Cattell, who has repeatedly argued that they are much less susceptible to cultural factors, and his claim is accepted by Vernon (1960, p. 90) to the extent that such tests give a fairer picture of intelligence among linguistically handicapped people.

On the other hand, we have a rather consistent picture of failure to discount the effect of social class differences by these means and some direct evidence in the opposite direction. Lawrence (1931) found a correlation of about ·3 between score on a performance test and parents' class and income. The correlation with social class was lower for boys than girls. In experiments such as that of Findlay and McGuire (1957) lower-class and middle-class children were matched on a verbal test to test the hypothesis that on a non-verbal or relatively 'culture-fair' test the working-class group would prove superior. Exactly the opposite was found. Similarly, Tsakalos (1966) investigated the relative social-class differences in performance on (a) the Jenkins non-verbal intelligence test No. 1 (published by the N.F.E.R.), (b) Moray House verbal reasoning test No. 71, (c) Moray House English test No. 36, (d) Moray House arithmetic test No. 36. His main aim was to discover whether a non-verbal test was any more resistant to social-class influences or more 'culture-fair' than the three Moray House tests. His findings were that all four tests showed significant differences in performance when administered to some four hundred eleven-year-old Edinburgh children. The order of differences (descending order of size) was English, verbal reasoning, Jenkins non-verbal, arithmetic.

The synthesis and resolution of these conflicting findings is an urgent task for future research workers. Most of the present evidence is based on correlational studies and on group comparisons. More work is needed on individual cases, and the rather crude distinction between verbal and non-verbal measures needs closer experimental study, since non-verbal tests may often be most effectively coped with by implicit verbalisation. In addition, it would obviously be wrong to think of differences in performance on verbal and non-verbal tests as only due to factors such as social class. There will clearly also be individual differences in interests and specialised abilities within classes that affect such differential scores (Welsh, 1967). More comprehensive research is required and the recommendations made in Chapter 3 about a closer liaison between correlational and experimental workers might well bear fruit also in this area.

IMPLICATIONS FOR EDUCATIONAL POLICY

The research surveyed in this chapter has been selected so as to emphasise (a) demonstrated relations between social and cultural conditions and measured intelligence, and (b) attempts to minimise and allow for resulting bias. Another large body of literature has recently grown up, concerned with educational opportunity in Britain and making explicit the inequalities that remain, even when measured ability is taken at its face value. A review of the millions of words that have been written in the last few years about educational opportunity in Britain is not possible within the scope of this book, but one or two points must be mentioned. Floud, Halsey and Martin (1956), for instance, demonstrated social inequality (although diminished during the two or three decades before their survey) in opportunities for selective secondary education as between wealthy Southern areas and poorer Northern ones. Comprehensive secondary education may reduce but cannot in itself remove such inequalities, which are due less to 'inefficient' selection procedures than to deep-seated class attitudes. Jackson and Marsden (1962) have documented in detail the factors that can make it psychologically difficult for a bright working-class child to adopt the new attitudes inevitably associated with grammar-school sixth form and higher education. To adopt them whole-heartedly may often appear a kind of disloyalty to his family, friends and class.

There is a tendency for these restricting consequences of working-class membership to move up the age-scale, so to speak. Very soon, if not already, social pressures on the working-class boy and even more on the working-class girl to leave school before entering the sixth form will appear a more potent source of wasted talent and inequality of opportunity than any systematic social handicap at an earlier stage. Certainly estimates of the national resources of talent by, among others, Headmasters of Grammar schools have been, even in the recent past, grossly restrictive and pessimistic. Jackson and Marsden quote some such estimates, including one by Rée in 1953 (then Headmaster of Watford Grammar School) that the huge majority of boys leaving school after taking 'O' level GCE had approached their academic ceiling and that sixth-form studies would to them be a waste of time. Jackson and Marsden's comment that he could hardly have been more experienced or more wrong, though harsh, is not unjustified. In the recent past, in fact, this stage has probably been the one at which most high-level talent was wasted from social causes, since Furneaux (1961) found that once pupils had entered advanced sixth forms, the selective effects of social class determinants ceased to operate. (But one cannot bank on this continuing, as perhaps in the past only exceptional individuals from working-class homes reached that stage.) Moreover, even if performance is less affected at this level, and it seems particularly so at Oxbridge, where there is some evidence of a *negative* correlation between social class and student performance (Dale, 1963), this is a relatively minor point. The good performance of working-class pupils in sixth forms and still more at Universities such as Oxford and Cambridge (perhaps also University College, London. See Malleson, 1960) is presumably due to the wastage of working-class pupils of high, but not exceptionally high ability and motivation. The Robbins Committee report showed that of children born in 1940–1 of equally high ability, the proportion entering degree-level courses was twice as high for middle-class as for working-class children, and further recent evidence of this wastage has been provided by Armstrong (1967).

Psychological views of intelligence have played some part in this underestimating and wastage of national resources. The idea of a fixed, unalterable IQ has led to the idea of a fixed, unalterable quantity of national talent. Enough evidence has been summarised in this chapter, however, to show rather conclusively that, whatever proportion of variance in intelligence we ascribe to hereditary or genetic endowment, for practical purposes we must act and plan as though environmental influences were crucial. If this conclusion seems self-contradictory, the paradox can be partly resolved as follows. There is a strong likelihood that the genes set a limit or ceiling on cognitive ability, but that in most people's lives environmental circumstances impose a much lower one. Studies of identical twins, for instance, allow no other conclusion than that inherited dispositions in interaction with social circumstances must be taken into account. Social organisation, however, is capable of such a degree of change and development that 'what is given at birth' may, in different forms of society, assume almost any degree of relative importance.

It is therefore unfortunate to write, as in the title of Macintosh's (1959) book, about a 'pool of ability', and to imply that there is a fixed proportion of people in the population capable of a certain level of cognitive performance. Convenient as this idea may be in the short term to the administrator, it cannot be justified by a dispassionate view of relevant research and leads to policies that perpetuate an arbitrary stratification in society. The more informed and humane view is expressed by Vernon who points out (1960, p. 185) that the supply of adequate students, for instance, depends much less upon the distribution of IQ than on such factors as the educational and vocational aspirations of the family, the traditions and current attitudes in the schools, the effectiveness of teaching methods and the prestige of occupations requiring university training.

Suggested additional reading

KLINEBERG, O. (Ed.), *Characteristics of the American Negro*. New York: Harper (1944).

DREGER, R. M., and MILLER, U. S., 'Comparative psychological studies of Negroes and Whites in the United States'. *Psychol. Bull.* 57, 361–402 (1960).

WARBURTON, F. W., 'The ability of the Gurkha recruit'. *Brit. J. Psychol.*, 42, 123–133 (1951).

PRINGLE, M. L. KELLMER, *Depreviation and Education*. London: Longmans (1965).

WISEMAN, S., *Education and Environment*. Manchester: Manchester Univ. Press (1964).

FLOUD, J., HALSEY, A. H., and MARTIN, F. M., *Social Class and Educational Opportunity*. London: Heinemann (1956).

SWIFT, D. F., 'Social Class and Educational Adaptation'. In *Educational Research in Britain* (Ed. H. J. Butcher). London: Univ. of London Press (1968).

XI

Ability, Personality and Achievement

TERMAN'S STUDIES OF GIFTED CHILDREN

In 1921 Lewis M. Terman, who was already well known for the construction of the Stanford-Binet test, and who had played a large part
in organising the mass testing of American recruits with the Army
Alpha test in the First World War, began a study of highly intelligent
11-year-old children in California. In 1925, assisted by a number of
other distinguished psychologists, including Florence Goodenough and
T. L. Kelley, he produced the first volume of a series with the rather
question-begging title of 'Genetic Studies of Genius'.

This was the initial report of a massive research, in which the aim
was to follow the group of gifted people, numbering about 1,500,
throughout their lives and to observe their achievements, using the
word in a wide sense, including not only success in studies and career,
but also interests, hobbies, marital state, health, death rate, and a host
of other data. Terman himself died in 1956, but the survey is still
continuing under the supervision of his principal collaborator, Melita
Oden, and will hardly be fully complete before the year 2000.

Five volumes have appeared (Terman, 1925; Cox, 1926; Burks,
Jensen and Terman, 1930; Terman and Oden, 1947; Terman and
Oden, 1959). Four of these describe successive findings about the
Californian gifted group; the book by Cox is on different lines, being an
attempt to assess retrospectively the intelligence of men and women of
genius over several centuries.

Before summarising the results to date of this monumental study, one
may pay tribute to Terman's admirable single-mindedness and capacity
for planning. The cost of the survey up to 1959 was about $250,000,
and of this Terman contributed more than one fifth out of his own
pocket, and in addition he and the other authors ploughed back into the
research all royalties from any publications resulting from it. One of
the most remarkable features of this survey, as Oden points out in her
preface to the fifth volume, and as anyone who has attempted even a

modest follow-up study will appreciate, is that, more than 35 years after it was started, over 95% of the surviving subjects were still actively participating and providing very detailed and intimate information. This is the more striking in that by this time many of them had become quite eminent, with correspondingly heavy demands on their time, and with increasing hazards to anonymity.

The three most important conclusions to have emerged from this mass of research are: (1) A rebuttal of the popular idea that intellectual gifts generally imply compensating weaknesses or deficiencies in other respects, such as in character, stability, or health; (2) A confirmation of the rarity and unpredictability of creative and original talent, whether aesthetic, literary, scientific or administrative. No Picasso, Benjamin Britten, or W. H. Auden; no Robert Oppenheimer, Rutherford or J. B. S. Haldane; no John Kennedy or Henry Ford appears to have been caught in the net; (3) An overwhelming demonstration of the value of general intelligence, measured by conventional tests, as the most important psychological variable that can at present be assessed, and (despite large individual changes in IQ) the most stable and predictive over the life span. Other factors, broadly classifiable under the headings of personality and motivation, must, one would suppose, be of equal total importance, but in spite of attempts to demonstrate their usefulness in prediction (e.g. Cattell and Butcher, 1968) they remain in general so elusive, variable and multifarious that, even in combination, their practical predictive efficiency is lower than that of general intelligence. In the present state of psychological knowledge, it is hard to imagine that, by selecting on the basis of any other variable, even on such apparently promising personality variables as introversion/extraversion and neuroticism or on motivational factors such as the need for achievement, one could produce such impressive long-term results as Terman foresaw half a century ago.

The children who have been studied in such detail and for so long were chosen by various means from schools in the larger towns of California. Practical and financial difficulties prevented a representative proportion of country children from being included, so that the group was never claimed to include the thousand or so *most* intelligent children in California. But within half a dozen of the larger cities, a careful search was made, and the coverage later checked by a further programme of tests, so that probably between 75% and 90% of the most intelligent children within those urban districts (so far as they could be identified at that age) were included. Means of selection varied within the whole sample, and the criteria of selection were adapted to meet as far as possible the needs of one or two special groups, such as children of foreign-born parents. The first screening for most of the children included the National group intelligence test and an abbreviation of the Stanford-Binet. Those with an IQ of 130 or higher, as shown by this preliminary testing, were selected for further study, and at the second and final stage for children aged 11 or under, the acceptance level was a Stanford-Binet IQ (on the complete scale) of 140; in the case of older children, it was a point or two lower, since the version used was known to grade gifted children of 12 or 13 rather too low.

Apart from details of how the group was selected, the first volume is mainly concerned with a careful investigation of the correlates of high intelligence and with a demonstration of the *general* slight superiority of these children, even in characteristics only very remotely related (as one would suppose) to measured intelligence.

Terman found, for instance, that they had been rather heavier at birth than the average child, that they had learned to walk earlier, had talked (on the average) about three months earlier, that they were, when tested, larger and heavier than the average of American and Californian children at that time, and that they matured physically at an earlier age. Their general health was found to be better than that of an unselected group, although it was admitted that this judgment was partly subjective. They were reported, by age 12, to sleep almost an hour longer than the average child.

Besides this detailed physical and anthropometric investigation, attempts were made to study the group's interests, play habits, temperamental traits and social and moral development. No evidence was found that in any of these respects the gifted group fell below the average degree of development, and in almost every area there were indications, at least, of superior attainment. In general, this part of the survey appears to have demolished conclusively the popular opinion that high intelligence tends to be associated with deficiencies in general development. No differences were found, for instance, in 'masculinity' of interests among the boys or 'femininity' of interests among the girls, as compared with general norms, except for a slightly higher 'masculinity' rating among the gifted boys at most ages. Terman also found a greater maturity of interests in his selected group in the sense that their preferences were for activities that among children in general showed increasing rather than decreasing popularity between the ages of eight and fourteen. In terms of sociability and popularity, there appeared to be only small differences between the gifted group and all other children. The former were rather less involved in social and competitive games, played by themselves slightly more on the average, preferred playmates older than themselves more often, and were more often reported to be 'queer' or 'different', but were apparently no more frequently teased or bullied.

The gifted group, or rather some 600 members of it who formed the main core, having been selected by the most careful procedure, were compared with a control group of a similar number of children of average intelligence on a large number of temperamental and character traits as rated by teachers. The main results were interpreted as showing that the children selected for exceptionally high intelligence were in no way inferior, and often highly superior, to the general level in those traits to which a judgment of 'superior' or 'inferior' was relevant. Some 'halo' effect was no doubt present, resulting in the almost universal tendency to rate people high on practically every trait once a generally favourable impression has been formed; but even when allowance had been made for this effect, no suggestion of deficiency in temperament or character on the average could be detected. These findings have since been confirmed in a number of other researches, e.g. by Witty (1940) and by Lightfoot (1951).

Most emphasis has been given in this account to Terman's findings about characteristics not obviously related to general intelligence, and correspondingly less to scholastic achievement and examination success. Even greater superiority was demonstrated in this sphere, but no summary will be provided, for two reasons. Firstly, such results were more to be expected, and therefore of less interest than those concerned with apparently more remote characteristics such as health, interests and social maturity; secondly, the relation between measured intelligence and academic performance has been extensively studied by other investigators and will be reviewed in later sections of this chapter.

Terman's facts were clearly collected with meticulous care and scientific rigour, but many of the comments and interpretations now appear naive and dubious in the light of subsequent research and changing views about intelligence. Very many of these interpretations are in terms of inherited differences, and while this may be correct, we should nowadays consider more carefully alternative explanations in terms of environmental influences. Thus in the summaries at the end of Chapters 4, 5 and 6 in the first volume (concerned with racial and social origins, number of intellectually superior relatives, and vital statistics, respectively) Terman argues, for instance, that the high proportion of Jewish subjects in the group, the existence of a large number of intellectually distinguished relatives of members of the group, and the average intellectual pre-eminence of firstborn children, all support the hereditarian argument. He is also impressed by the relatively early age at which differences in intelligence become apparent. He may indeed be right in these interpretations, but very few psychologists would now agree with them without considerable reservations. More recent studies both of early child development and of sociological factors have shown how early and how crucially influences such as those of social class, and of consequent degree of intellectual stimulation, can operate.

Interesting as are the early findings, perhaps the main value of this huge research consists in the life-long following up of the gifted group, carefully planned before the first volume was written. The third of the five reports (Burks, Jensen and Terman, 1930) follows the group to the final stages of their school careers and in some cases to their entry to college. The results recorded are very much in line with many of the findings five or six years earlier. As in the earlier study, no evidence was found for intellectual one-sidedness, emotional instability, lack of social achievement or any form of general maladjustment. These were all found, of course, in isolated cases, but on the average the group was notably free of any such weaknesses. Some of the exceptions, however, are very interesting to read about, and copious case histories are provided.

Most of the group were 'accelerated', reaching various milestones of school progress at an earlier age than their contemporaries. This 'acceleration' during the period covered by the third volume averaged about one-sixth of the child's chronological age, but Terman and his associates found that their actual progress in school work as assessed by achievement tests represented an acceleration of about 40%. In their last year in secondary school, the group's average performance was in the top 10%. This is more impressive than it sounds for two reasons. Firstly, these schoolchildren were generally younger than their fellows in the same class, and secondly a considerable degree of selection had already taken place by this stage, so that the comparison was not with an unselected population but with other pupils who were themselves well above the average in scholastic achievement. More than 90% of the boys in the group went on to college, and more than 80% of the girls. This latter figure is impressive, and it would be interesting to know what was the corresponding figure for highly intelligent girls in Britain in 1928 – interesting, and probably distressing. Even in about 1960 in Scotland, Macdonald, Gammie and Nisbet (1964) found that 73% of highly intelligent boys (IQ over 130) went on to a university, and only 52% of the girls.

In the fourth volume (Terman and Oden, 1947) we witness a very large chronological jump; the group is now aged about 35 and has passed through the Second World War. This summary has already become fairly lengthy, so that the findings about the gifted group as adults must necessarily be severely precised. Up to about the age of 35, mortality rates in the gifted group were appreciably lower than in the general population, being over a period of 18 years, 4·14% among males and 3·98% among females, as against 5·02% and 4·68%. Suicides seem to have been no commoner than in the general population. Delinquency and crime were also below the average rate. War records were, on the average, highly satisfactory, and occupational status and earnings after the war well above average. Marriage rate, age at marriage and divorce rate showed only small differences from corresponding figures in the general population. Mean IQ of 384 offspring of the group (Stanford-Binet) was about 128, that is to say approximately what would be expected on Galton's principle of filial regression, or perhaps rather higher. About 28 times as many of these offspring were found to have an IQ of 150+ as in the general population. An attempt was also made to see whether members of the group with IQ 170+ differed systematically from the rest of the group in any of the characteristics studied. The results were nearly all negative, except that these people with exceptionally high intelligence (even as compared with the rest of the group) had achieved a higher proportion of distinctions at college and also had attained rather higher occupational status. By the age of 35, the group had published about 90 books and 1,500 articles, but a high percentage of these were due to a few prolific individuals. One, for instance, had over a hundred research publications to his credit before he was 35.

The latest volume to be published (Terman and Oden, 1959) contains information obtained in surveys conducted in 1950 and 1955. At the latter date, most of the group were aged about 45. 104 members had died, and contact had been completely lost with another 28 of the original 1500+. Almost all the remainder were still actively co-operating. New findings are, however, relatively slight as compared with those in the earlier reports, as is perhaps to be expected. The general picture is of a consolidation of careers well under way. The incomes earned by many of the group in 1954, when they were in their early forties, are quite impressive even by American standards. In the five best-paid professions, containing about a quarter to a third of the men, they averaged over $15,000. The average earned income of all men in the group was just under $10,000. The 36 doctors averaged $23,500, and the six highest earners in the group had annual incomes between $100,000 and $400,000. Literary and scientific achievement as assessed by volume of publication had also accelerated sharply. The group now had to its credit about 2,000 scientific papers and 230 patents, also 33 novels and many hundreds of shorter literary productions.

But even the $400,000 income men had hardly proved themselves geniuses, and it is perhaps unfortunate that Terman and his collaborators described their project in such terms. Substitute 'talent' for 'genius', and no complaint can be made. On the contrary, an overwhelming proportion of Terman's subjects have shown themselves richly talented. This single study remains the most convincing demonstration of how astonishingly well the one much criticised variable, measured intelligence, can predict level of achievement for decades.

INTELLIGENCE AND SCHOLASTIC PERFORMANCE IN SCHOOL
AND UNIVERSITY

Most of the relevant British research about the relation between intelligence and performance has been done in connection with selection procedure for admission to different kinds of secondary school, the so called 11+ selection. It is not within the purpose of this chapter to discuss in detail the educational and social rights and wrongs of these procedures, but, since this question nearly always rouses strong feelings, I had better briefly state my own views, so that any bias in presentation may be discounted. The organisation of secondary education into three distinct kinds of school, providing different kinds of education, seems basically indefensible. Not only is there a strong case against such a system on grounds of social justice, but comparison with other democratic countries suggests that it is not even superior in producing an intellectual élite. Faced with the existence of this system, however, which clearly could not be changed overnight, and faced previously with the even less socially just system prevailing before 1944, educationalists and psychologists devoted a great deal of careful and unbiased research into means of allocating children so that they could derive most benefit from the kinds of secondary school in existence. In practice, because of the small numbers of technical schools available, and because of the greatly superior scholastic standards and social prestige of the grammar schools, 'allocation' meant 'selection'. Any attempts to achieve 'parity of esteem' were, it now appears, foredoomed to failure. One consequence of the unfortunate British (and particularly English) system whereby an advanced technology of mental testing has been used to some degree to prop outdated social distinctions – not through defects in the psychological techniques, but through uncritical assumptions about the power and limitations of mental testing – has been that almost all sociologists, whose data have uncompromisingly revealed the crudities of social stratification, have reacted passionately against the whole system, including the use of mental tests (e.g. Glass, 1964). In the USA, by contrast, it has been easier to produce a cool and balanced assessment of the social impact of testing as such, with an adequate appreciation of its positive potentialities as well as its dangers. An excellent example of a sociological study of this kind is the book by Goslin (1965).

It is important to distinguish the social justice or injustice of the tripartite system from that of the methods of selection. Given the existence of the former, a very high degree of success was attained in devising the fairest and most effective means of selection, so far as could be judged from the research results available. As was pointed out in Chapter 1, it is ironic that the tests commonly used, such as the Moray House tests, originally devised by Sir Godfrey Thomson, should in many minds be associated with the perpetuation of social injustice, since they were first constructed with the aim, which was very largely fulfilled, of decreasing and greatly mitigating such injustice, by providing instruments which would be less influenced by social differences than any others available, and at the same time be most predictive of scholastic aptitude in the grammar school or senior secondary school. Thomson himself was an uncompromising enemy of social privilege in education, and a major part of his considerable achievement consisted in the successful reduction of it, not least by his programme of test construction.

Undoubtedly, however, as we saw in the last chapter, it is virtually impossible to produce an intelligence test, which shall be a useful predictor of performance and at the same time produce equal average scores for children of different social classes. This is as true in other countries as in Britain. It is possible, however, to produce a test of intelligence or reasoning which will be on the whole a better predictor of general scholastic success several years later than any other single measure so far discovered, largely independently of social class influences. Here again, however, the separation of children into different kinds of secondary school greatly complicates the issue of validation, and it has rightly been urged that the confirmation of such prediction is to some extent a 'self-fulfilling prophecy' (a useful phrase coined by the sociologist Robert Merton) since the abler children also receive better conditions and greater encouragement. Two points are worth making about the 'self-fulfilling prophecy' aspect of selection. Firstly, the demonstrated validity of the procedures employed is largely unaffected by criticisms of this kind; validatory studies have generally relied on differences in performance of pupils *within* grammar schools or selective secondary schools (Vernon, 1957), and not on differences *between* kinds of school. Secondly, the effect of grading children in this way and the reasonable theory that lower expectations of teachers and others will result in lower performance have until recently been only a belief, though an extremely plausible one. Experimental evidence has been available, however, in the last year or so that this is more than just a likely occurrence (Rosenthal and Jacobson, 1966).

With the advent of comprehensive secondary schools, social injustice in the educational system may be greatly lessened, but no one should suppose that selection, implicit or explicit, will disappear in the fore-seeable future. Within existing comprehensive schools, children tend to be labelled fairly early as likely to obtain GCE passes, likely to obtain CSE passes, or unlikely to obtain either. There is also the growing importance of the 18+ and the increasingly difficult problem of allocating university places to the candidates who will make best use of them. In spite of the large expansion that has taken place following the recommendations of the Robbins Committee report and the much larger number of places now available in institutions of higher education, it is increasingly evident that there is a still larger number of young people who could make good use of them.

Lavin (1965) has produced a useful summary of American research on the prediction of scholastic achievement, surveying some 300 books and articles published mainly between 1953 and 1961. Some of his general conclusions are worth stressing here, and his evaluation of the importance of non-cognitive factors will be discussed in the next section. Firstly, with considerable justification, he criticises descriptions of students as 'under-achievers' and 'over-achievers' on the basis of discrepancies between scores on intelligence tests and measures of academic achievement. This is to expect too much, by implication, of measured intelligence as a predictor, suggesting that it is in effect the *only* factor, and that other influences are in some way surprising or abnormal. There are also logical and technical difficulties inherent in this approach, particularly if 'achievement quotients' are calculated. Logically, 'over-achievement' should be uncommon, or impossible, if measures of ability are taken at their face value. Difficulties also arise from the well-known statistical phenomenon of 'regression to the mean'. Since measures of ability and achievement universally show a positive correlation, regression effects may lead to false conclusions.

These can be largely avoided by comparing *actual* and *predicted* (by a regression equation) achievement scores, rather than actual raw scores in both cases, but the whole approach encounters considerable hazards. Two other valid points made by Lavin are (a) the increased likelihood of curvilinear relations and of threshold effects (such as described in Ch. 4 p. 102) when the joint predictive power of cognitive and non-cognitive factors is considered, and (b) the need for more longitudinal studies. These are scarce in spite of the vast literature on the prediction of academic achievement, and, as we have already seen in Chapter 7, often yield different findings from those of static, correlational researches.

Besides these important methodological points, Lavin's survey summarises some of the clearest substantive findings as follows. The commonest criterion of achievement in studies of college students is 'grade-point' average. The correlation of single tests of ability or intelligence with this criterion is typically around $+\cdot5$; the multiple correlation of batteries of such tests or of combinations of tests and previous scholastic measures is usually around $\cdot65$. Average grade in high school is generally the single best predictor. Whether success at particular subjects in college can be predicted much better than the average grade is not entirely clear; many studies have produced conflicting results. One fairly consistent finding that emerges from this extensive survey is that the college performance of women in the USA is more consistent, more in line with their measured ability, and consequently more predictable than that of men.

Corresponding work in Britain on the prediction of academic success among university students has been much more scattered, piecemeal and unsystematic, but is by no means negligible. Relevant summarising articles have been written by Eysenck (1947), Warburton (1952), Drever (1963), Kelsall (1963), Albrow (1967) and Butcher (1968a), among others.

NON-INTELLECTUAL FACTORS CONTRIBUTING TO ACHIEVEMENT

Discussion of achievement in the preceding sections may easily have given the impression that it is only to be interpreted in a narrow or even philistine and materialistic way in terms of such criteria as marks obtained in GCE, income earned and promotion gained in one's chosen occupation, or inclusion at an early age in 'Who's Who'. There are obvious objections to any such analysis. Firstly, many of the men and women who in a long view achieve most, elude any such crude assessment. Mozart was buried in a pauper's grave, Bertrand Russell was turned out of his fellowship at Cambridge, some of Mendel's most important papers lay unnoticed (though published) for several decades. Level of income, promotion and public recognition are all crude criteria. Again, although most of us have a rough and ready idea that certain occupations are of greater social usefulness and more demanding of developed talent in those who practise them than other humbler and less skilled jobs, most of us would equally be hesitant, and rightly so, about placing occupations firmly on one simple scale as representing degrees of 'achievement'. Add to this the fact that there may be more variation in effectiveness within occupations than between them, and one is forced to the conclusion that occupational achievement, and a fortiori 'achievement' as used in a wider sense, is capable of only very approximate and provisional assessment.

All the same, it would be even more absurd for applied psychology to omit this whole topic, or to maintain that all men are equal in this respect. Just as both common usage and scientific enquiry suggest that men are not equal in their potentialities, they also indicate that men are no more equal in the extent to which they are able to develop the talents they have. Absolute criteria for assessing this degree of development are even harder to find than for assessing the potentiality itself. Psychologists, as so often, find themselves in the position of trying to validate one theoretical concept that is easy to criticise against another that is even fuller of holes. When an attempt is made, in spite of these difficulties, to assess achievement in a broader sense, non-intellectual factors begin to assume a much greater importance.

Social and environmental factors, as discussed in the last chapter, play an important part in determining the extent to which potentialities are realised. So do individual differences in personality and motivation, and in practice these are perhaps even more important. From rags to riches, from a Scottish croft to a seat in the cabinet, from a ghetto or an East End slum to a chair in theoretical physics, all these progressions, although uncommon, occur sufficiently often hardly to cause surprise. They cannot occur, however, without both an adequate, above average, degree of intelligence and a high degree of drive or ambition.

The researches already reviewed in some detail show clearly enough that, statistically speaking, measured intelligence, even when tested at quite an early age, is a surprisingly effective predictor of future achievement throughout the whole of life. This conclusion of Terman's has been established with such a weight of evidence as hardly to be disputable, and is not invalidated by demonstrations of quite striking changes in the IQ of individuals. But, from another point of view that is of equal interest and importance, the individual people who are the statistical exceptions require detailed study.

To sum up these remarks so far, there is a real psychological question concerned with the extent to which people develop fully and make good use of their intellectual gifts. A few, for instance, of Terman's gifted group were in mid-life employed as bar-tenders or truck drivers, in marked contrast with the majority in professional or management posts. Thus high measured intelligence predicts to a considerable degree in Western industrial societies, but by no means infallibly, the occupational status likely to be attained. The status of the occupation attained and the degree of promotion within the occupation serve as a very approximate indication of vocational achievement. They are only interpretable as approximate indicators even of vocational success, since it is almost impossible to arrange occupations on a unidimensional scale without either begging too many questions or omitting some of the most interesting professions.

Accepting for the moment, however, that occupational status and the other rather crude criteria will serve up to a point as measures of vocational achievement, what kinds of factor other than intellectual, such as the 'drive' and 'ambition' already mentioned are relevant? As far as the individual person is concerned, two or perhaps three other kinds of factor must be invoked to explain the variation that is not predictable from general intelligence and special abilities. Personality and motivational variables are the two kinds to be included for certain; 'chance' factors are the doubtful third kind, doubtful because to the behavioural or social scientist they are a residue of uninvestigated probably small and numerous influences that are however capable of investigation in principle.

The distinction between personality traits and motivational or dynamic variables is relative rather than absolute, but in practice a useful one. Personality traits are more static, change less quickly, are more easily assessed by tests and ratings, and there is a tolerable amount of agreement among psychologists about what kinds of trait are most important in accounting for the largest range of individual difference as averaged over a large population of people. Correlations of tests and factor analyses, as described in Chapter 2, have been applied to personality data, and as with ability factors, the resulting traits may operate at different levels of generality. There are broad general traits such as introversion/extraversion and anxiety or 'neuroticism' which are analogous in this respect to general intelligence; there are more specific,

or at least rather less general ones (such as the 16 assessed by Cattell's
16 P-F test) which are analogous to Thurstone's primary mental
abilities.

The success of personality assessment and the reliability and objectivity of the individual differences revealed are held by almost all
psychologists to be lower than those of intelligence testing. The same is
true to an even greater extent of motivational variables, which present
additional difficulties in assessment. How much progress then has been
made in measuring these elusive traits and in linking them with scholastic achievement, vocational success and other criteria of achievement?
Herculean efforts to define stable traits, both of personality and of
motivation, have been made by Cattell, who has also attempted to show
their usefulness in the prediction of achievement (Cattell, 1957; Cattell
and Butcher, 1968). Earlier attempts of this kind by other workers have
shown this to be a field in which it is far from easy to obtain positive
results of practical significance. Cattell's results at least show that there
are important relations between personality factors and achievement,
but in most cases the correlations, although statistically significant, are
too small as yet for practical use in guidance and prediction. A cross-
cultural study (Butcher, Ainsworth and Nesbitt, 1963; Ainsworth,
1967) is fairly typical in demonstrating consistent but small degrees of
relation between Cattell's personality factors and attainment in various
school subjects. A number of studies linking these personality factors
with other aspects of achievement and non-achievement, e.g. with
success in arts and crafts (Cross, Cattell and Butcher, 1967), athletic
performance, various aspects of vocational performance, and delinquency and criminality, have been carried out both in the USA and in
England. Many of these are summarised by Cattell (1957, 1965a) and a
survey by Warburton of the English results, mostly unpublished except
in theses, is due to appear in 1968.

Many English workers, however, have preferred to use Eysenck's two
broader factors of introversion-extraversion and neuroticism (e.g. Lynn,
1957; Callard and Goodfellow, 1962; Child, 1964; Savage, 1966). Here
too, results are promising rather than sensational. There is a fair
amount of evidence that introversion is allied with superior performance
in university work (though not in school work), but the relation is not
very clear-cut. It is very possible that these factors are too broad and
that some of the relations found with Cattell's more specific traits
may be to some extent cancelling each other out. The use of broader
traits permits the construction of longer scales, with consequently
higher reliability, but to describe individual differences in personality in

terms of only two dimensions must involve rather drastic over-simplification.

Other methods of personality assessment that have been employed include (a) clinical instruments such as the Minnesota Multiphasic Personality Inventory (MMPI) and (b) projective techniques such as the Rorschach and the Thematic Apperception Test (TAT). These have not generally proved very effective or reliable forecasters of academic performance in the researches where ability has been partialled out or otherwise controlled. Lavin's review, for instance, shows that in more studies than not scores on the MMPI were unrelated to academic performance. Similarly he finds the Rorschach to have been of little use in this respect, though some of the researches suggest that it might be useful for predicting criteria other than college marks or grades. Studies of the TAT show it to have been somewhat more useful, and the use of this technique will be reviewed later in this section.

The use of motivational factors to predict scholastic achievement has also been attempted, but is subject to great difficulties and uncertainties. In principle, these factors appear at least as important as the more static personality traits, but there is less agreement about how to classify and to assess them. Cattell has been the main pioneer in this area and, deeply influenced by the taxonomy of McDougall, has developed a number of techniques for the indirect, disguised assessment of attitudes. Correlation and factor analysis of these measures has revealed a number of dynamic traits classified as either 'ergs' or sentiments. The former are akin to drives or instincts, and include such basic human motivating forces as sex and aggressiveness; the latter are clusters of attitudes concentrated around social institutions such as church, home and occupation. Much of this work by Cattell and his associates (e.g. Cattell, 1947; Cattell and Baggaley, 1956; Cattell, Sweney and Radcliffe, 1960; Cattell, Horn and Butcher, 1962) has been characterised by boldness in conceptualisation and by sophisticated techniques of measurement and analysis. Its main weakness has been a reliance for the most part on factorial validity and an inbred dependence on marker items from one test being assumed to be valid in a succeeding one, with a corresponding lack of demonstrated external, real-life validity. In two recent studies, however (Pierson et al., 1964; Cattell, Sealy and Sweney, 1966), attempts have been made to link these motivational factors with external criteria.

The other main approach to motivation as an influence on achievement, both in individuals and in social and national groups, has been exemplified in the work of McClelland on the 'need for achievement'.

(See, in particular, McClelland et al., 1953). This has arisen from the theoretical classification by Murray of human needs, of which the most satisfactory summary is provided by Hall and Lindzey (1957, Chapter 5). 'Need for achievement' is generally assessed in one of two ways, either by responses to TAT pictures or by questionnaires, such as the Edwards Personal Preference Schedule. Results have been moderately promising but inconsistent (Lavin, p. 77). On balance the questionnaire method has been rather more successful for predictive purposes, probably on account of the low reliability of the projective measures. Lavin concludes that, even apart from such technical defects and difficulties, achievement motivation, as conceived by McClelland and as embodied in these measures, is not likely to correlate particularly highly with academic achievement, being multidimensional and containing some components that are irrelevant or even inversely related.

Two recent British researches in this area deserve comment. Both Robinson (1964) and Bruckman (1966) have found among school children a positive correlation between intelligence (as measured, for instance, by a Moray House verbal reasoning test) and 'need for achievement' as assessed by McClelland's techniques. This is to be expected, and the causation probably works in both directions. It is reasonable to suppose both that a high need for achievement is conducive to obtaining good test scores, and that success in tested performance reinforces motivation and confidence. What is not clear about the complex interaction between intelligence, motivation and achievement is whether it is intelligence or success in school work that is the more crucial in affecting level of motivation. Robinson argues for the latter, showing that, when the variable of school success is partialled out (i.e. its effect removed by a statistical technique), the positive relation between need for achievement and intelligence disappears. Bruckman's study, on the other hand, shows that, when the effect of intelligence is partialled out, the relation between need for achievement and school success, as indicated by stream to which the child is allocated, disappears. These results are not easy to interpret or summarise, and probably are affected (as Robinson points out) by age, type of school, degree of selection in sample and so on. Further research in this area would be particularly profitable and important.

There has also been considerable interest among educational psychologists in recent years on other kinds of non-intellectual factor relevant both to success in college and to success in career; besides attempts such as those of Cattell and Eysenck to show the importance of basic personality traits, a wide range of interests and biographical data have been explored. There has been a growing realisation that in the prediction of success in higher education as the population becomes increasingly selected by ability from high school to post-graduate study, the best possible measures of ability can be expected to show diminishing efficiency, and that individual differences other than in ability become relatively more important. Increasing specialisation seems to be important here, as well as the selection by ability. Juola (1966) has shown that the predictive power of ability tests administered on entrance to an American college falls off sharply after a few terms, but improves in usefulness if the student switches courses.

Two important variables that have been quite commonly examined in research are (a) work and study habits and (b) clarity or certainty of subject and vocational choice. Lavin reviews research findings in these two areas (1965, p. 66 and p. 72), and concludes that, with ability controlled, both good study habits and a high degree of certainty on the part of the student about his future plans and career have been shown to be predictive of academic success.

Finally, one or two extensive recent researches have included a very wide range of variables, intellectual, temperamental and biographical. Typical of these is the ambitious study described by Nichols and Holland (1963). Their population of subjects was of very high ability, such that measures of intelligence and aptitude could hardly be expected to discriminate sharply; it was composed of 10,000 Merit Finalists selected from some half a million candidates under the American National Merit Scholarship scheme. These 10,000 were the highest scorers on two scholastic aptitude tests, including the well-known SAT. A one-in-six random sample of these 10,000 were the subjects of the research. More than 150 measures were obtained, ranging over personality, interests and biographical data, and correlated with 14 criteria of first-year college achievement, such as, for example, average grade, rating on leadership, scientific achievement, artistic achievement. The degree of selection involved and the consequent attenuation in predictive power of normally efficient ability measures is demonstrated by the fact that first-year college grades did not correlate significantly either with verbal or mathematical score on the well-known and generally effective Scholastic Aptitude Test. These grades did however correlate significantly (around $+\cdot20$) with high school rank. The non-intellectual variables which proved to be significant predictors of first-year college grades (out of the vast mass studied) appeared to be measures of two main traits – (a) perseverance and motivation to achieve, (b) conformity and socialisation. An especially interesting finding was that most of the measures in these two clusters were still significant as predictors when

high school record was partialled out, which seems to imply that level of
motivation and determination to succeed assume a new importance at
university level, as distinct from being just a continuation of already
well-established habit.

Several important recent papers, both British and American, make
related points. Rodger (1965) discusses capacity and inclination for
University courses in Britain, and emphasises that these two require-
ments must always be carefully distinguished. Racial groups may clearly
differ in the extent of their desire for education, even where there is no
evidence of any systematic difference in intelligence or capacity. A
student who obtains first-class honours in psychology may not be
sufficiently interested in the subject to continue studying it. It is certainly possible to assume too readily that ability and interest in a particular subject always go together. Statistically they certainly tend to,
but where patterns of interest and ability have been studied *within the
individual*, usually by expressing his scores in ipsative form, that is to say
as deviations from his own mean, relatively low correlations are typical
(Wesley, Corey and Stewart, 1950).

Holland and Richards (1965) studied students in 24 American Universities and Colleges in an attempt to assess the relation between, on the
one hand academic potential and performance, and, on the other, non-
academic accomplishment as shown by, for example, musical, literary,
dramatic, scientific and social activities. Their conclusion was that, even
in this 'academic' group, academic potential and performance formed
only one of several fairly independent areas of talent, and that, although conventional tests of ability and aptitude remained the best
techniques available for predicting college success in scholastic subjects,
if a sponsor also wishes to find college students who will do outstanding
things outside the classroom and in later life, then he should continue
to make an effort to secure a better record of the student's competence
and achievements in high school (p. 173).

Nichols (1966) reports another survey in which non-intellective
factors were found to be important in the prediction of first-year college
grades in American universities. The best predictor of college grades
was rank in high school class, followed by the non-intellective grade
scales and finally by aptitude test scores. More important, perhaps, than
the specific findings is Nichols' discussion of the present climate of
opinion in America among psychologists most concerned with the prediction of success in higher education. Several of the points made serve
also to reinforce the conclusions of this section.

Firstly, in spite of all the technical sophistication employed, methods

K

of selection and prediction, typically depending on a combination of an aptitude test with high school scholastic record, appear to be too narrow. However unsatisfactory and undeveloped at present are the available methods of assessing personality, motivation and extra-curricular accomplishment, future improved methods of selection and allocation will need to take these into account. In addition, validity, as measured by the correlation between selection variables and average academic performance at university is not enough. Academic gradings are both too unreliable and too narrow to provide a satisfactory criterion, and themselves have only low correlation with later 'real-life' success. The attempt to select students in such a way as to maximise academic success may, if pursued too narrowly and rigorously, impoverish firstly the universities, and eventually society itself.

This chapter began with a detailed account of the evidence for the far-reaching importance of general intelligence. This should not be forgotten when we consider the complementary importance of non-intellectual traits. The two, although conceptually separate, interact in practice in all kinds of subtle ways, with the result that, even when one studies personality traits, it may often be advisable to consider their effect at different intelligence levels. Spielberger and Katzenmeyer (1959), for instance, present findings which they suggest show that degree of general anxiety is relevant to academic achievement, but principally at intermediate intelligence levels, since the highest and lowest intelligence groups tend to succeed or fail, irrespective of anxiety level.

Intelligence is without doubt associated with high achievement in a very wide range of tasks and occupations. But even in those to which it is most directly relevant, it accounts for no more than about half the variation in performance, and in some situations and groups, much less. Educational and applied psychologists are at present deeply concerned with analysing other relevant factors, particularly those associated with level of motivation.

Suggested additional reading

TERMAN, L. V., and ODEN, M. H., *The Gifted Group at Mid-life*. Stanford, California: Stanford Univ. Press (1959).

WARBURTON, F. W., 'The measurement of personality'. *Educ. Res.* 4, 2–18, 115–132, 193–206 (1961–62).

LAVIN, D. E., *The Prediction of Academic Performance*. New York: Russell Sage Foundation (1965).

CATTELL, R. B., and BUTCHER, H. J., *The Prediction of Achievement and Creativity*. Indianapolis, Indiana: Bobbs-Merrill (1968). Chs. 10 and 13.

MCCLELLAND, D. C., *The Achievement Motive*. New York. Appleton-Century-Crofts (1953).

NICHOLS, R. G., and HOLLAND, J. L., 'Prediction of the first-year college performance of high-aptitude students'. *Psychol. Monogr.* 77, No. 7. Whole No. 570 (1963).

Bibliography

ABI RAFI, A. (1967) 'The Progressive Matrices (1938) and the Dominoes (D48) tests: a cross-cultural study', *Brit. J. educ. Psychol.*, **37**, 117-118.

ADLER, A. (1965) *Superiority and Social Interest.* (A collection of later writings edited by H. L. and R. R. Ansbacher.) London: Routledge.

AIKEN, L. R. (1965) 'The probability of chance success on objective test items', *Educ. Psychol. Measmt.*, **25**, 127-134.

AINSWORTH, M. E. (1967) 'The relation between motivation, personality, intelligence and school attainment in a secondary modern school', *Brit. J. educ. Psychol.*, **37**, 135-136. (Thesis abstract.)

ALBROW, M. C. (1967) 'Ritual and reason in the selection of students', *Univ. Quart.*, **21**, 141-151.

ALEXANDER, W. P. (1935) 'Intelligence, concrete and abstract', *Brit. J. Psychol.*, Monogr. Suppl. 19.

ALPER, T. G., and BORING, E. G. (1944) 'Intelligence test scores of Northern and Southern white and Negro recruits in 1918', *J. abnorm. soc. Psychol.*, **39**, 471-474. Reprinted in Jenkins and Paterson.

ALTUS, G. T. (1956) 'Some correlates of the Davis-Eells tests', *J. consult. Psychol.*, **20**, 227-232.

ALTUS, W. D. (1965) 'Birth order and scholastic aptitude', *J. consult. Psychol.*, **29**, 202-205.

AMERICAN PSYCHOLOGICAL ASSOCIATION (1954) 'Technical recommendations for tests', *Psychol. Bull.*, **51**, pt. 2.

ANASTASI, ANNE (1956) 'Intelligence and family size', *Psychol. Bull.*, **53**, 187-209.

ANASTASI, ANNE (1958a) *Differential Psychology.* New York: Macmillan.

ANASTASI, ANNE (1958b) 'Heredity, environment and the question "How?" ', *Psychol. Rev.*, **65**, 197-208.

ANASTASI, ANNE (1961) *Psychological Testing* (2nd edn.). New York: Macmillan.

ANASTASI, ANNE, and D'ANGELO, R. Y. (1952) 'A comparison of negro and white preschool children in language development and Goodenough draw-a-man IQ', *J. genet. Psychol.*, **81**, 147-165.

ANDERSON, C. C. (1962) 'The relationship between inhibition of motor response and cognitive performance', *Brit. J. educ. Psychol.*, **32**, 234-240.

ANDERSON, J. E. (1939) 'The limitations of infant and preschool tests in the measurement of intelligence', *J. Psychol.*, **8**, 351-379.

ANDERSON, R. C., and AUSUBEL, D. P. (1965) (Eds.) *Readings in the Psychology of Cognition.* Holt, Rinehart and Winston: New York and London.

ARMER, P. (1963) 'Attitudes toward intelligent machines', in *Computers and Thought* (eds. E. A. Feigenbaum and J. Feldman).

ARMSTRONG, H. G. (1967) 'Wastage of ability amongst the intellectually gifted', *Brit. J. educ. Psychol.*, 37, 257–259.

BAJEMA, C. J. (1963) 'Estimation of the direction and intensity of natural selection in relation to human intelligence by means of the intrinsic rate of natural increase', *Eugen. Quart.*, 10, 175–187.

BAKER, B. O., HARDYCK, C. D., and PETRINOVICH, L. F. (1966) 'Weak measurements versus strong statistics: an empirical critique of S. S. Stevens' proscriptions on statistics', *Educ. Psychol. Measmt.*, 26, 291–309.

BALINSKY, B. (1941) 'An analysis of the mental factors of various age groups from nine to sixty', *Genet. Psychol. Monogr.*, 23, 191–234.

BANNISTER, D. (1962) 'Personal construct theory: a summary and experimental paradigm', *Acta Psychol.*, 20, 104–120.

BARRON, F. (1955) 'The disposition toward originality', *J. abnorm. soc. Psychol.*, 51, 478–485.

BARRON, F. (1963) *Creativity and Psychological Health.* Princeton, N.J.: Van Nostrand.

BARTLETT, F. C. (1958) *Thinking. An Experimental and Social study.* London: Allen and Unwin.

BAYLEY, NANCY (1949) 'Consistency and variability in the growth of intelligence from birth to eighteen years', *J. genet. Psychol.*, 75, 165–196.

BAYLEY, NANCY (1955) 'On the growth of intelligence', *Amer. Psychologist*, 10, 805–818.

BAYLEY, NANCY (1957) 'Data on the growth of intelligence between sixteen and twenty-one years as measured by the Wechsler–Bellevue scale', *J. Gen. Psychol.*, 90, 3–15.

BAYLEY, NANCY (1966) 'Learning in adulthood: the role of intelligence', Ch. 8 in H. J. Klausmeier and C. W. Harris (Eds.) *Analyses of Concept Learning.*

BELOFF, J.R. (1962) *The Existence of Mind.* London: MacGibbon and Kee.

BENJAMIN, B. (1966) 'Social and economic differences in ability', in *Genetic and Environmental Factors in Human Ability* (Ed. J. E. Meade and A. S. Parkes.) Edinburgh: Oliver and Boyd.

BERGER, L., BERNSTEIN, A., KLEIN, E., COHEN, J., and LUCAS, G. (1964) 'Effects of Aging and Pathology on the Factorial Structure of Intelligence', *J. Consult. Psychol.*, 28, 199–207.

BERLYNE, D. E. (1957) 'Recent developments in Piaget's work', *Brit. J. educ. Psychol.* 27, 1–12.

BERLYNE, D. E. (1963) 'Soviet research on intellectual processes in children', *Monogr. Soc. Res. Child Devel.*, 28, 165–184.

BERLYNE, D. E. (1965) *Structure and Direction in Thinking.* New York and London: Wiley.

BERNSTEIN, B. (1959) 'A public language: some sociological implications of a linguistic form', *Brit. J. Sociol.,* 9, 159–174.

BERNSTEIN, B. (1960) 'Language and social class', *Brit. J. Sociol.,* 11, 271–276.

BERNSTEIN, B. (1961a) 'Social class and linguistic development: A theory of social learning', in *Education, Economy and Society* (Eds. A. H. Halsey, J. Floud and A. Anderson). Glencoe, Illinois: The Free Press.

BERNSTEIN, B. (1961b) 'Social structure, language and learning', *Educ. Res.:* 3, 163–176.

BERNSTEIN, B. (1962) 'Linguistic codes, hesitation phenomena and intelligence', *Language and Speech,* 5, 31–45.

BERNSTEIN, B., and YOUNG, D. (1966) 'Some aspects of the relationship between communication and performance in tests', in J. E. Meade and A. S. Parkes (Eds.) *Genetic and Environmental Factors in Human Ability.* Edinburgh: Oliver and Boyd.

BERRY, J. W. (1966) 'Temne and Eskimo perceptual skills', *Internat. J. Psychol.,* 1, 207–229.

BIESHEUVEL, S. (1949) 'Psychological tests and their application to non-European peoples', *Yearbook of Education,* 87–126. Evans Bros.

BIESHEUVEL, S., and LIDDICOAT, R. (1959) *J. Nat. Inst. Personnel Res.,* 8, 3–14.

BIGGS, J. B. (1959) 'The development of number concepts in young children', *Educ. Res.,* 1, 2, 17–34.

BINET, A., and SIMON, T. (1908) 'The development of intelligence in the child'. *Anneé Psychol.,* 14, 1–90. Translated version in Goddard, 1916, q.v.

BIRREN, J. E. (1965) 'Age changes in speed of behaviour: its central nature and physiological correlates', Ch. 10, pp. 191–216 in *Behaviour, Ageing and the Nervous System* (Ed. A. T. Welford and J. E. Birren). Springfield: C. C. Thomas.

BIRREN, J. E., and MORRISON, D. F. (1961) 'Analysis of WAIS subtests in relation to age and education', *J. Gerontol.,* 16, 363–368.

BITZER, D. L., and BRAUNFELD, P. G. (1965) 'Plato: a computer-controlled teaching system'. Ch. 6 in Sass, M.A. and Wilkinson, W. D. *Computer Augmentation of Human Reasoning.*

BLEWETT, D. B. (1954) 'An experimental study of the inheritance of intelligence', *J. ment. Sci.,* 100, 922–933.

BLOOM, B. S. (1964) *Stability and Change in Human Characteristics.* New York: Wiley.

BONARIUS, J. C. J. (1965) 'Research in the personal construct theory of George A. Kelly: Role construct. repertory test and basic theory', in Maher, B.A. (Ed.) *Progress in Experimental Personality Research,* 2. New York and London: Academic Press.

BOOTE, D. W. (1967) 'An experimental study of concept attainment with reference to concrete and formal modes of thinking', *M.Ed. thesis*, Univ. of Manchester.

BORKO, H. (Ed.) (1962) *Computer Applications in the Behavioral Sciences*. Englewood Cliffs. N.J.: Prentice-Hall.

BORTNER, M. (1965) 'Review of Progressive Matrices Tests', in O. K. Buros (Ed.). *Sixth Mental Measurements Yearbook*. New Jersey: Gryphon Press.

BOURNE, L. E. (1963) 'Factors affecting strategies used in problems of concept-formation', *Amer. J. Psychol.*, **76**, 229–38.

BRADWAY, KATHERINE P., and THOMPSON, CLARE W. (1962) 'Intelligence at Adulthood: A Twenty-Five Year Follow Up', *J. educ. Psychol.*, **53**, 1–14.

BRADWAY, K. P., THOMPSON, C. W., and CRAVENS, R. B. (1958) 'Preschool IQs after twenty-five years', *J. educ. Psychol.*, **49**, 278–281.

BRANCH, M., and CASH, A. (1966) *Gifted Children*. London: Souvenir Press.

BREARLEY, M., and HITCHFIELD, E. (1966) *A Teacher's Guide to Reading Piaget*. London: Routledge.

BRIDGMAN, P. W. (1931) *Dimensional Analysis*. New Haven: Yale Univ. Press.

BROADBENT, D. E. (1961) *Behaviour*. London: Eyre and Spottiswoode.

BROADBENT, D. E. (1966) 'The well ordered mind', *Amer. Educ. Res. J.*, **3**, 281–295.

BRODBECK, M. (1963) 'Logic and scientific method in research on teaching', Ch. 2 in N. L. Gage (Ed.) *Handbook of Research on Teaching*. Chicago: Rand McNally.

BROMLEY, D. B. (1963) 'Age differences in conceptual abilities', Ch. 5, pp. 96–112, in *Processes of Ageing, Social and Psychological Perspectives*, **1**, R. H. Williams, C. Tibbitts and Wilma Donahue, Eds., New York: Atherton Press.

BROMLEY, D. B. (1966) *The Psychology of Human Ageing*. London: Penguin Books.

BROVERMAN, D. M. (1960) 'Cognitive style and intra-individual variation in abilities', *J. Personal.*, **28**, 240–256.

BROVERMAN, D. M. (1964) 'Generality and Behavioral Correlates of Cognitive Styles', *J. consult. Psychol.*, **28**, 487–500.

BROWN, R. (1965) *Social Psychology*. New York: Free Press.

BROWN, R. and MCNEILL, D. (1966) 'The "tip-of-the-tongue" phenomenon', *J. verb. Learning verb. Behav.*, **5**, 325–337.

BRUCKMAN, I. R. (1966) 'The relationship between achievement motivation and sex, age, social class, school stream and intelligence', *Brit. J. soc. clin. Psychol.*, **5**, 211–221.

BRUNER, J. S. (1959) 'Inhelder and Piaget's "The Growth of Logical Thinking." A psychologist's viewpoint', *Brit. J. Psychol.*, **50**, 363–370.

BRUNER, J. S. (1961) *The process of Education.* Cambridge, Mass.: Harvard Univ. Press.

BRUNER, J. S. (1964) 'The Course of Cognitive Growth', *American Psychologist*, **19**, 1–15.

BRUNER, J. S. (1966) *Toward a Theory of Instruction.* Cambridge, Mass. Harvard University Press.

BRUNER, J. S., GOODNOW, J. J., and AUSTIN, G. A. (1956) *A Study of Thinking.* New York: Wiley.

BRUNER, J. S., OLVER, R. R., and GREENFIELD, PATRICIA M. (1966) *Studies in Cognitive Growth.* New York and London: Wiley.

BRYAN, W. L., and HARTER, N. (1899) 'Studies on the telegraphic language', *Psychol. Rev.*, **6**, 345–75.

BURKE, H. R. (1958) 'Raven's Progressive Matrices: a review and critical evaluation', *J. genet. Psychol.*, **93**, 199–228.

BURKS, B. S., JENSEN, D. S., and TERMAN, L. M. (1930) 'The Promise of Youth', *Genetic Studies of Genius*, **III.** Stanford, California: Stanford Univ. Press.

BURNS, R. B. (1966) 'Age and mental ability: re-testing with thirty-three years' interval', *Brit. J. educ. Psychol.*, **36**, 116. (Thesis abstract.)

BUROS, O. K. (Ed.) (1965) *The Sixth Mental Measurements Year Book.* New Jersey: Gryphon Press.

BURT, C. (1909) 'Experimental tests of general intelligence', *Brit. J. Psychol.*, **3**, 94–177.

BURT, C. (1940) *The Factors of the Mind.* London: Univ. of London Press.

BURT, C. (1949) 'The structure of the mind: A review of the results of factor analysis', *Brit. J. educ. Psychol.*, **19**, 100–114, 176–199.

BURT, C. (1955a) 'The evidence for the concept of intelligence', *Brit. J. educ. Psychol.*, **25**, 158–177.

BURT, C. (1955b) The meaning and assessment of intelligence. *Eugen. Rev.*, **47**, 81–91.

BURT, C. (1958) 'The inheritance of mental ability', *Amer. Psychologist*, **13**, 1–15.

BURT, C. (1959) 'General ability and special aptitudes', *Educ. Res.*, **1, 2**, 3–16.

BURT, C. (1960) 'The factor analysis of the Wechsler scale', *Brit. J. statist. Psychol.*, **13**, 82–87.

BURT, C. (1962) Critical Notice of 'Creativity and Intelligence' by Getzels and Jackson. *Brit. J. educ. Psychol.*, **32**, 292–298.

BURT, C. (1963) 'Is intelligence distributed normally?' *Brit. J. statist. Psychol.*, **16**, 175–190.

BURT, C. (1965) Critical notice of 'The Home and the School' (J. W. D. Douglas) *Brit. J. educ. Psychol.*, **35**, 259–264.

BURT, C. (1966) 'The appropriate uses of factor analysis and analysis of variance', Ch. 8 in R. B. Cattell, *Handbook of Multivariate Experimental Psychology.* Chicago: Rand McNally.

BURT, C., and HOWARD, M. (1956). 'The multifactorial theory of intelligence', *Brit. J. statist. Psychol.*, **9**, 115–125.

BURT, C., and HOWARD, M. (1957) 'The relative influence of heredity and environment on assessments of intelligence', *Brit. J. statist. Psychol.*, **10**, 99–104.

BUTCHER, H. J. (1968a) 'University Education', in *Educational Research in Britain* (Ed. H. J. Butcher). London: Univ. of London Press.

BUTCHER, H. J. (1968b) 'Creativity', in *Multivariate Personality Research: contributions to the understanding of personality in honour of R. B. Cattell* (Ed. R. M. Dreger).

BUTCHER, H. J. (1968c) 'Sampling', in *Research Methods in Education and Training* (Eds. K. Miller and S. Cotgrove).

BUTCHER, H. J. (1968d) 'Human abilities', in *Development in Learning*. Vol. 3 (Eds. E. A. Lunzer and J. Morris). London: Staples Press.

BUTCHER, H. J. (Ed.) (1968e) *Educational Research in Britain*. London: Univ. of London Press.

BUTCHER, H. J. (1969) 'Predicting arts and science specialisation in a group of Scottish secondary schoolchildren'. *Brit. J. educ. Psychol.*, **39**.

BUTCHER, H. J., AINSWORTH, M., and NESBITT, J. E. (1963). 'Personality factors and school achievement', 'A comparison of British and American children', *Brit. J. educ. Psychol.*, **33**, 276–285.

CALLARD, M. P., and GOODFELLOW, C. L. (1962) 'Neuroticism and extraversion in schoolboys as measured by the J.M.P.I.', *Brit. J. educ. Psychol.*, **32**, 241–250.

CAMERON, MARION B. (1967) An 'investigation of cognitive differences in first-year arts and science students'. *M.Ed. thesis.* Univ. of Aberdeen.

CAMPBELL, A. C. (1963) 'Solution procedures and item writing', *Austral. J. Psychol.*, **15**.

CAMPBELL, A. C. (1964) 'Concentration versus dispersion of figural properties in nonverbal test items', *Educ. Psychol. Measmt.*, **24**, 285–289.

CAMPBELL, A. C. (1965) 'On the solving of code items demanding the use of indirect procedures', *Brit. J. Psychol.*, **56**, 1, 45–51.

CAMPBELL, D. T. (1960) 'Blind variation and selective retention in creative thought as in other knowledge processes', *Psychol. Rev.*, **67**, 380–400.

CAMPBELL, W. J. (1952) 'The influence of home environment on the educational progress of selective secondary school children', *Brit. J. educ. Psychol.*, **22**, 89–100.

CARMENT, D. W., MILES, C. G., and CERVIN, V. B. (1965) 'Persuasiveness and persuasibility as related to intelligence and extraversion', *Brit. J. soc. clin. Psychol.*, **4**, 1–7.

CARNE, E. B. (1965) *Artificial Intelligence Techniques.* London: Macmillan.

CARROLL, J. B. (1953) 'An analytical solution for approximating simple structure in factor analysis', *Pmka.*, **18**, 23–28.

CARTER, C. O. (1962) *Human Heredity.* Harmondsworth: Penguin Books.

K*

CARTER, C.O. (1966) *Differential fertility by intelligence*, in Meade, J. E. and Parkes, A. S. (Eds.) *Genetic and Environmental Factors in Human Ability*.

CATTELL, PSYCHE (1940) *The Measurement of Intelligence of Infants and Young Children*. New York: Psychological Corporation.

CATTELL, R. B. (1947) 'The ergic theory of attitude and sentiment measurement', *Educ. Psychol. Measmt.*, **45**, 598–618.

CATTELL, R. B. (1950) 'The fate of national intelligence: test of a thirteen year prediction', *Eugen. Rev.*, **42**, 136–148.

CATTELL, R. B. (1953) 'Research design in psychological genetics with special reference to the multiple variance analysis method', *Amer. J. Hum. Genet.*, **5**, 76–93.

CATTELL, R. B. (1957) *Personality and Motivation Structure and Measurement*. New York: World Book Co.

CATTELL, R. B. (1960) 'The multiple abstract variance analysis equations and solutions for nature – nurture research on continuous variables'. *Psychol. Rev.*, **67**, 353–372.

CATTELL, R. B. (1963a) 'The interaction of hereditary and environmental influences', *Brit. J. statist. Psychol.*, **16**, 191–210.

CATTELL, R. B. (1963b) 'Theory of fluid and crystallized intelligence: a critical experiment', *J. educ. Psychol.*, **54**, 1–22.

CATTELL, R. B. (1963c) 'The personality and motivation of the researcher from measurements of contemporaries and from biography', in Taylor and Barron, *Scientific Creativity*. New York: Wiley.

CATTELL, R. B. (1963d) 'Validity and reliability: a proposed more basic set of concepts', *J. educ. Psychol.*, **55**, 1–22.

CATTELL, R. B. (1965a) *The Scientific Analysis of Personality*. Harmondsworth: Penguin Books.

CATTELL, R. B. (1965b) 'Methodological and conceptual advances in evaluating hereditary and environmental influences and their interactions', in Vandenberg, S. G. (Ed.) *Methods and Goals in Human Behavior Genetics*. Academic Press.

CATTELL, R. B. (1967) 'The theory of fluid and crystallised general intelligence checked at the 5–6 year old level', *Brit. J. educ. Psychol.* **37**, 209–224.

CATTELL, R. B., and BAGGALEY, A. R. (1956) 'The objective measurement of attitude motivation: development and evaluation of principles and devices', *J. Personal.*, **24**, 401–423.

CATTELL, R. B., BLEWETT, D. B., and BELOFF, J. R. (1955) 'The inheritance of personality: a multiple variance analysis determination of approximate nature-nurture ratios for primary personality factors in Q-data', *J. Amer. Hum. Genet.*, **7**, 122–146.

CATTELL, R. B., and BUTCHER, H. J. (1968) *The Prediction of Achievement and Creativity*. Indianapolis, Indiana: Bobbs Merrill.

CATTELL, R. B., and DREVDAHL, J. E. (1955) 'A comparison of the personality profile of eminent researchers with that of eminent teachers and administrators and of the general population', *Brit. J. Psychol.*, **46**, 248–261.

CATTELL, R. B., HORN, J. L., and BUTCHER, H. J. (1962) 'The dynamic structure of attitudes in adults; a description of some established factors and of their measurement by the Motivational Analysis Test', *Brit. J. Psychol.*, **53**, 57–69.

CATTELL, R. B., KRISTY, N., and STICE, G. F. (1952) 'A first approximation to nature-nurture ratios for eleven primary personality factors in objective tests', *J. abnorm. soc. Psychol.*, **54**, 143–159.

CATTELL, R. B., SEALY, A. P., and SWENEY, A. B. (1966) 'What can personality and motivation source trait measurements add to the prediction of school achievement?', *Brit. J. educ. Psychol.*, **36**, 280–295.

CATTELL, R. B., SWENEY, A. B., and RADCLIFFE, J. A. (1960) 'The objective measurement of motivation structure in children', *J. clin. Psychol.*, **16**, 227–232.

CHAMBERS, E. G. (1943) 'Statistics in psychology and the limitations of the test method', *Brit. J. Psychol.*, **33**, 189–199.

CHARLES, D. C., and JAMES, S. T. (1964) 'Stability of average intelligence', *J. genet. Psychol.*, **105**, 105–111.

CHILD, D. (1964) 'The relationship between introversion-extraversion, neuroticism and performance in school examination', *Brit. J. educ. Psychol.*, **34**, 187–196.

CIEUTAT, V. J. (1965) 'Examiner differences with the Stanford–Binet I.Q.', *Percept. motor skills.* **20**, 317–318.

CLARKE, C. M., VELDMAN, D. J., and THORPE, J. S. (1965) 'Convergent and divergent thinking abilities of talented adolescents', *J. educ. Psychol.*, **56**, 157–163.

CLARKE, H. H., and OLSON, A. L. (1965) 'Characteristics of 15-year-old boys who demonstrate various accomplishments or difficulties', *Child Develpm.*, **36**, 559.

CLARKE, P. R. F. (1962) 'Complexities in the concept of Intelligence', *Psychological Reports*, **11**, 411–417.

CLINE, V. B., RICHARDS, J. M., and ABE, C. (1962) 'The validity of a battery of creativity tests in a high school sample', *Educ. Psychol. Measmt.*, **22**, 781–784.

CLINE, V. B., RICHARDS, J. M., and NEEDHAM, W. E. (1963) 'Creativity tests and achievement in high school science', *J. appl. Psychol.*, **47**, 184–189.

COCHRAN, W. G., and COX, GERTRUDE M. (1950) *Experimental Designs*. New York: Wiley.

COHEN, J. (1964) 'A perspective for psychology', Ch. 1 in *Readings in Psychology* (Ed. J. Cohen). London: Allen and Unwin.

COLEMAN, W., and WARD, A. W. (1955) 'A comparison of Davis-Eells and Kuhlmann–Finch scores of children from high and low socio-economic status', *J. educ. Psychol.*, **46**, 465–469, 403.

COLER, M. A. (Ed.) (1963) *Essays on Creativity in the Sciences*. New York: University Press.

COLLINGWOOD, R. G. (1940) *An Essay on Metaphysics*. Oxford: Oxford Univ. Press.

COLLINS, N. L., and MICHIE, D. (1967) *Machine Intelligence I*. Edinburgh: Oliver and Boyd.

CONWAY, J. (1959) 'Class differences in general intelligence', *Brit. J. stat. Psychol.*, **12**, 5–14.

CORNWELL, J. (1952) *An orally presented group test of intelligence*. London: Methuen.

COX, C. M. (1926) 'The early mental traits of three hundred geniuses', *Genetic Studies of Genius, Vol. II*. Stanford, California: Stanford Univ. Press.

COX, R. (1967) Examinations and higher education. *Univ. Quarterly*, **21**, 352–358.

CRONBACH, L. J. (1951) 'Coefficient alpha and the structure of tests', *Pmka.*, **16**, 297–334.

CRONBACH, L. J. (1957) 'The two disciplines of scientific psychology', *Amer. Psychologist*, **12**, 671–684.

CRONBACH, L. J. (1960) *Essentials of Psychological Testing* (2nd edn.). New York: Harper.

CRONBACH, L. J. (1967) 'How can instruction be adapted to individual differences?' Ch. 2 in Gagné, R. M. (Ed.) *Learning and Individual Differences*. Columbus, Ohio: Merrill.

CRONBACH, L. J., and GLESER, GOLDINE C. (1965) *Psychological Tests and Personnel Decisions* (2nd ed.). Urbana, Univ. of Illinois Press.

CRONBACH, L. J., RAJARATNAM, N., and GLESER, G. C. (1963) 'Theory of generalizability. A liberalization of reliability theory', *Brit. J. statist. Psychol.*, **16**, 137–164.

CROOKES, T. G. (1963) 'A note on intelligence and date of birth', *Brit. J. med. Psychol.*, **36**, 355–356.

CROPLEY, A. J. (1964) 'Differentiation of Abilities, Socioeconomic Status, and the WISC', *J. consult. Psychol.*, **28**, 512–517.

CROPLEY, A. J. (1966) 'Creativity and Intelligence', *Brit. J. educ. Psychol.*, **36**, 259–266.

CROSS, P., CATTELL, R. B., and BUTCHER, H. J. (1967) 'The personality pattern of creative artists', *Brit. J. educ. Psychol.*, **37**, 292–299.

DALE, R. R. (1963) 'Reflections on the influence of social class on student performance at the university', *Sociol. Rev. Monogr.*, No. 7, 131–140.

DAMON, A. (1965) 'Discrepancies between findings of longitudinal and cross-sectional studies in adult life: physique and physiology', *Human Developm.*, **8**, 16–22.

DARLINGTON, C. D. (1963) 'Psychology, genetics and the process of history', *Brit. J. Psychol.*, **54**, 293–298.

DATTA, L. (1964a) 'The Remote Associates Test as a predictor of creativity in engineers', *J. appl. Psychol.*, **48**, 183.

DATTA, L. (1964b) 'A note on the Remote Associates Test, U.S. culture,
and creativity', *J. appl. Psychol.*, **48**, 184.

DAVIES, ANN D. M. (1965) 'The perceptual maze test in a normal
population', *Percept. mot. Skills*, **20**, 287–93.

DAVIES, ANN D. M. (1966) *Some Tests of Mental Functioning and Their
Relation to Ageing and to Brain Damage.* Ph.D. Thesis. University of
Liverpool.

DAVIES, ANN D. M., and DAVIES, M. G. (1965) 'The difficulty and graded
scoring of Elithorn's perceptual maze test', *Brit. J. Psychol.*, **56**, 295–302.

DAVIES, F. B. (1964) *Educational Measurements and their Interpretation.*
Belmont, California: Wadsworth.

DAVIES, G. A. (1966) 'Current status of research and theory in human
problem solving', *Psychol. Bull.*, **66**, 36–54.

DAVIES, M. G., and DAVIES, A. D. M. (1965) 'Some analytical properties
of Elithorn's Perceptual Maze', *J. math. Psychol.*, **2**, 371–380.

DAVIES, P. C. (1956) 'A factor analysis of the Wechsler–Bellevue scale',
Educ. Psychol. Measmt., **16**, 127–146.

DAVITZ, J. R. (1964) *The Communication of Emotional Meaning.* New
York: McGraw-Hill.

DEARBORN, W. F., and ROTHNEY, J. W. M. (1941) *Predicting the Child's
Development.* Cambridge, Mass.: Sci-Act.

DÉCARIE, THÉRÈSE G. (1966) *Intelligence and Affectivity in Early Childhood. An experimental study of Jean Piaget's object concept and object
relations.* New York: International Universities Press.

DE FINETTI, B. (1965) 'Methods for discriminating levels of partial
knowledge concerning a test item', *Brit. J. math. stat. Psychol.*, **18**,
87–123.

DE GROOT, A. D. (1965) *Thought and Choice in Chess.* The Hague:
Mouton.

DE GROOT, A. D. (1966) 'Perception and memory versus thought: some old
ideas and recent findings', Ch. 2 in *Problem Solving: Research, Method
and Theory* (Ed. B. Kleinmuntz). New York: Wiley.

DE MILLE, R., and MERRIFIELD, P. R. (1962) Review of 'Creativity and
Intelligence', by Getzels and Jackson. *Educ. Psychol. Measmt.*, **22**, 803–
808.

DENNIS, W. (1943) 'Animism and related tendencies in Hopi children',
J. abnorm. soc. Psychol., **38**, 21–36.

DENNIS, W., and MALLENGER, B. (1949) 'Animism and related tendencies in senescence', *J. Gerontol.*, **4**, 218–221.

DENNIS, W., and NAJARIAN, P. (1957) 'Infant development under
environmental handicap', *Psychol. Monogr.*, **71**, No. 7, whole No. 463.

DENNIS, W., and RUSSELL, R. W. (1940) 'Piaget's questions applied to
Zuni children', *Child Develpm.*, **11**, 181–187.

DEPARTMENT OF EDUCATION AND SCIENCE (1967) *Children and Their Primary Schools* (*The Plowden Report*). London: H.M. Stationery Office.

DEUTSCHE, JEAN M. (1937) 'The Development of Children's Concepts of Causal Relations', *Minnesota Univ. Inst. Child Welfare Monogr.*

DIENES, Z. P., and JEEVES, M. A. (1965) *Thinking in Structures.* London: Hutchinson.

DOBZHANSKY, T. (1967) 'Of flies and men', *Amer. Psychologist*, **22**, 41–48.

DONALDSON, M. C. (1956) *The relevance to the theory of intelligence testing of the study of errors in thinking.* Ph.D. Thesis, Edinburgh Univ. Library.

DONALDSON, M. C. (1959) 'Positive and negative information in matching problems', *Brit. J. Psychol.*, **50**, 253–262.

DONALDSON, M. C. (1963) *A Study of Children's Thinking.* London: Tavistock.

DOUGLAS, J. W. B. (1964) *The Home and the School.* London: Mac-Gibbon and Kee.

DOUGLAS, J. W. B., and ROSS, J. M. (1964) 'The later educational progress and emotional adjustment of children who went to nursery schools or classes', *Educ. Res.*, **7**, 73–80.

DRAKE, R. M. (1959) 'Review of the Davis-Eells Games' in Buros, O. K., *Fifth Mental Measurements Yearbook.* New Jersey: Gryphon Press.

DREGER, R. M., and MILLER, K. S. (1960) 'Comparative psychological studies of Negroes and whites in the United States', *Psychol. Bull.*, **57**, 361–402.

DREVDAHL, J. E. (1956) 'Factors of importance for creativity', *J. clin. Psychol.*, **12**, 21–26.

DREVDAHL, J. E., and CATTELL, R. B. (1958) 'Personality and creativity in artists and writers', *J. clin. Psychol.*, **14**, 107–111.

DREVER, J. (1963) 'Prediction, placement and choice in university selection', Annex A. to appendix 2 (B) of Robbins committee report.

DREVER, J. (1967) 'The nurture of intelligence', *Scott. Educ. Studies*, **1**, 3–7.

DUNCAN, D. R., and BARRETT, A. M. (1961) 'A longitudinal comparison of intelligence involving the Wechsler–Bellevue I and the WAIS', *J. clin. Psychol.*, **17**, 318–319.

DUNCANSON, J. P. (1966) 'Learning and measured abilities', *J. educ. Psychol.*, **57**, 220–229.

DUNCKER, K. (1945) 'On problem solving', *Psychol. Monogr. 58, whole No. 270.*

DUNNETTE, M. D. (1964) 'Critics of psychological tests: basic assumptions: how good?' *Psychol. in the Schools*, **1**, 63–69.

EDWARDS, M. P., and TYLER, L. E. (1965) 'Intelligence, creativity and achievement in a non-selective public junior high school', *J. educ. Psychol.*, **56**, 96–99.

EELLS, K., DAVIS, A., HAVIGHURST, R. J., HERRICK, V. E., and TYLER, R. W. (1951) *Intelligence and Cultural Differences.* Chicago: Chicago Univ. Press.

EIFERMANN, R. R. (1965a) 'Response patterns and strategies in the dynamics of concept attainment behaviour', *Brit. J. Psychol.*, 56, 217–222.

EIFERMANN, R. R. (1965b) 'Selection strategies in concept attainment: a re-examination,' in *Scripta Hierosolymitana*. 14. *Studies in Psychology*. Jerusalem: Magnes Press.

ELCOCK, E. W., and MURRAY, A. M. (1967) 'Experiments with a learning component in a Go-Moku playing program', in *Machine Intelligence* (Ed. N. L. Collins and D. Michie). Edinburgh: Oliver and Boyd.

ELITHORN, A., JONES, D., KERR, M., and LEE, D. (1964) 'The effects of the variation of two physical parameters on empirical difficulty in a perceptual maze test', *Brit. J. Psychol.*, 55, 31–37.

ELITHORN, A., KERR, M., and JONES, D. (1963) 'A binary perceptual maze', *Amer. J. Psychol.*, 76, 506–8.

ELITHORN, A., KERR, M., and MOTT, J. (1960) 'A group version of a perceptual maze test', *Brit. J. Psychol.*, 51, 19–26.

EL KOUSSY, A. A. H. (1935). 'The visual perception of space', *Brit. J. Psychol.*, *Monogr. Suppl.*, No. 20.

ELLIS, H. (1904) *A Study of British Genius*. London: Hurst and Blackett.

EMMETT, W. G. (1949) 'Evidence of a Space Factor at 11 + and Earlier', *Brit. J. Psychol.*, *Stat. Sec.*, 2, 3–16.

EMMETT, W. G. (1954) 'The Intelligence of urban and rural children', *Population Studies*, 7, 207.

ENTWISLE, DORIS R. (1966) *Word Associations of Young Children*. Baltimore: Johns Hopkins Press.

ERLENMAYER-KIMLING, L. and JARVIK, L. F. (1963) 'Genetics and intelligence', *Science*, 142, 1477–1479.

EYSENCK, H. J. (1939) 'Primary Mental Abilities', *Brit. J. educ. Psychol.*, 9, 270–275.

EYSENCK, H. J. (1944) 'The effect of incentives on neurotics, and the variability of neurotics as compared with normals', *Brit. J. med. Psychol.*, 20, 100–3.

EYSENCK, H. J. (1947) 'Student selection by means of psychological tests – a critical survey', *Brit. J. educ. Psychol.*, 17, 20–39.

EYSENCK, H. J. (1952) *The Scientific Study of Personality*. London: Routledge.

EYSENCK, H. J. (1953) *Uses and Abuses of Psychology*. London: Penguin Books.

EYSENCK, H. J. (1966) 'Personality and experimental psychology', *Bull. Brit. Psychol. Socy.*, 19, 1–28.

EYSENCK, H. J. (1967) 'Intelligence assessment: a theoretical and experimental approach', *Brit. J. educ. Psychol.*, 37, 81–98.

EYSENCK, H. J., and WHITE, P. O. (1964) 'Personality and the measurement of intelligence', *Brit. J. educ. Psychol.*, 34, 197–201.

FEIGENBAUM, E. A., and FELDMAN, J. (Eds.) (1963) *Computers and Thought*. New York: McGraw-Hill.

FERGUSON, G. A. (1954) 'On learning and human ability', *Canad. J. Psychol.*, **8**, 95–112.

FERGUSON, G. A. (1956) 'On transfer and the abilities of man', *Canad. J. Psychol.*, **10**, 121–131.

FERGUSON, G. A. (1965) 'Human Abilities', *Ann. Rev. Psychol.*, **16**, 39–62.

FERRON, O. M. (1967) 'The Linguistic Factor in the Test Intelligence of West African Children', *Educ. Res.*, **9**, 113–122.

FIELD, J. C. (1960) 'Two types of tables for use with Wechsler's intelligence scales', *J. clin. Psychol.*, **16**, 3–7.

FINDLEY, D. C., and MCGUIRE, C. (1957) 'Social status and abstract behaviour', *J. abnorm. soc. Psychol.*, **54**, 135–137.

FISHER, M. (1966) 'Intelligence', *in Proc. of the ann. conference of the Philosophy of Education Society of Great Britain, 1966.* London: Univ. of London Institute of Education.

FLAVELL, J. H. (1963) *The Developmental Psychology of Jean Piaget.* Princeton, N.J.: Van Nostrand.

FLEISHMAN, E. A., and HEMPEL, W. E. (1954) 'Change in factor structure of a complex psychomotor task as a function of practice', *Pmka.* **19**, 239–252.

FLESCHER, I. (1963) 'Anxiety and achievement of intellectually gifted and creatively gifted children', *J. Psychol.*, **56**, 251–268.

FLETCHER, T. J. (ed.) (1964) *Some Lessons in Mathematics.* Cambridge: Cambridge Univ. Press.

FLOUD, J. E. (1963) Review of 'Studies in Individual Differences' (Eds. J. J. Jenkins and D. G. Paterson). New Society, 1, 30, 26.

FLOUD, J. E., HALSEY, A. M., and MARTIN, F. M. (1956) *Social Class and Educational Opportunity.* London: Heinemann.

FLUGEL, J. C. (1947) 'An inquiry as to popular views on intelligence and related topics', *Brit. J. educ. Psychol.*, **17**, 140–152.

FLUGEL, J. C., and WEST, D. J. (1964) *A Hundred Years of Psychology* (3rd edn.). London: Methuen.

FOGEL, L. J., OWENS, A. J., and WALSH, M. J. (1966) *Artificial Intelligence through Simulated Evolution.* New York and London: Wiley.

FORREST, G. M. (1961) 'An experimental study of concept attainment in children', *M.Ed. thesis.* Univ. of Manchester.

FOULDS, C. A., and RAVEN, J. C. (1948) 'Normal changes in the mental abilities of adults as age advances', *J. Ment. Sci.*, **94**, 135–142.

FRANCE, N. (1964) 'The use of group tests of ability and attainment: a follow-up study from primary to secondary school'. *Brit. J. educ. Psychol.*, **34**, 19–33.

FRANDSEN, A. N. (1950) 'The Wechsler–Bellevue Intelligence Scale and high school achievement', *J. appl. Psychol.*, **34**, 406–411.

FREEMAN, F. S. (1962) *Theory and Practice of Psychological Testing* (3rd edn.). New York: Holt.

FREUD, S. (1910) *Eine Kindheitserinnerung des Leonardo da Vinci*. Transl. Alan Tyson and publ. in Pelican books 1963.

FREYBERG, P. S. (1966) 'Concept development in Piagetian terms in relation to school attainment', *J. educ. Psychol.*, **57**, 164–168.

FREYMAN, R. (1965) 'Further evidence on the effect of date of birth on subsequent school performance', *Educ. Res.*, **8**, 58–64.

FRIJDA, N. H. (1967) 'Problems of computer simulation', *Behav. Sci.*, **12**, 59–67.

FRUCHTER, B. (1966) 'Manipulative and Hypotheses-Testing Factor-Analytic Experimental Designt', Ch. 10 in R. B. Cattell, *Handbook of Multivariate Experimental Psychology*. Chicago: Rand McNally.

FULLER, J. L. (1960) 'Behaviour genetics', *Ann. Rev. Psychol.*, **11**, 41–70.

FULLER, J. L., and THOMPSON, W. R. (1960) *Behaviour Genetics*. New York.

FUQUA, (1967) Research described in Times Educ. Supplt. No. 2715, p. 1859 (issue of 2nd June).

FURNEAUX, W. D. (1960) 'Intellectual abilities and problem-solving behaviour', Ch. 5 in H. J. Eysenck (Ed.) *Handbook of Abnormal Psychology*. London: Pitman Medical Publishing Co.

FURNEAUX, W. D. (1961) *The Chosen Few*. London: Oxford Univ. Press.

GAGE, N. L. (Ed.) (1963) *Handbook of Research in Teaching*. Chicago: Rand McNally.

GAGNÉ, R. M. (1964) 'Problem Solving' in Melton, A. W. (Ed.) *Categories of Human Learning*. New York Academic Press.

GAGNÉ, R. M. (1965) *The Conditions of Learning*. New York: Holt, Rinehart and Winston.

GAGNÉ, R. M. (Ed.) (1967) *Learning and Individual Differences*. Columbus, Ohio: Merrill.

GALANTER, E. (1966). *A Textbook of Elementary Psychology*. San Francisco: Holden-Day.

GALTON, F. (1870) *Hereditary Genius*. New York: Appleton.

GARRETT, H. E. (1946) 'A developmental theory of intelligence', *Amer. Psychologist*, **1**, 372–378.

GESELL, A. (1925) *The Mental Growth of the Pre-School Child*. New York: Macmillan.

GESELL, A. (1940) *The First Five Years of Life*. New York: Harper.

GETZELS, J. W., and JACKSON, P. W. (1962) *Creativity and Intelligence*. New York: Wiley.

GHISELIN, B. (1952) (Ed.) *The Creative Process*. London: Cambridge University Press.

GIST, N. P., and CLARK, C. D. (1939) 'Intelligence as a selective factor in rural-urban migration', *Amer. J. Sociol.*, **44**, 36–58.

GLANZER, M., HUTTENLOCHER, J., and CLARK, W. H. (1963) 'Systematic operations in solving concept problems: a parametric study of a class of problems', *Psychol. Monogr.*, **77**, No. 1.

GLASER, R. (1967) 'Some implications of previous work on learning and individual differences', in *Learning and Individual Differences* (Ed. R. M. Gagné). Columbus, Ohio: Merrill.

GLASS, D. V. (1964) Introduction to J. W. B. Douglas 'The Home and the School', London: MacGibbon and Kee.

GODDARD, H. H. (1916) Publication of the Vineland Training School No. 11. Vineland, N.J.

GOLANN, S. E. (1963) 'Psychological study of creativity', *Psychol. Bull.*, 60, 548–565.

GOLDBERG, S. (1966) 'Probability judgements by pre-school children: task conditions and performance', *Child Develpm.*, 37, 157–167.

GOLDFARB, W. (1945) 'Effects of psychological deprivation in infancy and subsequent stimulation', *Amer. J. Psychiat.*, 102, 18–33.

GOLDMAN, R. J. (1964) 'The Minnesota Tests of Creative Thinking', *Educ. Res.*, 7, 3–14.

GOLDMAN, R. J. (1965) 'The application of Piaget's scheme of operational thinking to religious story data by means of the Guttman scalogram,' *Brit. J. educ. Psychol.*, 35, 158–170.

GOLDMAN, R. J., and CLARKE, D. F. (1967) 'The Minnesota tests of creative thinking – a note on scorer reliability in follow-up studies with English primary school children', *Brit. J. educ. Psychol.*, 37, 115–116.

GOLDMAN, R. J., and TAYLOR, F. M. (1966a) 'Coloured immigrant children: a survey of research studies and literature on their educational problems and potential – in the U.S.A.', *Educ. Res.*, 9, 22–43.

GOLDMAN, R. J., and TAYLOR, F. M. (1966b) 'Coloured immigrant children: A survey of research studies and literature on their educational problems and potential – in Britain', *Educ. Res.*, 8, 163–184.

GOOCH, S., and PRINGLE, M. L. KELLMER (1967) *Four Years On.* London: Longmans.

GORDON, H. (1923) *Mental and scholastic tests among retarded children.* London: Board of Education pamphlet No. 44.

GOSLIN, D. A. (1963) *The Search for Ability.* New York: Russell Sage Foundation.

GOTTESMAN, I. I. (1963) 'Heritability of personality: a demonstration' *Psychol. Monogr.*, 77 (9).

GOWAN, J. C., and DEMOS, G. D. (1964) *The Education and Guidance of the Ablest.* Springfield, Illinois: Thomas.

GREEN, B. F. (1964) *Digital computers in research.* New York: McGraw-Hill.

GREEN, B. F. (1966a) 'The computer revolution in psychometrics', *Pmka.* 31, 437–446.

GREEN, B. F. (1966b) 'Current Trends in Problem Solving', in *Problem Solving: Research, Method and Theory* (Ed. B. Kleinmuntz). New York and London: Wiley.

GREEN, R. F., and BERKOWITZ, B. (1964) 'Changes in Intellect with Age: II. Factorial Analysis of Wechsler–Bellevue Scores', *J. genet. Psychol.*, 104, 3–18.

GREGORY, R. L. (1966) 'Visual Illusions', in *New Horizons in Psychology* (Ed. B. Foss). Pelican Books.

GREGORY, R. L. (1967) *Eye and Brain*. London. Weidenfeld & Nicolson.

GRIFFITHS, RUTH (1954) *The Abilities of Babies*. London: Univ. of London Press.

GRIZE, J. B. (1965) 'Genetic epistemology and psychology', in *Scientific Psychology*, Welman and Nagel (Eds.), pp. 460–473.

GRUBER, H. E., TERRELL, G., and WERTHEIMER, M. (Eds.) (1962) *Contemporary Approaches to Creative Thinking*. New York: Atherton Press.

GUERTIN, W. H., FRANK, G. H., and RABIN, A. I. (1956) 'Research with the WB Intelligence Scale: 1950–1955', *Psychol. Bull.*, **53,** 235–257.

GUERTIN, W. H., LADD, C. E., FRANK, G. H., RABIN, A. I., and HIESTER, D. S. (1966) 'Research with the Wechsler Intelligence Scales for Adults', *Psychol. Bull.*, **66,** 385–409.

GUERTIN, W. H., RABIN, A. I., FRANK, G. H., and LADD, C. E. (1962) 'Research with the Wechsler Intelligence Scales for Adults: 1955–1960', *Psychol. Bull.*, **59,** 1–26.

GUILFORD, J. P. (1950) 'Creativity', *Amer. Psychologist*, **5,** 444–454.

GUILFORD, J. P. (1956) 'The structure of intellect', *Psychol. Bull.*, **53,** 267–293.

GUILFORD, J. P. (1959) 'Three faces of intellect', *Amer. Psychologist*, **14,** 469–479. Reprinted in Anderson and Ausubel (1965).

GUILFORD, J. P. (1961) 'Factorial angles to psychology', *Psychol. Rev.*, **68,** 1–20.

GUILFORD, J. P. (1963) 'Potentiality for creativity and its measurement', in *'Proceedings of the 1962 invitational conference on testing problems'*. Princeton, N.J.: E.T.S.

GUILFORD, J. P. (1964) 'Some new looks at the nature of creative processes', Ch. 7 in N. Frederikson and H. Gulliksen (Eds.) *Contributions to Mathematical Psychology*.

GUILFORD, J. P., (1965) *Fundamental Statistics in Psychology and Education* (4th edn.). New York: McGraw-Hill.

GUILFORD, J. P. (1967) *The Nature of Human Intelligence*. New York: McGraw-Hill.

GUILFORD, J. P. and HOEPFNER, R. (1963) 'Current summary of structure-of-intellect factors and suggested tests', *Reports from Psychol. Lab.*, Univ. of S. California, No. 30.

GUILFORD, J. P., and HOEPFNER, R. (1966) 'Structure-of-intellect factors and their tests 1966', *Reports from the Psychol. Lab.*, Univ. of S. California, No. 36.

GULLIKSEN, H. (1950) *Theory of Mental Tests*. New York: Wiley.

GUTTMAN, L. (1965) 'A faceted definition of intelligence', in R. Eifermann (Ed.) *Scripta Hierosolymitana*, **14.** Jerusalem: Magnes Press.

HAAN, NORMA (1963) 'Proposed model of ego functioning: coping and defence mechanisms in relationship to I.Q. change', *Psychol. Monogr.*, **77**, No. 8.

HADAMARD, J. (1945) *The Psychology of Invention in the Mathematical Field*. Princeton: Princeton University Press. Reprinted 1954 by Dover books.

HADDON, F. A., and LYTTON, H. (1968) 'Teaching approach and the development of divergent thinking abilities in primary schools', *Brit. J. educ. Psychol.*, **38**, 171–180.

HAEFELE, J. W. (1962) *Creativity and Innovation*. New York: Reinhold.

HAGGARD, E. (1954) 'Social status and intelligence. An experimental study of certain cultural determinants of measured intelligence', *Genet. Psychol. Monogr.*, **49**, 141–186.

HALL, C. S., and LINDZEY, G. (1957) *Theories of Personality*. New York: Wiley.

HALSEY, A. H. (1958) 'Genetics, social structure and intelligence', *Brit. J. Sociol.*, **9**, 15–28.

HALSEY, A. H. (1959) 'Class differences in general intelligence', *Brit. J. statist. Psychol.*, **12**, 1–4.

HAMILTON, V. (1967) 'Size constancy and intelligence: a re-examination', *Brit. J. Psychol.*, **57**, 319–328.

HANSEN, D. N. (1966) 'Computer assistance with the educational process', *Rev. educ. Res.*, **36**, 588–603.

HARRELL, T. W., and HARRELL, M. S. (1945) 'Army general classification test scores for civilian occupations', *Educ. Psychol. Measmt.*, **5**, 229–239.

HARRIS, C. W. (1963) (Ed.) *Problems in Measuring Change*. Madison: Univ. of Wisconsin Press.

HARRIS, C. W. (1964) 'Some recent developments in factor analysis', *Educ. Psychol. Measurement*, **24**, 2, 193–206.

HARRIS, C. W. (1965) (Ed.) *Proceedings of the 1964 International Conference on Testing Problems*. Princeton, N.J.: Educational Testing Service.

HARRIS, C. W. (1966) 'Canonical Factor Models for the Description of Change', Ch. 12 in R. B. Cattell, *Handbook of Multivariate Experimental Psychology*. Chicago: Rand McNally.

HARTOG, P., RHODES, E. C., and BURT, C. (1936) *The Marks of Examiners*. London: Macmillan.

HASAN, PARWEEN (1965) 'Intelligence and Creativity', *B. Ed. thesis*, Univ. of Edinburgh Library.

HASAN, PARWEEN, and BUTCHER, H. J. (1966) 'Creativity and intelligence: a partial replication with Scottish children of Getzels and Jackson's study', *Brit. J. Psychol.*, **57**, 129–135.

HAUGEN, E. (1961) 'The bi-lingual individual', in S. Saporta (Ed.) *Psycholinguistics*, pp. 395–407. New York: Holt, Rinehart and Winston.

HAYES, K. J. (1962) 'Genes, drives and intellect', *Psychol. Reports.*, **10**, 299–342.

HEARNSHAW, L. S. (1964) *A Short History of British Psychology*. London: Methuen.

HEBB, D. O. (1949) *The Organisation of Behavior*. New York: Wiley.

HEBB, D. O. (1966) *A Textbook of Psychology*. Philadelphia, London: W. B. Saunders Co. (2nd edn.).

HEBRON, MIRIAM E. (1966) *Motivated Learning: A developmental study from birth to the senium*. London: Methuen.

HEIM, ALICE W. (1954) *The Appraisal of Intelligence*. London: Methuen.

HEIM, ALICE W. (1955) 'Adaptation to level of difficulty in intelligence testing', *Brit. J. Psychol.*, **46**, 211–224.

HEIM, ALICE W. (1957) 'Psychological adaptation as a response to variations in difficulty', *J. gen. Psychol.*, **56**, 193–211.

HELMSTADTER, G. C. (1966) *Principles of Psychological Measurement*. London: Methuen.

HEMPEL, C. G. (1965) *Aspects of Scientific Explanation and Other Essays in the Philosophy of Science*. New York: Free Press.

HEMPEL, C. G. (1966) *Philosophy of Natural Science*. Englewood Cliffs, N.J.: Prentice-Hall.

HENDRICKSON, A. E., and WHITE, P. O. (1964) 'Promax: a quick method for rotation to oblique simple structure', *Brit. J. stat. Psychol.*, **17**, 65–70.

HENDRICKSON, A. E., and WHITE, P. O. (1966) 'A method for the rotation of higher-order factors', *Brit. J. math. statist. Psychol.*, **19**, 97–104.

HESS, R. D. (1955) 'Controlling cultural influence in mental testing: an experimental test', *J. educ. Res.*, **49**, 53–58, 403.

HIGGINS, J. V., REED, E. W., and REED, S. C. (1962) 'Intelligence and family size: a paradox resolved', *Eugen. Quart.*, **9**, 84–90.

HILGARD, E. R., and ATKINSON, R. C. (1967) *Introduction to Psychology* (4th edn.). New York: Harcourt, Brace.

HILGARD, E. R., and BOWER, G. H. (1966) *Theories of Learning* (3rd edn.) New York: Appleton-Century-Crofts.

HIMELSTEIN, P. (1966) 'Research with the Stanford-Binet, form L–M.', *Psychol. Bull.*, **65**, 156–164.

HIMMELWEIT, H. T. (1961) 'The role of intelligence in modifying social class differences in outlook', *Acta Psychologica*, **19**, 273–281.

HIMMELWEIT, H. T., and WHITFIELD, J. W. (1949) 'Mean intelligence scores of a random sample of occupations', *Brit. J. industr. Med.*, **1**, 224–226.

HINDLEY, C. B. (1965) 'Stability and change in abilities up to five years: group trends', *J. child psychol. psychiat.*, **6**, 85–100.

HIRSCH, J. (1963) 'Behavior genetics and individuality understood', *Science*, **142**, 1436–42.

HIRSCH, J. (1967) 'Behavior-genetic or "experimental" analysis: the challenge of science versus the lure of technology', *Amer. Psychologist*, **22**, 118–130.

HODGES, W. F., and FOX, R. (1965) 'Effect of arousal and intelligence on binocular rivalry rate', *Percept. motor skills*. 20, 71–75.

HOFSTAETTER, P. R. (1954) 'The changing composition of "intelligence": a study in T-technique', *J. genet. Psychol*. **85**, 159–164.

HOLLAND, J. L., and RICHARDS, J. M. (1965) 'Academic and non-academic accomplishment: correlated or uncorrelated?', *J. educ. Psychol*., **56**, 165–174.

HOLLINGDALE, S. H., and TOOTILL, G. C. (1965) *Electronic Computers*. London: Penguin.

HOLLOWAY, G. E. T. (1967a) *An introduction to the Child's Conception of Space*. London: Routledge.

HOLLOWAY, G. E. T. (1967b) *An introduction to the Child's Conception of Geometry*. London: Routledge.

HONZIK, M. P. (1957) 'Developmental studies of parent-child resemblance in intelligence', *Child Develpm*., **28**, 215–228.

HONZIK, M. P. (1963) 'A Sex Difference in the Age of Onset of the Parent-Child Resemblance in Intelligence', *J. educ. Psychol*., **54**, 231–237.

HOPKINS, K. D. (1964) 'Extrinsic reliability: estimating and attenuating variance from response styles, chance and other irrelevant sources' *Educ. Psychol. Measmt*., **24**, 875–894.

HORN, J. L. (1966) 'Motivation and Dynamic Calculus Concepts from Multivariate Experiment', Ch. 20 in R. B. Cattell, *Handbook of Multivariate Experimental Psychology*. Chicago: Rand McNally.

HORN, J. L., and BRAMBLE, W. J. (1967) 'Second-order ability structure revealed in right and wrongs scores', *J. educ. Psychol*., **58**, 115–122.

HORN, J. L., and CATTELL, R. B. (1966) 'Refinement and test of the theory of fluid and crystallized general intelligences', *J. educ. Psychol*., **57**, 253–270.

HORN, J. L., and CATTELL, R. B. (1967) 'Age differences in fluid and crystallised intelligence', *Acta Psychologica*, **26**, 107–129.

HORST, P. (1966) *Psychological Measurement and Prediction*. Belmont, California: Wadsworth.

HOUSSIADAS, L. (1964) 'Effects of "set" and intellectual level on the perception of causality', *Acta Psychologica*, **22**, 155–161. Reprinted in *Experiments in Visual Perception* (Ed. M. D. Vernon). London: Penguin Books (1966).

HOVLAND, C. I. (1960) 'Order of consideration of different types of concepts', *J. exp. Psychol*., **59**, 220–225.

HOVLAND, C. I., and WEISS, W. (1953) 'Transmission of information concerning concepts through positive and negative instances', *J. exper. Psychol*., 1953, **45**, 175–182.

HUANG, I. (1943) 'Children's concepts of physical causality: a critical summary', *J. genet. Psychol.*, **63**, 71–121.

HUDSON, L. (1960) 'A differential test of arts/science aptitude', *Nature* **186**, 413.

HUDSON, L. (1965) 'Intelligence: convergent and divergent', in *Penguin Science Survey*, 1965, B.

HUDSON, L. (1966) *Contrary Imaginations*. London: Methuen.

HULL, C. L. (1920) 'Quantitative aspects of evolution of concepts', *Psychol. Monogr.* (whole No. 123).

HULL, C. L. (1928) *Aptitude Testing*. New York: World Book Co.

HUMPHREYS, L. G. (1962) 'The organisation of human abilities', *Amer. Psychol.*, **17**, 475–483.

HUMPHREYS, L. G., and BOYNTON, P. L. (1950) 'Intelligence and intelligence tests' in *Encyclopaedia of Educational Research* (Ed. W. S. Munroe). New York: Macmillan, pp. 600–612.

HUNT, E. B. (1962) *Concept Learning*. New York: Wiley.

HUNT, J. MCV. (1961) *Intelligence and Experience*. New York: Ronald Press.

HUNTLEY, R. M. C. (1966) 'Heritability of Intelligence', in Meade, J. E. and Parkes, A. S. *Genetic and Environmental Factors in Human Ability*.

HURLEY, J. R., and CATTELL, R. B. (1962) 'The procrustes program: producing direct rotation to test a hypothesized factor structure', *Behav. Sci.*, **7**, 258–262.

HUSEN, T. (1951) 'The influence of schooling upon I.Q.', *Theoria*, **17**.

HUSEN, T. (Ed.) (1967) *International Study of Achievement in Mathematics*. Stockholm: Almquist and Wiksell. New York and London: John Wiley.

HUTTENLOCHER, J. (1962) 'Some effects of negative instances on the formation of simple concepts', *Psychol. Reports*, **11**, 35–42.

INGLIS, J. J. (1967) *Selection and Comprehensive Secondary Education*. Godfrey Thomson Lecture.

INHELDER, BÄRBEL (1953) 'Criteria of the stages of mental development', Ch. 3 in *Discussions on Child Development* (Eds. J. M. Tanner and B. Inhelder). Vol. I. London: Tavistock.

INHELDER, BÄRBEL (1962) 'Some aspects of Piaget's genetic approach to cognition', in W. Kessen and C. Kuhlmann (Eds.) *Monogr. Soc. Res. Child Devel.*, **27**, 2 (whole No. 83).

IRVINE, S. H. (1965) 'Adapting tests to the cultural situation: a comment', *Occup. Psychol.*, **39**, 13–23.

IRVINE, S. H. (1966) 'Towards a rationale for testing attainments and abilities in Africa', *Brit. J. educ. Psychol.*, **36**, 24–32.

ISAACS, N. (1963) *The Growth of Understanding in the Young Child* (2nd edn.). London: Educational Supply Association.

ISAACS, S. (1930) *Intellectual Growth in Young Children*. London: Routledge.

JACKSON, B., and MARSDEN, D. (1962) *Education and the Working Class*. London: Institute of Community Studies Report No. 6.

JACKSON, R. A. (1955) 'Guessing and test performance', *Educ. Psychol. Measmt.*, 15, 74-9.

JAHODA, G. (1956) 'Assessment of abstract behavior in a non-western culture', *J. abnorm. soc. Psychol.*, 53, 237-243.

JAHODA, G. (1958) 'Child animism: I. A critical survey of cross-cultural research', *J. soc. Psychol.*, 47, 197-212.

JAHODA, M. (1967) 'Examining university examinations', *Univ. Quart,.* 21, 269-270.

JENKINS, J. J., and PATERSON, D. G. (1961) (Eds.) *Studies in Individual Differences*. London: Methuen.

JENSEN, A. R. (1966) 'Individual differences in concept learning', Ch. 9 in H. J. Klausmeier and C. W. Harris (Eds.) *Analyses of Concept Learning.*

JENSEN, A. R. (1967) 'Varieties of individual differences in learning', Ch. 6 in *Learning and Individual Differences* (Ed. R. M. Gagné). Columbus, Ohio: Merrill.

JOHNSON, D. M. (1966) 'Solution of Anagrams', *Psychol. Bull.*, 66, 371-384.

JOHNSON, J. P. (1966) 'Factors affecting transfer in concept-identification problems', *J. exper. Psychol.*, 72, 655-660.

JONES, H. E. (1959) 'Intelligence and problem solving', Ch. 20, pp. 700-738 in *Handbook of Aging and the Individual: Psychological Aspects* (Ed. J. E. Birren). University of Chicago Press.

JONES, H. E., and CONRAD, H. S. (1933) 'The growth and decline of intelligence: a study of a homogeneous group', *Genet. Psychol. Monogr.*, 13, 223-298.

JONES, SHEILA (1967) 'Decoding a deceptive instruction', *Brit. J. Psychol.*, 57, 405-411.

JUOLA, A. E. (1966) 'Prediction of successive terms' performance in college from tests and grades', *Amer. educ. res. J.*, 3, 191-197.

KAGAN, J. (1964) 'The child's sex role classification of school objects', *Child Develpm.*, 35, 1051-1056.

KAGAN, J. (1966) 'Learning, attention and the issue of discovery', Ch. 11 in *Learning by Discovery, A critical Appraisal* (Eds. L. S. Shulman and E. R. Keislar). Chicago: Rand McNally.

KAISER, H. F. (1958) 'The Varimax criterion for analytic rotation in factor analysis', *Pmka.*, 23, 187-200.

KEIR, G. (1965) 'The psychological assessment of the children from the island of Tristan da Cunha', in C. Banks and P. L. Broadhurst (Eds.) *Stephanos, Studies in Psychology presented to Cyril Burt*, pp. 129-172.

KELLEY, T. L. (1928) *Crossroads in the Mind of Man*. Stanford, California: Stanford Univ. Press.

KELLY, G. A. (1955) *The Psychology of Personal Constructs*. New York: Norton.

KELLY, G. A. (1965) 'The strategy of psychological research', *Bull. Brit. Psychol. Soc.*, **18**, 59, 1–15.

KELSALL, R. K. (1963) 'University student selection in relation to subsequent academic performance. A critical appraisal of the British evidence', *Sociol. Rev. Monogr. No. 7* (Ed. P. Halmos). 99–115.

KENDLER, H. H. (1964) 'The Concept of the Concept', in Melton, A.W. (Ed.) *Categories of Human Learning*, pp. 212–233. New York: Academic Press.

KENDLER, H. H., and KENDLER, T. S. (1959) 'Reversal and nonreversal shifts in kindergarten children', *J. exper. Psychol.*, **58**, 56–60.

KENDLER, H. H., and KENDLER, T. S. (1962) 'Vertical and horizontal processes in problem solving', *Psychol. Rev.*, **69**, 1–16.

KENDLER, T. S. (1963) 'Development of mediating responses in children', *Monogr. Soc. Res. Child. Devel.*, **86**, 33–47.

KENDLER, T. S. (1964) 'Learning and Problem Solving: Comments on Prof. Gagné's paper', in Melton, A. W. (Ed.) *Categories of Human Learning*.

KENNEDY, W. A., NELSON, W., LINDNER, R., MOON, H., and TURNER, J. (1960) 'The ceiling of the new Stanford-Binet', *J. clin. Psychol.*, **17**, 284–286.

KESSEN, W., and KUHLMAN, CLEMENTINA (1962) (Eds.) 'Thought in the Young Child', *Monogr. Soc. Res. Child Develpm.*, **27**, No. 2, Serial No. 83.

KIDD, ALINE H. (1962) 'The Culture-Fair Aspects of Cattell's Test of g: Culture-Free', *J. genet. Psychol.*, **101**, 343–62.

KIPNIS, D. (1965) 'Intelligence as a modifier of the behaviour of character disorders', *J. appl. Psychol.*, **49**, 237–242.

KLAUSMEIER, H. J., and HARRIS, C. W. (1966) *Analyses of Concept Learning*. New York and London: Academic Press.

KLAUSMEIER, H. J., and WIERSMA, W. (1964) 'Relationship of sex, grade level, and locale to performance of high I.Q. students on divergent thinking tests', *J. educ. Psychol.*, **55**, 114–119.

KLEINMUNTZ, B. (Ed.) (1966) *Problem Solving Research, Method and Theory*. New York and London: Wiley.

KLINEBERG, O. (1935) *Negro Intelligence and Selective Migration*. New York: Columbia Univ. Press.

KLINEBERG, O. (Ed.) (1944) *Characteristics of the American Negro*. New York: Harper.

KLINEBERG, O. (1963) 'Negro-white differences in intelligence test performance: a new look at an old problem', *Amer. Psychologist*, **18**, 198–203.

KNELLER, G. F. (1965) *The Art and Science of Creativity*. New York and London: Holt, Rinehart and Winston.

KODLIN, D., and THOMPSON, D. J. (1958) 'An appraisal of the longitudinal approach to studies in growth and development', *Monogr. Soc. Res. Child. Devel.*, **23**, Serial 67, No. 1.

L

KOESTLER, A. (1964) *The Act of Creation*. London: Hutchinson.

KOGAN, N., and WALLACH, M. (1964) *Risk taking: A study in cognition and personality*. New York: Holt, Rinehart and Winston.

KOHLBERG, L., and ZIGLER, E. (1967) 'The impact of cognitive maturity on the development of sex-role attitudes in the years four to eight', *Genet. Psychol. Monogr.*, **75**, 89–165.

KOHNSTAM, G. A. (1967) *Piaget's Analysis of Class Inclusion: right or wrong?* The Hague: Mouton.

KRECH, D. (1962) 'Cortical localization of function', Ch. 2 in L. Postman (Ed.) *Psychology in the Making*. New York: Knopf.

KRETSCHMER, E. (1931) *The Psychology of Men of Genius*. London: Kegan Paul.

KUBIE, L. S. (1958) *Neurotic Distortion of the Creative Process*. Lawrence: Univ. Kansas Press.

KUENNE, M. R. (1946) 'Experimental investigation of the relation of language to transposition behaviour in young children', *Amer. Psychologist*, 1946, **1**, 259–260.

LAUGHERY, K. R., and GREGG, L. W. (1962) 'Simulation of human problem-solving behavior', *Pmka.*, **27**, 265–82.

LAURENDEAU, MONIQUE, and PINARD, A. (1962) *Causal Thinking in the Child: A Genetic and Experimental Approach*. New York: International Universities Press.

LAVIN, D. E. (1965) *The Prediction of Academic Performance*. New York: Russell Sage Foundation.

LAWLEY, D. N. (1950) 'A method of standardizing group-tests', *Brit. J. Psychol.* (Stat. Sect.) **3**, 86–89.

LAWRENCE, E. M. (1931) 'An investigation into the relationship between intelligence and environment', *Brit. J. Psychol. Monogr. Suppl.*, No. 16.

LEE, E. S. (1951) 'Negro intelligence and selective migration: a Philadelphia test of the Klineberg hypothesis', *Amer. sociol. Rev.*, **16**, 227–233.

LEFFORD, A. (1946) 'The influence of emotional subject-matter on logical reasoning', *J. gen. Psychol.*, **34**, 127–151.

LENNEBERG, E. H. (1967) *Biological Foundations of Language*. New York: Wiley.

LESSER, G. S., FIFER, G., and CLARK, D. H. (1965) 'Mental abilities of children from different social-class and cultural groups', *Monogr. Soc. Res. Child Develop.*, **30**, No. 4.

LEVINSON, B. M. (1961) 'Subcultural values and I.Q. stability', *J. genet. Psychol.*, **98**, 69–82.

LEWIS, D. G. (1967) 'Commentary on "the genetic determination of differences in intelligence: a study of monozygotic twins reared together and apart", by Cyril Burt.' *Brit. J. Psychol.*, **57**, 431–433.

LEWIS, D. G., and GREGSON, A. (1965) 'The effects of frame size and intelligence on learning from a linear program', *Programmed Learning*, **1**, 170–175.

LIGHTFOOT, G. F. (1951) 'Personality characteristics of bright and dull children', *Teachers Coll., Columbia Univ. contrib. to educ.*, No. 969.

LINDHOLM, B. W. (1964) 'Changes in conventional and deviation IQs', *J. educ. Psychol.*, **55**, 110–113.

LINDQUIST, (1951). (Ed.) *Educational Measurement.* Washington D.C.: American Council on Education.

LITTELL, W. M. (1960) 'The Wechsler intelligence scale for children – a review of a decade of research', *Psychol. Bull.*, **57**, 132–162. (Reprinted as Ch. 6 in Savage, R.D. (Ed.) 1966.)

LITTLE, A., and WESTERGAARD, J. (1964) 'The trend of class differentials in educational opportunity in England and Wales', *Brit. J. Sociol.*, 15, 301–16.

LITTLE, E. B. (1962) 'Overcorrection for guessing in multiple-choice test scoring', *J. Educ. Res.*, **55**, 245–52.

LITTLE, E., and CREASER, J. (1966) 'Uncertain responses in multiple-choice examinations', *Psychol. Rep.*, **18**, 801–2.

LIVERANT, S. (1960) 'Intelligence: a concept in need of re-examination', *J. Consult. Psychol.*, **24**, 101–109.

LORD, F. M. (1958) 'Further problems in the measurement of growth', *Educ. Psychol. Measmt.*, **18**, 437–451.

LORD, F. M. (1964) 'Nominally and rigorously parallel test forms', *Pmka.*, **29**, 335–345.

LORENZ, K. (1966) *On Aggression.* London: Methuen.

LOVELL, K. (1955) 'A study of the problem of intellectual deterioration in adolescents and young adults', *Brit. J. Psychol.*, **46**, 199–210.

LOVELL, K. (1964) *The Growth of Basic Mathematical and Scientific Concepts in Children* (3rd edn.). London: Univ. of London Press.

LOVELL, K. (1966) 'Concepts in Mathematics.' Ch. 13 in H. J. Klausmeier and C. W. Harris (Eds.) *Analyses of Concept Learning.*

LUNZER, E. A. (1965) 'Problems of formal reasoning in test situations', *Monogr. Soc. Res. Child Develpm.* No. 100, 19–46.

LUNZER, E. A. (1968) 'Children's thinking', in *Educational Research in Britain* (Ed. H. J. Butcher) London: Univ. of London Press.

LURIA, A. R., and VINOGRADOVA, O. S. (1959) 'An objective investigation of the dynamics of semantic systems', *Brit. J. Psychol.*, **50**, 89–105.

LYNN, R. (1957) 'Temperamental characteristics related to disparity of attainment in reading and arithmetic', *Brit. J. educ. Psychol.*, **27**, 62–67.

LYONS, J., and WALES, R. (1967) *Psycholinguistic Papers.* Edinburgh: Edinburgh Univ. Press.

MACARTHUR, R. S., and ELLEY, W. B. (1963) 'The reduction of socio-economic bias in intelligence testing', *Brit. J. educ. Psychol.*, **33**, 1–119.

MCCLEARN, G. E., and MEREDITH, W. (1966) 'Behavior genetics', *Ann. Rev. Psychol.*, **17**, 515–550.

MCCLEARY, R. A., and MOORE, R. Y. *Subcortical mechanisms of behaviour; the psychological and primitive parts of the brain*, New York, 1965.

MCCLELLAND, D. C. (1958) 'Issues in the identification of talent', in *Talent and Society* (Ed. D. C. McClelland). Princeton: Van Nostrand.

MCCLELLAND, D. C., ATKINSON, J. W., CLARK, R. A., and LOWELL, E. L. (1953) *The Achievement Motive*. New York: Appleton-Century-Crofts.

MCCLELLAND, W. (1942) *Selection for Secondary Education*. London: Univ. of London Press.

MCDADE, D. F. (1967) 'Language, intelligence and social class', *Scott. Educ. Studies.*, **1**, 34–39.

MACDONALD, B., GAMMIE, A., and NISBET, J. (1964) 'The Careers of a Gifted Group', *Educational Research*, **6**, 216–219.

MCEWAN, P. J. M. (1965) 'Climate and intelligence', *Brit. J. soc. clin. Psychol.*, **4**, 8–13.

MCINTOSH, D. (1959) *Educational Guidance and the Pool of Ability*. London: Univ. of London Press.

MACKAY, G. W. S., and VERNON, P. E. (1963) 'The measurement of learning ability', *Brit. J. educ. Psychol.*, **33**, 177–186.

MCKELLAR, P. (1957) *Imagination and Thinking*. London: Cohen and West.

MACKINNON, D. W. (1962) 'The nature and nurture of creative talent'. *Amer. Psychologist*, **17**, 484–495.

MACNAMARA, J. (1964) 'Zero error and practice effects in Moray House English quotients', *Brit. J. educ. Psychol.*, **34**, 315–320.

MCNEMAR, Q. (1938) 'Newman, Freeman, and Holzinger's twins: a study of heredity and environment', *Psychol. Bull.*, **35**, 237–249.

MCNEMAR, Q. (1940) 'A critical examination of the University of Iowa studies of environmental influences on the IQ', *Psychol. Bull.*, **37**, 63–92,

MCNEMAR, Q. (1942) *The revision of the Stanford-Binet scale*. Boston, Mass.

MCNEMAR, Q. (1958) 'On growth measurement', *Educ. Psychol. Measmt.*, **18**, 47–55.

MCNEMAR, Q. (1964) 'Lost: Our Intelligence? Why?', *Amer. Psychologist*, **19**, 871–882.

MAIER, H. W. (1965) *Three Theories of Child Development*. New York and London: Harper and Row.

MAIER, N. R. F. (1930) 'Reasoning in humans: I. On direction', *J. comp. Psychol.*, **10**, 115–143.

MAIER, N. R. F. (1933) 'An aspect of human reasoning', *Brit. J. Psychol.*, **24**, 144–155.

MAIER, N. R. F. (1937) 'Reasoning in rats and human beings', *Psychol. Rev.*, **44**, 365–378.

MAIER, N. R. F. (1945) 'Reasoning in humans: III. The mechanisms of equivalent stimuli and reasoning', *J. exper. Psychol.*, **35**, 349–360.

MAIER, N. R. F., and BURKE, R. J. (1967) 'Response availability as a factor in the problem-solving performance of males and females', *J. Personal Soc. Psychol.*, **5**, 304–310.

MAIER, N. R. F., and HOFFMAN, L. R. (1961) 'Organization and creative problem solving', *J. appl. Psychol.*, **45,** 277–80.

MALLESON, N. (1960) 'University student 1953. II. Schooling', *Univ. Quarterly*, **14,** 156–164.

MARCUS, A. (1963) 'The effect of correct response location on the difficulty level of multiple-choice questions', *J. appl. Psychol.*, **47,** 48–51.

MARQUHART, D. L., and BAILEY, L. L. (1955) 'An evaluation of the culture free test of intelligence', *J. genet. Psychol.*, **86,** 353–58.

MARSH, R. W. (1964) 'A statistical re-analysis of Getzels and Jackson's data', *Brit. J. educ. Psychol.*, **34,** 91–93.

MAXWELL, J. (1954) 'Intelligence, fertility and the future', *Eugen. Quart.*, **I,** 244–247. (Reprinted in J. J. Jenkins and D. G. Paterson, Studies in Individual Differences, Methuen 1961.)

MAXWELL, J. (1961) *The level and trend of national intelligence.* London: Univ. Lond. Press.

MAXWELL, J., and PILLINER, A. E. G. (1960). 'The intellectual resemblance between sibs', *Ann. Hum. Genet.*, **24,** 23–32.

MAYS, W. (1966) 'A philosophic critique of intelligence tests', *Educ. Theory.*, **16,** 318–332.

MEADE, J. E., and PARKES, A. S. (Eds.) (1966) *Genetic and Environmental Factors in Human Ability.* Edinburgh. Oliver and Boyd.

MEDNICK, S. A. (1962) 'The associative basis of the creative process', *Psychol. Rev.*, **69,** 220–232.

MEER, B., and STEIN, M. I. (1955) 'Measures of intelligence and creativity', *J. Psychol.*, **39,** 117–126.

MELAMETSA, L. (1965) 'The influence of training on the level of test performance and the factor structure of intelligence tests', *J. Scand. Psychol.*, **6,** 19–25.

MEREDITH, P. (1966) *Instruments of Communication.* London: Pergamon.

MERRIFIELD, P. R. (1966) 'An analysis of concepts from the point of view of the structure of intellect', Ch. 2 in *Analyses of Concept Learning* (Eds. H. J. Klausmeier and C. W. Harris).

MEYER, W. J. (1964). *Developmental Psychology.* New York: The Center for Applied Research in Education.

MEYERS, C. E., DINGMAN, H. F., ORPET, R. E., SITKEI, E. G., and WATTS, C. A. (1964). 'Four ability-factor hypotheses at three pre-literate levels in normal and retarded children', *Monogr. Soc. Res. Child Develpt.*, No. 96, **29,** No. 5.

MILES, C. C. (1934) 'The influence of speed and age on the intelligence scores of adults', *J. gen. Psychol.*, **10,** 208–10.

MILES, T. R. 'On defining intelligence'. *Brit. J. educ. Psychol.*, **27,** 153–165.

MILLER, E. H. (1955) 'A study of difficulty levels of selected types of fallacies in reasoning and their relationships to the factors of sex, grade level, mental age, and scholastic standing', *J. educ. Res.*, **49,** 123–129.

MILLER, G. A., GALANTER, E., and PRIBRAM, K. H. (1960) *Plans and the Structure of Behavior*. New York: Holt.

MILLMAN, J., and GLOCK, M. D. (1965) 'Trends in the measurement of general mental ability', *Rev. educ. res.*, **35**, 17–24.

MINSKY, M. (1963) 'Steps toward artificial intelligence', in Feigenbaum, E. A., and Feldman, J. (Eds.) *Computers and Thought*. New York: McGraw-Hill.

MINSKY, M. (1966) 'Artificial intelligence'. *Scientific American*, 215, 3, 246–260.

MISCHEL, W., and METZNER, R. (1962) 'Preference for delayed reward as a function of age, intelligence, and length of delay interval', *J. abnorm. soc. Psychol.*, **64**, 425–431.

MOGENSEN, A. (1964) 'Raven's Progressive Matrices in uniovular twins brought up apart', *J. Scandinav. Psychol.*, **5**, 50–52.

MOORE, R. (1966) 'The relation of intelligence to creativity', *J. Res. in Music Educ.*, **14**, 143–253.

MOORE, T. (1967) 'Language and intelligence: a longitudinal study of the first eight years', *Hum. Develpm.*, **10**, 88–106.

MORETON, C. A., and BUTCHER, H. J. (1963) 'Are rural children handicapped by the use of speeded tests in selection procedures?', *Brit. J. educ. Psychol.*, **33**, 22–30.

MORGAN, J. B., and MORTON, J. T. (1944) 'The distortion of syllogistic reasoning produced by personal convictions', *J. soc. Psychol.*, **20**, 39–59.

MORRIS, JOYCE M. (1966) *Standards and Progress in Reading*. N.F.E.R. research reports, 2nd series, No. 1.

NASH, C. B., and NASH, C. S. (1964) 'Correlations between ESP scores and intelligence', *Int. J. Parapsychol.*, **6**, 309–323.

NEUHAUS, J. O., and WRIGLEY, C. (1954) 'The Quartimax method: an analytic approach to orthogonal simple structure', *Brit. J. stat. Psychol.*, **7**, 81–91.

NEWELL, A., SHAW, J. C., and SIMON, H. (1958) 'Elements of a theory of human problem solving', *Psychol. Rev.*, **65**, 151–166.

NEWELL, A., and SIMON, H. A. (1961) 'Computer simulation of human thinking', *Science*, **134**, 2011–2017.

NEWELL, A., and SIMON, H. A. (1963a) 'GPS, a program that simulates human thought', in Feldman and Feigenbaum, pp. 279–296.

NEWELL, A., and SIMON, H. A. (1963b) 'Computers in psychology', Ch. 7 in R. D. Luce, R. R. Bush and E. Galanter (Eds.) *Handbook of Mathematical Psychology*, **I**. New York: Wiley.

NEWLAND, T. E. (1962) 'The assessment of exceptional children', Ch. 2 in W. M. Cruickshank (Ed.) *Psychology of Exceptional Children and Youth*.

NEWMAN, H. H., FREEMAN, F. N., and HOLZINGER, K. J. (1937) *Twins: A Study of Heredity and Environment*. Chicago: Chicago Univ. Press.

NICHOLS, R. C. (1966) 'Non-intellective predictors of achievement in college', *Educ. Psychol. Measmt.*, **26**, 899–915.

NICHOLS, R. C., and HOLLAND, J. L. (1963) 'Prediction of the first year college performance of high aptitude students', *Psychol. Monogr.* **77**, no. 7, whole no. 570.

NISBET, J. D. (1953) 'Family Environment', *Occasional Papers on Eugenics*. No. 8.

NISBET, J. D. (1957) 'Intelligence and Age: Retesting with twenty-four years' interval', *Brit. J. educ. Psychol.*, **27**, 190–198.

NISBET, J. D., and BUCHAN, J. (1959) 'The long-term follow-up of assessments at age eleven', *Brit. J. educ. Psychol.*, **29**, 1–8.

NISBET, J. D., and ENTWISTLE, N. J. (1967) 'Intelligence and family size', 1949–1965. *Brit. J. educ. Psychol.*, **37**, 188–193.

NISBET, J. D., and GAMMIE, A. (1961). 'Over 135 I.Q.', *Educ. Res.*, **4**, 53–55.

NISBET, J. D., and ILLSLEY, R. (1963). 'The influence of early puberty on test performance at the age of eleven', *Brit. J. educ. Psychol.*, **33**, 169–176.

NISBET, J. D., ILLSLEY, R., SUTHERLAND, A. E., and DOUSE, M. J. (1964) 'Puberty and test performance: a further report', *Brit. J. educ. Psychol.*, **34**, 202–203.

OHNMACHT, F. W. (1966) 'Achievement, anxiety and creative thinking'. *Amer. Educ. Res. J.*, **3**, 131–138.

OJHA, H. A., KELVIN, R. P., and LUCAS, C. J. (1966) 'A note on season of birth and intelligence', *Brit. J. educ. Psychol.*, **36**, 94.

OLIVER, R. A. C. (1932) 'The comparison of the abilities of races with special reference to East Africa', *East Afr. Med. J.*, **9**, 160–204.

OLIVER, R. A. C. (1933) 'Adaptation of intelligence tests to tropical Africa', *Overseas Educ.* 4 (4) and 5 (1).

OLIVER, R. A. C. (1934) 'Mental tests in the study of the African', *Africa.*, **7**, 40–46.

ORPET, R. E., and MEYERS, C. E. (1966) 'Six structure-of-intellect hypotheses in six-year-old children', *J. educ. Psychol.*, **57**, 341–346.

OSLER, SONIA F., and FIVEL, M. W. (1961) 'Concept attainment: I. The role of age and intelligence in concept attainment by induction', *J. exper. Psychol.*, **62**, 1–8.

OSLER, SONIA F., and TRAUTMAN, GRACE E. (1961) 'Concept attainment: II. Effect of stimulus complexity upon concept attainment at two levels of intelligence', *J. exper. Psychol.*, **62**, 1–8.

OSLER, SONIA F., and WEISS, SANDRA R. (1962) 'Studies in concept attainment: III. Effect of instructions at two levels of intelligence', *J. exper. Psychol.*, **63**, 528–533.

O'SULLIVAN, MAUREEN, GUILFORD, J. P., and DE MILLE, R. (1965) *Measurement of Social Intelligence*. Report No. 34. Psych. Lab., Univ. of S. Calif., Los Angeles.

OWENS, W. A. (1953). 'Age and mental abilities: a longitudinal study', *Genet. Psychol. Monogr.*, **48**, 3–54.

OWENS, W. A. (1959). 'Is age kinder to the initially more able?', *J. Gerontol.*, **14**, 334–7.

OWENS, W. A. (1966). 'Age and Mental Abilities: a second adult follow-up', *J. educ. Psych.*, **57**, 311–325.

PARNES, S. J., and BRUNELLE, E. A. (1967) 'The literature of creativity: Part I', *J. creative Behav.*, **1**, 52–109.

PARNES, S. J., and HARDING, H. F. (1962) *A Source Book of Creative Thinking.* New York: Scribner.

PEEL, E. A. (1956) *The Psychological Basis of Education.* Edinburgh: Oliver and Boyd.

PEEL, E. A. (1959) 'Experimental examination of some of Piaget's schemata concerning children's perception and thinking and discussion of their educational significance', *Brit. J. educ. Psychol.*, **29**, 98–103.

PEISACH, ESTELLE C. (1965) 'Children's comprehension of teacher and peer speech', *Child Develpm.*, **36**, 467–480.

PENROSE, J. (1966) 'The psychology of chess', *New Society* No. 222 (29th Dec.) 967–968.

PENROSE, L. S. (1963) *Outline of Human Genetics.* (2nd edn.) London: Heinemann.

PIAGET, J. (1925) 'De quelques formes primitives de causalité chez l'enfant', *L'année Psychol.*, **26**, 31–71.

PIAGET, J. (1927) 'La causalité chez l'enfant', *Brit. J. Psychol.*, **18**, 276–301.

PIAGET, J. (1936) *La Naissance de L'Intelligence.* Neuchatel: Delachaux et Niestlé.

PIAGET, J. (1937) 'Le problème de l'intelligence et de l'habitude: réflexe conditionné, "Gestalt" ou assimilation', *Proc. 11th Int. Congr. Psychol.*, 170–183.

PIAGET, J. (1950) *The Psychology of Intelligence.* London: Routledge.

PIAGET, J. (1951) 'Principal factors determining intellectual evolution from childhood to adult life', Chs. 6 and 7 in D. Rapaport (Ed.) *Organization and Pathology of Thought.* New York: Columbia Univ. Press.

PIAGET, J. (1953) 'Les relations entre l'intelligence et l'affectivité dans le développement de l'enfant', *Bull. Psychol.*, Paris, **7**, 143–150, 346–361, 522–535, 699–701.

PIAGET, J. (1954) 'Ce qui subsiste de la théorie de la Gestalt dans la psychologie contemporaine de l'intelligence et de la perception', *Rev. Suisse Psychol.*, **13**, 72–83.

PIAGET, J. (1955) 'Ce qui subsiste de la théorie de la Gestalt dans la psychologie contemporaine de l'intelligence et de la perception', in *J. de Ajuriaguerra, et. al.*, Aktuelle Probleme der Gestalt theorie. Bern: Hans Huber, Pp. 72–83.

PIAGET, J. (1956) 'Les relations entre la perception et l'intelligence dans le développement de l'enfant', *Bull. Psychol.*, *Paris*, **10**, 376–381, 751–760.

PIAGET, J. (1958) *The Growth of Logical Thinking*. London: Routledge.

PIDGEON, D. A. (1965) 'Date of birth and scholastic performance', *Educ. Res.*, **8**, 3–7.

PIDGEON, D. A. (1967) *Achievement in Mathematics: A National Study in Secondary Schools*. London: National Foundation for Educational Research in England and Wales.

PIERSON, G. R., BARTON, V., and HAY, G. (1964) 'S.M.A.T. motivation factors as predictors of academic achievement of delinquent boys', *J. Psychol.*, **57**, 243–249.

PILKINGTON, G. W., and HARRISON, G. T. (1967) 'The relative value of two high-level intelligence tests, advanced level, and first-year university examination marks for predicting degree classification', *Brit. J. educ. Psychol.*, **37**, 382–388.

PILLINER, A. E. G. (1965) 'The application of analysis of variance in psychometric experimentation', *Ph.D. thesis*, Univ. of Edinburgh Library.

PILLINER, A. E. G. (1968) 'Examinations' in *Educational Research in Britain* (Ed. H. J. Butcher). London: Univ. of London Press.

PINNEAU, S. R. (1961) *Changes in Intelligence Quotient: Infancy to Maturity*. Boston: Houghton Mifflin.

PONT, H. B. (1963) 'A review of the use of information theory in psychology and a study of the effect of age on channel capacity', *Ed.B. thesis*, Univ. of Aberdeen Library.

PORTEUS, S. D. (1955) *The Maze Test: Recent Advances*. Palo Alto, Calif., Pacific Books.

PORTEUS, S. D. (1959a) *The Porteus Mazes. The Supplement Series of Mazes*. New York: Psychological Corp.

PORTEUS, S. D. (1959b) 'Recent Maze Test Studies', *Brit. J. med. Psychol.*, **32**, 38–43.

PORTEUS, S. D. (1965) *Porteus Maze Test – Fifty Years' Application*. London: Harrap.

POSNER, M. I. (1965) 'Memory and thought in human intellectual performance', *Brit. J. Psychol.*, **56**, 197–216.

PRESTON, R. C. (1965) 'The multiple-choice test as an instrument in perpetuating false concepts', *Educ. Psychol. Measmt.*, **25**, 111–116.

PRIBRAM, K. H. (1960) 'A review of theory in physiological psychology', *Ann. Rev. Psychol.*, **11**, 1–40.

PRINGLE, M. L. K. (1965) *Deprivation and Education*. London: Longmans.

PRINGLE, M. L. K., BUTLER, N. R., and DAVIE, R. (1967) *11,000 Seven-Year-Olds. First Report of the National Child Development Study (1958 Cohort)*. London: Longmans.

QUERESHI, M. Y. (1967) 'Patterns of psycholinguistic development during early and middle childhood', *Educ. Psychol. Measmt.*, **27**, 353–365.

RABIN, A. I., and GUERTIN, W. H. (1951) 'Research with the WB test: 1945–1950', *Psychol. Bull.*, **48**, 211–248.

RADFORD, J. (1966) 'Verbalisation effects in a "non-verbal" intelligence test', *Brit. J. educ. Psychol.*, **36**, 33–38.

RAPAPORT, D. (Ed.) (1951) *Organization and Pathology of Thought.* New York: Columbia Univ. Press.

RAPAPORT, G. M., and BERG, I. A. (1955) 'Response sets in a multiple-choice test', *Educ. Psychol. Measmt.*, **15**, 58–62.

RAPOPORT, A. (1964) 'The uses of mathematics in psychology', Ch. 6 in B. B. Wolman (Ed.) *Scientific Psychology.* New York: Basic Books.

RAVEN, J. C. (1948) 'The comparative assessment of intellectual ability', *Brit. J. Psychol.*, **39**, 12–19.

READER, D. H. (1963) 'African and Afro-European research: a summary of previously unpublished findings in the National Institute for Personnel Research', *Psychologia Africana*, **10**, 1–18.

REESE, H. (1962) 'Verbal mediation as a function of age level', *Psychol. Bull.*, **59**, 502–509.

REEVES, JOAN W. (1965) *Thinking about Thinking.* London: Secker and Warburg.

REID, JESSIE F. (1962) 'Intelligence tests – a comment', *Scott. Educ. J.*, **45**. 211–212.

REID, JESSIE F. (1968) 'Reading', in *Educational Research in Britain* (Ed. H. J. Butcher). London: Univ. of London Press.

REITMAN, W. R. (1965) *Cognition and Thought.* New York and London: Wiley.

RENSHAW, T. (1952) 'Factor rotation by the method of extended vectors', *Brit. J. Psychol.* (Stat. Sect.) **5**, 7–13.

RIPPLE, R. E., and MAY, F. B. (1962) 'Caution in comparing creativity and I.Q.', *Psychol. Rep.*, **10**, 229–230.

ROBERTS, A. O. H. (1962) 'The maximum reliability of a multiple-choice test', *Psychologia Africana*, **9**, 286–93.

ROBINSON, W. P. (1964) 'The achievement motive, academic success and intelligence test scores', *Brit. J. soc. clin. Psychol.*, **4**, 98–103.

RODGER, A. (1949) 'Symposium on the selection of pupils for different types of secondary schools – VIII. An industrial psychologist's point of view', *Brit. J. educ. Psychol.*, **19**, 154–159.

RODGER, A. (1965) 'Capacity and inclination for university courses', *Occup. Psychol.*, **39**, 37–43.

ROE, ANNE (1953) 'A psychological study of eminent psychologists and anthropologists, and a comparison with biological and physical scientists', *Psychol. Monogr.*, **67**, No. 2.

ROEN, S. R. (1960) 'Personality and Negro-White intelligence', *J. abnorm. soc. Psychol.*, **61**, 148–150.

ROGERS, C. A. (1956) 'Measuring intelligence in New Zealand', *Auckland Univ. Coll. Monogr. Series No. 2.*

ROSENTHAL, R. (1964) 'Experimenter outcome-orientation and the results of the psychological experiment', *Psychol. Bull.*, **61**, 405–12.

ROSENTHAL, R. (1966) *Experimental Effects in Behaviour Research.* N.Y. Appleton-Century-Crofts.

ROSENTHAL, R. (1967) 'Covert communication in the psychological experiment', *Psychol. Bull.*, **67**, 356–367.

ROSENTHAL, R., and JACOBSON, L. (1966) 'Teachers' expectancies: determinants of pupils' I.Q. gains', *Psychol. Reports.*, **19**, 115–118.

ROSS, T. (1938) 'The synthesis of intelligence – its implications', *Psychol. Rev.*, **45**, 185–189.

ROUSSEAU, H. J. (1962) 'Ability in a multi-cultural community: Rhodesia and Nyasaland', in G. Z. F. Bereday and J. A. Lauwerys (Eds.) *The Gifted Child:* The Yearbook of Education. New York: Harcourt.

ROYCE, J. R. (1957) 'Factor theory and genetics', *Educ. Psychol. Measmt.*, **17**, 361–376.

ROYCE, J. R. (1966) 'Concepts generated in comparative and physiological psychological observations', Ch. 21 in R. B. Cattell, (Ed.) *Handbook of Multivariate Experimental Psychology.* Rand McNally: Chicago.

RYLE, G. (1949) *The Concept of Mind.* London: Hutchinson.

SAMUEL, A. L. (1959) 'Machine learning using the game of checkers', *I.B.M. Journ. of Res. and Devel.*, **3**, 211–229. (Reprinted in Feigenbaum and Feldman, pp. 71–105.)

SASS, M. A., and WILKINSON, W. D. (1965) *Computer Augmentation of Human Reasoning.* Washington, D.C.: Spartan Books.

SAUGSTAD, P. (1955) 'Problem-solving as dependent upon availability of functions', *Brit. J. Psychol.*, **46**, 191–198.

SAUGSTAD, P. (1957) 'An analysis of Maier's pendulum problem', *J. exper. Psychol.* **54**, 168–179.

SAVAGE, R. D. (1966) 'Personality factors and academic attainment in junior school children', *Brit. J. educ. Psych.*, **36**, 91–92.

SCHAIE, K. W. (1965) 'A general model for the study of developmental problems', *Psychol. Bull.*, **64**, 92–107.

SCHAIE, K. W., and STROTHER, C. R. (1964) 'The effect of time and cohort differences on the interpretation of age changes in cognitive behavior', *Amer. Psychologist.*, **19**, 546 (abstract).

SCHMADEL, E. (1963) 'The relationship of creative-thinking abilities to school achievement', *Appendix A in Reports from the Psychol. Lab.*, Univ. of S. California, No. 27.

SCHÖNEMANN, P. H. (1966) 'A generalized solution of the orthogonal Procrustes problem', *Pmka.*, **31**, 1–10.

SCHURDAK, J. J. (1967) 'An approach to the use of computers in the instructional process and an evaluation', *Amer. Educ. Res. J.*, **4**, 59–73.

SCHVANEVELDT, R. W. (1966) 'Concept identification as a function of probability of positive instances and number of relevant dimensions', *J. exper. Psychol.*, **72**, 649–654.

SCOTTISH COUNCIL FOR RESEARCH IN EDUCATION. (1933) *The Intelligence of Scottish Children*. Pub. No. 5. Univ. of London Press.

SCOTTISH COUNCIL FOR RESEARCH IN EDUCATION. (1949) *The Trend of Scottish Intelligence*. Pub. No. 30. Univ. of London Press.

SCOTTISH COUNCIL FOR RESEARCH IN EDUCATION. (1953) *Social Implications of the 1947 Scottish Mental Survey*. Pub. No. 35. Univ. of London Press.

SCOTTISH COUNCIL FOR RESEARCH IN EDUCATION. (1958a) *Eleven-year-olds Grow up*. Univ. of London Press.

SCOTTISH COUNCIL FOR RESEARCH IN EDUCATION (1958b) *Educational and Other Aspects of the 1947 Scottish Mental Survey*. Univ. of London Press.

SCOTTISH COUNCIL FOR RESEARCH IN EDUCATION. (1967) *The Scottish Standardisation of the Wechsler Intelligence Scale for Children*. London: Univ. of London Press.

SEASHORE, H., WESMAN, A., and DOPPELT, J. (1950) 'The standardization of the Wechsler Intelligence Scale for Children', *J. consult. Psychol.*, **14**, 99–110.

SELFRIDGE, O. (1965) 'Reasoning in game playing by machine', Ch. 1 in Sass, M. A., and Wilkinson, W. D. (Eds.). *Computer Augmentation of Human Reasoning*. Washington, D.C.: Spartan Books.

SEMEONOFF, B., and TRIST, E. (1958) *Diagnostic Performance Tests: A Manual for Use with Adults*. London: Tavistock.

SEMLER, I. J., and ISCOE, I. (1966) 'Structure of intelligence in negro and white children', *J. educ. Psychol.*, **57**, 326–336.

SEREBRIAKOFF, V. (1966) *I.Q. A Mensa Analysis and History*. London: Hutchinson.

SHAPIRO, R. J. (1965) 'The integrating of remotely associated concepts as a process in scientific creativity', *Psychologia Africana*, **11**, 40–48.

SHAPIRO, R. J. (1966) 'The identification of creative research scientists', *Psychologia Africana*, **11**, 99–132.

SHARP, STELLA E. (1899) 'Individual psychology: a study in psychological method', *Amer. J. Psychol.*, **10**, 329–391.

SHAW, G. B. (1911) *The Sanity of Art: An Exposure of the Current Nonsense about Artists being Degenerate*. London: Constable.

SHERMAN, M., and KEY, C. B. (1932) 'The intelligence of isolated mountain children', *Child Develpm.*, **3**, 279–290.

SHIELDS, J. (1962) *Monozygotic Twins*. London: Oxford University Press.

SHOLL, D. A. (1956) *The Organisation of the Cerebral Cortex*. London: Methuen.

SHUEY, A. M. (1966) *The Testing of Negro Intelligence* (3rd edn.). New York: Social Science Press.

SIMON, H. A., and KOTOVSKY, K. (1963) 'Human acquisition of concepts for sequential patterns', *Psychol. Rev.*, **70**, 534–546.

SKEELS, H. M., and HARMS, I. (1948) 'Children with inferior social histories; their mental development in adoptive homes', *J. genet. Psychol.*, **72**, 283–94.

SKEMP, R. R. (1964) *Understanding Mathematics*. London: Univ. of London Press (2 vols.).

SKINNER, B. F. (1957) *Verbal Behavior*. New York: Appleton-Century-Crofts.

SKODAK, MARIE (1939) 'Children in foster homes: a study of mental development', *Univ. of Iowa Stud. Child Welfare*, **16**, No. 1.

SKODAK, MARIE, and SKEELS, H. M. (1949) 'A final follow-up study of one hundred adopted children', *J. genet. Psychol.*, **75**, 85–125.

SLAKTER, M. J. (1967) 'Risk taking on objective examinations', *Amer. Educ. Res. J.*, **4**, 31–50.

SMART, R. C. (1965) 'The changing composition of "intelligence": A replication of a factor analysis', *J. genet. Psychol.*, **107**, 11–116.

SMITH, C. M. (1948) *Mental Testing of Hebridean Children in Gaelic and English*. London: Univ. of London Press.

SMITH, F., and MILLER, G. A. (1966) *The Genesis of Language*. Cambridge, Mass. M.I.T. Press.

SMITH, I. M. (1964) *Spatial Ability. Its Educational and Social Significance*. London: Univ. of London Press.

SMOKE, K. L. (1932) 'An objective study of concept formation', *Psychol. Monogr.*, **42**, No. 4.

SMYTHIES, J. R. (Ed.) (1965) *Brain and Mind*. London: MacGibbon and Kee.

SORENSON, A. G. (1963) 'The use of teaching machines in developing an alternative to the concept of intelligence', *Educ. Psychol. Measmt.*, **23**, 323–329.

SPEARMAN, C. E. (1904) ' "General intelligence" objectively determined and measured', *Amer. J. Psychol.*, **15**, 72–101.

SPEARMAN, C. E. (1923) *The Nature of Intelligence and the Principles of Cognition*.

SPEARMAN, C. E. (1927) *The Abilities of Man*. London: Macmillan.

SPEARMAN, C. E. (1931) 'Our need of some science in place of the word "intelligence" ', *J. educ. Psychol.*, **30**, 1–16.

SPEARMAN, C. E., and WYNN JONES, LL. (1950) *Human Ability*. London: Macmillan.

SPENCER, H. (1855) *The Principles of Psychology*. Williams and Norgate.

SPIELBERGER, C. D., and KATZENMEYER, W. G. (1959) 'Manifest anxiety, intelligence and college grades', *J. consult. Psychol.*, **23**, 278.

SPIKER, C. C., and MCCANDLESS, B. R. (1954) 'The concept of intelligence and the philosophy of science', *Psychol. Rev.*, **61**, 255–266.

STEPHENSON, W. (1931) 'Tetrad-differences for non-verbal sub-tests. Tetrad-differences for verbal sub-tests. Tetrad-differences for verbal-sub-tests relative to non-verbal sub-tests', *J. educ. Psychol.*, **22**, 167–185, 255–267, 334–350.

STERN, C., and KEISLAR, E. R. (1967) 'Acquisition of problem solving strategies by young children, and its relation to mental age', *Amer. Educ. Res. J.*, **4**, 1–12.

STEVENS, S. S. (1951) 'Mathematics, measurement and psychophysics', in *Handbook of Experimental Psychology* (Ed. S. S. Stevens). New York: Wiley.

STEWART, L. H., DOLE, A. A., and HARRIS, Y. Y. (1967) 'Cultural differences in abilities during high school', *Amer. Educ. Res. J.*, **4**, 19–30.

STEWART, N. (1947) 'A.G.C.T. scores of army personnel grouped by occupation', *Occupations*, **26**, 5–41.

STODDARD, G. D. (1943) *The Meaning of Intelligence.* New York: Macmillan.

STOTT, D. H. (1967) 'Commentary on "The genetic determination of differences in intelligence: a study of monozygotic twins reared together and apart" by Cyril Burt: congenital influences on the development of twins', *Brit. J. Psychol.*, **57**, 423–29.

STOTT, L. H., and BALL, R. S. (1965) 'Infant and Pre-school Mental tests: review and evaluation', *Monogr. Soc. Res. Child Develpm.*, **30**, No. 3. Serial No. 101.

SULTAN, E. E. (1962) 'A factorial study in the domain of creative thinking', *Brit. J. educ., Psychol.*, **32**, 78–82.

SUPPES, P. (1966) 'The uses of computers in education', *Scientific American*, 215, 3, 206–223.

SWIFT, D. F. (1965) 'Meritocratic and social class selection at age eleven', *Educ. Research*, **8**, 65–72.

SWIFT, D. F. (1967) 'Family environment and 11 + success: some basic predictors', *Brit. J. educ. Psychol.*, **37**, 10–21.

SWIFT, D. F. (1968) 'Social class and educational adaptation', in *Educational Research in Britain* (Ed. H. J. Butcher). London: Univ. of London Press.

TANNER, J. M. (1961) *Education and Physical Growth.* London: Univ. of London Press.

TATSUOKA, M. M. (1966) *Review of Harris, C. W. (ed.), Proceedings of the 1964 Invitational Conference on Testing Problems.* Princeton: E.T.S.

TAYLOR, C. W. (Ed.) (1964) *Creativity: Progress and Potential.* New York: McGraw-Hill.

TAYLOR, C. W., and BARRON, F. (1963) *Scientific Creativity: Its Recognition and Development.* New York: Wiley.

TAYLOR, C. W., and HOLLAND, J. (1964) 'Predictors of creative performance', in C. W. Taylor (Ed.) *Creativity: Progress and Potential.* New York: McGraw-Hill.

TEMPLIN, M. (1957) *Certain Language Skills in Children, Their Development and Interrelationships.* Minneapolis: Univ. of Minnesota Press.

TERMAN, L. M. (1925) *Mental and Physical Traits of a Thousand Gifted Children. Genetic Studies of Genius,* **I.** Stanford, California: Stanford Univ. Press.

TERMAN, L. M., and MERRILL, M. A. (1937) *Measuring Intelligence.* London: Harrap.

TERMAN, L. M., and MERRILL, M. A. (1960) *Stanford-Binet Intelligence Scale.* Boston: Houghton Mifflin.

TERMAN, L. M., and ODEN, M. H. (1947) *The Gifted Child Grows Up. Genetic Studies of Genius,* **IV.** Stanford, California: Stanford Univ. Press.

TERMAN, L. M., and ODEN, M. H. (1959) *The Gifted Group at Mid-life. Genetic Studies of Genius,* **V.** Stanford, California: Stanford Univ. Press.

THOMPSON, J. W. (1963) 'Bi-polar and unidirectional scales', *Brit. J. Psychol.,* **54,** 15–24.

THOMPSON, W. R. (1966) 'Multivariate experiment in behavior genetics', Ch. 23 in R. B. Cattell, *Handbook of Multivariate Experimental Psychology.* Chicago: Rand McNally.

THOMSON, G. H. (1942) 'Following up individual items in a group intelligence test', *Brit. J. Psychol.,* **32,** 310–317.

THOMSON, G. H. (1945) 'The distribution of intelligence among university and college students', *Brit. J. educ. Psychol.,* **15,** 76–79.

THOMSON, G. H. (1949) 'Intelligence and fertility', *Eug. Rev.,* No. 4.

THOMSON, G. H. (1951) *The Factorial Analysis of Human Ability* (5th edn.). London: Univ. of London Press.

THOMSON, R. (1959) *The Psychology of Thinking.* London: Penguin Books.

THORNDIKE, R. L. (1963). 'Some methodological issues in the study of creativity', *Proc. of 1962 Invitational Conference on Testing Problems,* 40–54 (ETS, Princeton).

THORNDIKE, R. L. (1966). 'Intellectual status and intellectual growth', *J. educ. Psychol.,* **57,** 121–127.

THOULESS, R. H. (1959). 'Effect of prejudice on reasoning', *Brit. J. Psychol.,* **50,** 289–93.

THURSTONE, L. L. (1924). *The Nature of Intelligence.* London: Kegan Paul, Trench, Trubner & Co. Ltd.

THURSTONE, L. L. (1938). 'Primary mental abilities', *Psychometr. Monogr.* No. 1.

THURSTONE, L. L. (1955). 'The differential growth of mental abilities', Chapel Hill, North Carolina. *Report of Univ. of N. Carolina Psychometric Laboratory* No. 14.

THURSTONE, L. L., and THURSTONE, T. G. (1941). 'Factorial studies of intelligence', *Psychometr. Monogr.*, No. 2.

THURSTONE, L. L., THURSTONE, T. G., and STRANDSKOV, H. H. (1953). 'A psychological study of twins. I. Distribution of absolute twin differences for identical and fraternal twins', *Res. Rep. No. 4, Psychometric Lab.*, *Univ. of N. Carolina.*

THURSTONE, T. G. (1941). 'Primary mental abilities of children', *Educ. Psychol. Measmt.*, **1**, 105–116.

TIBER, N., and KENNEDY, W. A. (1964) 'The effects of incentive on the intelligence test performance of different social groups', *J. consult. Psychol.*, **28**, 187.

TOMKINS, S. S., and MESSICK, S. (1962). *Computer Simulation of Personality.* New York and London: Wiley.

TORRANCE, E. P. (1960) 'Educational achievement of the highly intelligent and the highly creative: eight partial replications of the Getzels-Jackson study', (*Research Memorandum* BER-60-18). Bureau of Educ. Research, Univ. of Minnesota.

TORRANCE, E. P. (1962) *Guiding Creative Talent.* Englewood Cliffs, N.J.: Prentice-Hall.

TORRANCE, E. P. (1963) *Education and the Creative Potential.* Minneapolis: Univ. of Minnesota Press.

TORRANCE, E. P. (1964) 'Education and Creativity', Ch. 3 in C. W. Taylor (Ed.) *Creativity: Progress and Potential.* New York: McGraw-Hill.

TORRANCE, E. P. (1965) *Rewarding Creative Behaviour.* Englewood Cliffs, N.J.: Prentice Hall.

TSAKALOS, P. (1966) 'Is a non-verbal a culture-fair test?', *B.Ed. thesis*, Univ. of Edinburgh Library.

TUDDENHAM, R. D. (1948) 'Soldier intelligence in world wars I and II', *Amer. Psychologist*, **3**, 54–56.

TUDDENHAM, R. D. (1961)' The nature and measurement of intelligence', Chapter 8 in L. Postman, *Psychology in the Making.* New York: Knopf.

TUDDENHAM, R. D. (1966) 'Jean Piaget and the world of the child', *Amer. Psychologist*, **21**, 207–217.

TURING, A. M. (1950) 'Computing machinery and intelligence', *Mind* 59, 433–460. (Reprinted in Feigenbaum and Feldman).

TYLER, L. E. (1965) *The Psychology of Human Differences* (3rd edn.). New York: Appleton-Century-Crofts.

VANDENBERG, S. G. (1956) 'The hereditary abilities study', *Eugen. Quart.*, **3**, 94–99.

VANDENBERG, S. G. (1962) 'The hereditary abilities study: hereditary components in a psychological test battery', *Amer. J. Hum. Genet.*, **14**, 220–37.

VANDENBERG, S. G. (Ed.) (1965) *Methods and Goals in Human Behavior Genetics.* New York and London: Academic Press.

VANDENBERG, S. G. (1966) 'Contributions of twin research to psychology', *Psychol. Bull.*, **66**, 327–352.

VARON, EDITH J. (1935) 'The development of Alfred Binet's psychology', *Psychol. Monogr.*, **46**, No. 3.

VERNON, P. E. (1938) 'Intelligence test sophistication', *Brit. J. educ. Psychol.*, **8**, 237–244.

VERNON, P. E. (1948) 'Indices of item consistency and validity', *Brit. J. Psychol.* (Statist. sect.) **1**, 152–166.

VERNON, P. E. (1950) *The Structure of Human Abilities*. London: Methuen.

VERNON, P. E. (1956) *The Measurement of Abilities* (2nd edn.). London: Univ. of London Press.

VERNON, P. E. (1957) *Secondary School Selection. A British Psychological Society Inquiry*. London: Methuen.

VERNON, P. E. (1960) *Intelligence and Attainment Tests*. London: Univ. of London Press.

VERNON, P. E. (1963) 'The pool of ability', in *Sociol. Rev. Monogr.* No. 7.

VERNON, P. E. (1964a) 'The psychology of intelligence and G.', Ch. 17 in *Readings in Psychology* (Ed. J. Cohen). London: Allen and Unwin.

VERNON, P. E. (1964b) 'Creativity and intelligence', *Educ. Res.*, **6**, 163–169.

VERNON, P. E. (1965) 'Abilities and attainments in the Western Isles', *Scott. Educ. J.*, **48**, 948–950.

VERNON, P. E. (1966) 'Educational and intellectual development among Canadian Indians and Eskimos', *Educ. Rev.*, **18**, 79–91 and 186–195.

VERNON, P. E. (1967) 'A cross-cultural study of "creativity tests" with 11-year boys', *New Res. in Educ.*, **1**, 135–246.

VERNON, P. E., and PARRY, J. B. (1949) *Personnel Selection in the British Forces*. London: Univ. of London Press.

VINCENT, D. F. (1952) 'The linear relationship between age and score of adults in intelligence tests', *Occup. Psychol.*, **26**, 243–249.

VOGEL, W., and BROVERMAN, D. M. (1964) 'Relationship between EEG and intelligence: a critical review', *Psychol. Bull.*, **62**, 132–144.

VOGT, O. (1951) 'Study of the ageing of the nerve cells', *J. Gerontol.* **6**.

VYGOTSKY, L. S. (1962) *Thought and Language*. Cambridge, Mass. M.I.T. Press.

WALL, W. D., and PRINGLE, M. L. KELLMER (1966) 'The clinical significance of standard score discrepancies between intelligence and social competence.' *Human Development*, **9**, 121–151.

WALLACE, J. G. (1965) *Concept Growth and the Education of the Child*, Slough, Bucks: N.F.E.R. (Occasional publication No. 12).

WALLACH, M. A. (1963) 'Research on Children's Thinking', *Child Psychology*. (Edited by Harold W. Stevenson.) *Sixty-second Yearbook, Part I, National Society for the Study of Education*. University of Chicago Press, Ch. 6, pp. 236–76.

WALLACH, M. A., and KOGAN, N. (1965a) *Modes of Thinking in Young Children*. New York: Holt, Rinehart and Winston.

WALLACH, M., and KOGAN, N. (1965b) 'A new look at the creativity-intelligence distinction', *J. Personal.*, **33**, 348–369.

WALLAS, G. (1926) *The Art of Thought*. London: Watts.

WALTON, D. (1955) 'The validity and interchangeability of Terman-Merrill and Matrices test data', *Brit. J. educ. Psychol.*, **25**, 190–194.

WARBURTON, F. W. (1951) 'The ability of the Gurkha recruit', *Brit. J. Psychol.*, **42**, 123–133.

WARBURTON, F. W. (1952) *The Selection of University Students*. Manchester Univ. Press.

WARBURTON, F. W. (1955) 'The scientific status of mental measurement', *Brit. J. Psychol.*, **46**, 122–129.

WARBURTON, F. W. (1961) 'The measurement of personality—I', *Educ. Res.*, **4**, 2–17.

WARBURTON, F. W. (1962a) 'The measurement of personality—II', *Educ. Res.*, **2**, 115–132.

WARBURTON, F. W. (1962b) 'The measurement of personality—III', *Educ. Res.*, **2**, 193–206.

WARBURTON, F. W. (1963). 'Analytic methods of factor rotation', *Brit. J. statist. Psychol.*, **16**, 165–174.

WARBURTON, F. W. (1966). 'Construction of the new British Intelligence Scale', *Bull. Brit. Psychol. Socy.*, **19**, 68–70 (abstract).

WARD, J. (1967) 'An oblique factorization of Wallach and Kogan's "creativity" correlations', *Brit. J. educ. Psychol.*, **37**, 380–382.

WARREN, J. R. (1966) 'Birth order and social behavior', *Psychol. Bull.*, **65**, 38–49.

WASON, P. C. (1959) 'The processing of positive and negative information', *Quart. J. exper. Psychol.*, **11**, 92–107.

WEAVER, H. E., and MADDEN, E. H. (1949) 'Direction in problem solving', *J. Psychol.*, **27**, 331–345.

WEBB, A. P. A. (1963) 'A longitudinal comparison of the WISC and WAIS with educable mentally retarded Negroes', *J. clin. Psychol.*, **19**, 101–102.

WECHSLER, D. (1958) *The Measurement and Appraisal of Adult Intelligence* (4th edn.). London: Bailliere, Tindall and Cox.

WEINER, M. (1964) 'Organization of mental abilities from ages 14 to 54', *Educ. Psychol. Measmt.*, **24**, 573–587.

WEIR, RUTH H. (1962) *Language in the Crib*. The Hague: Mouton.

WELFORD, A.T. (1958) *Ageing and Human Skill*. Oxford: Oxford Univ. Press

WELSH, G. S. (1967) 'Verbal interests and intelligence: comparison of Strong VIB, Terman CMT and D-48 scores of gifted adolescents', *Educ. Psychol. Measmt.*, **27**, 349–352.

WERTHEIMER, M. (1959) *Productive Thinking* (2nd edn.). New York: Harper.

WESLEY, S. M., COREY, D. Q., and STEWART, B. M. (1950) 'The intra-individual relationship between interest and ability', *J. appl. Psychol.*, **34**, 193–197.

WEVRICK, L. (1962) 'Response set in a multiple-choice test', *Educ. Psychol. Measmt.*, **22**, 533–8.

WHEELER, L. R. (1942) 'A comparative study of the intelligence of East Tennessee mountain children', *J. educ. Psychol.*, **33**, 321–324.

WHITFIELD, J. W. (1951) 'An experiment in problem solving', *Quart. J. exper. Psychol.*, **3**, 184–197.

WIENER, N. (1948) *Cybernetics*. New York: Wiley.

WILLIAMS, J. D. (1965) *The Compleat Strategyst* (2nd edn.). New York: McGraw-Hill.

WILLIAMS, MOYRA (1965) *Mental Testing in Clinical Practice*. London: Pergamon Press.

WISEMAN, S. (Ed.) (1961) *Examinations and English Education*. Manchester: Manchester Univ. Press.

WISEMAN, S. (1964) *Education and Environment*. Manchester: Manchester Univ. Press.

WISEMAN, S. (1966) 'Environmental and innate factors and educational attainment', in *Genetic and Environmental Factors in Human Ability* (Eds. J. E. Meade and A. S. Parkes), pp. 64–80.

WISEMAN, S. (Ed.) (1967) *Intelligence and Ability*. Penguin Books.

WISSLER, C. (1901) 'The correlation of mental and physical tests', *Psychol. Rev. Monogr.*, **3**, 1–63.

WITTY, P. A. (1940) 'A genetic study of fifty gifted children', *Nat. Society for the Study of Education. 39th Yearbook.*

WITTY, P. A., and JENKINS, M. D. (1936) 'Intra-race testing and Negro intelligence', *J. Psychol.*, **1**, 179–192.

WODTKE, K. H. (1964) 'Some data on the reliability and validity of creativity tests at the elementary school level', *Educ. Psychol. Measmt.*, **24**, 399–408.

WOLFF, P. H. (1960) 'The developmental psychologies of Jean Piaget and psychoanalysis', *Psych. Issues*, **2** (1. whole No. 5).

WOOD, DOROTHY A. (1961) *Test Construction*. Columbus, Ohio: Merrill.

WOOLDRIDGE, D. E. (1963) *The Machinery of the Brain*. New York: McGraw-Hill.

YAMAMOTO, K. (1964a) 'Role of creative thinking and intelligence in high school achievement', *Psychol. Rep.*, **14**, 783–789.

YAMAMOTO, K. (1964b) 'Threshold of intelligence in academic achievement of highly creative students', *J. exper. Educ.*, **32**, 401–404.

YAMAMOTO, K. (1964c) 'A further analysis of the role of creative thinking in high-school achievement', *J. Psychol.*, **58**, 277–283.

YAMAMOTO, K. (1965a) 'Multiple achievement battery and repeated measurements: a postscript to three studies on creative thinking', *Psych. Reports*, **16**, 367–375.

YAMAMOTO, K. (1965b) 'Effects of restriction of range and test un-reliability on correlation between measures of intelligence and creative thinking', *Brit. J. educ. Psychol.*, 35, 300–305.

ZANGWILL, O. L. (1950), *An Introduction to Modern Psychology*. London: Methuen.

ZANGWILL, O. L. (1963). 'The cerebral localisation of cortical function', *Advancement of Science*, 20, 335–344.

ZIMMERMAN, D. W., and WILLIAMS, R. H. (1965). 'Chance success due to guessing, and non-independence of true scores and error scores in multiple-choice tests: Computer trials with prepared distributions', *Psychol. Rep.*, 17, 159–165.

Subject Index

Name Index